Sue Grant and Rich

Economics A Level

MV=PT

50p

MACMILLAN

Acknowledgements

First edition 1989
Revised 1991
Reprinted 3 times
Second edition 1996

Published by
MACMILLAN PRESS LTD
Houndmills, Basingstoke, Hampshire RG21 6XS
and London
Companies and representatives
throughout the world

ISBN 0–333–62573–0

A catalogue record for this book is available
from the British Library.

10   9   8   7   6   5   4
05   04   03   02   01   00

Printed in Hong Kong

To our families

The authors and publishers wish to thank the following who have kindly given permission for the use of copyright material: *The Economist* for extracts from various issues of *The Economist*. Copyright © *The Economist* 1995; *The Guardian* for Sally Weale, 'Dying girl in court fight for treatment', *The Guardian*, 10 March 1995, and 'The poor get poorer', *The Guardian*, 21 February 1995; *Financial Times* for an extract from 'Fall in MO eases rate rise pressure', *Financial Times*, 31 January 1995; The Controller of Her Majesty's Stationary Office for a table from *Britain 1995: An Official Handbook*, table 16.1, and the Central Statistical Office for material from *Social Trends 25*, 1992; Newspapers Publishing plc for an extract from Marie Woolf, 'Supermarket "real bread" ruins the small bakers', *Independent on Sunday*, 19 March 1995; Times Newspapers Ltd for David Smith, 'Britain's black economy soars to £50bn', *The Sunday Times*, 13 February 1995, Garth Alexander, 'Yen's unstoppable rise threatens to end in disaster', *The Sunday Times*, 12 March 1995, and Colin Narbrough, 'Leap in imports widens UK's world trade gap', *The Times*, 10 February 1995, Copyright Times Newspapers Ltd, 1995.

The author and publishers wish to thank the following examination boards for permission to use past questions: The Associated Examining Board; Joint Matriculation Board; Northern Ireland Council for the Curriculum, Examinations and Assessment; Scottish Examinations Board; Southern Universities' Joint Board; University of Cambridge Local Examinations Syndicate; University of London Examinations and Assessment Council; University of Oxford Delegacy of Local Examinations; Welsh Joint Education Committee. All examining groups wish to point out that worked examples included in the text are entirely the responsibility of the authors and have neither been provided nor approved by the board. They may not constitute the only possible solutions. The University of London Examinations and Assessment Council accepts no responsibility whatsoever for the accuracy or method of working in the answers given.

The authors are most grateful to the following Heads of Economics for their careful reading and correction of some or all of the original typescript: Clarrie Haynes, Marlborough School, Woodstock, Oxfordshire; Danny Myers, New College, Swindon, Wiltshire; Brian Sangster, Burford School, Oxfordshire; Jonathan Townsend, Abingdon School, Oxfordshire; Laurence Whitehouse, Farnborough Sixth Form College, Hampshire. A particular thanks should be given to Robert Ackrill for the long hours of invaluable assistance given freely in shaping the initial stages of the book. Past students of West Oxfordshire Technical College, Corrina Boreham, Angela Frost, Clare Guy and Robert Prior-Wandesforde, and Sally Trego, formerly of Matthew Arnold School, corrected many early errors. We also owe a huge debt to the many other students who have painstakingly worked through the examples. Robert Sulley of Macmillan has given the most helpful support.

Since this is a joint venture, both authors thank their families for their sacrifices, patience and understanding throughout.

Any failings which remain are entirely our own.

Every effort has been made to trace all the copyright-holders, but if any have been inadvertently overlooked the publishers will be pleased to make the necessary arrangement at the first opportunity.

Good design
for effective revision

The Economic Problem and Demand and Supply

Syllabus analysis
Ensures you only do the topics you need – no more, no less

Start and completion column Keeps tabs on your progress – see at a glance which areas still need to be worked through

Chapter breakdown
Shows you in detal what is covered in the chapters

Self-assessement
For you to note how well you've done or areas which to to be revised again

AEB	NEAB	OCSEB	UCLES	ULE	UODLE		Date begun	Date completed	Self-assessment
✓	✓	✓	✓	✓	✓	**Fact sheets**			
✓					✓	**Investigative study**			
✓	✓	✓	✓	✓	✓	**Data response**			
✓	✓	✓	✓	✓	✓	**Objective questions**			
✓	✓	✓	✓	✓		**Essays**			

Contents

Topic

Exam Board Addresses

For syllabuses and past papers contact the Publications office at the following addresses:

The Associated Examining Board
Publications Department
Stag Hill House
Guildford
Surrey
GU2 5XJ
Tel. 01483 302302

University of Cambridge Local
　Examinations Syndicate
1 Hills Road
Cambridge
CB1 2EU
Tel. 01223 553311

Northern Examinations and
　Assessment Board
12 Harter Street
Manchester
M1 6HL
Tel. 0161 953 1170
(Also shop at the above address)

University of London Examinations
　and Assessment Council
Stewart House
32 Russell Square
London
WC1B 5DN
Tel. 0171 331 4000

Oxford and Cambridge Schools
　Examination Board
Purbeck House
Purbeck Road
Cambridge
CB2 2PU
Tel. 01223 411211

University of Oxford Delegacy of Local
　Examinations
Ewert Place
Summertown
Oxford
OX2 7BZ
Tel. 01865 54291

Northern Ireland Council for the
　Curriculum, Examinations and
　Assessment
29 Clarendon Road
Belfast
BT1 3BG
Tel. 01232 261200
Fax 01232 261234

Welsh Joint Education Committee
245 Western Avenue
Llandaff
Cardiff
CF5 2YX

Remember to check your syllabus
number with your teacher!

Introduction

How to use this book

This book has been designed to help you prepare for your A Level examination in economics. Simply buying a revision text does not guarantee examination success. However, by working from this book over the months leading up to the final examination you will improve your ability to understand and apply key economic concepts.

Work Out Economics A Level is not intended as a textbook but as a comprehensive revision manual. If there are topics you have not covered in class, refer to a good textbook and make notes from the relevant chapter. Key economic terms are in *italic* type for emphasis and are clearly defined in the text.

The book is divided into self-contained chapters, each covering a major topic. At the beginning of each chapter you will find a summary of the essential economics you need to know. Make sure you become thoroughly familiar with the material in these summaries.

Each chapter contains a number of worked examples of the type of question you can expect in the final examination. For data response and essay-type questions, suggested solutions are given. It is absolutely essential that you do not treat the solutions provided as 'model' answers to be memorised and then copied out in the examination. In economics there is almost always more than one 'correct' solution to a given problem. This is particularly true in macroeconomics, where professional economists are divided as to the causes and cures for problems

such as inflation and unemployment. Use the solution given as an indication of the sort of analytical skills of evaluation and judgement that you should be using yourself.

The section on objective questions gives you a chance to test your knowledge and understanding of a topic. Do these questions without looking at the answers provided. If you give an incorrect solution to one of the questions refer back to the relevant section in the fact sheet.

Revision

Most courses in A Level economics are over two years. Ideally, preparation begins six months before the final examination. You cannot hope or expect to sustain intensive concentration for twenty-six weeks. Start by obtaining a copy of the syllabus from the appropriate examining group. Use the syllabus to write out a study plan, listing the topics you are going to revise each week. Spend most time studying the concepts and issues that are central to the subject. For instance you may find that some topics, such as welfare economics, are covered in more depth in *Work Out Economics A Level* than is required by your syllabus.

Build up to a period of intensive revision during the last four weeks before the exam. Many people find it helpful to write as they revise. Make notes on one side of loose-leaf paper, leaving generous margins in case you want to add new ideas. In particular, make sure that when you have finished a topic you can:

(1) Define economic terms
(2) List key points
(3) Apply important concepts
(4) Draw relevant graphs

It is important to be able to draw graphs quickly and accurately, and a little practice will be needed.

The number of hours you put in is far less important than what you put into those hours. Most students find that they can concentrate better and learn faster if they work in bursts of thirty minutes with regular breaks. Avoid uninterrupted three-hour slogs. Promise yourself a special 'treat' at the end of a successful revision session.

Try to review the material covered shortly after you have studied it, and again a few days later. At the beginning of the revision programme have a look at past questions and write down the main points you would make in an answer. Draw and label relevant graphs. Make sure you can explain in your own words important concepts such as crowding out and inferior goods. It may help to draw up your own glossary of key economic words. Find time to familiarise yourself with current economic trends in the UK by reading economic articles in the quality newspapers and journals. For instance, do you know the present rate of inflation or the balance of payments trend? Similarly, you should be aware of the current government's policy. Are you aware of the Chancellor's strategy for demand management of the economy? As the final exam approaches, practise answering questions in full and under examination conditions. You will soon find that your ability to apply economics has improved beyond all measure.

Make sure your study programme is balanced and allows time for enjoyment and relaxation. Work hard, do your best and look forward to the long summer holiday, when you can take a well-earned break.

The examination

You are bound to be slightly nervous on the day of the exam. So is everyone else. Remember, with careful revision and good examination techniques picked up by reading this book, you should do well. Arrive in good time. Do not forget to take the appropriate equipment for each paper. There are three main types of question in the final examination, although boards also make use of case studies and investigative studies – see the grid at the end of the Introduction.

(a) Essay questions

For this paper you are going to need two pens, a ruler, a pencil, a rubber and a watch. Correcting fluids such as Tipp-Ex are not allowed! Essay questions test your ability to evaluate arguments and express viewpoints. Most students find this type of question the hardest to tackle, and on average the marks earned in the essay paper are lower than those for data response and objective test papers.

Start by reading through the paper and identifying the topic covered by each question. Check the phraseology, taking particular note of key words as these will indicate what the examiner is looking for. For instance, *'compare and contrast'* means discuss similarities and differences, while *'elucidate'* means explain. Only answer questions on topics you have revised. Only attempt questions where you can answer each part. Once you have decided to attempt a question, briefly plan your answer. Many candidates like to gain confidence by tackling their best question first. Remember, there are two main reasons why capable students underachieve when writing essays:

(1) Candidates decide a question is about one topic (e.g. inflation) and then write all they know about that topic.
(2) Candidates copy out a memorised answer to a similar past question.

You will do much better if your answer is a well-reasoned explanation that is relevant to the set question. Develop a line of argument that has a beginning, a middle and an end. Try starting your essay by defining the important economic terms given in the question. Then make clear any assumptions you are going to make. For example, suppose the question is ' "In the long run, all firms earn normal profits, only." Discuss'. You might begin by defining firms and normal profits and then continue by initially assuming a perfectly competitive market structure. After establishing that the ability of firms to leave or enter the industry ensures that only normal profits are earned in perfectly competitive markets, in the long run, end the essay by evaluating an industry assuming imperfect competition.

Some questions, such as the one just discussed, lend themselves to a graphical analysis. Clear, neat and labelled graphs that are relevant to the set question can save a hundred words of explanation. It is always better to draw a series of graphs to advance an argument than to use one diagram for all stages of an argument. Avoid simply drawing diagrams and then ignoring them in your answer. Any graph should be an integral part of the essay. Draw the examiners' attention to a diagram by stating, say, 'in Figure 1 the firm sets output at Q'. Write in clear, simple short sentences. Often arguments are best developed by stating a point, explaining that point and then giving a real-world example. For instance, suppose part of a question asked, 'Explain the meaning of *ad valorem* taxes'. You might write:

> An *ad valorem* tax means value added tax [statement]. A given percentage is added to the selling price of a good and the resulting tax is passed on to the government by the seller [explanation]. For example, 17.5% VAT on the sale of a £200 camera would increase its market price to £235 and raise £35 of tax for the government [example].

Once a point has been fully developed, start a new paragraph. Try to relate your theory to the real world. Examiners are always impressed if a candidate can display an understanding of how economics influences the world around us. Remember, too, that good candidates avoid narrow interpretations and recognise that there is more than one valid approach. Do not use unacceptable abbreviations, for example, 'gov' instead of government. When using acceptable abbreviations, first write out the word or phrase in full with the abbreviation following in brackets. For instance, 'International Monetary Fund (IMF)'. Thereafter you may use the abbreviation.

It is absolutely essential that you complete the required number of questions. If you are running out of time and cannot complete an answer, do a full essay plan, including graphs where appropriate.

Be careful to avoid irrelevant answers – these not only earn no marks, but also waste valuable time that could have been used to earn marks from another question. No marks are earned by waffle or by repeating points made earlier in the essay. Do not spend too much time on one particular question. Set out your work clearly and neatly. Use your economics. Above all, make sure that what you are writing is relevant and answers the set question.

(b) Data response questions

For this paper you are going to need two pens, a ruler, a pencil, a rubber and a watch. Bring a calculator along. Remember to check that the batteries are not on the verge of running out. Data response questions are especially good at testing your ability to apply economics and to quantify. There are two types of data response questions: *statistical data*, displayed as graphs, tables, charts or diagrams, and *literary prose extracts* from newspapers, journals, etc. Each examining board tends to have its own 'house' style of data response question. Make sure you have familiarised yourself with examples drawn from previous papers. In the actual exam, allocate sufficient time for a careful study of the entire question. Here is a check-list of points to consider when tackling statistical data response questions:

(1) Ask yourself what key economic concepts are being tested by the question.
(2) Look at how the data have been obtained:
   (a) Are there any hidden assumptions or unsupported statements?
   (b) Is the evidence used selective or biased?
   (c) Is the survey *complete* (i.e. all the appropriate population have been included) or a *sample* (i.e. only some of the population have been included)?
(3) Identify major variables in the data:
   (a) Are the figures shown as absolute values, percentages, index numbers, billions of £s, thousands of people etc.?
   (b) Which is the largest item?
   (c) How do other items compare?
   (d) Which variables are *stock values* (i.e. an amount at a given moment in time) or *flow values* (i.e. an amount per time period)?
(4) Observe any trends (patterns) in the data:
   (a) Which variables are rising, falling or stable?
   (b) What is the percentage change in a variable? Use the equation:

$$\frac{\text{percentage}}{\text{change}} = \frac{(\text{present value} - \text{previous value})}{\text{previous value}} \times 100$$

   (c) Are any variables cyclical?
(5) Is there a direct relationship between any variables in the data? Look out for:
   (a) *Causal relationships*, where the value of one variable determines the value of a second variable. However, remember that unrelated variables sometimes move closely together.
   (b) *Lagged relationships*, where the current value of one variable is related to the previous value of a second variable.
(6) Relate your knowledge of theory to the data. Can

you give reasons for relationships, trends or cycles observed?

(7) Always look for relevant data to explain your assertions.

Gain confidence in handling and interpreting statistical data by familiarising yourself with typical examples. Much of the data used by economists is presented as *time series*, which show the value of a particular variable such as national income at different points in time. Great use is made of official statistics issued by the Central Statistical Office (CSO). Try to find time to look at CSO publications such as the 'Blue Book' (UK National Accounts) or the 'Pink Book' (Balance of Payments Statistics), which are kept in the reference section of most public libraries.

Literary data response questions present an extract and sometimes supporting tables for analysis. Spend time reading the section of prose carefully. Many of the check-list of points given above for use with statistical data can equally be applied to prose. You are almost certainly going to be asked to identify and express *in your own words* the main features of the data. Try to avoid making sweeping or vague statements that are unsupported by evidence. Instead, explain the essential features of the extract, quoting relevant phrases from the text only to support a point made in your own words. Always indicate such phrases by 'quotation marks'.

Many literary data response questions ask candidates to apply economic concepts. You are expected to relate relevant theories such as supply-and-demand or theory of the firm to the extract presented. Remember that a variety of approaches may be required. Diagrams should be used if appropriate.

You may be asked to evaluate the data and then predict future trends or outcomes. Look back at the extract and identify key variables, relationships and economic concepts. Use these as the basis of your predictions. Avoid making a series of random predictions unsupported by information contained in the data provided.

(c) Objective questions

For this paper you are going to need a pencil, rubber, ruler, watch and calculator. Objective questions are well suited to testing your knowledge and understanding of theories, and deal with 'certainty' areas of economics. Hence, objective questions are set on topics where economists are agreed that there is a single correct answer.

These *multiple-choice questions* contain a stem and a number of possible answers, of which only one is correct.

Example 1

STEM	Industrial inertia occurs when:

	A the share of manufacturing in national output declines	
DISTRACTORS {	**B** firms fail to exploit economies of scale	} OPTIONS
	C industry gains no cost advantage from any one site	
KEY	**D** the initial reasons for location have disappeared	

The *stem* sets the question and candidates have to choose between a number of incorrect *distractors* and the correct option, called the *key*. Some questions can be answered quickly. Look at the options and see where there are any that can be immediately eliminated or accepted. If not, it is important not to be delayed by those questions requiring deep thought or lengthy calculations. Remember: each question, whether easy or difficult, carries the same number of marks. Make a note of such questions for later consideration and carry on working through the paper.

A range of strategies can be used when tackling the objective question paper. Only one rule must be followed: answer all the questions. Some candidates prefer to work through the paper, answering each question in turn, irrespective of the amount of time or degree of difficulty involved. However we have already suggested that it may be better to delay answering time-consuming questions until you have worked through all other questions. Be sure to treat each question carefully and not to give a wrong answer through carelessly misreading the stem or options. Questions with 'not' in the stem are particularly dangerous! For this type of question, the option to which you can answer 'no' is the correct solution.

If you begin to run out of time, work through the remaining questions allowing yourself a maximum of, say, 20 seconds per question. If time is about to run out completely, make sure you scribble down some answer and hope that at least one or two will be right.

In any case, DON'T PANIC. Both authors wish you all the best and good luck in the final exams!

The new A Level syllabuses

All the newly approved syllabuses have the following characteristics in common:
- Less emphasis on some traditional areas of content, e.g. Keynesian 45° approaches.
- Greater emphasis on examining the strengths and weaknesses of the market economy.
- Reduced assessment weightings for knowledge and understanding, with most marks now being awarded for achievement of 'higher order' skills.
- Greater focus on the application of economics to contemporary issues.

There are also significant differences between the new syllabuses and these are illustrated in the following table.

Exam board	Changed assessment weightings[1]	Multiple choice	Coursework	Focused study[2]	Modularity
AEB	yes	yes	yes	yes	no
NEAB	yes	yes	no	no	no
Oxford	yes	yes	yes	yes	yes
O & C	yes	yes	no	yes	no
ULEAC (Nuffield)	n/a	no	yes	no	partial[1]
ULEAC (Traditional)	yes	yes	no	yes	no
UCLES Linear	yes	yes	no	no	no
UCLES Modular	n/a	no	no	yes	yes
WJEC	yes	yes	no	no	no

Notes:
[1] Choice between business studies and economics routes.
[2] Extended study of a particular economic issue/context.
Source: The Economics & Business Education Association.

The Economic Problem and Demand and Supply

PART I

AEB	NEAB	OCSEB	UCLES	ULE	UODLE	Topic	Date begun	Date completed	Self-assessment
✓	✓	✓	✓	✓	✓	**Fact sheets**			
✓					✓	**Investigative study**			
✓	✓	✓	✓	✓	✓	**Data response**			
✓	✓	✓	✓	✓	✓	**Objective questions**			
✓	✓	✓	✓	✓	✓	**Essays**			

The Economic Problem

1.1 Fact sheet

(a) The economic problem

(1) Wants and needs are satisfied through the consumption (use) of goods and services.

(2) *Outputs* (goods and services) are produced from inputs (resources) sometimes called *factors of production*. The four factors are land, labour, capital and entrepreneurs.

(3) The economic problem arises because, while our resources are finite, our wants and needs are infinite.

(4) All societies have to decide which goods and services to produce, how to produce them, and who is to receive them.

- *Resource allocation* refers to a particular use of land, labour, capital and entrepreneurs.

(b) Economic methodology

Economics is a social science that uses scientific methods:

(1) A *hypothesis* (prediction) is constructed about economic behaviour that may be right or may be wrong.

(2) A *model* is built describing the behaviour of economic variables (influencing factors) involved in the initial hypothesis.

(3) The hypothesis is tested against *empirical* (real world) evidence by use of the model.

(4) If the hypothesis cannot be disproved, it becomes an accepted *theory*.

- Economists isolate the relationship between two variables by assuming *ceteris paribus* – i.e. that all other influencing factors are held constant.

- *Positive economics* deals with statements of fact that can be proved or disproved, and shows how the economy actually works.

- *Normative economics* deals with statements of opinion that cannot be proved or disproved, and suggests what should be done to solve economic problems.

- *Microeconomics* considers the behaviour of an individual consumer, firm and industry, and is mainly interested in resource allocation and relative prices.

- *Macroeconomics* considers the behaviour of the economy as a whole, and is mainly interested in national output, employment, the balance of payments and the general price level.

(c) Opportunity cost

The decision to produce or consume one product involves the sacrifice of another product. The real or opportunity cost of an action is the next best forgone alternative.

- An economic good is in limited supply and possesses an opportunity cost – e.g. a car.

- However a free good is not scarce and has no opportunity cost – e.g. sunshine.

(d) Production possibility curves

A *production possibility curve* (PPC) is sometimes called an opportunity cost or transformation curve, and shows the combination of two goods a country can make in a given time period with resources fully employed (Figure 1.1). A PPC is drawn assuming a country has a fixed amount of resources and a constant state of technology.

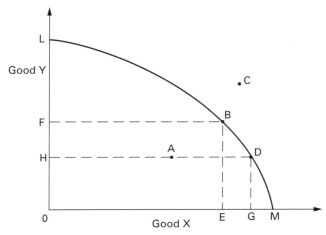

Figure 1.1 A production possibility curve

(1) LM is a PPC
(2) Points under the PPC (e.g. A) imply resource underutilisation.
(3) Points along the PPC (e.g. B) indicate a full employment of resources.
(4) Points outside the PPC (e.g. C) are beyond the current productive capacity of the economy.
(5) The opportunity cost of producing 0E amount of good X is LF of good Y.
(6) The opportunity cost of reallocating resources from B to D is FH of good Y.

* A concave (bowed outwards) production possibility curve indicates increasing opportunity cost. As more of good X is produced, increasing amounts of good Y have to be forgone to produce an extra unit of good Y.
* A straight line production possibility curve indicates a constant opportunity cost. As production of good X changes, the amount of good Y that has to be forgone to gain an extra unit of good X does not change.
* A convex (bowed inwards) production possibility curve shows a decreasing opportunity cost. As more of good X is produced, the cost of an extra unit good X in terms of forgone good Y declines.
* An increase in the quantity and/or quality of

resources will increase an economy's productive potential. This is shown by a shift to the right of the production possibility curve.

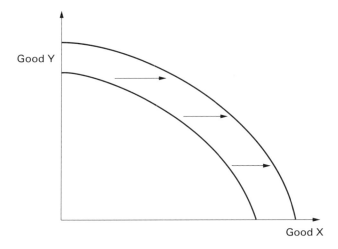

Figure 1.2 A shift of the production possibility curve

(e) Types of economic system

An *economic system* is the network of organisations used by a society to resolve the economic problem. There are three categories of economic system.

(i) Free market economy

* Resources are owned by households.
* Markets allocate resources through the *price mechanism*. An increase in demand raises price. The higher price encourages firms to switch additional resources into the production of that good.
* Income depends on the market value of a resource. Factors in scarce supply and high demand are best rewarded.

(ii) Planned or command economy

* Resources are owned by the state.
* The state allocates resources, and sets production targets and growth rates according to its own view of people's wants.
* Income distribution is decided by the state, and ignores the scarcity value of a particular factor.

(iii) Mixed economy

In practice all economies are mixed where:

* Some resources are owned by the public sector (i.e. the government).

Table 1.1 Problems of different economic systems

Market economy can result in	Planned economy can result in
The non-production of public goods	Production not satisfying consumers' real wants
Monopolies reducing competition	Reduced consumer sovereignty
Production ignoring externalities	Shortages and surpluses of products
An unequal distribution of income and wealth.	The forgone output of administrators
High unemployment	Reduced incentives lowering individual effort

- Some resources are owned by the private sector (i.e. households).

(f) Move from a command economy

In the transition from a command towards a market economy a number of problems may be encountered:

(1) Structural change as resources are reallocated to reflect the choices of households rather than the government.

(2) Inflation resulting from the removal of government price controls.

(3) Redistribution of income leaving some people unable to afford basic necessities.

(4) Lack of regulation of firms as it will take time to establish new regulatory bodies.

(5) Industrial unrest as workers and employers establish new wage rates, new working conditions and new terms of tenure.

See also chapter 13.

1.2 Investigative study

Example 1.1

A comparison of the macroeconomic performance of two formerly planned economies, e.g. the Czech Republic and Russia.

1.3 Data response

(a) What would be the opportunity cost of treating the 10-year-old girl? **(6 marks)**

(b) What would be the opportunity cost of not treating the 10-year-old girl? **(4 marks)**

(c) On what grounds might expenditure on treatment that has little chance of success be justified? **(4 marks)**

(d) In what sense are all economic decisions 'the judgment of Solomon'? **(5 marks)**

(e) Distinguish between how the quantity of resources to be allocated to health care is determined in a command and in a market economy. **(6 marks)**

Example 1.2

Dying girl in court fight for treatment

Sally Weale

A High Court judge will today rule on an application by the father of a 10-year old girl with leukaemia who is seeking to overturn a decision by his local health authority to refuse funding for further treatment which could save her life.

The court heard yesterday that the girl, who in January was given six to eight weeks to live, would die without the £75,000 treatment. It would involve intensive chemotherapy followed by a second bone marrow transplant.

Cambridge Health Authority argues that her chances of survival are so slight and the treatment so distressing that its limited resources might be better spent.

The judge, Mr Justice Laws, sitting in London's Law Courts on the opening day of the hearing yesterday, said the case centred on the most precious right of all, "namely the right to life"

Nigel Pitt, counsel for the health authority, said it was not a straightforward question of life and death. The girl's case was particularly difficult and the treatment proposed was debilitating with severe side effects, which "in all probability" she would not survive. The alternative was to adopt a palliative approach, enabling B to enjoy a few weeks or months of normal life.

Mr Pitt claimed the chances of success, using statistics provided by Peter Gravett, the consultant haematologist at the London Clinic, who would carry out the treatment, were in the region of 2.25 per cent.

Other figures quoted by Mr McIntyre suggested the chances were slightly higher. "Even if it's only in the order of 5 or 6 per cent, she has a significant chance of being cured."

According to Mr Pitt the treatment could not be justified on therapeutic grounds. The only basis on which it could be justified was for experimental or research reasons.

Mr Justice Laws asked: "How can it not be justified on therapeutic grounds when the alternative is certain death? It's what a betting man calls a risk against certainty. Every man who wanted to live would take that risk."

Mr Pitt described the balancing act performed by health authorities in deciding how to allocate limited resources. It was not the first desperately needed operation not to have received NHS funding, he said "It's the judgment of Solomon."

"If the health authority were to spend all its money on treatments which doctors had advised were extremely unlikely to succeed and then had no money left to treat hundreds of other patients who might have been effectively treated, what would the public have to say about that?"

He asked whether any particular patient had any more fundamental right to life from NHS money than any other.

The judge responded: "Well possibly a child close to death may be said to have a more pressing claim."

Mr Justice Laws will give his judgment today.

Source: Extract from the *Guardian*, 10 March 1995

Solution 1.2

(a) Opportunity cost is the best alternative forgone. Treating the girl would take up limited resources, including doctors', nurses' and theatre time. This means that other patients would forgo the opportunity of treatment. These patients might have a greater chance of recovery. The NHS has limited resources and choices have to be made as to who to treat. Demand for treatment exceeds supply. Treating the girl might also reduce the quality of the girl's life during the period of treatment.

(b) By not treating the girl there is a risk that the girl's life would be lost. The opportunity cost might also involve missing out on the opportunity to try out new forms of treatment and improving the quality of the lives of the girl's relatives.

(c) Expenditure on treatment that has little chance of success can be justified on the ground that it may improve medical knowledge and thereby increase the quality and length of people's lives in the future. When heart transplant operations were first carried out, for example, the success rate was low.

(d) All economic decisions, whether in terms of what to produce, what to buy or how to spend one's time, involve having to make choices. Just as it is not possible to treat everyone, given limited NHS resources, it is not possible to produce everything that people would like to consume, for example. These decisions can be very difficult and the opportunity cost high.

(e) In a command economy the quantity of resources to be devoted to health care is determined by the state. The state assesses the needs of the population and the resources available and then issues directives to state hospitals. In a market economy resources are allocated via the price mechanism. If people want more health care, the price of health care will rise and more resources will be allocated to health care. The price mechanism also rations goods. Those who can afford to pay will receive health care.

1.4 Objective questions

Example 1.3

A worker is currently earning £400 for a 40 hour week. The management offer a 12% wage increase or a basic wage of £410 and a reduction in the working week to 38 hours. What is the opportunity cost if the worker opts for a 38 hour week?

A 2 hours **B** 38 hours **C** £38 **D** £48

Example 1.4

A woman bought a car for £7000 but would like a new model costing £8200. She could obtain £5900 if she sold her car. What is the opportunity cost of her owning her current car?

A £1100 **B** £1200 **C** £5900 **D** £8200

Example 1.5

Which of the following is a normative economic statement?

A The state decides what is produced in a command economy
B A higher proportion of consumer goods is produced in a market economy than in a command economy
C Command economies have a higher rate of economic growth than market economies
D A market economy is a more desirable form of economic system than a command economy

Example 1.6

Which of the following is an example of a free good?

A Sea water
B State education
C An expenses-paid business trip
D A toy included in a cereal packet to encourage people to buy the cereal

Example 1.7

Which of the following would shift the production possibility frontier of an economy to the right?

A A more even distribution of wealth
B An increase in the stock of capital
C An increase in the number of people dependent on the working population
D An improvement in the efficiency with which factors of production are combined

Example 1.8

The figure overleaf illustrates the production possibility curve of a country.

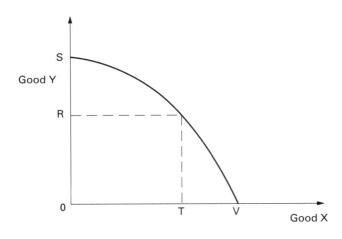

What is the opportunity cost of producing 0T amount of good X?

A   0R amount of good Y
B   RS amount of good Y
C   TV amount of good X
D   0V amount of good X

Example 1.9

What does a straight-line production possibility curve illustrate?

A   A constant rate of opportunity cost in the production of both goods
B   A decreasing rate of opportunity cost in the production of both goods
C   An increasing rate of opportunity cost in the production of both goods
D   A decreasing rate of opportunity cost in the production of one of the goods and an increasing rate of opportunity cost in the production of the other good.

Example 1.10

The figure below shows the production possibility frontier for a country currently producing at point K.

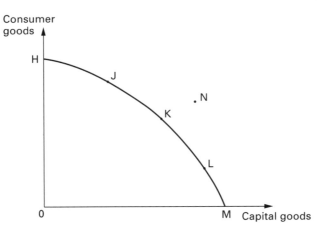

How could the economy eventually reach point N?

A   Move to point H
B   Move to point J
C   Move to point L
D   Employ idle resources

Example 1.11

What is the essential characteristic of a market economy?

A   Full employment
B   Producer surplus
C   Public corporations
D   Consumer sovereignty

Example 1.12

Only in a pure command economy does production

A   respond to prices
B   respond to directives
C   reflect the preferences of firms
D   reflect the preferences of households

1.5 Solutions to objective questions

Solution 1.3   Answer: **C**

A 12% wage increase on a 40 hour week would give a pay increase of £400 × 12/100 = £48. So a worker opting for a 40 hour week would earn £400 + £48 = £448. Therefore if the worker elects to work 38 hours and earn £410 he/she will be forgoing £38.

Solution 1.4   Answer: **C**

Opportunity cost is cost in terms of the best alternative forgone. By keeping her own car the woman is forgoing the opportunity to obtain £5900.

Solution 1.5   Answer: **D**

A normative statement is one based on opinion and cannot be proved or disproved against real world (empirical) evidence. Option **D** is a matter of opinion since people will disagree about what is a desirable form of economic system. Options **A**, **B** and **C** are all positive statements as they can all be assessed objectively. For instance, analysis of economic data may prove that some market economies actually have a higher rate of economic growth than some command economies.

Solution 1.6   Answer: **A**

A free good is one that does not require resources to produce it and is not scarce. Sea water is replenished naturally and has no opportunity cost. Whilst the good and services described in options **B**, **C** and **D** are free to the consumer, they all require resources to produce them that could have been put to alternative uses.

Solution 1.7   Answer: **B**

A production possibility curve (PPC) is sometimes called a production *possibility frontier*. A PCC is drawn on the assumption that a nation's stock of resources, including capital, is fixed. An increase in the stock of capital will increase the productive potential of a country and hence shift the PPC to the right.

B ⇒ A more even distribution of wealth may affect the patterns of consumption and production but its effect on the position of the PPC is uncertain.

C ⇒ An increase in the number of dependents will increase the burden on the working population but not the potential output of the country.

D ⇒ An improvement in the efficiency with which resources are combined would cause a movement from inside to near or on the production possibility curve.

Solution 1.8   Answer: **B**

If the economy is producing 0T amount of goal X, it

is also producing 0R amount of good Y. If it did not produce 0T amount of good X and devoted all its resources to good Y, it would be able to produce 0S amount of good Y. So by producing 0T amount of good X it is forgoing RS amount of good Y.

Solution 1.9   Answer: **A**

A straight-line production possibility curve illustrates a situation where resources are equally good at producing both types of good. In this situation the opportunity cost of producing an extra unit of either of the goods will remain constant. This is shown in the figure below. When the society increases its output of good X from 1 to 2 units, the opportunity cost is half a unit of good Y. Similarly to increase the output of good X from 14 to 15, half a unit of good Y has to be given up. The opportunity cost of producing good Y remains constant. To increase the output of good Y from 2.5 to 3 or from 8 to 8.5 will include forgoing 1 unit of X.

Option **B** would be illustrated by a bowed outwards (concave) PCC and option **C** by a bowed inwards (convex) PPC. The situation described in option **D** is not possible.

Solution 1.10   Answer: **C**

The movement from point K to point N can only come about if the production possibility curve (PPC) shifts to the right, to UW.

This requires an increase in the productive capacity of the economy. Moving along the PPC from K to L shifts resources out of the production of consumer goods and into the production of capital goods.

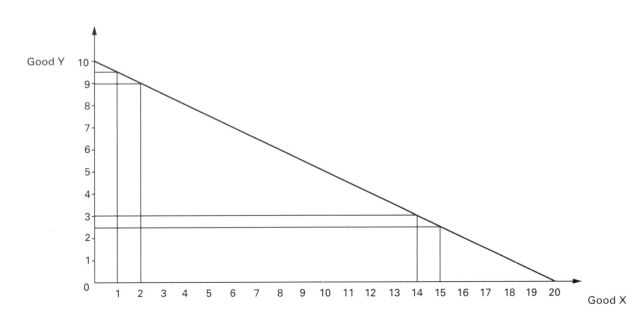

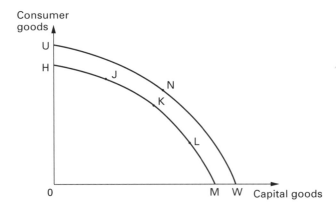

Additional capital goods can be used to make more consumer and capital goods and the economy can be at point N. Other options are wrong because:

A and **B** ⇒ reduce the productive capacity of the economy.

D ⇒ Point K lies on the PPC, so no idle resources are available.

Solution 1.11   Answer: **D**

In a market economy, households have consumer sovereignty and determine what is produced by 'voting' with their purchases. For instance, if consumers demand more of a product the price rises and more is supplied. Other options are wrong because:

A ⇒ Full employment is unlikely to occur in a market economy.

B ⇒ Firms do not necessarily enjoy producer surplus.

C ⇒ Public corporations are nationalised industries and a feature of mixed economies.

Solution 1.12   Answer: **B**

A command economy is run by the state and directives (instructions) are used to organise production. Other options are wrong because:

A ⇒ Prices are not used as a method of regulating production in a pure command economy.

C and **D** ⇒ In a pure command economy production reflects the decisions of the state and not the preferences of firms, nor directly the preferences of households.

1.6 Essays

Example 1.13

(a) Distinguish between 'market' and 'command' economies. **(10 marks)**

(b) A number of countries have recently decided to move from a command towards a market economy. On what grounds can it be judged which type of economic system is superior. **(15 marks)**

- In (a), establish criteria such as resource ownership for comparing market and command economies.
- In (b), (1) explain how welfare criteria can be used to judge the success of an individual economic system; (2) one economic system is superior to another only if it is better able to satisfy welfare criteria – discuss the evidence.
- Throughout, avoid making subjective, political statements of opinion.

Solution 1.13

(a) A market economy is an economic system where resources are owned by individuals and allocated by the price mechanism without government intervention. In a command economy, the government owns resources and decides on the type and quantity to be made. A study of comparative economic systems will try to identify and contrast characteristics common to both types of economy. For instance property rights are the rules that define the use to which resources may be put. In market economies, individuals are free to buy and sell land, labour and capital, provided that they do not infringe the legal property rights of others. In a command economy, individuals can own consumer goods but they are not allowed to own industrial plant or machinery. All non-labour resource are owned by the state.

Different economic systems have different methods of resolving the problem of scarcity. Market economies use the price mechanism to allocate resources. All goods, services and resources have a market price. An increase in consumer demand raises the price and encourages a firm to increase production of a good by transferring resources out of the manufacture of less profitable products. In command economies, the state allocates resources according to its own view of what people want. A body of central planners decides what proportion of resources to devote to consumer and producer goods. It then sets production targets and arranges for the supply of necessary inputs. Firms aim not to make a profit but to meet production targets.

It can be seen that the decision-making process in command economies is collectivist and centralised. The government is the single most important economic institution. On the other hand, decision making in market economies is highly individualistic and decentralised. The role of the state is limited to collecting taxes to pay for public goods such as defence, and enforcing property rights.

The method of motivating economic agents varies between the two systems. In market economies, jobs in high demand but short supply command high wages. Successful entrepreneurs receive profits for taking on the risk and responsibility of organising production. Hence income and wealth distributions are unequal. In command economies, limited wage differentials do exist to reward extra effort. However, it is the sense of 'shared purpose' springing from the common ownership of resources that is meant to act as the prime 'moral' incentive to work.

(b) The success of an economic system lies in its ability to use resources to satisfy as many wants as possible. Welfare economics supplies a number of tests that can be used to judge the absolute efficiency of an economic system. There are two main tests:
(1) Is it possible to reallocate resources and increase output?
(2) Is it possible to reallocate resources and make a consumer better off without making anyone else worse off?
The system that best meets these conditions will be superior. Before considering empirical evidence, it is important to note that real-world examples such as the USA and Cuba only approximate to theoretical market and command models.

Economic theory suggest that a competitive market economy automatically brings about an optimal resource allocation. However market failure occurs when some private-sector firms in the USA do not take full account of the spill-over effects of production such as pollution. Frictions in factor markets have resulted in mass unemployment and a general depression. Moreover efficiency criteria make no statement about the 'fairness' of an uneven distribution of income and wealth in the USA.

Data suggest that there is hardly any unemployment in Cuba. However critics argue that this has only been achieved by massive overmanning. Productivity and standards of living could be raised following a reallocation of resources. Modern economies are highly specialised, interdependent and complex. In the absence of market prices, planners have insufficient information upon which to base welfare-maximising decisions. Distorted information prevents planners from taking full account of production and consumption externalities.

It used to be thought that there would be little pollution in command economies as state planners would take into account social costs and benefits. However recent evidence has shown that pollution levels were very high in a number of former planned economies, including East Germany, Romania and Poland. In these cases the state was more concerned to increase output than to improve the quality of the environment.

In conclusion, it can be seen that comparing market and command economies is difficult and complex. The final judgement depends on the importance placed on a particular measure. For example, in terms of productivity, evidence suggests that market economies are superior to command economies; in terms of unemployment levels, evidence suggests that command economies are superior to market economies.

Example 1.14

(a) What fundamental economic principles are illustrated by a production possibility frontier? Explain the usual shape of a production possibility frontier. **(10 marks)**
(b) How does a production possiblity frontier illustrate 'economic inefficiency'? **(5 marks)**
(c) What can cause a movement of a production possibility frontier? **(5 marks)**
(d) What may enable an economy to consume a combination of goods outside its production possibility frontier? **(5 marks)**

• Devote most attention to part (a) as it carries the highest number of marks.
• In part (a):
  (1) discuss scarcity, choice, opportunity cost and efficiency, but efficiency only briefly as it comes into part (b);
  (2) explain, using an example, the usual shape of the production possibility frontier.
• In part (b) explain, by using a point inside a

production possibility frontier, the meaning of economic inefficiency.

- In part (c) consider factors that can cause a rightward shift in the production possibility frontier and illustrate these.
- In part (d) consider the significance of international trade.

Solution 1.14

(a) A production possibility frontier shows the maximum output that can be produced with the efficient use of existing resources. Figure 1 shows that if all resources are devoted to producing consumer goods, 200 consumer goods can be made, whereas if all resources are devoted to making capital goods, 50 can be made. It is also possible to produce any combination of capital and consumer goods along and inside the production possiblity frontier.

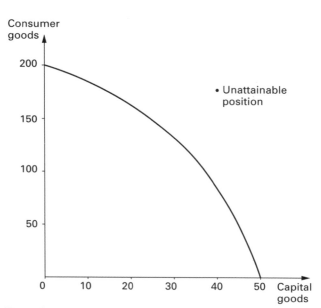

Figure 1

A production possibility frontier illustrates the principles of scarcity. Society may like to produce, say, 180 consumer goods and 40 capital goods, but Figure 1 shows that this is not possible (it is an unattainable position). Society's wants exceed resources. At any one time output potential is limited by the resources available.

A production possibility frontier also illustrates choice and opportunity cost. Figure 2 shows that society could choose to produce 150 consumer goods and 23 capital goods. If it decides to produce more capital goods it will have to produce fewer consumer goods. Society will be choosing to switch some resources from producing consumer goods to producing capital goods. A decision to increase the output of capital goods from 23 to 30 will involve forgoing 25 consumer goods.

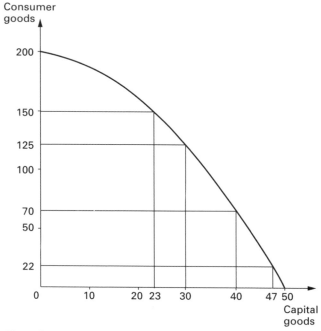

Figure 2

Production possibility frontiers are usually drawn as curves concave to the origin as it is thought that, in most cases, the opportunity cost of producing one category of good will increase as its output rises. In Figure 2 when the output of capital goods rises from 40 to 47 the opportunity cost rises from 25 to 48 consumer goods. Increasing opportunity cost occurs because resources are not equally good at producing both products. When the output of capital goods initially starts to rise, resources that are good at producing capital goods will be used. Then, as the output of capital goods increases, further resources that are better at producing consumer goods will have to be used. So more resources will have to switch from making consumer goods to achieve any given rise in output of capital goods, and hence the output of consumer goods will fall further.

Whilst any point outside the curve illustrates an unattainable position, any point on the curve represents full and efficient use of resources.

(b) Economic inefficiency can be illustrated by a point inside a production possibility frontier. Figure 3 shows a society producing at point A, making 100 consumer goods and 20 capital goods. This is an inefficient position that can result from unemployment or inefficient use of resources.

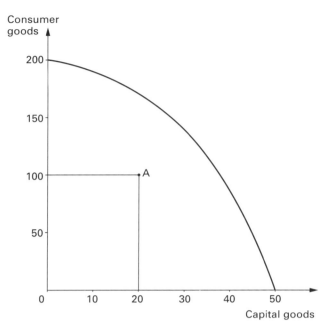

Figure 3

Society is not achieving its productive potential. Greater and more efficient use of resources will result in a rise in output without any opportunity cost. For instance the output of consumer goods could be increased to 165 without having to forgo any capital goods.

(c) A rightward shift of a production possibility curve indicates a rise in productive potential.

An increase in productive potential can be achieved by a rise in the quantity or quality of factors of production. For instance an increase in technology, a rise in the amount and quality of education and training and an increase in the labour force will all raise the output a society can produce. Barring natural disasters, wars and famine, most countries' production possibility frontiers move to the right over time.

(d) Although it is not possible to produce a combination of goods outside a production possibility

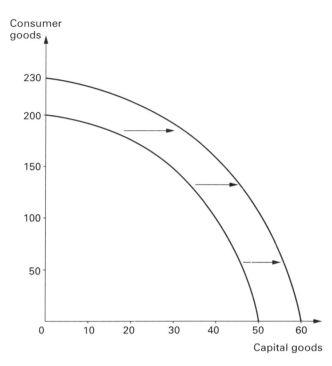

Figure 4

frontier, international trade may enable an economy to attain such a combination. By engaging in international trade countries can specialise in the goods they have comparative advantage in and then exchange some of these for other goods. If the exchange rate lies within the countries' respective opportunity cost ratios, the amount that the countries can consume will rise. In our example, the country can increase the output of capital goods from 23 to 30 by reducing the output of consumer goods from 150 to 125 (see Figure 2). However if it engages in international trade it may be able to exchange consumer goods on the basis of one consumer good for one capital good. This would enable the economy to consume 143 consumer goods and 30 capital goods, a combination that lies outside the production possibility frontier.

Demand

2.1 Fact sheet

(a) Definition of demand

- *Demand* is the amount of a good consumers are both willing and able to buy at a given price.
- A *demand curve* shows the amount of a good consumers are willing and able to buy at different prices.
- The amount of a good demanded depends on:
  (a) price;
  (b) the conditions of demand.

(b) Movements along a demand curve

- A change in price results in a movement along a demand curve, resulting in *a change in the quantity demanded*.

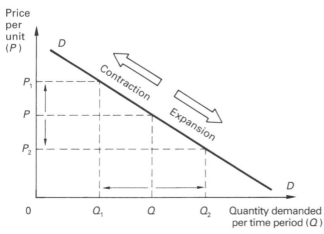

Figure 2.1 Movements along a demand curve

- A change in the price of a good *never* shifts the demand curve for that good.
- In Figure 2.1 an increase in price causes a *contraction* in demand, and a decrease in price results in an *expansion* (or *extension*) in demand.

(c) Individual and market demand

- Individual demand is one buyer's demand for a good.
- Market demand is the total demand for a good.
- A market demand curve is the horizontal summation of all the individual demand curves.

(d) Increases and decreases in demand

- A demand curve is drawn assuming *ceteris paribus* – i.e. that all factors influencing demand are being held constant except price. The *conditions of demand* refer to those factors held constant, and include:
  (a) the real income of consumers;
  (b) the price of other goods in (a) competitive demand (substitution), (b) joint demand (complements);
  (c) consumer taste;
  (d) advertising;
  (e) expectations about the economy;
  (f) the population size and structure.
- A change in one of these conditions affects the level of demand at all prices and results in a shift in the demand curve.

• Figure 2.2 illustrates the effect of a decrease in demand.

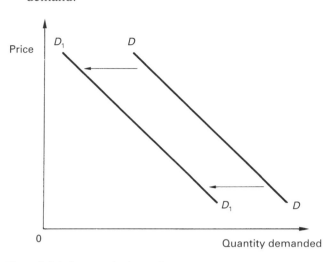

Figure 2.2 A decrease in demand

Causes

• A decrease in real income.
• An increase in the price of a complement.
• A decrease in the price of a substitute.
• An adverse movement in consumer taste.
• A reduction in advertising for this good.
• Reduced expectations about the economy.
• A decrease in the population.

Effect

• The demand curve shifts to the right.

(e)   Income and substitution effects

• The *income effect* occurs when the price of a good falls and the consumer can maintain current consumption for less expenditure. Provided that the good is normal, some of the resulting increase in real income is used to buy more of this product. If the good is inferior, an increase in income is used to buy more of a superior substitute and less of this product.
• The *substitution effect* occurs when the price of a good falls and the consumer substitutes more of this product for others.
• The demand curve of a *Giffen good* (a low-quality product) and of a *Veblen good* (a good purchased to show one's wealth) slope up from left to right. In the case of a Giffen good this is because the income and substitution effects work in opposite directions and the income effect outweighs the

substitution effect. In the case of a Veblen good the income and substitution effects also work in opposite directions, but this time it is the 'perverse' substitution effect that outweighs the income effect.

(f)   Utility

• *Utils* are used to measure satisfaction.
• *Total utility* is the amount of satisfaction obtained by consuming units of a good.
• *Marginal utility* (MU) is the extra satisfaction obtained from consuming one more unit of a good.
• The *law of diminishing marginal utility* states that the more a consumer has of a given commodity, the smaller the satisfaction gained from consuming each extra unit.
• Rational consumers spend their income in order to maximise satisfaction. Consumers compare:
  (a) the utils per extra pound spent on X, using the equation $MV_x P_x$, with
  (b) the utils per extra pound spent on Y, using the equation $MV_y P_y$.
• If the number of utils per pound spent on X is greater than the number of utils per pound spent on Y, consumers can increase their satisfaction by increasing their consumption of X.
• Satisfaction is maximised by arranging expenditure among commodities so as to achieve *equi-marginal returns*. This occurs when:

$$\frac{\text{marginal utility of X}}{\text{price of X}} = \frac{\text{marginal utility of Y}}{\text{price of Y}}$$

• Utility theory requires consumers to be able to measure satisfaction.

(g)   Indifference curves

• An *indifference curve* shows the combinations of two goods whose consumption yields equal total satisfaction to the consumer.
• A *budget line* or *income line* shows all the combinations of two goods the consumer can buy, given a fixed income and constant prices.
• A rational consumer maximises satisfaction by adjusting his or her expenditure between two goods so as to be at the point on the budget line tangential to (just touching) an indifference curve furthest from the origin – i.e. point A in Figure 2.3. In Figure 2.3, JK is the budget line of the consumer, and I_1 and I_2 are indifference curves. I_2

is further from the origin and yields a higher level of satisfaction that does I_1. To maximise satisfaction, the consumer will select point A and buy A amount of good X, and C amount of good Y.

- An increase in income would result in a parallel shift to the right in the budget line JK.
- An increase in price of good X would pivot the budget line around point J towards the origin.

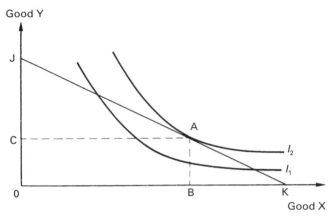

Figure 2.3 Consumer equilibrium

(h) Consumer surplus

- Consumer surplus is the difference between the maximum a consumer would pay for a good and the price actually paid.
- The area of consumer surplus is that above the price line and below the demand curve, as shown in Figure 2.4.

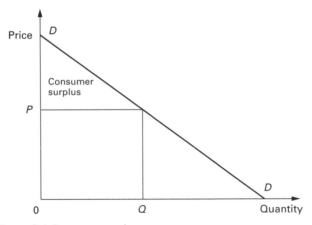

Figure 2.4 Consumer surplus

2.2 Investigative study

Example 2.1

An assessment of the effectiveness, over a period of time, of the measures producers can take to raise demand for their products, e.g. ice cream.

2.3 Data response

Example 2.2

Consumer expenditure at 1990 market prices (£ million). Examples of commodities:

Year	Furniture and floor coverings	Food	Tobacco	Total
1988	6864	41 541	8689	334 591
1989	6748	42 281	8677	345 406
1990	6422	41 816	8578	347 527
1991	6115	41 870	8336	339 993
1992	6303	42 380	7958	339 941

Source: CSO, *Annual Abstract of Statistics*, 1994.

(a) Explain what is meant by 'consumer expenditure at 1990 market prices'. **(3 marks)**
(b) What is the main influence on total consumer expenditure? **(2 marks)**
(c) Comment on changes in:
  (1) total consumer expenditure;
  (2) expenditure on furniture and floor coverings;
  (3) expenditure on food;
  (4) expenditure on tobacco **(13 marks)**
(d) Discuss the influence on demand for a product that you have not covered in **(b)** and **(c)**. **marks)**

Solution 2.2

(a) Consumer expenditure at 1990 market prices means that consumer spending has been adjusted for inflation using 1990 as a base year and has been measured in terms of the prices charged in the shops, so indirect taxes and subsidies have been taken into account.

(b) The main influence on total consumer expenditure is personal disposable income. As income rises total spending is likely to rise but the proportion spent may decline.

(c)

Year	% change in furniture and fittings	% change in food	% change in tobacco	Total
1989	−1.7	1.8	−0.1	3.20
1990	−4.8	−1.1	−1.1	0.60
1991	−4.8	0.1	−2.9	−2.2
1992	3.1	1.2	−4.5	−0.02

(1) Consumer expenditure rose relatively rapidly in 1989, its growth then slowed down in 1990 and fell in 1991 and 1992 during the recession.

(2) Expenditure on furniture and fittings showed the greatest fluctuations. Spending on furniture and fittings is influenced by the state of the housing market. When the housing market is doing well and more houses are being bought and sold, more furniture and fittings tend to be purchased. Expenditure on furniture and fittings, a category that includes some expensive items, is also significantly affected by changes in interest rates. This is because many people will buy, for example, a new sofa on borrowed funds. In 1989 the rate of interest rose quite significantly and in 1992 it fell by a significant amount.

(3) Expenditure on food was the most stable of the three commodities. Food is seen as an essential item and people do not significantly change the quantity they buy when income changes.

(4) Tobacco expenditure showed a downward trend throughout the period. Spending on tobacco has largely fallen because of increased awareness of the dangers to health it imposes and the connected cause of it becoming a less socially accepted habit.

(d) Demand for a product is influenced by a number of other factors. A rise in population size will increase the demand for most products. A change in the age structure will affect products differently. For instance a rise in the average age of the population will increase the demand for bungalows. Advertising can have a powerful impact on most products. A less even distribution of income will increase the demand for luxury goods. Changes in the price of substitute also influence demand, and for some products a change in weather conditions can affect demand, e.g. umbrellas.

2.4 Objective questions

Example 2.3

Which of the following is not held constant when a demand curve is drawn?
A Households' real income
B The price of the good itself
C The price of competing goods
D The price of complementary goods

Example 2.4

The demand curve for a normal good shifts to the left when:
A the price of the good itself rises
B the price of complements rises
C the price of substitutes rises
D an indirect tax is imposed on the good

Example 2.5

A basic assumption of demand theory is that consumers allocate their incomes so as to maximise their:
A present consumption
B savings
C total utility
D marginal utility

Example 2.6

The following table shows the total utility gained from consuming each of three goods:

Units of good	X	Y	Z
1	40	16	10
2	48	30	20
3	52	42	30
4	54	52	40
5	52	60	50

The consumer experiences diminishing marginal utility in the consumption of:
A X alone   B Y alone
C X and Y alone   D X, Y and Z

Example 2.7

Good	Price	Quantity	Marginal utility
A	20p	6	10
B	30p	2	?

If a consumer buys the quantities of A and B shown above and is maximising his utility, what is the marginal utility derived from good B?

A 3   **B** 5   **C** 10   **D** 15

Example 2.8

A consumer has the following demand schedule for chocolate:

Number of bars	1	2	3	4	5
Price	60p	50p	40p	30p	20p

If the price of chocolate is 40p and the consumer buys three bars, what is his or her consumer surplus?

A 30p   **B** 40p   **C** 50p   **D** 60p

Example 2.9

The diagram shows a demand curve for journeys over a toll bridge.

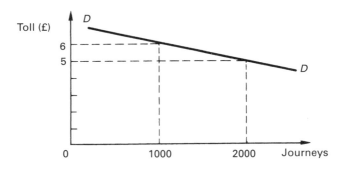

If the toll is reduced from £6 to £5, by how much will consumer surplus increase?

A £1100   **B** £1500   **C** £6000   **D** £7500

Example 2.10

The diagram shows a consumer's indifference map. RS is the consumer's budget line, and points J, K, L, M and N show different combinations of goods Y and X.

It can be seen that the consumer would prefer

A combination M to combination N
B combination N to combination J
C combination L to all others
D combination K to all others

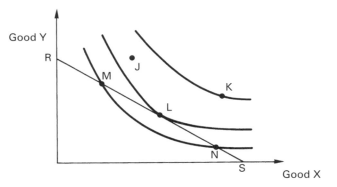

Example 2.11

The law of diminishing marginal utility states that the more a consumer has of a given commodity the:

A lower the total level of satisfaction enjoyed
B lower the price of each extra unit consumed
C lower the usefulness of each extra unit consumed
D lower the satisfaction from each extra unit consumed

Example 2.12

What is a Giffen good?

A A good whose demand rises with income
B A good whose demand rises with a rise in its price
C A good whose demand rises with a rise in the price of a complement
D A good whose income and substitution effects work in the same direction

2.5 Solutions to objective questions

Solution 2.3   Answer: **B**

When drawing a demand curve, all the factors influencing demand are held constant except one. Options **A**, **C** and **D** are incorrect because they are all examples of conditions of demand held fixed when a demand curve is drawn.

Solution 2.4   Answer: **B**

If the prices of complementary goods increase, the demand for this good decreases, resulting in the demand curve shifting to the left. Other options are incorrect because:

    A ⇒ causes a movement (contraction) along the demand curve.

C ⇒ increases demand for the product.

D ⇒ shifts the supply curve to the left.

Solution 2.5   Answer: **C**

In allocating their incomes it is assumed that rational consumers seek to maximise their total utility or satisfaction. **D** is incorrect because consumers maximise their total utility by ensuring that the marginal utility per penny or pound spend for each good is equal.

Solution 2.6   Answer: **C**

To answer this question it is necessary to calculate the marginal utility (MU) for each product. Marginal utility is the change (Δ) in total utility (TU) resulting from consuming one extra unit (Q) and is found, using the equation MU = ΔTU/ΔQ.

	X		Y		Z	
Units of good	TU	MU	TU	MU	TU	MU
1	40	40	16	16	10	10
2	48	8	30	14	20	10
3	52	4	42	12	30	10
4	54	2	52	10	40	10
5	52	−2	60	8	50	10

The calculations show that while the marginal utility of Z is constant, the marginal utilities of X and Y decline as consumption increases, Indeed, in the case of X disutility occurs – i.e. the consumption of the fifth unit causes total utility to decline.

Solution 2.7   Answer: **D**

Consumers will not change their pattern of expenditure if at present they are enjoying maximum total satisfaction. This occurs when the marginal utility (MU) of each good divided by its price (P) is equal, so that in each case:

$$\frac{\text{MU of A}}{P \text{ of A}} = \frac{\text{MU of B}}{P \text{ of B}} \text{ so that } \frac{10}{20} = \frac{?}{30}$$

Therefore

$$\frac{10}{20} = \frac{15}{30} \text{ so that } 0.5 = 0.5$$

Solution 2.8   Answer: **A**

Consumer surplus occurs when people are able to buy a good for less than they were willing to pay. The price of a chocolate bar is 40p, so:

Consumer surplus on first bar = 60p − 40p = 20p

Consumer surplus on second
bar = 50p − 40p = 10p

Consumer surplus on third
bar = 40p − 40p = 0p

Total consumer surplus = 20p + 10p = 30p

Solution 2.8   Answer: **B**

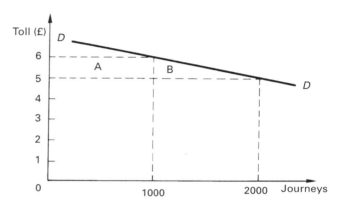

In the diagram, consumer surplus is shown by areas A + B. Those consumers who previously paid £6 now only have to pay £5. 1000 journeys are made at £1 less than people would have paid, so the increase in surplus is area A – i.e. £1000.

In addition, a further 1000 journeys are undertaken. The resulting increase in consumer surplus equals area B. Area B is given by the equation

$$0.5(P_1 − P_2) \times (Q_2 − Q_1)$$
$$= 0.5(£6 − £5(\times (2000 − 1000)$$
$$= 0.5(£1) \times (£1000)$$
$$= £0.5 \times 1000$$
$$= £500$$

Therefore the total increase in consumer surplus is area A + area B = £1000 + £500 = £1500.

Solution 2.10   Answer: **D**

Consumers will always prefer the point furthest away from the origin, i.e. K. Other options are incorrect because:

A ⇒ The consumer is indifferent between point M and point N, because the two are on the same indifference curve.

B ⇒ Point J is further from the origin than is point N.

C ⇒ While combination L is the consumer's point of equilibrium, the question asks which combination the consumer *prefers*.

Solution 2.11   Answer: **D**

Diminishing marginal utility means that the satisfaction gained from consuming extra units declines as consumption increases. Other options are incorrect because:

A ⇒ Total satisfaction (utility) usually rises as consumption increases.

B ⇒ The individual consumer is unable to influence the price at which the product is bought.

C ⇒ In economics, utility is concerned with satisfaction rather than usefulness.

Solution 2.12   Answer: **B**

A Giffen good is one with a direct relationship between price and demand. The other options are incorrect because:

A ⇒ describes a normal good.

C ⇒ Demand for the complement and the Giffen good would fall.

D ⇒ In the case of a Giffen good the income effect and the substitution effect work in opposite directions, with the income effect outweighing the substitution effect.

2.6 Essays

Example 2.13

(a)   Define 'demand' and explain the expected relationship between price and demand.

(8 marks)

(b)   Discuss the following two statements:
   (1) An increase in demand raises the price of a particular good.
   (2) An increase in price cuts demand for that good.   **(17 marks)**

• Briefly define demand.
• Use either income and substitution effects of marginal utility theory to explain the relationship between price and demand.
• Mention, briefly, that there are exceptions to the expected relationship.

• Distinguish between movements and shifts in demand curves.
• Make a careful distinction between the cause and effect of an increase in (1) demand and (2) price.
• Include demand and supply graphs.

Solution 2.13

(a) Demand refers to the amount of a good consumers are willing and able to buy at a given price. For most products, price and demand are inversely related. A rise in price will cause a fall in the quantity demanded. This is shown in Figure 1, where a rise in price from P to P_1 causes a contraction in demand from Q to Q_1.

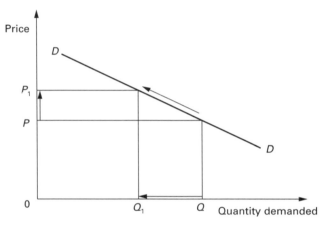

Figure 1

This relationship between price and demand can be explained by income and substitution effects. A rise in price will reduce people's real income (purchasing power) and so they will be less able to buy the good. It will also cause some people to switch to substitutes, so that the willingness to buy the product will decline.

In a few exceptional cases, price and demand vary directly. Veblen goods are goods that people buy, in part, to show how wealthy they are, and Giffen goods are poor-quality products the poor have to buy because they have insufficient purchasing power to switch to alternatives.

(b) The amount of a good consumers are initially willing and able to buy at different market prices is shown by the demand curve D in Figure 2.

Assume that the good in question is apples. The demand curve, D, is drawn by assuming that all factors influencing the demand for apples are held constant, except price. A change in a condition of demand invalidates this *ceteris paribus* assumption. For example a rise in the price of a substitute good,

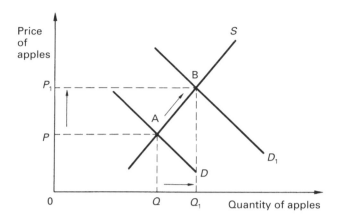

Figure 2

such as oranges, encourages consumers to switch to alternative commodities, such as apples. Hence the demand for apples increases at all prices. The increase in demand has the effect of shifting the demand curve to the right, to D_1. The price of apples rises from P to P_1, causing an expansion along the supply (S) curve from A to B. Initial analysis suggests that *an increase in demand raises the price of a particular good.*

An increase in the price of a good also affects the amount demanded by consumers. However, unlike an increase in demand, an increase in price does not shift the demand curve for the good. Again using apples as an example, an increase in price results in a fall in the quantity demanded, causing a contraction along the demand curve from A to B in Figure 3.

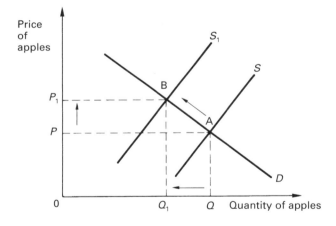

Figure 3

In fact the fall in the quantity demanded in Figure 3 can only have been caused by a decrease in supply causing the supply curve to shift to the left and the price to rise. In these circumstances, *an increase in price reduces the demand for that good.*

Analysis has so far supported both statements given in the question. By itself, an increase in demand does

raise the price of a good. However the price increase is the effect and not the cause of the increase in demand. By itself, an increase in price does cut demand. However the price increase is now the cause and not the effect of the fall in demand.

In conclusion, it can be seen that the two statements in the question are correct if considered separately, but are incorrect if linked together.

Example 2.14

(a) Explain the difference between marginal and total utility. **(5 marks)**
(b) How does marginal utility explain the shape of the demand curve? **(12 marks)**
(c) Why is the price of diamonds higher than the price of water? **(8 marks)**

- First define utility.
- Use a numerical example to explain the difference between marginal and total utility.
- Use a diagram and a numerical example to explain the shape of the demand curve.
- In examining the relative price of diamonds and water, distinguish between total and marginal utility.

Solution 2.14

(a) Utility is the satisfaction a person gains from consuming a good. Total utility is the total satisfaction gained from consuming a given quantity of a good. Marginal utility is the satisfaction gained from consuming an extra unit of a good. The table below shows that as more biscuits are consumed in a given period, total utility rises but at a diminishing rate. This is because the marginal utility declines.

No. of biscuits	Total utility	Marginal utility
1	20	20
2	38	18
3	53	15
4	63	10
5	68	5
6	70	2

(b) Most demand curves slope downwards from left to right. This can be explained by considering the marginal utility a person gains the more of a good she or he consumes and by examining what happens to demand when the price changes.

One way of assessing marginal utility is to ask people how much they would be prepared to pay for a good. This information can then be plotted on a graph. As marginal utility declines the more a person consumes, the amount she or he is prepared to pay for extra units will decline. The diagram below shows the marginal utility gained from biscuits.

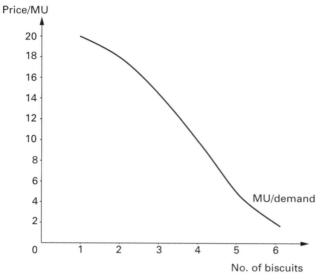

Figure 1

As marginal utility can be assessed by using price, the marginal utility curve is in effect the demand curve. People consume when $P = MU$.

The relationships between the demand curve and marginal utility can also be analysed by considering the effect of a price change. A consumer achieves maximum total utility when he or she equates marginal utility with the amount spent on the goods he or she buys, i.e.

$$\frac{\text{marginal utility of biscuits}}{\text{price of biscuits}} =$$

$$\frac{\text{marginal utility of apples, etc.}}{\text{price of apples}}$$

Initially this may be:

$$\frac{15}{5p} = \frac{45}{15p}$$

If the price of biscuits rises to 10p the consumer will maximise total utility by buying fewer biscuits and more apples, or more of another good. As fewer biscuits are bought, marginal utility will rise, and as more apples are bought, marginal utility will fall.

$$\frac{20}{10p} = \frac{30}{15p}$$

Thus a rise in price results in a fall in demand, and this inverse relationship is shown by a demand curve that slopes downwards from left to right.

(c) It may appear strange that diamonds, which are an unnecessary luxury, are more expensive than water, which is a necessity. Water does indeed have a higher total utility than diamonds. However the amount consumers are willing to pay is based on marginal utility and not total utility.

Consumers buy a combination of goods when the marginal utilities per pound spent are equal. Water will be consumed in large quantities up to the point when the last gallon of water used gives a low marginal utility and the price paid is relatively low. Most people do not buy diamonds, and the marginal utility gained from the last diamond bought and the price paid is relatively high. For example:

$$\frac{\text{marginal utility of water}}{\text{price of water}} =$$

$$\frac{\text{marginal utility of diamonds}}{\text{price of diamonds}}$$

$$\frac{10}{20p} = \frac{250}{£50}$$

3

Supply

3.1 Fact sheet

(a) Definition of supply

- *Supply* is the amount of a good that producers are both willing and able to sell at a given price.
- A *supply curve* shows the amount of a good that producers are willing and able to sell at different prices.
- The amount of a good supplied depends on:
  (a) price;
  (b) the conditions of supply.

(b) Movements along a supply curve

- A change in price results in a movement along a supply curve, resulting in a *change in the quantity supplied*.
- A change in the price of a good *never* shifts the supply curve for that good.
- In Figure 3.1 an increase in price causes an *expansion* (or *extension*) of supply, and a decrease in price results in a *contraction* of supply.

(c) Individual and market supply

- *Individual supply* is one producer's supply of a good.
- *Market supply* is the total supply of a good.
- A *market supply curve* is the horizontal summation of all the individual supply curves.

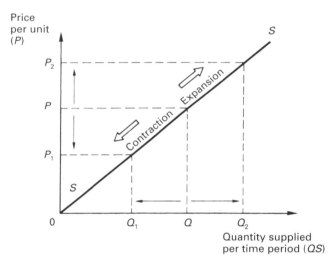

Figure 3.1 Movements along a supply curve

(d) Increases and decreases in supply

- A supply curve is drawn assuming *ceteris paribus* – i.e. that all factors influencing supply are being held constant, except price. The *conditions of supply* refer to those factors held constant and include:
  (1) *Average* (or *unit*) costs of production.
  (2) The current state of technology.
  (3) The price of other goods:
     (a) in *competitive supply* (i.e. alternative products the firm could make);
     (b) in *joint supply* (i.e. by products from manufacture).

(4) Unforeseen circumstances (e.g. a drought ruining a wine crop).
(5) Taxes and subsidies.
(6) The number of firms in the industry.
(7) The goals of producers.

- A change in one of these conditions affects the level of supply at all prices and results in a shift in the supply curve.
- Figure 3.2 illustrates the effect of an increase in supply.

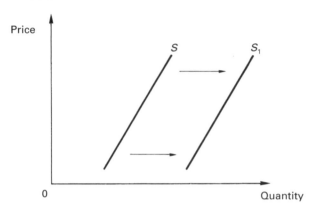

Figure 3.2 An increase in supply

Causes

- A decrease in unit costs of production.
- Improved technology.
- A fall in the price of a good in competitive supply.
- A rise in the price of a good in joint supply.
- Beneficial unforeseen circumstances.
- A subsidy given to producers.
- New firms entering the industry.
- A firm changing its objective from profit to sales maximisation.

Effect

- The supply curve shifts to the right.

(e) Producer surplus

- *Producer surplus* is the difference between the minimum price a producer would accept to supply a given quantity of a good and the price actually received.
- The area of producer surplus is that above the supply curve and below the price line in Figure 3.3.

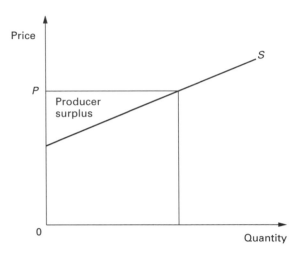

Figure 3.3 Producer surplus

3.2 Investigative study

Example 3.1

A study of the impact of changes in technology in an industry, e.g. banking, on the quality of service, costs and price.

3.3 Data response

Example 3.2

Year	Output at current factor cost (£ million) Coal mines and nuclear fuel	Total production industries
1988	2913	121 361
1989	2452	130 031
1990	2154	134 365
1991	2528	132 672
1992	2373	135 637
1993	1655	144 435

Source: CSO, *Blue Book*, 1994; United Kingdom National Accounts.

(a) Calculate and comment on the change in the output of coal mines and the nuclear fuel industry for the period shown. **(8 marks)**
(b) Do you think coal has an elastic or inelastic supply? Explain your answer. **(8 marks)**
(c) What factors do you think could reverse the trend you have observed and shift the supply curve in the opposite direction? **(8 marks)**
(d) In which sector – primary, secondary or tertiary – are coal mining and nuclear fuel placed? **(1 mark)**

Solution 3.2

(a)

Year	% change in output of coal mines and nuclear fuel	% share of coal mines and nuclear fuel in total output of production industries
1988		2.4
1989	−15.8	1.9
1990	−13.8	1.6
1991	17.4	1.9
1992	−6.1	1.7
1993	−30.3	1.1

Over the whole period there was a sharp decline in the actual output of coal and nuclear fuel, and this industry's share of the total output of all production industries. There was one exception to this: 1991 witnessed an increase in both output and the share of the total of all production industries. The most marked decline came in 1993, when output fell by more than a third. This reflected the large-scale closure of pits by the government.

(b) The formula for measuring elasticity of supply is:

$$PES = \frac{\% \text{ change in quantity supplied}}{\% \text{ change in price}}$$

Whether at any particular time the supply of coal is elastic or inelastic is determined by two key factors: the level of stocks held and the extent of spare capacity. If stocks are high and mines are not being fully worked, a rise in price could bring about a significant rise in supply. However if stocks are low and mines are being worked to full capacity, it will be difficult to adjust supply to a rise in price and supply will be inelastic.

(c) A number of factors could cause supply of coal to increase and thereby shift the supply curve to the right. New deposits of coal could be discovered away from existing coal mines or new seams could be found at mines currently being operated. The government could subsidise coal production. Improvements in technology may enable new seams to be tapped. These factors are also likely to reduce production costs, as will a fall in unit labour costs, perhaps because of an improvement in productivity.

(d) Coal mining and nuclear fuel are extractive industries and are therefore placed in the primary sector.

3.4 Objective questions

Example 3.3

Why does a normal supply curve for corn slope upwards from left to right?
A Farmers' profits increase as price increases
B Farmers increase supply following increases in demand
C Farmers charge more to cover a rise in the price of seed
D Farmers are willing to produce more corn as price increases

Example 3.4

The supply of a good is represented by the equation $P = 10 + 0.8 Q_s$, where P refers to the price in pounds (£) and Q_s is the quantity of the good sold. At what price will the producer sell 20 units?
A £10 B £16 C £20 D £26

Example 3.5

Which of the following would cause a shift of the supply curve to the right?
A A decrease in VAT
B A decrease in specific subsidies
C An increase in production costs
D An increase in the price of the product

Example 3.6

Goods X and Y are in competitive supply. Other things being equal, what will be the effect of a decrease in demand for good Y?
A An increase in the supply and price of good X
B A decrease in the supply and price of good X
C An increase in the supply and a decrease in the price of good X
D A decrease in the supply and in increase in the price of good X

Example 3.7

Which of the following will cause the supply curve for peaches to shift to the left?
A A rise in the price of apples
B A successful advertising campaign for cream

C   A reduction in EU subsidies to fruit growers
D   An increase in the total number of consumers of peaches

Example 3.8

At a price of £10 the quantity supplied is 800. If elasticity of supply is 1.5, what will be the quantity supplied if the price rises to £11?
A 680   **B** 720   **C** 840   **D** 920

Example 3.9

Goods that are in joint supply are:
A sold together
B consumed together
C produced together
D produced by the same firm

Example 3.10

Which of the following would cause an expansion in the supply of chicken?
A A fall in the price of beef
B A rise in the price of chicken
C A rise in vegetarianism
D A rise in the price of chicken feed

Example 3.11

Why is the supply of fresh salmon more inelastic than the supply of tinned salmon?
A Fresh salmon cannot be stored
B Fresh salmon is in more demand than tinned salmon
C Producers of tinned salmon are more efficient than producers of fresh salmon
D There are more substitutes for tinned salmon than for fresh salmon

Example 3.12

Which of the following would increase the elasticity of supply of a product?
A A rise in its price
B A rise in the capacity utilisation of the industry
C A fall in the time it takes to produce the product
D A fall in the mobility of the factors of production that produce the good

3.5 Solutions to objective questions

Solution 3.3   Answer: **D**

A supply curve slopes upwards from left to right, since higher prices induce producers to extend their supply. Other options are incorrect because:
   A ⇒ Profitability cannot be assessed without further information about revenue and costs.
   B ⇒ An increase in demand for corn causes a rise in price and an extension in supply, not an increase in supply.
   C ⇒ When drawing a supply curve all variables are held constant except price. A rise in the price of seed shifts the supply curve to the left.

Solution 3.4   Answer: **D**

The equation $P = 10 + 0.8Q_s$ simply means price equals 10 plus whatever quantity is being supplied multiplied by 0.8. Therefore
$P = 10 + (0.8 \times 20) = 10 + 16 = 26$.

Solution 3.5   Answer: **A**

A decrease in VAT increases supply and shifts the supply curve to the right. The other options are incorrect because:
   A and **C** ⇒ would result in a decrease in supply, which would shift the supply curve to the left.
   D ⇒ would cause a movement along the supply curve (expansion) and not an increase.

Solution 3.6   Answer: **C**

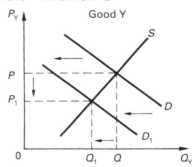

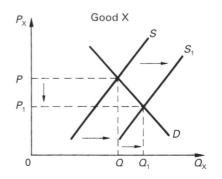

The top diagram shows that a decrease in the demand for good Y reduces its price. Since good Y and good X are in competitive supply, a fall in the price of Y encourages producers to increase their supply of X. The bottom diagram shows that an increases in the supply of X reduces its price.

Solution 3.7   Answer: **C**

A reduction in EU subsidies to fruit growers would decrease the supply of all fruit, including peaches.

Options **A**, **B** and **D** all describe events that would increase the demand for peaches, thereby causing their price to rise and supply to expand.

Solution 3.8   Answer: **D**

$$\text{PES} = \frac{\%\Delta QS}{\%\Delta P}$$

In this case:

$$1.5 = \frac{\%\Delta QS}{10}, \text{ so}$$

$$1.5 \times 10 = \%\Delta QS$$

$$15\% = \%\Delta QS$$

A rise in price will cause an expansion in supply, so supply will now be:

$$800 + 15\% = 800 + 120 = 920$$

Solution 3.9   Answer: **C**

Goods in joint supply are produced together. An example is beef and leather.

   A ⇒ Any types of good may be sold together.
   B ⇒ Goods consumed together are complements.
   C ⇒ Goods produced by the same firm are not necessarily in joint supply. Indeed they may be in competitive supply.

Solution 3.10   Answer: **B**

An expansion in supply is a movement along an existing supply curve and can only be caused by a change in the price of the good concerned, in this case chicken. A higher price will encourage chicken farmers to sell more chicken.

   A ⇒ A fall in the price of beef may encourage some people to switch from consuming chicken to consuming beef. This will decrease the demand for chicken, lower its price and cause supply to contract.

   C ⇒ A rise in vegetarianism will again cause a decrease in the demand for chicken, a fall in its price and a contraction in supply.

   D ⇒ A rise in the price of chicken feed will increase the cost of chicken feed and result in a decrease in supply.

Solution 3.11   Answer: **A**

As fresh salmon is perishable its supply cannot be easily adjusted in response to price changes. For instance if the price of fresh salmon falls it cannot be withdrawn from the market – it will still have to be sold.

Solution 3.12   Answer: **C**

If the product can be produced more quickly, producers will be able to alter supply more easily in response to changes in price.

   A ⇒ Elasticity of supply measures how supply responds to a change in price, it is not determined by it.

   B and **D** ⇒ would make it more difficult to alter supply and hence make supply more inelastic.

3.6 Essays

Example 3.13

(a)   What is the relationship between supply and price?   **(10 marks)**
(b)   What factors could cause an increase in supply? **(15 marks)**

•   Use a diagram to illustrate the usual relationship between supply and price.
•   Refer to extensions and contractions in supply.
•   Briefly acknowledge that there are exceptions to the expected relationship.
•   Illustrate an increase in supply.
•   Distinguish between a movement along and a shift in the supply curve.
•   Discuss the main causes of an increase in supply and give examples.

Solution 3.13

(a) Supply is the quantity of a good that producers are willing and able to offer for sale at a given price. In most cases supply and price vary directly, so that a rise in price causes an extension in supply and a fall in price causes a contraction in supply. Figure 1 shows that a rise in price from P to P_1 causes an extension in supply from Q to Q_1.

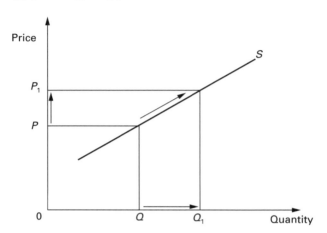

Figure 1

A rise in price usually causes an extension in supply because it enables the higher costs that are likely to result from a rise in output to be covered and may increase the profitability of producing the good.

In a few cases the supply curve may not be upward sloping. It is possible for a supply curve to be horizontal (perfectly elastic), vertical (perfectly inelastic) or downward sloping. The last example can occur in the case of some labour markets where a rise in the wage rate causes some already well-paid workers to reduce the number of hours they work.

(b) An extension in supply results in more of a good being supplied because of a rise in its price, other influences being held constant. An increase in supply also results in more of a good being supplied, but in this case because of a change in an influence on the supply of a good other than its price.

An increase in supply is illustrated by a shift in the supply curve to the right, with more being supplied at each and every price. This is shown in Figure 2.

There are a number of causes of an increase in supply. One of the main causes is a fall in the cost of production, for example an improvement in technology will enable producers to increase the quantity and probably the quality of output at a lower unit cost. In the last twenty years technological advances have significantly lowered the production costs and prices of a number of products, including calculators and personal computers.

A change in the profitability of other goods is another influence. If the profitability of goods in

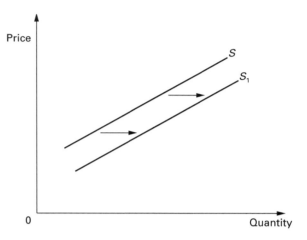

Figure 2

competitive supply falls and/or the profitability of goods in joint supply rises, the supply of this good will increase. For example if the profitability of pork production falls and the profitability of leather hides rises, the supply of beef is likely to increase.

A government subsidy or the reduction or abolition of an indirect tax will increase the supply of a product. The EU subsidy on linseed oil in the early 1990s resulted in an increase in the amount of linseed grown.

Producers will also supply more now if they believe that prices will fall in the future, or if they change their objectives, for instance from profit to sales maximisation.

An increase in the number of firms in the industry will increase supply. In some cities deregulation has resulted in a rise in the number of bus companies covering popular routes.

A change in unforeseen circumstances can also cause a change in conditions of supply. The ending of a war is likely to result in a rise in the range of civilian goods produced. A favourable spell of weather is likely to increase the supply of a number of agricultural crops, including apples, wheat and wine.

Example 3.14

(a) Explain how the supply curve of a firm in perfect competition is determined. **(15 marks)**

(b) How can the market supply curve be derived? **(10 marks)**

• This question can be answered relatively briefly.
• Consider both the short-run and long-run supply curves.
• Draw diagrams to illustrate how the supply curves are determined.

- Distinguish between individual and market supply curves.

Example 3.14

The supply curve of a firm shows the amount the firm is willing and able to sell at different prices. When plotting a supply curve the only influence that is being changed is price.

The supply curve of a firm operating under conditions of perfect competition is based on its marginal cost curve. It is assumed that firms in this market structure are profit maximisers and will therefore produce an output where $MC = MR$. As perfectly competitive firms are price takers, marginal revenue will equal average revenue (and hence price), so these firms will produce where $MC = P$. Figure 1 shows the marginal cost curve for a perfectly competitive firm. At a price of P, Q will be supplied, at a price of P_1, Q_1 will be supplied, at a price of P_2, Q_2 will be supplied and so on.

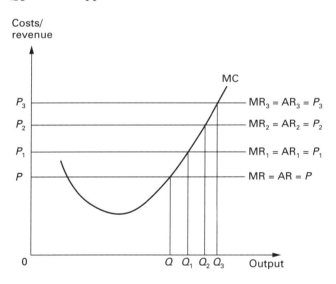

Figure 1

Therefore the amount that will be supplied can be found from the marginal cost curve.

In the short run firms will stay in the industry provided that at least their variable costs can be covered. So in the short run the supply curve is based on the MC curve from X to Y (i.e. at and above average variable cost).

In the long run all costs have to be covered and the supply curve is based on the marginal cost curve at and above the average cost curve (i.e. from Y to Z).

(b) An individual supply curve shows the quantity that one firm will supply at different prices. A market

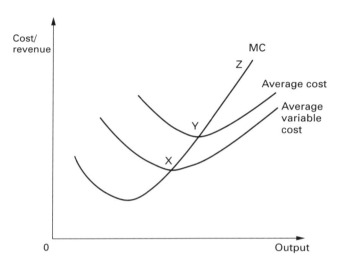

Figure 2

supply curve is the total amount that will be supplied by all the firms in the industry at different prices. It is found by the horizontal summation of all the individual supply curves (and hence MC curves). This means the amount that each individual firm would supply at each price is added together and then plotted on a supply graph. For example Figure 3 shows the supply curve of three firms (this is obviously a simplification because a perfectly competitive industry would contain far more firms).

At a price of £1 the market supply is 20 (7 + 7 + 6), at £2 it is 30 (11 + 10 + 9) and at £3 it is £42 (15 + 14 + 13).

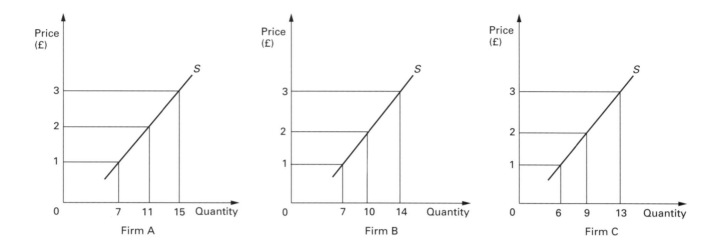

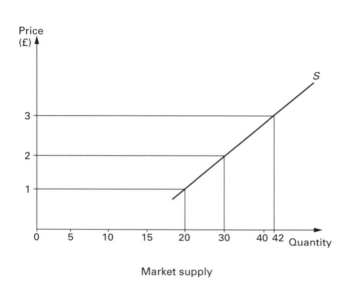

Market supply

Figure 3

Price Determination

4.1 Fact sheet

(a) Equilibrium price

- In Figure 4.1, *excess supply* occurs at prices above *P*, because producers are prepared to sell more than consumers are willing to buy. Attempts to maintain a *minimum price* above the market price (e.g. the Common Agricultural Policy) results in *structural surpluses*.
- *Excess demand* occurs at prices below *P*, because consumers want to buy more than producers are prepared to sell. Attempts to maintain a *maximum price* below the market price (e.g. by rationing) results in *artificial shortages*.
- Equilibrium is a state of balance – i.e. a situation where there is no tendency for change. There is only one market price where the amount that producers want to sell equals the amount that consumers want to buy. The forces of demand and supply ensure that *P* is the *equilibrium market price*.

(b) Changes in equilibrium price

- An increase in demand will cause price to rise and supply to expand.
- A decrease in demand will cause price to fall and supply to contract.
- An increase in supply will cause price to fall and demand to expand.
- A decrease in supply will cause price to rise and demand to contract.

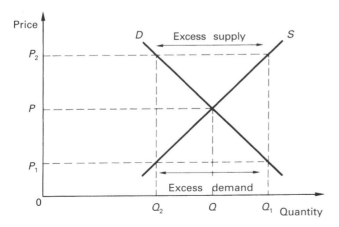

Figure 4.1 Equilibrium and non-equilibrium prices

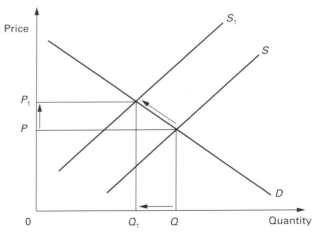

Figure 4.2 The effect of a decrease in supply

(c) Indirect taxation

An *indirect tax* (T_i) is a surcharge on price imposed on the sale of goods and services by the government and can be:

(1) *specific* – i.e. a fixed amount per unit;
(2) *ad valorem* – i.e. a percentage of the selling price.

- The effect of an indirect tax is shown by adding the amount of the tax to the supply curve.
- *Tax incidence* refers to the burden of a tax. The more price-inelastic the demand for a good, the greater the tax incidence borne by the consumer.

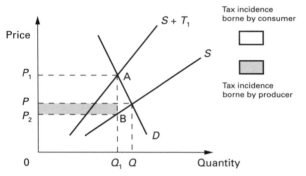

Figure 4.3 An ad valorem *indirect tax. Area P_2P_1AB equals the total amount of tax revenue raised*

(d) Subsidies

- A *subsidy* (SU) is a discount on price given by the government.
- A subsidy can be *specific* or *ad valorem*.
- The effect on a supply curve is shown by deducting the amount of a subsidy from the supply curve.
- The more price-inelastic the demand for a good, the greater the share of the subsidy going to the consumer.

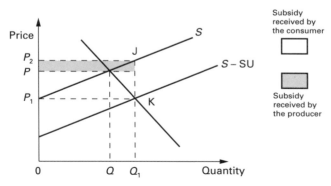

Figure 4.4 A specific subsidy. Area P_1PJK equals the total amount of subsidy paid

(e) Price instability

- Products with stable conditions of supply and demand will have stable prices from year to year.
- Products with unstable conditions of supply and demand will experience price fluctuations from year to year.
- Products with seasonal variations in demand, such as hotel accommodation, tend to be price-unstable.
- Agricultural prices tend to be unstable because:
  (a) supply changes from one time period to the next because of variable weather conditions;
  (b) the effects of changes in supply is amplified by price-inelastic demand (see Chapter 5);
  (c) the effect of changes in demand is amplified by price-inelastic supply;
  (d) *supply lags* (delays) exist between the decisions to produce and the produce coming onto the market. The resulting *cobweb model* is explained in Example 4.14.

(f) Interrelationships between markets

A decrease in the supply of product A will cause:

(1) a rise in the price and a contraction in demand for product A;
(2) an increase in demand for product B (a substitute) a rise in its price, and an expansion in its supply.
(3) a decrease in demand for product C (a complement), a fall in its price and a contraction in its supply;
(4) a decrease in supply of product D (a good in joint supply), a rise in its price, and a contraction in its demand;
(5) an increase in supply of product E (a good in competitive supply), a fall in its price and an expansion in its demand;
(6) a decrease in demand for the factors of production that produce product A, a fall in their price a contraction in their supply.

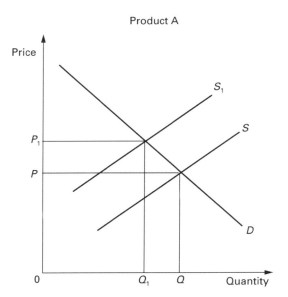

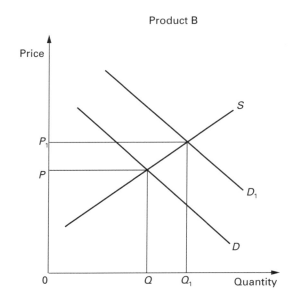

Figure 4.5 The effect of a decrease in the supply of product A on the market for product A and on the market for product B, a substitute.

4.2 Investigative study

Example 4.1

An analysis of the price movements of a particular commodity, e.g. coffee, their causes and effects.

4.3 Data response

Example 4.2

The following table refers to an imaginary market for corn. Farmers are assumed to plan next year's production on the basis of last year's price.

Year	Price per tonne (£)	Amount bought and sold (tonnes)
1990	150.0	3000
1991	200.0	1000
1992	125.0	4000
1993	162.5	2500
1994	145.0	3250
1995	150.0	3000
1996	150.0	3000

(a) Describe the annual variations in the price of corn. **(5 marks)**

(b) Given that demand conditions are unchanged, how would you explain the annual variations in the price of corn shown in the table? **(10 marks)**

(c) What pricing policies for corn might a government adopt for the period shown? **(10 marks)**

Solution 4.2

(a) Figure 1 indicates that the price of corn fluctuated above and below £150 per tonne between 1990 and 1996. The highest price, £200 per tonne, was achieved

Figure 1

in 1991 and the lowest, £125 per tonne, in the following year. Note that the magnitude of the oscillation diminishes.

(b) Market prices are determined by the interaction of supply and demand. Market equilibrium occurs when there is a stable, long-run market price from which there is no tendency to move. A change in any of the conditions of supply or demand would affect equilibrium by causing a shift in a supply or demand curve, hence a change in price.

Agricultural goods such as corn are particularly prone to unforeseen weather conditions, which affect supply from one year to another. The fact that the price of corn stood at £150 in three separate years would tend to suggest that this is the long-run equilibrium price for corn. The initial change in price in 1991 is likely to have been the result of an unexpectedly poor harvest brought about by, say, frost damage. The resultant fall in supply shown in Figure 3 raised the price to £200, with only 1000 tonnes bought and sold.

Figure 2 shows the path the market might have followed in moving back to equilibrium. Long-run disequilibrium occurred between 1991 and 1995, because farmers were unable accurately to predict next year's price. In 1992 they produced too much, and the price fell to remove the excess supply. In 1993 farmers produced too little and the price rose to remove excess demand. By 1995 the amount producers wanted to sell at £150 equalled the amount consumers wanted to buy, and the price remained stable into 1996.

(c) Pricing policy refers to the government's ability to leave markets free to set their own price or to intervene to stabilise price. Price intervention in the corn market requires the government to keep a buffer stock. For instance Figure 3 shows that the effect of the poor harvest of 1991 on price could have been overcome by the government selling 2000 tonnes from stock at the prevailing price of £150. Such price intervention would have allowed avoidance of the subsequent 'cobweb' shown in Figure 2.

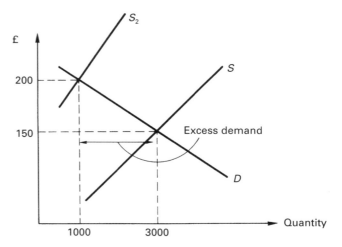

Figure 3

4.4 Objective questions

*Examples 4.3 to 4.6 refer to the following diagram, which shows the supply of and demand for British-made lawnmowers. The market is initially in equilibrium at point X. Starting from point X each time, indicate the new equilibrium position – **A**, **B**, **C** or **D** – after each of the events described.*

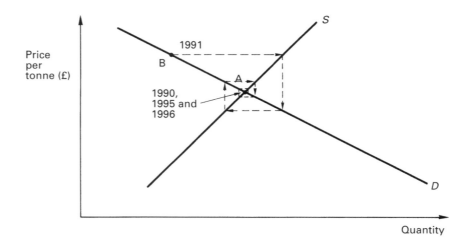

Figure 2

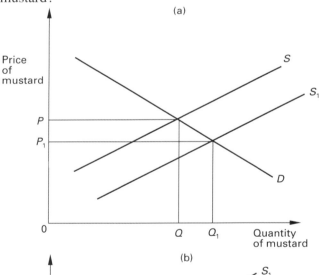

Example 4.3

What will be the new market price following the introduction of labour-saving technology?

Example 4.4

What will be the new market price if the price of imported lawnmowers falls considerably?

Example 4.5

What will be the new market price if there is a successful advertising campaign for lawnmowers, while at the same time the government introduces an indirect tax on the sale of lawnmowers?

Example 4.6

A subsidy is given to a product whose demand is price elastic but whose supply is price inelastic. Who will benefit from the subsidy?
A Producers will keep the entire subsidy
B Most of the subsidy will be kept by producers
C Consumers will receive the full benefit of the subsidy
D Most of the subsidy will be passed on to the consumers

Example 4.7

The diagram below indicates the conditions of demand and supply of wheat. What would be the effect of the government setting a minimum price of P_x?
A No effect
B Cause an excess supply of wheat
C Make the market demand curve P_xLM
D Require the intervention buying of $Q - Q_1$ amount of wheat

Example 4.8

The market demand for a good Y is given by the equation $Y = 80 - 10P$ and the market supply for good Y is given by the equation $Y = -40 + 20P$, where P denotes the price of good Y. The equilibrium price for the good is
A 2P   **B** 4P   **C** 10P   **D** 20P

Example 4.9

Which of the following diagrams illustrates the effect that a rise in the price of beef has on the market for mustard?

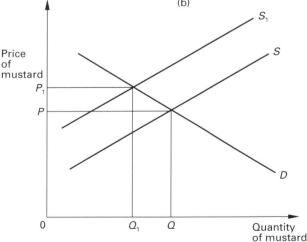

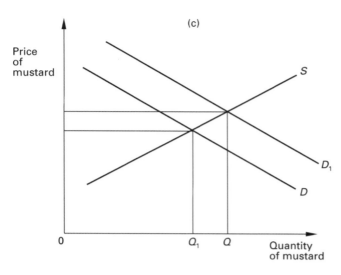

(c)

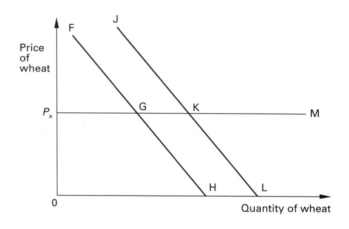

	Demand	Price	Supply
A	Increase	Increase	Expand
B	Expand	Decrease	Increase
C	Contract	Increase	Decrease
D	Decrease	Decrease	Contract

Example 4.12

The original demand curve for wheat is FGH. The government then introduces a guaranteed minimum price of $0P_x$, maintaining this price for intervention buying for stockpile. What is the new effective demand curve?

A FGM   **B** P_xGM   **C** P_xGH   **D** JKL

(d)

Example 4.10

The supply of a particular good is directly related to price and its demand is inversely related to price. During a certain period 5000 units are sold at £9 and during a later period 4000 units are sold at £8. Which of the following, other things being equal, could account for this change?

A An increase in consumers' incomes
B An increase in the cost of raw materials
C A decrease in the price of a substitute product
D A decrease in the productivity of factors of production

Example 4.11

As a result of improved training there is a rise in the productivity of car workers. If the rise in productivity outweighs the rise in training costs, what effect will this have on the demand, price and supply of cars?

4.5 Solutions to objective questions

Solution 4.3   Answer: **C**

The introduction of labour-saving technology reduces unit costs, increases supply and shifts the supply curve to the right to S_2. The new equilibrium position is given by the intersection of S_2 and D – i.e. point C.

Solution 4.4   Answer: **B**

A fall in the price of a substitute good for home-produced lawnmowers reduces demand and shifts the demand curve to D_2. The new equilibrium position is given by the intersection of D_2 and S – i.e. point B.

Solution 4.5   Answer: **A**

A successful advertising campaign shifts the demand curve for lawnmowers to the right to D_1. A tax on the sale of lawnmowers shifts the supply curve to the left to S_1. The equilibrium position is A.

Solution 4.6   Answer: **B**

It almost always helps to draw a diagram to illustrate details given in a question. D represents a price elastic demand curve and S represents a price inelastic supply curve. To show the effect of a subsidy, deduct an amount (say $P_2 - P_1$) from the supply curve at all output levels and label the new supply curve S_1. The initial market price is P, with Q amount bought and sold. The subsidy has increased supply and reduced the equilibrium price to P_1. While consumers pay only P_1, producers receive P_2 per unit sold. Because demand is price elastic and supply is price inelastic, the bulk of the subsidy goes to the producer (area A). A smaller proportion (area B) goes to the consumer.

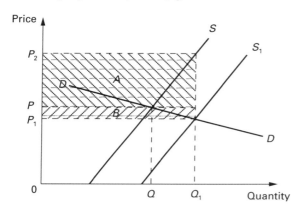

Solution 4.7   Answer: **B**

At the minimum price producers want to sell more (Q_1) than consumers want to buy (Q_2). So there is an excess supply of wheat of $Q_2 - Q_1$. The other options are incorrect because:

$A \Rightarrow$ A minimum price would have no effect if it was set below the equilibrium price.

$C \Rightarrow$ Above point L the market demand curve is unaffected by government action; beyond point L the government is prepared to intervene and buy up any amount of wheat necessary to maintain the price at P_1 – the demand curve becomes perfectly elastic at L and extends to M – it becomes KLM.

$D \Rightarrow$ To maintain the minimum price would require intervention buying of $Q_2 - Q_1$ amount of wheat.

Solution 4.8   Answer: **B**

In equilibrium, the two equations given in the question must equal each other. Remember when

manipulating equations that whatever is done to one side of the equation must also be done to the other side. The market price is found as follows:

	quantity demanded = quantity supplied
substitute	$80 - 10P = -40 + 20P$
add 10P	$80 = -40 + 30P$
add 40	$120 = 30P$
divide by 30	$4 = P$

Solution 4.9   Answer: **D**

Beef and mustard are complements. A rise in the price of beef will cause a contraction in demand for beef and a decrease in demand for mustard. The fall in demand for mustard will cause the price of mustard to decrease and its supply to contract, as shown in diagram (d).

Solution 4.10   Answer: **C**

The price of the product has fallen and a lower quantity is being bought and sold. This could have been caused by a decrease in demand for the product, as shown in the diagram below.

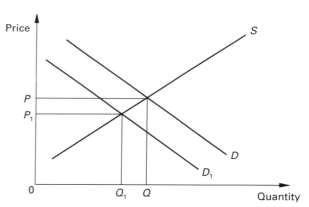

A decrease in the price of a substitute product would cause an expansion in demand for that product and a decrease in demand for this product.

$A \Rightarrow$ An increase in consumers' incomes would increase demand for the product, which would increase both the price of the product and the quantity traded.

B and $D \Rightarrow$ would cause the cost of production to rise, which in turn would result in a decrease in supply, a fall in price and an increase in the quantity traded.

Solution 4.11   Answer: **B**

An increase in the productivity of car workers would lower the cost of production. This would increase supply, which in turn would lower price and result in an expansion in demand, as shown below.

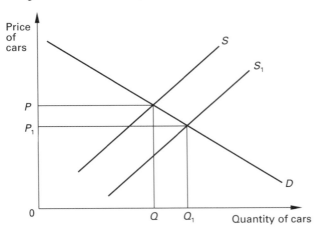

Solution 4.12   Answer: **A**

Above the guaranteed minimum price the government will allow market forces to operate and therefore the original demand curve will operate from F to G. However when the minimum price is reached the government will buy up any extra quantity supplied to prevent the price from falling below $0P_x$. So at G demand becomes perfectly elastic. The effect of the government's action is illustrated in the diagram below.

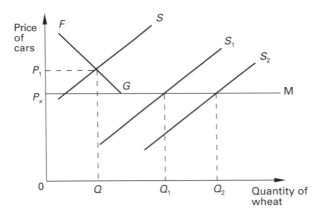

4.6 Essays

Example 4.13

Analyse the effect, in the short run only, on the price of coffee of (1) a severe frost, (2) a fall in the rate of VAT and (3) the introduction of rationing.

(25 marks)

- You are not expected to have a detailed knowledge of the coffee industry.

- Consider in each case which curve – demand or supply – is likely to shift.
- Apply your understanding of general demand and supply analysis.
- Make assumptions about the price elasticity of supply and demand for coffee and then draw flat or steep curves to match.

Solution 4.13

In a market economy the price of coffee is determined by the interaction of supply (the amount of a good that producers are willing and able to sell) and demand (the amount of a good that consumers are willing and able to buy).

(1) In Figure 1, S shows supply and D demand at different prices. P is the initial equilibrium market price and Q the initial amount of coffee bought and sold. The relatively long time taken to grow coffee plants means that supply is price inelastic. Demand is relatively price inelastic, because analysis suggests that there are few close substitutes for coffee. S and D are drawn assuming *ceteris paribus* (all other things being equal). A severe frost will invalidate this assumption and cause a decrease in the quantity of coffee supplied at all market prices, causing the supply curve in Figure 2 to shift to the left, to S_1. The decrease in supply causes a rise in price to P_1 and a contraction in demand.

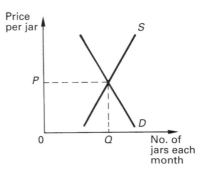

Figure 1

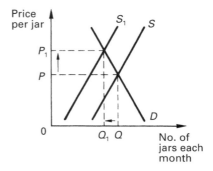

Figure 2

The more severe the frost the greater the decrease in supply, and the greater the resulting increase in price. The more price inelastic the demand the greater the increase in price for a given fall in supply.

(2) VAT is an *ad valorem* (according to value) indirect tax on the sale of goods and services. In Figure 3, the effect of VAT on coffee is found by adding the amount of the tax to the original supply curve at each level of output. A fall in VAT rates reduces the amount of tax received at each level of output and the supply curve moves to the right, to $S + T_1$. The assumption of inelastic demand means a significant fall in price, to P_1.

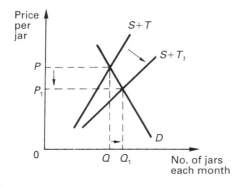

Figure 3

(3) Rationing, which usually occurs in response to a crisis such as war, is when the government intervenes in a market to fix the price and output of a good. In Figure 4, the government fixes the output of coffee at Q_1. Given that supply is now totally unresponsive to changes in price, S_1 is perfectly price inelastic and price rises to P_1. Often rationing authorities consider high free-market prices to be unfair to those on low incomes and unable to buy coffee, so Q_1 coupons are issued to consumers, allowing them to buy a fixed amount of the good each month at, say, price P.

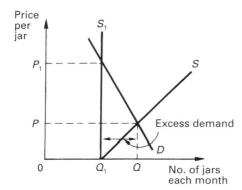

Figure 4

The final effect on the legal price is indeterminate. The government may decide to offer the good above, at or below the price prevailing before the introduction of rationing. However the existence of excess demand at prices below P_1 encourages the development of an illegal black market, where the price is likely to be higher than that set by the government.

Example 4.14

Explain why the prices of some goods change more than those of other goods. **(25 marks)**

- Explain why unstable conditions of supply and demand result in price changes.
- Explain why price inelasticity amplifies the effect on price of changes in supply and demand.
- Introduce time lags and apply the cobweb theory.
- Make use of graphs and relevant examples.

Solution 4.14

Equilibrium is a situation of balance from which there is no tendency to change. Equilibrium prices change only if there has been a change in a condition of demand or supply. It follows that products whose conditions of demand and supply are inherently unstable are subject to greater price fluctuations than those with more stable demand and supply conditions.

For instance, goods for which demand varies according to the time of year will display price instability. For example the price of coal falls during the summer but rises in the winter. Similarly a rise in incomes increases the demand for all normal goods. *Ceteris paribus*, the greater the increase in demand the greater the rise in price. Therefore goods with a low income elasticity of demand usually possess greater price stability. Goods with a low cross elasticity of demand with respect to all other goods have few substitutes or complements and are likely to show price stability. Similarly, products with few goods in joint or competitive supply are less likely to be subject to price changes.

Empirical (real-world) evidence suggests that agricultural goods have fluctuating prices. Farm products are particularly prone to unforeseen events such as bad weather and disease. Figure 1 shows that as the weather changes, so does supply. The effect on price of each change in supply is exaggerated by inelastic demand. Agricultural products have a low price elasticity of demand (PED) because they are inexpensive and consumers tend to buy much the same amount regardless of price.

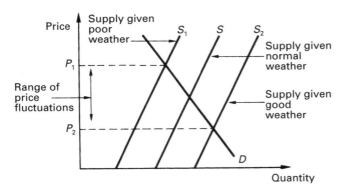

Figure 1

The cobweb theory explains why the price of some goods fluctuates more than others. Assume that farmers expect to sell their next crops at the same market price as in the previous season. This means that this year's price has no effect on current production but instead determines next year's supply. In Figure 2 the initial price is P. A 'shock' to the system (e.g. an unexpectedly poor harvest) causes price to rise to P_1. Farmers expect price P_1 in the next time period and produce Q_1. However consumers are only prepared to pay P_2 to buy up Q_1. Farmers then expect the next market price to be P_2 and so produce Q_2. Because supply is more inelastic than demand, the cobweb converges and the long-run equilibrium price of P is eventually restored. Had demand been more inelastic the resulting divergent cobweb would have caused even greater price variations over time.

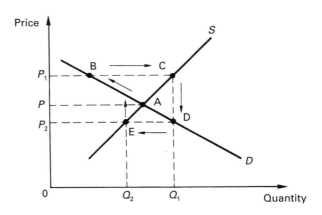

Figure 2

In conclusion, it can be seen that the prices of some commodities fluctuate more than those of others because of differences in the stability of the underlying conditions of demand and supply.

Elasticity

5.1 Fact sheet

(a) Concept of elasticity

Elasticity measures how one variable responds to a change in another variable.

(b) Price elasticity of demand

Price elasticity of demand (PED) measures the responsiveness of demand to a given change in price. The PED coefficient (value) is calculated by use of either of the following equations:

$$PED = \frac{\text{percentage change in quantity demanded}}{\text{percentage change in price}}$$

$$= \frac{\%\Delta O_D}{\%\Delta P}$$

$$\text{or } \frac{P}{Q_D} \times \frac{\Delta Q_D}{\Delta P}$$

where P is the initial price, Q_D is the initial quantity demanded and Δ means 'the change in'. From Figure 5.1, PED is calculated as follows:

PED between points A and B

$$= \frac{\%\Delta Q_D}{\%\Delta P} = \frac{400\%}{66.7\%} = 6$$

or

$$= \frac{P}{Q_D} \times \frac{\Delta Q_D}{\Delta P} = \frac{3}{1} \times \frac{4}{2} = 6$$

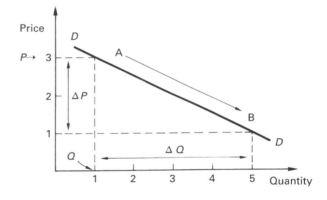

- The PED coefficient can be between zero and infinity (∞).
- If PED is less than 1, demand is inelastic.
- If PED is greater than 1, demand is elastic.
- PED is usually treated as a positive number and any minus signs are often ignored.

Figure 5.2 shows that the gradient (slope) of a demand curve generally reflects its PED. However great care should be taken when interpreting the gradient of a demand curve.

(1) The slope of a demand curve is not necessarily a guide to price elasticity. The scale of each axis affects PED.
(2) On a steep demand curve, PED at points near the *y*-axis can be elastic.
(3) On a flat demand curve, PED at points near the *x*-axis can be inelastic.
(4) PED falls as you move down a linear demand curve.

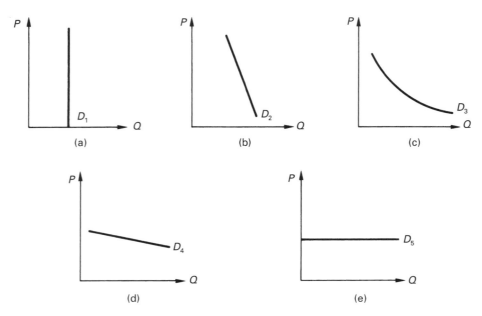

Figure 5.2 Demand curves with different price elasticities. In (a) the demand curve is a vertical line; demand is perfectly inelastic; the PED coefficient is equal to 0; and a price rise means no decrease in Q_D. In (b) the demand curve is a steep line; demand is relatively inelastic; the PED coefficient is greater than 0 but less than 1; and a price rise means a smaller percentage decrease in Q_D. In (c) the demand curve is a rectangular hyperbola; demand is unitary elastic; the PED coefficient is equal to 1; and a price rise means an equal percentage decrease in Q_D. In (d) the demand curve is a shallow line; demand is relatively elastic; the PED coefficient is greater than 1 but less than ∞; and a price rise means a greater percentage decrease in Q_D. In (e) the demand curve is a horizontal line; demand is perfectly elastic; the PED coefficient is equal to ∞; and a price rise means consumers buying perfect substitutes.

Table 5.1 Determinants of price elasticity of demand

Determinant	The demand for a good is relatively price-inelastic because:
Number of substitutes	If there are few substitutes for a good, consumers are unlikely to switch products
Consumer loyalty	If consumers are in the habit of buying a good, they are unwilling to use substitutes
Absolute price of the good	If a good is inexpensive, a large percentage change in price represents only a few pence
Proportion of income	If the good takes up only a small proportion of income, consumers will not react significantly
Number of complements	If the good has many complements, the product is needed if the other items are used.
Consumer adjustment	If consumers are slow to react to a change in price, the amount bought is largely unaffected
Width of definition	If the good is broadly defined, there will be few substitutes for it.

(5) A demand curve shifting to the left becomes more elastic.

(c) Price elasticity of demand and revenue

The effect of a price change on revenue depends on the elasticity of demand. Figure 5.3 shows how a change in price can increase or decrease revenue.

- If PED is elastic, a fall in price increases revenue.
- If PED is inelastic, a rise in price increases revenue.
- If PED is unitary, a price change leaves revenue unchanged.

The relationship between PED and marginal revenue is analysed in Figure 9.1.

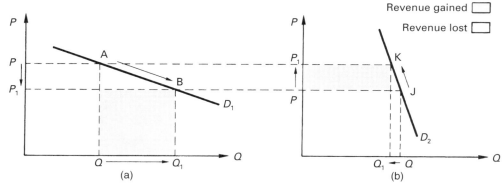

Fig 5.3 (a) Elastic demand and revenue. Since the price decrease results in a proportionately larger increase in quantity demanded, revenue rises. (b) Inelastic demand and revenue. Since the price increase results in a proportionately smaller decrease in quantity demanded, revenue rises.

(d)   Income elasticity of demand

Income elasticity of demand (YED) measures the responsiveness of demand to a given change in income.

$$\text{YED} = \frac{\text{percentage change in quantity demanded}}{\text{percentage change in income}}$$

$$= \frac{\%\Delta Q_D}{\%Y}$$

$$\text{or } \frac{Y}{Q_D} \times \frac{\Delta Q_D}{\Delta Y}$$

- Since YED can be negative, it is important to include minus signs when applicable.
- If YED is negative, the product is an inferior good.
- If YED is positive, the product is a normal good.
- If YED is positive and greater than 1, the product is a superior good.

An *Engel curve* shows the amount of a good demanded at different levels of income. Figure 5.4 shows that the slope of an Engel curve reflects its YED.

(e)   Cross-elasticity of demand

- *Cross-elasticity of demand* (XED) measures the responsiveness of demand for good A to a given change in the price of good B:

$$\text{XED}$$
$$= \frac{\text{percentage change in the quantity of A demanded}}{\text{percentage change in the price of B}}$$

$$= \frac{\%\Delta Q_D \text{ of A}}{\%\Delta P \text{ of B}}$$

$$\text{or } \frac{P_B}{Q_{DA}} \times \frac{\Delta Q_{DA}}{\Delta P_B}$$

- Since XED can be negative, it is important to include minus signs when applicable.
- If XED is positive, the two goods are in competitive demand – i.e. are substitutes.
- If XED is negative, the two goods are in joint demand – i.e. are complements.
- If XED is zero, the two products are unrelated – i.e. are independent goods.

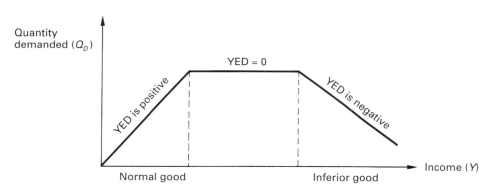

Figure 5.4 An Engel curve with different income elasticities

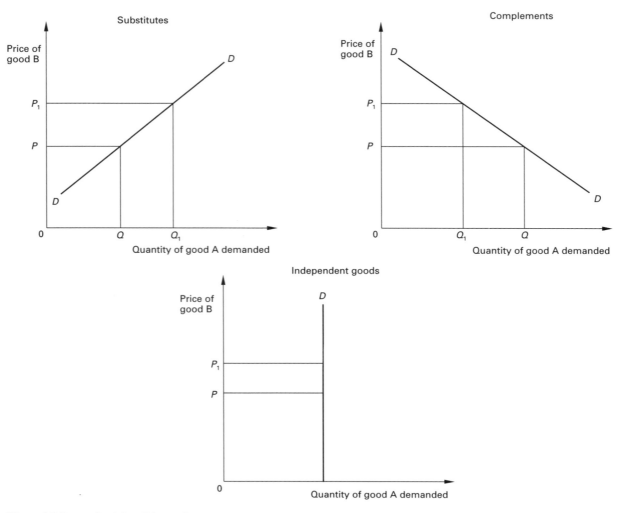

Figure 5.5 Cross elasticity of demand

Figure 5.5 illustrates the three possible types of cross-elasticity of demand.

(f)   Price elasticity of supply

Price elasticity of supply (PES) measures the responsiveness of supply to a given change in price:

$$\text{PES} = \frac{\text{percentage change in quantity supplied}}{\text{percentage change in price}}$$

$$= \frac{\%\Delta Q_S}{\%\Delta P}$$

or $\dfrac{P}{Q_S} \times \dfrac{\Delta Q_S}{\Delta P}$

- The PES coefficient can be between zero and infinity (∞)
- If PES is less than 1, supply is inelastic.
- If PES is greater than 1, supply is elastic.

Figure 5.6 shows that the gradient of a supply curve generally reflects its PES.

It is important to remember that for linear supply curves:

- PES is inelastic at all points when the supply curve intersects the *x*-axis first.
- PES is elastic at all points when the supply curve intersects the *y*-axis first.
- PES is unitary at all points when the supply curve intersects the origin.

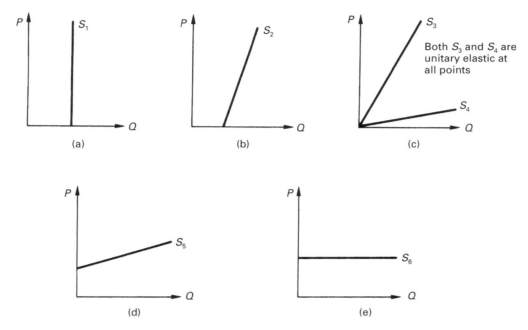

Figure 5.6 Supply curves with different price elasticities. In (a) supply is perfectly inelastic; the PED coefficient is equal to 0; and a price fall means no decrease in Q_S. In (b) supply is relatively inelastic; the PED coefficient is greater than 0 but less than 1; and a price fall means a smaller percentage decrease in Q_S. In (c) supply is unitary elastic; the PED coefficient is equal to 1; and a price fall means an equal percentage decrease in Q_S. In (d) supply is relatively elastic; the PED coefficient is greater than 1 but less than ∞; and a price fall means a greater percentage decrease in Q_S. In (e) supply is perfectly elastic; the PED coefficient is equal to ∞; and a price fall means that suppliers halt production.

Table 5.2 Determinants of price elasticity of supply

Determinant	The supply for a good is relatively price-elastic because:
Time	In the long run, firms can adjust all factor inputs to change supply easily
Production time	If a good is manufactured quickly, supplies can be changed easily
Stocks	If a firm has a large amount of stocks, supplies can be changed easily
Capacity	If labour and capital are underused, supplies can be changed easily
Factor mobility	If resources can move in and out of the industry, supplies can be changed easily

5.2 Investigative study

Example 5.1

A study of the effect of a change in the rate of tax – direct or indirect – on the market for a particular product.

5.3 Data response

Example 5.2

Products X, Y and Z are produced in goods and labour markets that operate under conditions of perfect competition. Product X has an income elasticity of demand of −0.2, product Y an income elasticity of demand of 0.6 and product Z an income elasticity of demand of 1.5.

Firms produce X, Y or Z, and at the start of the period all the firms in each industry are in long-run equilibrium. In the next year there is a rise of 5% in average real consumer disposable income.

(a) What term would you use to describe:
   (1) good X
   (2) good Y
   (3) good Z   **(5 marks)**
(b) Calculate how the change in income will affect the demand for each good.   **(5 marks)**
(c) Using diagrams, explain the changes that will occur over time in the product and factor markets.   **(12 marks)**
(d) In assessing future changes in product markets, which other elasticities should be taken into account?   **(3 marks)**

Solution 5.2

(a)(1) A good with negative income elasticity of demand is known as an inferior good. An increase in income results in a fall in demand for this type of good.

(2) A good with positive income elasticity of demand is known as a normal good. An increase in income results in an increase in demand for this type of good.

(3) A good with positive income elasticity of demand greater than one is known as a superior good. In this case an increase in income results not only in an increase in demand but a greater percentage increase than the rise in income. It has income elastic demand.

(b) Income elasticity of demand (YED) is calculated from the equation:

$$YED = \frac{\text{percentage change in quantity demanded}}{\text{percentage change in income}}$$

For good X: $-0.2 = ?/5\% = -1\%$ (demand for X falls by 1%)
For good Y: $0.6 = ?/5\% = 3\%$ (demand for Y rises by 3%)
For good Z: $1.5 = ?/5\% = 7.5\%$ (demand for Z rises by 7.5%)

(c) Answer (b) indicates that the demand for good X falls by 1% over one year. This will cause demand for the good to fall, price to fall and supply to expand. As less of the good will be produced, demand for the factors of production to produce it will decline. Figure

1 shows the effect on the good market (a) and the product market (b).

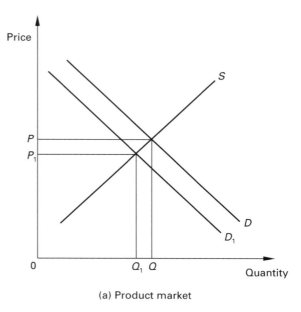

(a) Product market

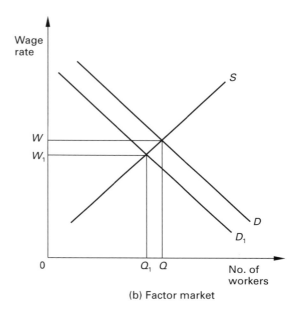

(b) Factor market

Figure 1

Figure 2 shows the increase in demand for good Y that follows an increase in income. The demand curve for good Y shifts to the right. The resultant rise in supply is achieved by attracting additional resources such as labour into the industry. The increase in the demand for the final product will increase the demand for inputs used in the manufacture of Y, and cause the demand for the inputs to shift to the right.

The effect on the product and good market in the case of good Z is similar, except that the increase in demand, the price rises and the payments for factors of production will be greater.

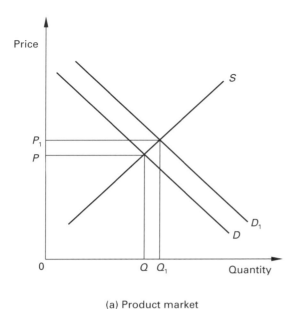

(a) Product market   (b) Factor market

Figure 2

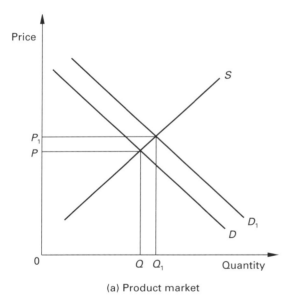

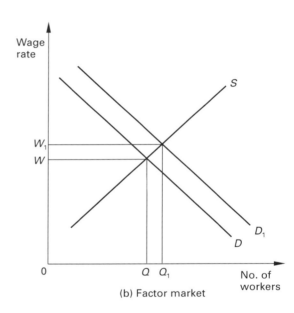

(a) Product market   (b) Factor market

Figure 3

The increase in payments for factors of production in the case of Y and Z will attract redundant factors of production from X. The reallocation of resources is achieved through a change in the relative price of products and factors of production between the product and factor markets.

(d) It would also be useful to consider price and cross-elasticity of demand and price elasticity of supply. For example a rise in the price of a good will result in a greater percentage fall in demand and a fall in revenue if demand is elastic. It will also cause an increase in demand for substitutes (positive cross-

elasticity of demand) and a decrease in demand for complements (negative cross-elasticity of demand). If supply is inelastic a rise in price will result in a smaller percentage extension in supply.

5.4 Objective questions

Example 5.3

The following table shows a demand schedule for a particular good:

Price (£)	1	2	3	4	5
Quantity demanded (kilos)	40	35	30	25	20

In which range does the price elasticity of demand (expressed as a positive number) lie for a rise in price from £3 to £4?

A 0.0–0.3 **B** 0.4–0.7 **C** 0.8–1.1 **D** 1.2–1.5

Example 5.4

If the demand curve for a normal good is linear, the price elasticity of demand for the good:
A decreases as the amount bought increases
B increases as the amount bought increases
C is always less than 1
D is unity

Example 5.5

Which of the following diagrams illustrates the relationship between two normal goods that are in joint demand?

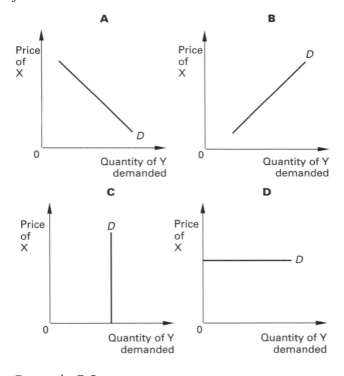

Example 5.6

If market price falls by 5% following a rise in supply, and there is no change in the quantity bought, the demand curve is:
A relatively elastic
B relatively inelastic
C completely elastic
D completely inelastic

Example 5.7

Which one of the following graphs refers to a good that exhibits a negative income elasticity of demand at all levels of income?

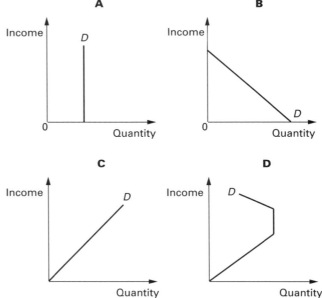

Example 5.8

The following table gives an individual's demand for three goods at two different income levels:

| | Income (£000) | |
	20	24
Units of A	10	15
Units of B	8	10
Units of C	10	11

It follows that the proportionate rise in income leads to:
A a proportionately greater increase in the amount of A demanded
B a proportionately greater increase in the amount of C demanded
C a proportionately greater increase in the demand for good B than for good A
D a proportionately greater increase in the demand for good C than for good B

Example 5.9

A cinema ceases to offer half-price mid-week tickets and instead charges full price. As a result the cinema experiences a fall in its total revenue from mid-week sales. What can be concluded from this information?

A At these prices the demand for mid-week tickets is elastic

B At these prices the demand for mid-week tickets is inelastic

C The demand for mid-week tickets is more elastic than the demand for weekend tickets

D The demand for mid-week tickets is more inelastic than the demand for weekend tickets

Example 5.10

Price elasticity of supply will be smaller:

A the longer the time period under consideration

B The larger the amount of stocks held by firms

C the more immobile the factors of production used

D the shorter the time period required to train the labour used

Example 5.11

The diagram below shows three supply curves. Which of the following statements relating to these supply curves is correct?

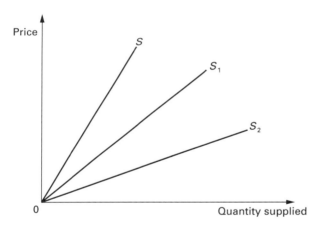

A Supply curve S_2 is more elastic than supply curve S

B Supply curve S_1 is more elastic than supply curve S_2

C All three supply curves illustrate elastic supply

D All three supply curves illustrate unit elasticity of supply

Example 5.12

If the price of a product rises by 10% and total revenue remains constant, price elasticity of demand is:

A unity

B elastic

C inelastic

D perfectly inelastic

5.5 Solutions to objective questions

Solution 5.3   Answer: **B**

Price elasticity of demand (PED) can be calculated by using either of the following equations:

$$PED = \frac{P}{Q_D} \times \frac{\Delta Q_D}{\Delta P}$$

$$or\ PED = \frac{\%\Delta Q_D}{\%\Delta P}$$

where P is the initial price, Q_D is the original quantity demanded, ΔQ_D is the change in quantity demanded and ΔP is the change in price.

Using the first equation:

$$PED = \frac{3}{30} \times \frac{(30-25)}{(4-3)} = \frac{3}{30} \times \frac{5}{1} = \frac{15}{30} = 0.5$$

and using the second equation

$$PED = \frac{16.67\%}{33.33\%} = 0.5$$

Note that the question states PED 'expressed as a positive number'. By convention, all negative signs are usually ignored when calculating PED.

Solution 5.4   Answer: **A**

A 'linear' demand curve is a straight line. The phrase 'a normal good' simply tells you that the demand curve in question slopes downwards from left to right. Consider the following diagram:

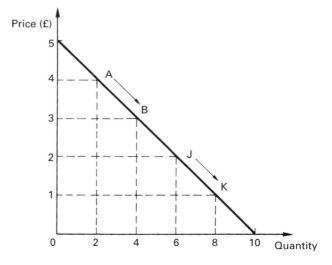

As you move down a demand curve, you are dividing a smaller percentage change in quantity demanded $(\%)\Delta Q_D$ by a larger percentage change in price $(\%\Delta P)$. For example:

A to B

$$\%\Delta Q_D = \frac{\text{change in } Q_D}{\text{original } Q_D} \times 100 = \frac{2}{2} \times 100 = 100\%$$

$$\%\Delta P = \frac{\text{change in } P}{\text{original } P} \times 100 = \frac{1}{3} \times 100 = 33.3\%$$

PED A to B

$$= \frac{\%\Delta Q_D}{\%\Delta P} = \frac{100}{33.3} = 3 \text{ (i.e. PED is elastic)}$$

J to K $\%\Delta Q_D = \dfrac{2}{6} \times 100 = 33.3\%$

$$\%\Delta P \quad = \frac{1}{2} \times 100 = 50\%$$

$$\therefore \text{PED J to K} = \frac{33.3}{50} = 0.67 \text{ (i.e. PED is inelastic)}$$

Solution 5.5   Answer: **A**

Two goods in joint demand are complements. Complements have a negative cross-elasticity of demand (XED). If the price of one good (e.g. electricity) rises, the demand for a complement (e.g. electric fires) falls. This type of relationship between price and demand is only shown in portion A. Other options are incorrect because:

B $\Rightarrow$ shows positive XED, which is possessed by substitutes.

C $\Rightarrow$ shows zero XED, which occurs when goods are independent.

D $\Rightarrow$ does not show a relationship. The quantity of Y demanded is changing for a reason unconnected with the price of X, which is remaining constant.

Solution 5.6   Answer: **D**

A completely inelastic demand curve is a vertical straight line. The 5% decrease in price results in no change in the quantity bought.

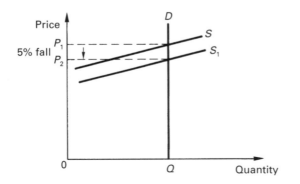

Solution 5.7   Answer: **B**

A good with a negative income elasticity of demand (YED) is an inferior good – i.e. as income rises, the quantity demanded falls. As you move up the y-axis, income rises but the quantity demanded continues to decline. Other options are incorrect because:

A $\Rightarrow$ shows zero YED as the same amount is demanded no matter what the level of income.

C $\Rightarrow$ shows positive YED throughout.

D $\Rightarrow$ shows a positive YED up to a certain level of income, then YED becomes zero and finally negative.

Solution 5.8   Answer: **A**

The question requires the calculation of (a) the percentage change in income, and (b) the resulting percentage change in the amount of each good demanded.

The percentage change ($\%\Delta$) of income (Y) is calculated by using the equation:

$$\%\Delta Y = \frac{\Delta Y}{Y} \times 100 = \frac{£24\,000 - £20\,000}{£20\,000} \times 100$$

$$= \frac{£4000}{£20\,000} \times 100 = 20\%$$

The percentage change in demand for each good equals the change in demand, divided by the original demand, times 100:

$$\%\Delta A \quad = \frac{5}{10} \times 100 = 50\%$$

$$\%\Delta B \quad = \frac{2}{8} \times 100 = 25\%$$

$$\%\Delta C \quad = \frac{1}{10} \times 100 = 10\%$$

The 20% increase in income results in a proportionately greater increase (50%) in the quantity demanded of A. Good C has an income inelastic demand and good A has a more income elastic demand than good B, which in turn has a more income elastic demand than good C.

Solution 5.9   Answer: **A**

The effect of discontinuing half-price mid-week tickets is to increase price. If elasticity of demand for mid-week tickets is greater than 1 but less than infinity (i.e. elastic), then the increase in price brings about a greater percentage fall in sales. Hence total revenue falls.

Option **B** is incorrect since, if the demand for mid-week tickets is inelastic, price and total revenue will move in the same direction. More information would be needed to conclude whether the demand for mid-week tickets is more elastic or more inelastic than the demand for weekend tickets.

Solution 5.10   Answer: **C**

'Price elasticity will be smaller' means 'supply becomes more inelastic'. Firms will not be able to adjust supply quickly if they are unable to increase or reduce the quantity of factors of production they employ easily. Options **A**, **B** and **D** would all make it easier to adjust supply and hence would make supply elastic.

Solution 5.11   Answer: **D**

Any straight-line supply curve that passes through the origin has unit elasticity of supply.

Solution 5.12   Answer: **A**

For total revenue to remain constant as price changes, the quantity demanded must change by the same percentage but in the opposite direction. This occurs when elasticity of demand is unity. If demand is elastic (option **B**) a rise in price will cause a fall in total revenue, whereas if demand is inelastic (option **C**) a rise in price will cause a rise in total revenue. When demand is perfectly inelastic a rise in price will cause a proportionate rise in total revenue – demand will remain constant but consumers will pay more for the same number of goods. For instance if demand was originally 90 and price £10, total revenue would be £900. A 10% rise in price to £11 would have no effect on demand, which would stay at 90, but would cause total revenue to rise to $90 \times £11 = £990$, which is a 10% rise in revenue.

5.6 Essays

Example 5.13

(a)   Explain what is meant by:
   (1) price elasticity of demand;
   (2) cross elasticity of demand;
   (3) income elasticity of demand.   **(10 marks)**
(b)   What relevance do these terms have for the sales director of a firm of travel agents?   **(15 marks)**

- Apply your general understanding of demand elasticity.
- Analyse each type of demand elasticity in separate paragraphs.
- Use diagrams and relevant formulae.
- Be careful to ensure that arguments are supported with worked examples relevant to a travel firm.
- A detailed knowledge of the travel and tourism industry is not expected.

Solution 5.13

(a) Elasticity of demand measures the responsiveness of demand to changes in other variables. There are three types of elasticity of demand.
   (1) Price elasticity of demand (PED) measures the responsiveness of quantity demanded to a given change in price:

$$\text{PED} \frac{= \% \text{ change in quantity demanded}}{\% \text{ change in price}}$$

Most goods have either elastic or inelastic demand. Elastic demand means that a change in price causes a greater percentage change in demand, whereas inelastic demand means that a change in price causes a smaller percentage change in demand.
   In most cases price elasticity of demand is negative, so that price and demand will move in opposite directions. Indeed so common is negative price elasticity of demand that usually the sign is omitted.
   (2) Cross-elasticity of demand (XED) measures the responsiveness of demand for one good to a given change in the price of a second good:

$$\text{XED} = \% \frac{\text{change in quantity demanded of good B}}{\% \text{ change in price of good A}}$$

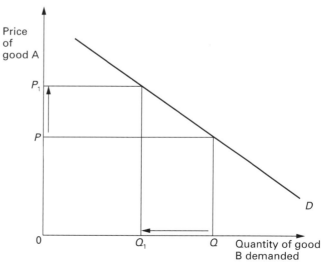

Figure 1

The XED value indicates which pair of products are substitutes (+XED coefficient), complements (−XED coefficient) or independent goods (XED = 0). Figure 1 illustrates negative cross-elasticity of demand. A rise in the price of good A causes a decrease in the demand for its complement, good B.

(3) Income elasticity of demand (YED) measures the responsiveness of demand to a given change in income:

$$\text{YED} = \frac{\%\ \text{change in quantity demanded}}{\%\ \text{change in income}}$$

Most goods have positive income elasticity of demand, which means that demand for them will vary directly with income. These goods are referred to as normal goods, although those with a positive income elasticity of demand that is greater than one (income elastic demand) are called superior goods. Figure 2 shows positive income elasticity of demand with a rise in income causing a rise in demand.

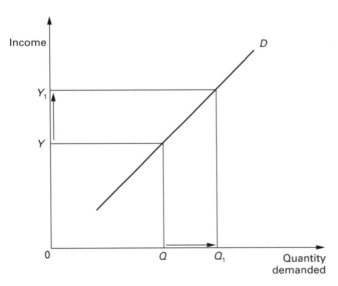

Figure 2

Inferior goods have negative income elasticity of demand, which means that income and demand vary inversely so that a rise in income will cause a fall in demand.

(b) The PED of a product will be of relevance to a sales director contemplating a price change and needing to know the probable effect on revenue.

Figure 3 shows two possible demand curves for coach day trips. D_1 is relatively price inelastic and D_2 is relatively price elastic. At the initial price of £10, 100 trips are sold and the firm's total revenue (price × quantity) is £10 × 100 = £1000. A 'special

offer' campaign where price is reduced by 20% affects revenue according to the PED for trips. Given d_1, total revenue becomes £8 × 110 = £880. Given D_2, total revenue is £8 × 150 = £1200. Therefore the special offer only increases the revenue of the firm if PED is elastic.

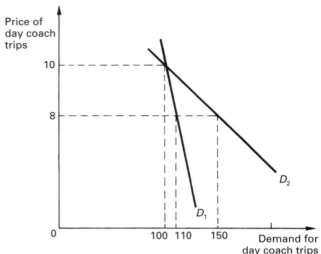

Figure 3

Demand for holiday excursions, which are expensive and have a number of close substitutes, is likely to be elastic.

A knowledge of XED enables a director to estimate the wider effects of discounting one holiday. Assume that the XED coefficient between holidays A and B is 2. A 10% reduction in the price of holiday A would cause a 20% fall in the quantity of B (a substitute holiday). This is likely to discourage the director from discounting the price of A.

XED also permits the firm to assess the effect of a loss-leader strategy, where the price of one good is heavily reduced in the hope that additional purchases of other products will compensate. Loss-leader campaigns are most effective when the XED of the other product with respect to a large number of other goods sold by the firm is negative and greater than 1, e.g. −4. The loss made on one item is made up by the profit from the sale of complements.

A knowledge of YED allows the sales director to predict the likely pattern of future demand for travel as consumers' real incomes rise. For example, assume that the firm has to decide between increasing the number of coach day trips or introducing a new luxury tour service. If market research shows that the YED for day trips is negative, then demand will fall over time and the firm will operate in a declining market. If the survey finds that the YED for luxury tours is positive and greater than 1, then demand will rise proportionately faster over time than income and the market will expand. The sales director may also try to change the image of trips and holidays that have negative income elasticity of demand from inferior to normal goods, e.g. by advertising, improving the service etc.

Example 5.14

(a) Explain what is meant by price elasticity of supply. **(7 marks)**
(b) Why is the price elasticity of margarine likely to vary over time? **(18 marks)**

- Give the formula for price elasticity of supply.
- Explain what is meant by elastic and inelastic supply.
- Include diagrams.
- Distinguish between the short run and long run.
- Cover the main influence on price elasticity of supply.

Solution 5.14

(a) Price elasticity of supply (PES) measures the responsiveness of quantity supplied to a given change in price. PES is calculated by comparing the proportionate change in price and quantity supplied by use of the equation:

$$PES = \frac{\text{percentage change in quantity supplied}}{\text{percentage change in price}}$$

Within a given time period, the elasticity of supply depends largely on the ability of a firm to vary output

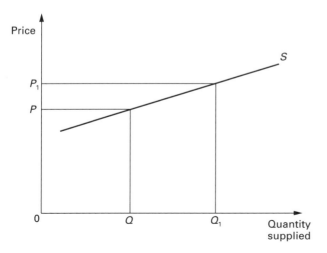

Figure 1

in response to price changes. If output is adjusted easily in response to price changes, then PES is elastic and hence greater than one. Figure 1 illustrates elastic supply.

Products whose output cannot be varied easily possess low PES. Figure 2 shows inelastic supply.

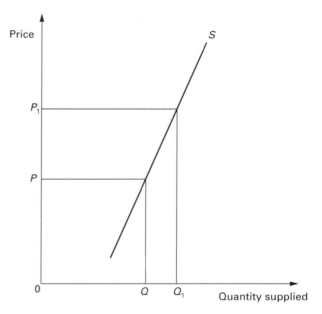

Figure 2

Analysis of the factors determining elasticity of supply requires a careful analysis of the factors determining the ability of a firm to vary output.

(b) The short run is defined as the period of time in which a firm is unable to alter the amount of at least one factor of production, such as capital used in production.

There are a number of reasons for believing that, in the short run, margarine output can be readily adjusted and the PES of margarine is elastic. For instance margarine is a relatively simple manufactured good that requires little time for mass production. Output can be expanded rapidly by operating overtime or by working night shifts. Margarine can be refrigerated and stored for long periods. Stocks can then be used to effect changes in the quantity supplied.

On the other hand there are several factors that would make the short-run PES of margarine inelastic. The impact of diminishing returns and the difficulty of substituting one factor of production for another raises short-run unit costs and makes supply inelastic. If margarine factories are operating at or near full capacity, output cannot be expanded rapidly in response to a price rise. Again, if the labour used to operate machinery requires specialist training, it is also difficult to expand production rapidly.

The long run is defined as the period of time when the firm is able to vary the amount of any factor of production. In the long run PES is more elastic than in the short run, for a variety of reasons. In the long run firms have an opportunity to overcome diminishing returns (which can occur in the short run) by adjusting the mix of labour and capital. The difficulties of factor immobility can be overcome through training.

Supply is elastic in the long run because firms have longer to plan their production decisions and more time to manufacture the good. For example machinery used to produce similar products such as cheese spreads can be switched into our out of the production of margarine. The industry can adjust production capacity by installing or removing machines. If the firm decides on a very large adjustment in capacity, a new factory can be built or an existing plant can be closed down. Moreover, provided that there are no barriers to entry, new firms can enter the industry. Alternatively, existing firms can switch into the production of another good. It is also likely that supply will be affected by the development of new technologies that improve production techniques and increase PES.

Costs of Production

6.1 Fact sheet

(a) Factors of production

Output is produced with *factors of production* (inputs). These are:

(1) *Land* – all natural resources, e.g. fishing grounds, farm land.
(2) *Capital* – man-made goods used in the production of goods and services, e.g. factories and machines.
(3) *Labour* – mental and physical effort expended in the production of goods and services.
(4) *Entrepreneurship* – entrepreneurs bear the uncertain and uninsurable risks of production.

* A *production function* shows the relationship between the amount of factors of production used and the amount of output produced.

(b) Short-run product curves

The *short run* is the period of time when the quantity of at least one factor of production is unchanged. Firms may be able to increase output by adding extra units of labour to a fixed amount of capital.

* The addition to output made by each extra worker is called *marginal product of labour* (MPL).
* Output per worker is called *average product of labour* (APL).

The concept of *returns* compares the percentage change in favour of production, e.g. labour ($\%\Delta L$) with the resulting percentage change in output ($\%\Delta Q$ – Table 6.1).

* The *law of diminishing returns* states that, as extra units of a variable factor are combined with a given amount of a fixed factor, the marginal products of the variable factor will eventually fall (Figure 6.1).
* If only diminishing returns are referred to, this is taken to mean diminishing marginal returns.

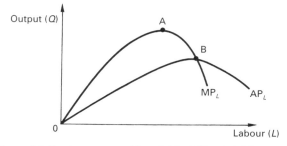

Figure 6.1 Product curves: $AP = Q/L$; $MP = \Delta Q/\Delta L$. A is the point of diminishing returns; B is the point of diminishing average returns

Table 6.1 Types of return

Type of return	Description	Marginal product
Increasing returns	$\%\Delta L$ is smaller than the resulting $\%\Delta Q$	Rising
Constant returns	$\%\Delta L$ is equal to the resulting $\%\Delta Q$	Constant
Decreasing returns	$\%\Delta L$ is greater than the resulting $\%\Delta Q$	Falling

(c) Costs of production

Table 6.2 Types of cost

Term	Symbol	Definition	Equation
Total cost	TC	The amount spent on producing a given output	$TC = FC + VC$
Variable costs	VC	Production expenses *dependent* on the level of output	$VC = TC - FC$
Fixed costs	FC	Production expenses *independent* of the level of output	$FC = TC - VC$
Average cost	AC	The amount spent on producing *each* unit	$AC = TC \div Q$
Average variable cost	AVC	Unit variable cost *dependent* on the level of output	$AVC = VC \div Q$
Average fixed cost	AFC	Unit fixed costs *independent* of the level of output	$AFC = FC \div Q$
Marginal cost	MC	The amount spent on producing *one extra* unit	$MC = \Delta TC \div \Delta Q$

- Accountancy and economic definitions of costs are different.
- Economists use the concept of *opportunity cost* when calculating productions costs.
- If resources are owned by the firm, the *inputed* (estimated) transfer earnings of the factor is included as a cost.

(d) Short-run cost curves

There are two main methods of illustrating short-run cost curves. In Figure 6.2:

- MC curve rises given diminishing returns.
- AC curve rises if MC is greater than AC.
- MC is made up entirely of changes in VC.
- Optimum output is where AC is lowest (point A).

In Figure 6.3

- TC curve rises if output increases.

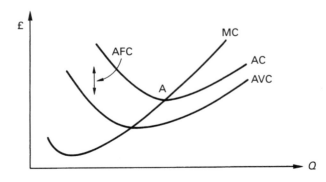

Figure 6.2 Unit cost curves

- VC curve rises if output increases.
- FC stay constant as output increases.

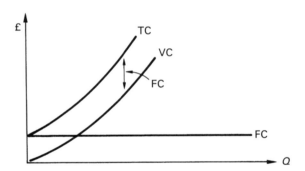

Figure 6.3 Total cost curves

(e) Economies of scale

In the long run the firm can increase output by varying all factors of production. Economies of scale (EOS) are reductions in long-run average (unit) costs that occur from an increase in production.

- Internal EOS occur within the firm as output rises. These can be divided into:
  - (1) plant economies: the benefits gained from factories, offices and machines growing in size;
  - (2) firm economies – the benefits gained from the company growing in size.
- External EOS occur outside the firm and are independent of the size of the individual firm.

Table 6.3 Types of internal economy of scale

Types of internal EOS	Description
Specialisation	Large firms have more scope for the division of labour than have small firms
Indivisibilities	Some machines are of a minimum size that can only be kept fully occupied by large firms
Increased dimension	The cost of capital does not increase in proportion with the output of each machine
Principle of multiples	Large firms use a machine combination that eliminates bottlenecks caused by different machines working at different speeds
Linked processes	Bringing together different stages of production in one factory reduces costs
Managerial	Big firms can spread the cost of employing the best managers over a large level of output. Managerial costs do not increase in proportion with output
Financial	Large firms offer more security and pay a lower rate of interest on loans than do small firms. Large firms can raise capital cheaply through a rights issue
Commercial	Large firms buy raw materials and components in bulk and are therefore given a discount
Marketing	Transportation and advertising costs do not increase in proportion with output
Research and development	Large firms can spread the cost of improving products over a large level of output

Table 6.4 Types of external economy of scale

Types of external EOS	Description
Infrastructure	Proximity to a good transport and communications network
Ancillary firms	Local back-up forms supply specialist support services or components
Skilled local labour	An area may have trained workers looking for jobs
Education	An area may have colleges providing specialist training

(f) Diseconomies of scale

Diseconomies of scale (DOS) are increases in long-run costs that occur from an increase in production.

(1) *Internal* DOS occur within the firm when increases in output raise long-run costs. They occur mainly because of managerial difficulties in oversized firms:
   (a) managers are unable to exercise effective control or coordination;
   (b) internal communications within the company are difficult;
   (c) workers feel isolated and out of touch with managers, and industrial relations decline.

(2) *External* DOS occur outside the firm when the long-run costs of all local firms rise when:
   (a) local road congestion causes transportation delays;
   (b) local land and factories become scarce and rents rise;
   (c) labour shortages develop within the area and wages rise.

(g) Long-run cost curves

- A *short-run average cost curve* (SAC) shows the unit cost associated with a given size of plant.
- A *long-run average cost curve* (LAC) shows the minimum unit cost of producing each level of output, allowing the size of plant to vary.
- An LAC curve is found by drawing a line tangential to each SAC curve.
- Each SAC curve shows the unit cost from plants of different size.
- The size of plant associated with SAC_2 is the smallest needed to minimise unit cost – i.e. *minimum efficient plant size* (MEPS).
- The slope of the LAC curve is determined by internal EOS.
- The position of the LAC curve is determined, in part, by external EOS.

The concept of *returns to scale* compares the percentage change in inputs (%Δ inputs) with the resulting percentage in output (%ΔQ). Table 6.5 explains the relationship between returns to scale and economies of scale that usually exists.

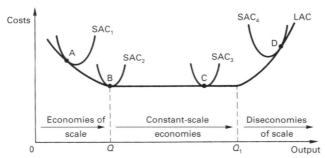

Figure 6.4 Long-run average cost curve

6.2 Investigative study

Example 6.1

A comparative study of the performance of two firms in the same industry – one large and one small.

6.3 Data response

Example 6.2

A profitable UK airline is considering whether to expand by introducing a new flight to New York. It is faced with the following costs per flight:

	£
Depreciation	1 500
Fuel charges	29 400
Insurance	600
Interest	800
Labour	10 000
Landing charges	1 000
Other fixed costs	6 700

(a) State which of the above costs are fixed costs and which are variable. Explain your choice.
(5 marks)

(b) (1) If the maximum number of passengers per flight is 500, what is the minimum price per seat that the airline must charge on this flight to operate it in the short run? **(6 marks)**
(2) What is the minimum price that would have to be charged to make the flight viable in the long run? **(6 marks)**

(c) Explain the factors that are likely to determine the actual price charged. **(8 marks)**

Solution 6.2

(a) Fixed costs are costs of production that are independent of the number of flights undertaken. An allowance for depreciation has to be made irrespective of whether or not an aeroplane flies. In a given time period the amount of insurance paid, or interest owed on loans, does not change with the number of flights made. Variable costs are costs that are dependent on

Table 6.5 Returns to scale and scale economies

Returns to scale	Description	Scale economies	Scope of LAC curve
Increasing returns to scale	%Δ inputs is smaller than the resulting %ΔQ	Economies of scale	Falling
Constant returns to scale	%Δ inputs is equal to the resulting %ΔQ	Constant	Horizontal
Decreasing returns to scale	%Δ inputs is greater than the resulting %ΔQ	Diseconomies of scale	Rising

the number of flights undertaken. Fuel charges, landing charges and labour costs are incurred after each flight. This assumes that labour is paid per flight and can be laid off at zero cost if no flights are made.

(b)(1) In the short run, a firm will continue to operate at a loss, provided that variable costs are covered. From the table, the total variable cost of each flight is £29 400 for fuel, £1000 for landing charges and £10 000 for labour, making a total of £40 400. Assuming that all 500 seats are sold, £40 400/500 = £80.80. So in the short run the minimum price that would have to be charged would be £80.80. In this case the operating loss is less than the total fixed costs that would have to be met if the flight were cancelled.

(2) In the long run all costs have to be met. From the table the total cost of each flight is £60 000. When divided by seating capacity this gives a price of £120. However the table does not include a specific figure for normal profit. This is considered to be a cost of production and may have been included in the 'other fixed costs' category. If not, the airline may operate a 'cost-plus' pricing policy and add, say, 20% onto costs (£24), giving a flight price of £140.

It is also highly unlikely that the airline will be able to sell all 500 seats for each flight. Therefore the minimum price that must be charged is total cost divided by average seating. For example, assume that 400 seats are sold for each flight. The minimum price becomes £60 000/400 = £150.

(c) Airline flights are subject to international agreements between countries. These agreements are highly restrictive and can specify the number of flights each week, the timing of flights and the prices that can be charged. Hence the market for international flights is highly imperfect and essentially oligopolistic in nature. Evidence suggests that even when more than one transatlantic airline flies between two cities, companies operate as a cartel and the price is fixed above the likely market price. With each airline charging the same price, non-price competition and branding is used to differentiate products.

The actual price charged, then, is likely to be affected by the cost structure of each flight, the number of seats sold on average, and the degree of competition between airlines on the transatlantic route.

6.4 Objective questions

Example 6.3

The addition to total output from the use of an extra unit of one factor is:
A marginal cost
B marginal product
C average cost
D average product

Example 6.4

A firm has fixed costs of £2000. Its average total cost is £10 and its average variable cost is £6. What is the firm's output?

A 125 units   B 200 units
C 333.3 units   D 500 units

Example 6.5

In the diagram below, MP shows the marginal product of labour and AP shows the average product of labour, at each level of output. Does the law of diminishing returns begin to operate at level **A**, **B**, **C** or **D**?

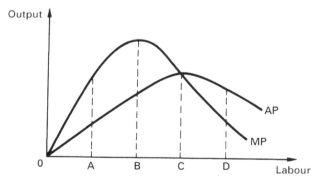

Example 6.6

The table below shows the weekly output of a firm and its total costs.

Output (tonnes)	0	10	20	30	40
Total costs (£)	120	180	200	210	225

At which level of output is average variable cost lowest?
A 10   B 20   C 30   D 40

Example 6.7

The diagram below shows short-run per unit cost curves for a firm.

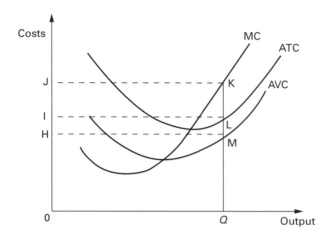

Which of the following areas represents total fixed cost?

A 0HM*Q*   B HILM
C IJKL   D 0IL*Q*

Example 6.8

If a firm's average variable cost curve is U-shaped, then, as output increases from zero, marginal cost must:

A always increase
B always decrease
C initially decrease and then increase
D initially increase and then decrease

Example 6.9

The diagram below shows the total cost curve of a firm.

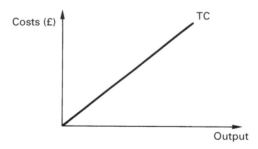

It follows from the diagram that, as the level of output increases, marginal cost must:

A always increase
B remain constant
C initially decrease and then increase
D initially increase and then decrease

Example 6.10

A firm increases the amount of labour, raw materials and capital used in production by 25%. If output increases by 15%, the firm is subject to:

A diseconomies of scale
B decreasing returns to capital
C decreasing returns to labour
D the law of diminishing returns

Example 6.11

The short-run total costs (TC) of a firm are given by the equation $TC = £30\ 000 + 5Q^2$, where Q is the level of output. What is the firm's fixed costs?

A £0   B £30 000
C $5Q^2$ D $£30\ 000/5Q^2$

Example 6.12

If average cost is falling:

A marginal cost must equal average cost
B marginal cost must also be decreasing
C marginal cost must be lower than average cost
D marginal cost must be greater than average cost

6.5 Solutions to objective questions

Solution 6.3 Answer: **B**

Marginal product refers to the addition to total product following the employment of an extra unit of a variable factor.

Solution 6.4 Answer: **D**

Average total cost = average variable cost + average fixed cost, so:

£10 = £6 + average fixed cost
£10 − 6 = average fixed cost = £4

Average cost = total fixed cost/output
£4 = 2000/output
£4 × output = 2000
output = 2000/4 = £500

Solution 6.5 Answer: **B**

Unless otherwise stated, the law of diminishing returns refers to diminishing *marginal* returns. In the diagram, the apex (top) of the marginal product curve shows the point of diminishing returns and this corresponds to output level B.

Solution 6.6   Answer: **D**

Fixed costs have to be paid out by the firm even if it produces zero output. There are no variable costs when output is zero. The table indicates that the total cost of zero production is £120. Therefore the firm's fixed costs must be £120.

Total cost minus fixed cost gives variable cost and variable cost divided by the level of output gives average variable cost. The table below shows that minimum average variable cost is reached where output is 40 units.

Output (tonnes)	0	10	20	30	40
Total cost (£)	120	180	200	210	225
Fixed cost	120	120	120	120	120
Variable cost	0	60	80	90	105
Average variable cost	—	6	4	3	2.63

Solution 6.7   Answer: **B**

Total fixed cost is average fixed cost multiplied by output. Average fixed cost is average total cost minus average variable cost. From the diagram, average fixed cost is LM. So total fixed cost is the area HILM. The area given in option **A** (0HMQ) is total variable cost and the area given in option **D** (0ILQ) is total cost.

Solution 6.8   Answer: **C**

Fixed costs are not affected by changes in output. Therefore marginal cost (MC) determines changes in variable costs. Figure 6.2 shows a U-shaped average variable cost (AVC) curve. Note that the AVC curve slopes downwards, provided that MC is less than AVC. The MC curve intersects AVC at its lowest point. Once MC is above AVC, the AVC curve begins to rise.

Solution 6.9   Answer: **B**

A linear total cost curve means the cost of making each extra unit – marginal cost – remains the same.

Solution 6.10   Answer: **A**

Returns to scale compares the percentage change in all factors of production with the resulting change in output. Since a 25% increase in factors of production results in a smaller percentage increase in output (15%), the firm is experiencing decreasing returns to scale. Decreasing returns to scale are usually associated with diseconomies of scale. This is because, if the cost of production remains constant, output rising by a smaller percentage than inputs will increase average (unit) cost.

Options **B**, **C** and **D** are incorrect as the question states that all three factors of production are changing. **B**, **C** and **D** are short-run concepts.

Solution 6.11   Answer: **C**

The equation $TC = £3000 \times 5Q^2$ means 'total cost is found by multiplying a fixed sum £3000 by 5 times the particular level of output, squared.' Fixed costs are £3000. Variable costs are 5 times the particular level of output, squared.

Solution 6.12   Answer: **C**

To answer this question it is useful to draw the marginal and average cost curves.

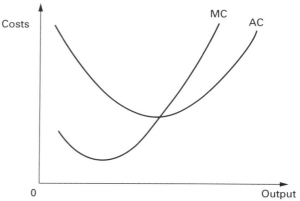

From the diagram it can be seen that when average cost is falling, marginal cost is below average cost.

6.6 Essays

Example 6.13

(a) Explain the difference between fixed and variable costs.   **(8 marks)**
(b) What effect will an increase in output have on average fixed, average variable and average total costs?   **(17 marks)**

- In defining fixed and variable costs, give examples.
- In part (b):
  (1) concentrate on the short run;
  (2) explain the relationship between marginal cost and average variable cost;
  (3) explain the relationship between AFC, AVC and ATC.
- Use diagrams and numerical examples.

Solution 6.13

(a) Fixed costs are costs that do not change with output. They are incurred even if output is zero and can also be referred to as indirect or overhead costs. Examples of fixed costs include rent and business rates. The amount of rent paid for a factory or office of a given size will not alter if the firm increases its output by, say, 6%, or if it closes down for two weeks over the Christmas period.

Variable costs are costs that do change with output. They can also be called direct or prime costs. For example if an insurance company attracts more customers its telephone bill is likely to increase.

Some costs will be fixed and some will be variable in the short run. This is because in the short run at least one factor of production will be fixed. In our example above it was the size of the factory or office, making rent the fixed cost. However in the long run all factors of production can be altered, including the size and number of factories and offices, and so all costs are variable.

(b) Average fixed cost is total fixed cost divided by output. As fixed cost is constant, AFC falls with output. This is shown in Table 1 and illustrated in Figure 1.

Output	Total cost	Fixed cost	Average fixed cost
0	100	100	—
1	180	100	100.0
2	250	100	50.0
3	300	100	33.3
4	320	100	25.0
5	360	100	20.0

Average variable cost is total variable cost divided by output. AVC is likely to fall initially as output rises and then increase. The shape of the AVC curve is influenced by the shape of the marginal cost curve. Marginal cost is the change in total cost resulting from a change in output of one. Both the MC and AVC curves are U-shaped. When output first begins to rise, increasing returns are experienced and marginal cost falls. Then diminishing returns are experienced and marginal cost rises. The marginal cost curve cuts AVC at its lowest point (Figure 2).

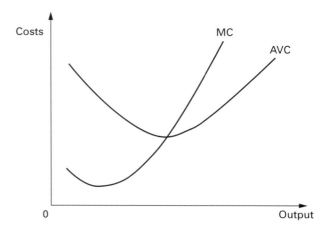

Figure 2

Average total cost is total cost divided by output. It is sometimes referred to as just average cost and consists of AFC + AVC. The short run average cost curve is also U-shaped. It falls at first because fixed costs are spread over more units and because of

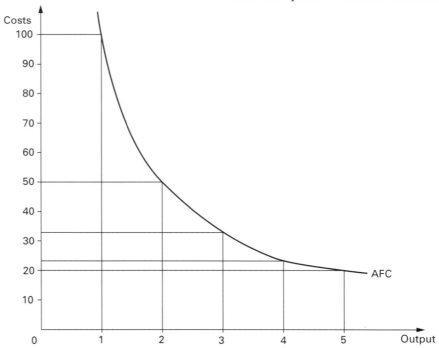

Figure 1

increasing returns. It then rises due to diminishing returns. As with AVC, it is cut at its lowest point by MC. Figure 3 illustrates ATC, AVC and MC. The vertical distance between ATC and AVC is AFC, and so this distance declines as output rises since AFC falls with output.

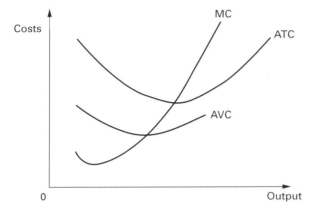

Figure 3

Table 2 shows how ATC and AVC fall and then rise with output. It also illustrates, as does Figure 3, that average cost is above marginal cost when average cost is falling and average cost is below marginal cost when average cost is rising.

Table 2

Output	Total cost	Variable cost	Average total cost	Average variable cost	Marginal cost
0	100	—	—	—	—
1	180	80	0.0	80.0	80
2	250	150	125.0	75.0	70
3	300	200	100.0	66.7	50
4	320	220	80.0	55.0	20
5	360	260	72.0	52.0	40
6	420	320	70.0	53.3	60
7	500	400	71.4	57.1	80
8	600	500	75.0	62.5	100
9	720	620	80.0	68.9	120

So AFC will fall with output and AVC and ATC will fall and then rise.

Example 6.14

How is a firm's average cost curve determined in:

(a) the short run?   (**13 marks**)

(b) the long run?   (**12 marks**)

- The question tests your understanding of returns and returns to scale.
- Make good use of accurate graphs.
- Use examples to develop important points.

Solution 6.14

(a) A firm is a unit that organises the production of goods and services. Traditional new classical theory assumes that firms use only two factors to produce output: labour and capital. Furthermore it assumes that firms can only increase output in the short run by adding extra units of labour to a fixed number of machines.

Marginal cost (MC) refers to the cost of producing an extra unit. Extra units are manufactured by employing additional workers. Assume that each worker receives the same wage. Initially each extra worker is able to produce more than the previous worker because, at first, marginal workers have easy access to a fixed number of machines and the division of labour principle can be applied. Since the firm is initially obtaining an increasing return for a constant outlay on wages, marginal costs are falling and the MC curve in Figure 1 slopes downwards. Beyond Q_1, the law of diminishing returns operates and the firm receives a decreasing return for a constant outlay on wages. Workers experience delayed access to machines and the opportunities for the division of labour have been fully exploited.

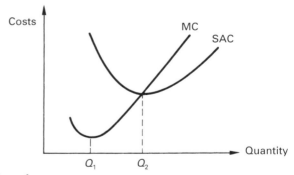

Figure 1

Average cost is the unit cost of producing a given level of output. The shape of the short-run average cost curve (SAC) in Figure 1 depends critically on the behaviour of marginal costs. SAC slopes downwards until Q_2 because marginal cost is less than unit cost. Beyond Q_2 marginal cost exceeds average cost and the SAC curve begins to rise.

It has been established that the shape of the short-run average cost curve is determined by the shape of the marginal cost curve, which in turn is determined by the law of diminishing returns. The type of return experienced depends on the degree of access workers have to machines and on the scope for the division of labour.

In the short run the firm is constrained to its current SAC curve. In the long run the firm can increase plant (production unit) size and move to a new SAC curve. Increasing the amount of capital employed shifts the SAC curve to the right. The type of scale economy then experienced determines whether or not the new SAC curve also shifts upwards or downwards. SAC shifts downwards if the firm experiences economies of scale (Figure 2), upwards if diseconomies of scale begin to come into effect (Figure 3) and horizontally given constant scale economies (Figure 4).

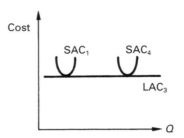

Figure 4

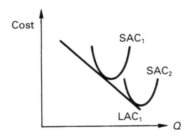

Figure 2

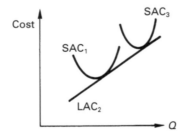

Figure 3

(b) A long-run average cost curve (LAC) is the envelope of the firm's SAC curves. The shape of the LAC curve is determined by the type of internal scale economies experienced by the firm. For example, the manufacture of cars offers significant potential technical economies of scale. Highly automated production lines populated with robot arms reduce LAC. As more cars are produced, the firm's greater requirement for raw materials such as steel allows it to negotiate substantial discounts with suppliers. Initially the LAC curve of a car manufacturer slopes downwards, as in Figure 2. However, beyond a certain level of output LAC begins to rise, as in Figure 3. Management becomes more difficult when the activities of the firm become more complex. Additional strata of middle managers (e.g. foremen) increase wages with no corresponding increase in output. Productivity may fall if workers feel alienated by impersonal mass production techniques.

In conclusion, it has been demonstrated that the firm's average cost curve is determined by the type of return experienced in the short run and the type of scale economy enjoyed in the long run.

PART II — Market Structure

AEB	NEAB	OCSEB	UCLES	ULE	UODLE	Topic	Date begun	Date completed	Self-assessment
✓	✓	✓	✓	✓	✓	**Fact sheets**			
✓					✓	**Investigative study**			
✓	✓	✓	✓	✓	✓	**Data response**			
✓	✓	✓	✓	✓	✓	**Objective questions**			
✓	✓	✓	✓	✓	✓	**Essays**			

MV-DP Size of Firms

7.1 Fact sheet

(a) How firms grow

Firms may grow in one of two ways;

(1) *Internal growth* – this is when a firm gets larger by increasing its own output.
(2) *External growth* – this is when a firm increases its size by taking over or merging with another firm (integration).

(b) Integration

Integration occurs when two firms combine. The new firm will probably enjoy significant economies of scale, and require fewer managers and workers.

- A *merger* is when the two firms agree to form a new company.
- A *takeover* is when one company buys a controlling interest in a second against the wishes of that company's directors.

There are three types of integration:

(1) *Horizontal*, between two companies in the same industry and at the same stage of production.
(2) *Vertical*, between two companies in the same industry but at different stages of production, either:
   (a) forwards, with a firm further up the chain of production, or
   (b) backwards, with a firm lower down the chain of production.

(3) *Conglomerate*, between two companies in different industries.

(c) Demergers

- A *demerger* is when a firm either:
   (a) divides into two or more firms, or
   (b) sells off some of its subsidiaries.
- The motives for demerging include:
   (a) improving managerial control;
   (b) reducing or avoiding internal diseconomies of scale;
   (c) increasing profitability.

(d) Small firms

- The size of firms can be measured in terms of:
   (a) number of people employed;
   (b) turnover;
   (c) profit;
   (d) capital employed.
- Small firms exist because:
   (a) they are easy to set up;
   (b) they can provide a personal service;
   (c) the minimum efficient scale may be small;
   (d) they are able to react quickly to changing market conditions;
   (e) they may be able to take work that is subcontracted from larger firms;
   (f) entrepreneurs may be unwilling to expand;
   (g) demand for some products is low because (1) they have a high price, (2) they are specialised, (3) they are sold locally.

7.2 Investigative study

Example 7.1

An analysis of a recent merger – the form taken, the motives behind the merger, its advantages and disadvantages.

7.3 Data response

Example 7.2

Annual turnover (£'000)	Number of businesses* 1993	Employment size	Number businesses* 1993	Employment 1991
1–34	26 838	1–9	90 672	280 805
35–49	12 894	10–19	13 934	194 481
50–99	25 598	20–49	14 314	437 656
100–249	33 176	50–99	5 628	390 344
250–499	19 633	100–199	3 234	448 027
500–999	13 974	200–499	2 138	656 131
1000–1999	9 208	500–999	686	469 360
2000–4999	7 230	1000+	516	1 381 514
10 000+	4 024			
Total	155 675	Total	131 122	4 258 318

* Defined as legal units, which includes companies, partnerships, sole proprietors, general government and non-profit-making bodies.
Source: *Britain 1995: An Official Handbook* (London: HMSO).

(a) How many people do most UK manufacturing businesses employ? **(3 marks)**

(b) What percentage of manufacturing workers did the typically sized business employ in 1991? **(5 marks)**

(c) What is meant by annual turnover? **(2 marks)**

(d) What is meant by a sole proprietor? **(4 marks)**

(e) Which form of business entity – public limited companies, private limited companies, partnerships or sole proprietorships – do you think has the highest annual turnover? **(3 marks)**

(f) How can a small business increase its annual turnover? **(6 marks)**

(g) Identify one other measure of business size. **(2 marks)**

Solution 7.2

(a) Most UK manufacturing businesses are small. The table shows that most businesses – 90 672 out of a total of 131 122 – employ between one and nine workers.

(b) The typically sized business, i.e. the small business, employed only 6.59% of the total number of manufacturing workers employed (280805/4258318 × 100).

(c) Annual turnover is the total sales of a business during the period of a calendar year.

(d) A small proprietorship is a business owned by a single person. This type of business is typically small. It has a number of advantages, including flexibility, speed of decision making and the provision of a personal service. However it also has disadvantages, including lack of capital and limited liability.

(e) Public limited companies, which are typically large companies, have the highest annual turnover. For instance the annual turnover of British Telecommunications was £13.2 billion in 1992.

(f) A small business can increase its annual turnover by internal or external growth. Internal growth involves a firm increasing its production by, for instance, taking on more workers or opening a new factory. External growth can be achieved by merging with another business – this may be in the form of a horizontal, vertical or conglomerate merger.

(g) Another measure of business size is the market share that businesses enjoy.

7.4 Objective questions

Example 7.3

Horizontal integration occurs when a car manufacturer:

A buys a chain of garages
B merges with a steel firm
C merges with a second car manufacturer
D combines with a company producing an unrelated product

Example 7.4

What is the main source of investment finance?
A Retained profits
B The issue of shares
C Borrowing from the banking sector
D Government financial assistance

Example 7.5

An oil company acquires a chain of petrol stations. This is an example of:
A a conglomerate merger
B a horizontal merger
C a forward vertical merger
D a backward vertical merger

Example 7.6

Which are the two main motives behind horizontal mergers?
A To diversify and gain control of supplies
B To increase market share and to take advantage of economies of scale
C To lower prices to consumers and improve the quality of the product
D To ensure an adequate number of outlets and to keep up with competitors.

Example 7.7

Which of the following is the most likely potential advantage of a demerger?

A Increase market share
B Improved staff facilities
C Improved management control
D Increased ability to borrow at low rates of interest

Example 7.8

Which of the following is an example of internal growth?
A The merger of two supermarkets
B A chemical company opening a new plant
C A tobacco company buying a television manufacturer
D A car manufacturer merging with a steel company

Example 7.9

A three-firm industrial concentration ratio of 80% indicates that:
A there are only a few firms in the industry
B the industry is dominated by a monopolist
C the majority of the industry's output is produced by only a few firms
D most of the firms in the industry are based in one geographical area

Example 7.10

Which of the following potential outcomes of a merger is most likely to benefit consumers?
A Economies of scale
B Increased bureaucracy
C Increased market share
D Reduction in competition

Example 7.11

The optimum size of a firm may be small because:
A raw material costs are high
B the market for the goods is small
C the process offers scope for mass production techniques
D there are significant potential economies of scale

Example 7.12

Which of the following sources of investment finance is not available to a sole trader?
A Retained profits
B The issue of shares
C Loans from banks
D Overdrafts from banks

7.5 Solutions to objective questions

Solution 7.3 Answer: C

Horizontal integration occurs when two firms are at the same stage of production and in the same industry. Other options are incorrect because:

A and B ⇒ are examples of vertical integration.

D ⇒ would be a conglomerate merger.

Solution 7.4 Answer: A

Retained profits, the issuing of shares, borrowing and government aid may all be used by a firm to finance expenditure on, for example, machinery and plant. However the most important source of investment finance is retained profits, which in any year will account for more than 60% of all investment finance.

Solution 7.5 Answer: C

A forward vertical merger occurs when a company merges with another company that is at a different stage of production and is nearer to marketing the product.

Solution 7.6 Answer: B

A horizontal merger is a direct way of reducing the number of competitors, and as the firms are in the same industry and at the same stage of production there may be the potential to take greater advantage of internal economies of scale, for instance commercial economies.

A ⇒ Diversification is more likely to be achieved by a conglomerate merger, whereas to gain control of supplies a firm may decide to engage in backward vertical integration.

C ⇒ Would be noble motives and may be stated by companies to be the reasons behind a merger. However in practice they are not the key motives.

D ⇒ To ensure an adequate number of outlets a firm may engage in forward vertical integration, and the desire to keep up with competitors could result in forward participation in any type of merger.

Solution 7.7 Answer: C

A demerger is when a company divides into two or more separate companies. This will occur if the company has become too large and is experiencing diseconomies of scale, one of which may be the problem of keeping control of all the company's activities.

A, B and D ⇒ are all potential benefits of a company growing in size rather than separating into smaller companies.

Solution 7.8 Answer: B

Internal growth occurs when a firm gets larger by increased investment and/or increase in its labour force. A chemical company that opens a new plant will grow in size.

A, C and D ⇒ are all examples of external growth. Option A is an example of a horizontal merger, option C of a conglomerate merger and option D of a backwards vertical merger.

Solution 7.9 Answer: C

Industrial concentration ratios are concerned with the extent to which the largest firms in an industry dominate the market. A three-firm industrial concentration ratio of 80% means that the largest three firms account for 80% of total sales or output.

A ⇒ There may be a large number of firms in the industry – the key point is that the largest three control 80% of the market.

B ⇒ If three firms have a market share of 80% the industry cannot be dominated by a pure monopoly. Taking the government definition of a monopoly, the industry could in theory contain three monopolies.

D ⇒ This refers to geographical concentration, which can give rise to external economies of scale.

Solution 7.10 Answer: A

Economies of scale may lead to lower costs of production and lower prices.

B, C and D ⇒ may result in disadvantages for consumers including higher prices and reduced quality, although with the exception of option B, which will raise costs, the effects are uncertain.

Solution 7.11 Answer: B

If demand for the product is small, a few small firms will be able to satisfy demand.

A, C and D ⇒ would mean that the optimum size of a firm would be large.

Solution 7.12   Answer: **B**

A sole trader can make use of retained profits and can borrow from banks in the form of loans or overdrafts. However sole traders do not issue shares.

7.6 Essays

Example 7.13

Why, despite the technical and financial advantages of large firms, are there so many small firms?

(25 marks)

- The questions tests your understanding of the technical and financial economies of scale that are open to large firms.
- Describe the circumstances in which small firms thrive.
- Where possible, use real-world examples.

Solution 7.13

It is important to distinguish between large and small firms. The Bolton Committee Report (1971) suggests that small businesses are firms that are managed by their owner(s) and have a relatively small share of the market. Small manufacturing firms employ fewer than 200 people. Large firms are typically incorporated (limited companies), where ownership and management are separated. Large companies that exploit economies of scale enjoy a cost advantage over small firms in the same industry. In particular, large firms have access to the following technical and financial economies.

Technical economies occur in the production of a good. As the firm expands, there is greater scope for specialisation and the division of labour. For example large factories can employ specialist skilled workers to do the same job all day with no time lost in changing tools or doing unfamiliar tasks. The indivisibility of certain types of capital means that many production processes, including that of chemicals, are impossible on a small scale. Mass production allows large firms to keep specialist capital fully utilised. Large firms can benefit by linking production processes that would otherwise be carried out in separate factories. For example a large manufacturer of shirts can reduce transport costs by combining the weaving and cutting of cotton under the same roof. Economies of increased dimensions mean that doubling the size of a machine results in a

more than double increase in output. The principle of multiples suggests that large firms can avoid the bottlenecks that occur when machines operate at different speeds, by installing a ratio of machines that keeps each fully utilised.

Financial economies allow large enterprises to raise capital on advantageous terms. Large firms are considered to be reliable and are therefore charged a low rate of interest. In particular, large firms have access to capital markets such as the stock exchange. Selling shares is a relatively inexpensive method of raising large amounts of capital.

Despite the cost advantage to large firms of producing in bulk, small businesses continue to survive for a variety of reasons. Limited opportunities for economies of scale allow them to find a niche by providing specialised products for small markets. For instance specialised design is non-uniform and cannot be manufactured in bulk. Service sectors such as hairdressing cannot easily achieve a large scale of operation, and therefore tend to be dominated by small firms. An irregular or limited demand for a product prevents mass production.

Small firms have the flexibility and low overheads needed to undertake 'one-off' projects, e.g. building construction. Often small firms survive by accepting subcontracting work from large companies. In industries such as printing, where fixed costs form only a small percentage of total costs, low set-up costs encourage the development of small firms. Where the market for a good is restricted and highly localised, small firms survive, e.g. village shops.

In an attempt to stimulate the supply side of the economy the government has introduced a number of schemes to help small firms to survive. For instance the Enterprise Allowance is a weekly sum paid to the unemployed while they are setting up their own businesses. The Business Expansion Scheme provides relief against income tax to investors in unquoted companies.

Example 7.14

Glaxo bought out Wellcome, another drug company, in 1995.

(a)   What type of merger was this?   **(5 marks)**
(b)   What are the main motives behind this type of merger?   **(10 marks)**
(c)   What are the potential advantages and disadvantages of this type of merger for society?   **(10 marks)**

- Distinguish briefly between horizontal, vertical and conglomerate mergers.
- Consider the main motives behind a horizontal merger.
- Relate at least some of the advantages and disadvantages of a horizontal merger to the drug industry – although detailed knowledge of the drug industry is not required.

Solution 7.14

(a) There are three main types of merger: horizontal, vertical and conglomerate. A horizontal merger occurs when two firms in the same industry and at the same stage of production merge. A vertical merger is when two firms in the same industry but at a different stage of production combine. Finally, a conglomerate merger is when two firms in different industries merge.

The merger between Glaxo and Wellcome was a horizontal merger as both firms were in the same industry and at the same stage of production. The industry is the drug (or pharmaceutical) industry and the stage of production is the secondary stage as both firms are manufacturing companies.

(b) There are a number of possible motives behind a horizontal merger, although the two main motives are increased market share and increased opportunity to take advantage of economies of scale. Merging with another company in the same industry is a direct way of removing a rival and a quick way of increasing its size relative to other firms. This in turn will reduce the chance of the new company being taken over as its larger size will mean that there will be fewer firms with access to sufficient financial resources to acquire it.

A larger firm will also be able to take greater advantage of internal economies of scale, thereby lowering average (unit) costs and increasing profitability. A larger company will, for example, probably be able to gain easier and cheaper access to finance, employ specialist staff, make use of larger and more cost-effective machinery, buy in bulk and advertise at competitive rates. In the drugs industry, research and development economies of scale are particularly significant. Drug firms spend a considerable amount of time and money developing new medicines and bringing them to the market. A merger between two drug companies researching into different areas of illnesses or using different ingredients will enable risks to be spread.

There may be a number of other possible motives behind a horizontal merger at a secondary stage, including increased ability to counterbalance the power of purchasing companies.

(c) A merger between any two drug companies will benefit consumers if it results in lower costs, higher product quality and better service. If the merged company passes on the benefit of lower costs achieved through economies of scale, and possibly rationalisation, in the form of lower prices consumers will gain. The increased research and development capacity may result in the development of new drugs that improve welfare by curing or alleviating illness. For instance development of a cure for AIDS would be a significant benefit. If a new merged company is a more efficient company it will be able to compete more effectively in the world drug market. This should improve the country's balance of payments position.

However there is no guarantee that a merger will increase efficiency or benefit consumers. The new company may be too large and may experience internal diseconomies of scale, thereby raising average costs and prices. The reduced competition may also result in a reduction in the range of drugs and a fall in quality, perhaps including a failure to test drugs adequately before they are put on the market. The move towards greater market power will reduce consumer surplus and increase producer surplus. A merger is often accompanied, at least initially, by a fall in employment as the new company seeks to rationalise production. This will have an adverse effect on redundant workers if they are unable to move to other, equally well-paid employment.

Market Structure

8.1 Fact sheet

(a) Definitions

- A *market* exists where buyers and sellers negotiate the exchange of a product.
- An *industry* is made up of firms producing similar products.
- *Market structure* refers to the number and type of firms in a particular industry.
- *Concentration ratios* measure the proportion of an industry's output or employment accounted for by, say, the five largest firms.

(b) Revenue

- The money received from the sale of output is called *revenue*.

(c) Profit

- Accountancy and economic definitions of profit are different.
- Economists regard normal profits as a cost of production.
- Revenue minus production costs equals *abnormal profit* π:

$$\pi = TR - TC = (AR - AC) \times Q$$

Table 8.1 Types of revenue

Term	Symbol	Definition	Equation
Total revenue	TR	The income received from the sale of a given output	$TR = AR \times Q$
Average revenue	AR	The amount received from the sale of each unit	$AR = TR \div Q$
Marginal revenue	MR	The amount received from selling one extra unit	$MR = \Delta TR \div \Delta Q$

Table 8.2 Types of profit

Term	Symbol	Definition	TR − TC is
Normal profit	$\pi = 0$	The minimum amount of profit the firm must receive to carry on producing (i.e. transfer income)	Zero
Abnormal profit	π	Profits exceed the amount the firm must receive to carry on producing (i.e. economic rent, super normal profit)	Positive
Abnormal loss	$-\pi$	Profits are below the amount the firm must receive to carry on producing (i.e. subnormal profit)	Negative

- New classical theory assumes that firms aim to maximise profits. However, where ownership and control of a company are in separate hands, managers may have a different aim, such as sales maximisation.

(d)   Perfect competition

- A *perfectly competitive industry* is made up of a large number of small firms, each selling homogeneous (identical) products to a large number of buyers.
- No individual customer receives preferential treatment.
- There are no *barriers to entry or exit*.
- Consumers and producers have perfect market knowledge.
- There is perfect mobility of factors of production.
- Each firm is a *price taker*, therefore MR = P(AR) and both are constant.
- The *profit-maximising level of output* occurs where marginal cost (MC) rises to equal marginal revenue (MR) – i.e. when MR = MC.

In Figure 8.1 the representative firm has to decide whether or not to produce extra units. The firm compares the cost of the marginal unit (i.e. MC) with the revenue received from its sale (i.e. MR). An extra unit is only worth producing if MR exceeds MC. Since MC includes an amount of normal profit, the firm maximises its profits by increasing production up to and including Q.

(e)   Supply curves in perfect competition

In Figure 8.2 an increase in demand raises the market price to P_1. In the short run the firm earns an abnormal profit of $(P_1 - C_1) \times Q_1$. In the long run the entry of new firms increases supply and the supply curve shifts to the right. Assuming constant scale economies, the price falls back to P and normal profits are restored.

- The MC curve shows combinations of price and quantity supplied by a firm. Therefore the MC curve is the supply curve of the firm.
- The addition of each firm's MC curve gives the industry's short-run supply curve.

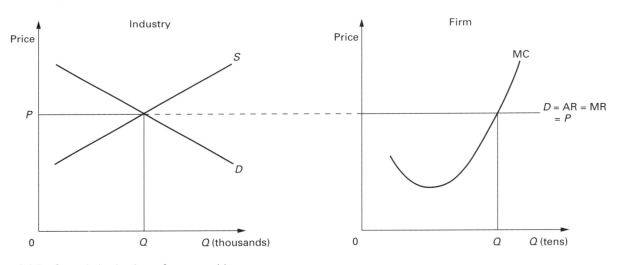

Figure 8.1 Profit maximisation in perfect competition

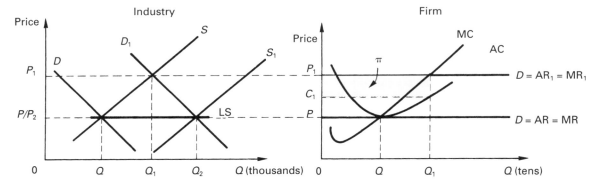

Figure 8.2 Long-run adjustment in a perfectly competitive market to an increase in demand

- The long-run supply curve (LS) shows the amount of a good supplied by the industry at different prices, allowing the number of firms and size of plant to vary.

(f) Abnormal losses in perfect competition

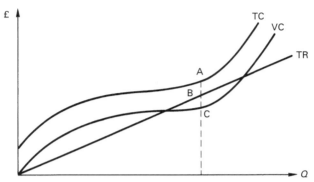

Figure 8.3 Revenue covers variable costs: losses are minimised by carrying on production because total revenue covers all variable costs and some (BC) of the fixed costs

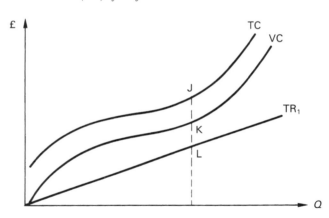

Figure 8.4 Variable costs exceed revenue: losses are minimised by ceasing production because total revenue fails to cover any variable costs and none of the fixed costs

- A loss-making firm carries on production in the short run, provided that:
  (a) it believes the situation will improve in the future;
  (b) it can cover its variable costs.
- In the long run, some firms making abnormal losses leave the industry, supply decreases and price rises. The total revenue curves in Figures 8.3 and 8.4 will shift upwards until normal profits are restored.

(g) Monopolistic competition

- *Monopolistic competition* is a market structure with a large number of firms producing differentiated products.

- There is spare capacity in the industry.
- Each firm is a *price maker*, so AR > MR and both fall the more the firms sells.
- There are no barriers to entry and exit.
- The firms are assumed to be profit maximisers and will produce where MC = MR.
- There will be non-price competition and possibly some price competition.
- The absence of barriers to entry and exit is likely to mean that normal profits will be earned in the long run, as shown in Figure 8.5.

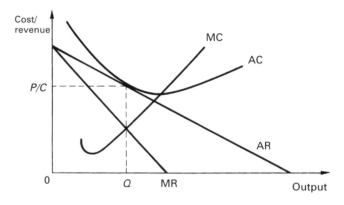

Figure 8.5 Long-run equilibrium output of a firm producing under conditions of monopolistic competition

(h) Oligopoly

- An *oligopolistic market* is one dominated by a few firms so there is a high concentration of sales.
- The firms may produce identical products (*perfect oligopoly*) or differentiated products (*imperfect oligopoly*).
- Each firm is a price maker, so AR > MR and both fall with output.
- There are barriers to entry and exit.
- Firms are interdependent. The behaviour of one firm will be influenced by the behaviour of its rivals.
- Firms may seek to maximise profits or adopt other pricing strategies – see Chapter 9.
- Supernormal profits are likely to be earned in the long run.
- Prices are likely to be stable because:
  (a) firms may believe that changing price will gain them no advantage – this is explained by the *kinked demand curve*, as shown in Figure 8.6;
  (b) firms may engage in *collusion*.

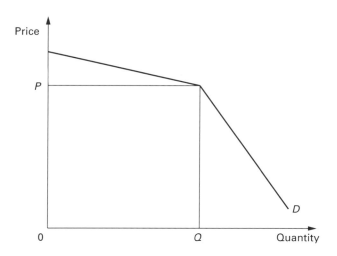

Figure 8.6 The kinked demand curve: above the price 0P demand is elastic as rival firms will not follow a price rise; below 0P demand is less elastic as rivals will match price reductions

- Firms wishing to increase sales are likely to use non-price competition such as:
  - (a) Advertising, where firms promote information about the company or a product. Advertising aims to: (1) increase demand for a products; (2) improve brand image and encourage consumer loyalty, thereby making demand more price-inelastic; and (3) create separate markets for the same product so that price discrimination can take place – e.g. soap powders.
  - (b) Organising promotion campaigns (e.g. free offers).
  - (c) Providing improved after-sales service.

(i) Monopoly

- A *pure monopoly* is a sole supplier. In this case the firm is the industry.
- The definition used in government policy is a firm that has at least a 25% share of the market.

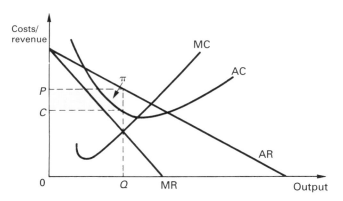

Figure 8.7 A monopolist earning supernormal profit

- There are significant barriers to entry and exit.
- Monopolists are price makers and can set price or output for their own product.
- Monopolists are usually assumed to be profit makers and can set price or output for their own product.
- Monopolists are likely to earn supernormal profits in the long run. In Figure 8.7 supernormal profit equals the area $(P - C) \times Q$.

8.2 Investigative study

Example 8.1

A study of public houses in the area to determine which market structure they operate in and the extent to which their behaviour conforms with the pattern predicted by theory.

8.3 Data response

Example 8.2

A feminist publishing company has decided to publish a novel by a new author, who agrees to be paid a percentage of the gross profits from the sale of the book. The diagram below illustrates the publisher's average revenue curve.

- (a) Draw in the publisher's marginal revenue curve and explain why you have drawn it where you have. **(3 marks)**
- (b) Explain the slope of both the marginal and average revenue curves **(6 marks)**
- (c) Where will the publisher set price? Illustrate your answer **(6 marks)**

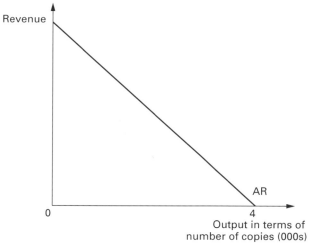

Figure 1

(d) Would spending on advertising increase the publisher's profits? **(4 marks)**

(e) If the writer renegotiated her contract to receive payments on the basis of, say 10% of the cover price of each book sold, explain and illustrate what output and price she would like to see.

(6 marks)

Solution 8.2

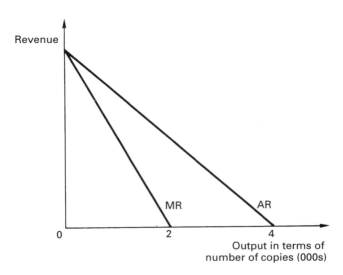

Figure 2

(a) Marginal revenue starts at the same point as average revenue and cuts the horizontal axis half way along from where average revenue would cut it.

(b) The average revenue curve is the consumers' demand curve for the book. The downward-sloping curve indicates that consumers are prepared to buy more copies of the book as price falls because of the substitution effect (the book is now relatively cheaper than substitutes) and the income effect (consumers can now afford to buy more copies of the text).

The marginal revenue curve slopes downwards because the publisher is a price maker. In order to sell more copies, price must fall not only for extra copies sold, but also on all preceding books. Hence marginal revenue is always less than price.

(c) The publisher will continue to print books up to the point where the cost of the extra unit (MC) equals revenue from the sale of the extra text (MR). This suggests a price of £15. (Note that the actual price charged depends on where the candidate draws the actual MC curve.)

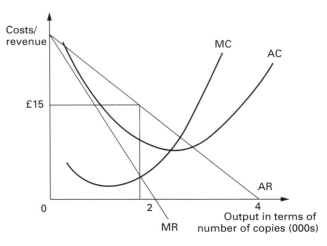

Figure 3

(d) Advertising would increase the cost of production and thus diminish profits. However, successful advertising would increase demand and shift the demand curve to the right, thereby increasing sales. Hence profits only increase if the net revenue from extra sales more than pays for the cost of the initial advertising.

(e) To receive the highest payment the writer would want to see sales revenue maximised. This is achieved at the point where MR intersects the x-axis, Up to this point marginal revenue is positive and revenue increases with sales. The author would want sales to be increased to 2000 by lowering the price to £10.

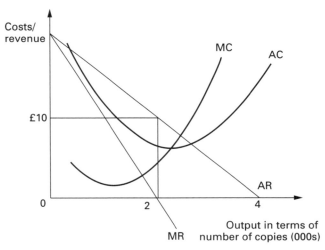

Figure 4

8.4 Objective questions

Example 8.3

Which of the following is a characteristic of a perfectly competitive industry?

A Firms are price takers

B Some differentiation of products
C The presence of barriers to entry
D Some firms offer discounts to important customers

Example 8.4

One difference between a firm operating in a perfectly competitive market and one operating in a monopolistically competitive market is that, for the latter only:
A some producers advertise
B average revenue equals price
C the number of producers is small
D all firms produce an identical product

Example 8.5

A tailor charges £100 per suit up to and including the fifth suit made. If more than five suits are ordered, the price charged for all suits falls to £80 per suit. What will be the marginal revenue to the tailor for the sixth suit?
A £100 **B** £80 **C** £0 **D** −£20

Example 8.6

The following table shows the cost and revenue conditions facing a firm. At what level of output would the firm be making maximum profit?

	Weekly output	Total cost	Total revenue
A	1	30	24
B	2	41	48
C	3	65	72
D	4	90	96

Example 8.7

The diagram shows a marginal revenue curve (MR). From the diagram it can be seen that as output increases from 0 to Q, total revenue is:
A increasing
B decreasing
C at a maximum
D at a minimum

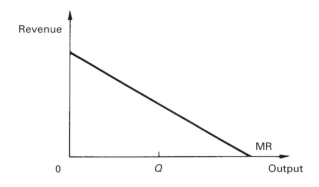

Example 8.8

The diagram below shows the total revenue (TR) and total cost (TC curves of a firm. Under which of the following market conditions is the firm operating?

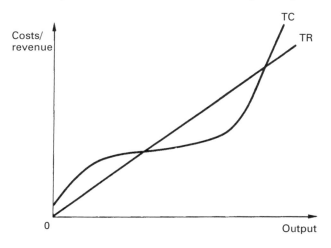

A Perfect competition in the short run
B Monopolistic competition in the short run
C Perfect competition in the long run
D Monopolistic competition in the long run

Example 8.9

A firm will continue production in the short run, provided that revenue covers:
A total cost
B average cost
C fixed cost
D variable cost

Example 8.10

Oligopolistic industries are usually characterised by:
A price stability
B firms being price takers
C firms' long-run average cost curves sloping upwards

D firms' average revenue equalling their marginal revenue

Example 8.11

A monopolist seeks to earn maximum profits. Will he or she produce output **A**, **B**, **C** or **D**?

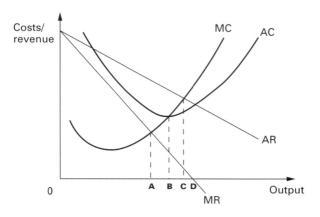

Example 8.12

Which of the following is a necessary condition for a firm to practice price discrimination?

A Seepage between the markets
B The firm is a price taker
C Different cost structures in each market
D Different price elasticities of demand in each market

8.5 Solutions to objective questions

Solution 8.3   Answer: **A**

A price taker is a firm that is unable to change market price by varying its own output. Firms producing under conditions of perfect competition are too small to affect price by changing their individual outputs. They are also unable to raise their price above the market price as their customers would switch to perfect substitutes from competitive firms. Since the firm is able to sell all its output at the going market price, there is no reason why it should sell any of its output for less.

B ⇒ Differentiated products means that consumers are able to tell the difference between the output of one firm and another. A condition of perfect competition is that the produce of each firm is identical.

C ⇒ A condition of perfect competition is that firms are free to enter or leave the industry at will.

D ⇒ In perfect competition, no one buyer is sufficiently large enough to be able to negotiate a discount on purchases.

Solution 8.4   Answer: **A**

Unlike a firm in perfect competition, monopolistically competitive firms produce a slightly different product from others in the industry. Therefore firms benefit from advertising because: (1) it increases demand for the product and (2) it improves the brand image of the good so that demand becomes more price-inelastic.

B ⇒ Average revenue equals price in all market structures.

C ⇒ There are a large number of producers in both perfect and monopolistic competition.

D ⇒ Whilst firms producing under conditions of perfect competition make an identical product, firms producing under conditions of monopolistic competition, as mentioned above, make differentiated products.

Solution 8.5   Answer: **D**

The marginal revenue of the sixth suit is the change in total revenue resulting from the sale of an extra suit. The total revenue from five suits is £100 × 5 = £500. The total revenue from six suits is £80 × 6 = £480. So selling the sixth suit has caused total revenue to fall by £20.

Solution 8.6   Answer: **C**

The firm will maximise profits when marginal revenue equals marginal cost. At three units MC = MR and at this point profits (including supernormal and normal) are maximised.

	Weekly output	Total cost	Marginal cost	Total revenue	Marginal revenue
A	1	30	—	24	24
B	1	41	11	48	24
C	1	65	24	72	24
D	1	90	25	96	24

It is not possible to calculate the marginal cost of

the first unit as it is not known what the cost of producing zero output was (i.e. the fixed cost). Note that the firm must be producing under conditions of perfect competition since AR = MR and both are constant.

Solution 8.7   Answer: **A**

Total revenue increases when marginal revenue is positive and is maximised when marginal is zero. It falls when marginal revenue is negative. Since Q is to the left of the point where the marginal revenue curve intersects the x-axis (and TR is maximised), total revenue is rising.

Solution 8.8   Answer: **A**

It can be ascertained that the firm is producing under conditions of perfect competition as the total revenue curve increases at a constant rate. Under conditions of monopolistic competition and other forms of imperfect competition, total revenue rises and then falls.

The firm is producing in the short run because it has fixed costs, as shown by the fact that at zero output there are costs. In the long run all costs will be variable.

Solution 8.9   Answer: **D**

If variable costs are covered then the direct costs of production can be met and the loss from continuing to manufacture is less than the total fixed costs that would have to be paid out if the firm halted production.

Solution 8.10   Answer: **A**

An oligopolistic industry is dominated by a few large firms and they are interdependent. For example if one firm reduces price to increase market share, other firms follow, thereby undermining the effectiveness of price competition. Oligopolists may also form cartels. So oligopolistic industries tend to show stable prices. Non-price competition such as special offers are used to increase sales.

B and **D** ⇒ Oligopolists are price makers and hence their average revenue exceeds their marginal revenue.

C ⇒ Oligopolists long-run average cost curves may be U-shaped or, because economies of scale are usually significant in what are often capital-intensive industries, may be L shaped or downward sloping.

Solution 8.11   Answer: **A**

A monopolist seeking to maximise profits will produce where MC = MR. Option **B** shows the productively efficient output, option **C** the allocatively efficient output and option **D** the sales maximisation output.

Solution 8.12   Answer: **D**

If the price elasticity of demand in each market is identical, then the gradient of each demand curve is the same and the firm is unable to charge different prices for the same product.

A ⇒ Seepage between the markets would mean that consumers will buy in the cheaper markets and sell in the more expensive markets, which will equal out the prices in the two markets.

B ⇒ To set price in different markets, the firm would have to be a price maker.

C ⇒ Price discrimination occurs when different prices are charged for goods or services that cost the same to produce.

8.6 Essays

Example 8.13

(a) What are the characteristics of a perfectly competitive industry?   **(7 marks)**
(b) What type of profits do perfectly competitive firms seek to earn?   **(5 marks)**
(c) What type of profits do perfectly competitive firms earn?   **(13 marks)**

• Cover the main characteristics of perfect competition and briefly explain them.
• Discuss profit maximisation.
Distinguish between the short and the long run.
• Include diagrams for the firm and industry.

Solution 8.13

(a) A perfectly competitive industry is one that includes a large number of buyers and sellers. Indeed there are so many buyers and sellers that the actions of any one buyer or seller will not affect price. The firms are price takers so that average revenue (price) equals marginal revenue. There is no product differentiation, the products are homogeneous and there is no attachment between consumers and producers. There are no barriers to entry and exit so that firms can enter the industry from outside and firms in the industry can switch production to other goods. There is perfect knowledge with consumers and producers being fully informed about, for example, price and profit levels. In addition there is perfect mobility of factors of production, so if a firm wishes to expand its output it will have no difficulty attracting new workers and buying more machinery.

(b) It is assumed that firms that operate under conditions of perfect competition are profit maximisers. This means that they will produce where marginal cost equals marginal revenue. The firms would like to earn the highest profits possible and would much prefer supernormal to normal profits. Given favourable market conditions firms may earn supernormal profits in the short run. However the forces of competition will drive down profits to the normal profit level in the long run. This is the minimum return entrepreneurs need to receive in the long run to keep them in the industry.

(c) In the short run, when at least one factor of production is fixed, any type of profit can be earned by a perfectly competitive firm. However in the long run, when all factors of production can be varied, only normal profits will be earned.

A rise in demand for the product will raise the price in the short run and cause existing firms to extend their supply. Figure 1 shows the effect on the industry of an increase in demand.

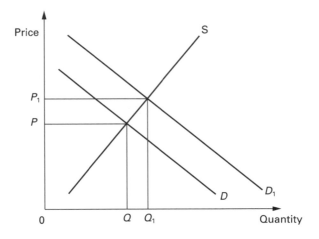

Figure 1

As a result of the rise in price the firms will experience supernormal (abnormal) profits. Figure 2

shows a firm producing where marginal cost (MC) equals marginal revenue (MR), but also where average revenue (AR) exceeds average cost (AC) and hence supernormal profits are earned.

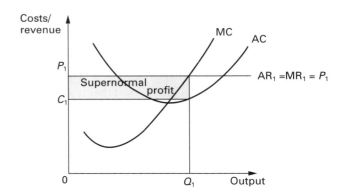

Figure 2

The absence of barriers to entry and the existence of perfect knowledge in this market structure means that firms outside the industry will be aware of the supernormal profits being made and will be able to enter the industry. This will cause an increase in supply in the industry, as shown in Figure 3.

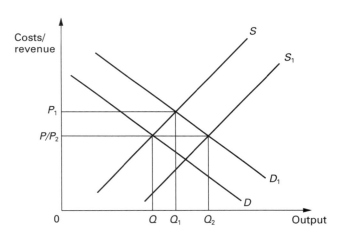

Figure 3

Firms will continue to enter the industry until price is driven down to the point where only normal profits are earned, i.e. where AR = AC. Figure 4 shows a firm earning normal profits.

Subnormal profits (losses) may be experienced by firms in the short run. Figure 5 shows the effect on a firm of a decrease in demand for the industry's product. It is producing where AC exceeds AR.

However, again this will be only a short-run situation. This is because the absence of barriers to exit will mean that some firms will leave the industry. These will be the firms that cannot cover their variable

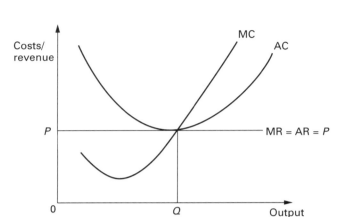

Figure 4

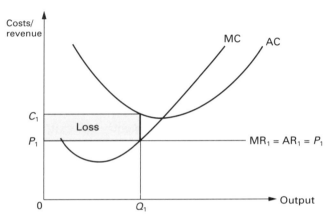

Figure 5

costs. The departure of firms from the industry will cause the industry's supply curve to shift to the left. Price will rise and firms that remain in the industry will now experience normal profits.

Example 8.14

(a) Is a private sector monopoly likely to achieve allocative efficiency? **(7 marks)**

(b) What advantages and disadvantages may consumers derive from private sector monopolies? **(18 marks)**

- Define allocative efficiency and monopoly.
- Concentrate on pure monopoly.
- Include a diagram showing monopoly output.
- Consider the effect of monopoly power on prices, output, quality and innovation.

Solution 8.14

(a) Allocative efficiency is achieved where price equals marginal cost. A private sector monopoly is a non-government firm. The legal definition of a

monopoly is a firm that has a 25% share of the market or more. A pure monopoly has a 100% share and in this case the firm is the industry.

A private sector monopoly is likely to seek to maximise profits. To do this it will produce when marginal cost (MC) equals marginal revenue (MR). This output is shown as $0Q$ in Figure 1, with a price being charged of $0P$.

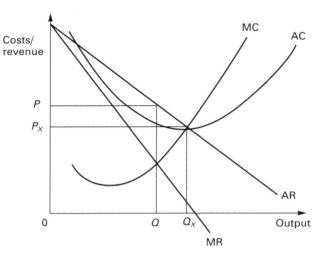

Figure 1

At this output, price exceeds MC and allocative efficiency is not achieved. The allocatively efficient output is $0Q_X$ and the allocatively efficient price is $0P_X$. The private sector monopolist restricts output to below $0Q_X$ in order to raise price and increase profits. So it underproduces and overcharges.

(b) Figure 1 also shows that the monopolist fails to achieve productive efficiency as it produces where average cost exceeds MC. It could produce more and lower its costs and prices. Consumers will suffer from its failure to do this.

Consumer surplus is likely to be low under conditions of monopoly. Figure 2, a simplified diagram, shows lower output and consumer surplus and higher price under a monopoly than under prefect competition.

In addition to lack of competition possibly enabling a monopolist to drive up price, it may also mean that the quality of the product may be low – dissatisfied consumers are unable to switch to rivals in the case of a pure monopoly.

The lack of competition may also mean that a monopolist is not pressed into improving its product through research and development and innovation. The monopolist's costs may also be high if the firm becomes too large and thereby experiences

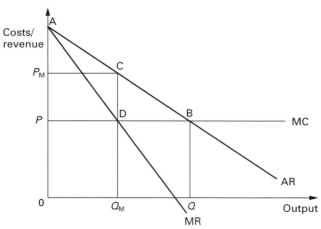

Perfect competition: price = 0*P*; quantity = 0*Q*;
                       consumer surplus = *PAB*

Monopoly: price = 0P_M; quantity = 0Q_M;
          consumer surplus = P_MAC;
          producer surplus = PP_MCD;

Figure 2

diseconomies of scale. It may also suffer from X-inefficiency.

However it is possible that consumers may actually benefit from monopoly. A monopolist may be able to take significant advantage of economies of scale. This may mean that even if it is earning a supernormal profit, the price it charges may be lower than that which would prevail in a competitive industry because of its substantially lower average costs. Indeed in the case of a natural monopoly situation, long-run average costs would be higher if the industry were to contain more than one firm.

A monopolist may also undertake more research and development and innovate to a greater extent than a firm in a competitive market. This is because it is likely to be earning supernormal profits and so will have more money to spend on research and development, and because it will believe that it will be able to protect any extra profits it earns through innovation due to the existence of barriers to entry into the industry.

These very barriers to entry lead some economists to argue that a monopoly market structure may encourage innovation. Schumpeter's theory of creative destruction argues that the only way to overcome a barrier to entry such as a patent will be to develop a new and superior version of the product. This theory sees one monopoly being replaced by a monopoly producing a better product and that monopoly in turn being replaced.

Where a monopoly exists in a contestable market, i.e. when there are no barriers to entry and exit, consumers may benefit. The firm will be able to enjoy economies of scale, but knowing that rival firms can enter the market it will have to keep price and profit levels low.

As there is uncertainty as to how a private sector monopoly will behave, in practice its relative advantages and disadvantages will have to be considered on a case-by-case basis.

Comparison of Market Structures

9.1 Fact Sheet

(a) Comparisons of market structure

In assessing how firms will behave in different market structures it is important to note the following:

(1) *Structure*, including:
  (a) the number of firms in the industry;
  (b) the size of the firms;
  (c) how easy or difficult it is for firms to enter or leave the market.
(2) *Conduct*, including:
  (a) the influence individual firms have over the price of their products;
  (b) the type of products produced;
  (c) how the firms compete.
(3) *Performance*, including:
  (a) the type of profits firms earn in the long run;
  (b) how efficient the firms are.

(b) Degrees of competition

- The most competitive market structure is perfect competition.
- *Imperfect competition* covers market structures between perfect competition and monopoly, i.e. monopolistic competition and oligopoly.
- The least competitive market structure is pure monopoly.

(c) Elasticity of demand

- The greater a firm's market share the more price inelastic demand will be for its product.
- Figure 9.1 shows the MR, AR and TR curves of an imperfectly competitive firm.

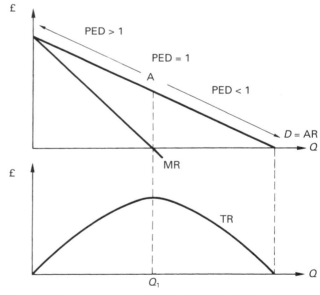

Figure 9.1 Revenue curves and price elasticity of demand (PED)

- The MR curve bisects the origin and the AR curve.
- To sell more output, the firm has to reduce price on the extra unit and all preceding units. Therefore, MR is always less than price.
- Up to Q, MR is positive, TR is rising and PED is elastic.

- Beyond Q, MR is negative, TR is falling and PED is inelastic.
- At A, PED is unitary.
- Total revenue is maximised at Q.
- Oligopolies have relatively inelastic demand and monopolies even more inelastic demand.
- Firms producing under conditions of monopolistic competition have relatively elastic demand.
- A perfectly competitive firm has perfectly elastic demand and hence a total revenue curve that increases at a constant rate. This is shown in Figure 9.2.

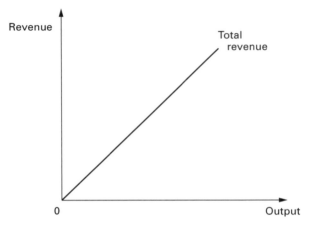

Figure 9.2 The total revenue curve of a perfectly competitive firm

(d)   Profit levels

The level of profits a firm earns depends on:
(a)   market conditions
(b)   market structure
(c)   the firm's objectives

- Monopolists and oligopolists do not automatically earn supernormal profits. Figure 9.3 shows a monopolist experiencing a loss.

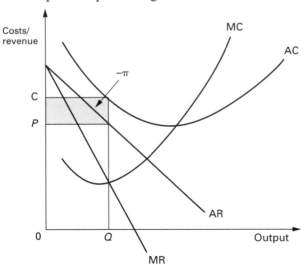

Figure 9.3 A monopolist experiencing a loss

- Given favourable market conditions, monopolists and oligopolists can earn supernormal profits in the long run due to barriers to entry.
- The absence of barriers to entry and exit means that firms producing under conditions of monopolistic competition and perfect competition earn normal profits in the long run.
- A *state-run monopoly* may seek to achieve allocative efficiency rather than profit maximisation.

(e)   Efficiency

- *Allocative efficiency* is achieved when a firm produces where MC = AR (marginal cost pricing).
- *Productive efficiency* exists when a firm produces at the lowest unit cost, i.e. where MC = AC.
- *Technical efficiency* is achieved when a firm produces a given quantity of output with the minimum number of inputs.
- *X-inefficiency* arises when a firm fails to produce on the lowest possible average and marginal cost curves.
- Perfectly competitive firms are always allocatively efficient and achieve productive and technical efficiency in the long run.
- Imperfectly competitive firms and monopolies are usually allocatively, productively and technically inefficient.
- Monopolies often experience organisation slack and so are X-inefficient.

(f)   Pricing strategies

(1) *Profit maximisation pricing*, i.e. producing where MC = MR and charging the corresponding price.
(2) *Price discrimination* occurs when the same product is sold in different markets for different prices (Figure 9.4). A discriminating monopoly is only able to practise price discrimination if it:
   (a) has some monopoly power and so can set price and exclude competitors;
   (b) is able to prevent the resale of the product;
   (c) has markets with different price elasticity of demand for the product.
   The monopolist adds together MR_1 from market A and MR_2 from market B to find the MR curve for both markets ($MR_1 + MR_2$). Output is fixed at the point where the MR_1 and MR_2 combined curve intersects the MC curve at Q. Q is then

Table 9.1 Market structure

Market structure	No. of firms	Nature of products	Substitutes	Price taker/maker	Barriers to entry	Above normal profits
Perfect competition	Many small	Homogeneous	Many perfect	Taker	None	Only in the short run
Monopolistic competition	Many small	Differentiated	Many close	Maker	None	Only in the short run
Oligopoly	Dominated by few large	Differentiated	Few	Maker	Some	Possible in the long run
Pure monopoly	One large	Unique	None	Maker	Complete	Possible in the long run

divided between the two markets by setting output at MC = MR in each market. Note that $QA + QB = Q$. Price is P_1 in market A and P_2 in market B. Price is higher in the market where demand is less elastic.

(3) *Cost-plus pricing* occurs when a firm adds a given percentage mark-up to average cost. A loss can be made if sales fall short of estimates.

(4) *Market penetration pricing* occurs when a firm reduces price to increase market share (the percentage of an industry's sales accounted for by one firm).

(5) *Limit pricing* occurs when a firm sets price just low enough to discourage possible new entrants.

(6) *Predatory pricing* occurs when a firm reduces price in the short run so as to force competitors out of the industry.

(7) *Skimming pricing* occurs when a firm charges a high initial price if some consumers are prepared to pay more for a new product. Eventually price is lowered to extend demand.

(g) Contestable markets

- The *theory of contestable markets* argues that what is important is not actual but potential competition.
- A market is *perfectly contestable* when the costs of entry and exit are zero.
- A *contestable market* is one where any entry costs can be recovered on exit, i.e. there are no sunk costs.
- In a perfectly contestable market the threat of entry by potential rivals will ensure that the firm or firms in the industry will:
  (a) earn normal profits;
  (b) achieve allocative, productive and technical efficiency.

9.2 Investigative study

Example 9.1

A study of a particular market analysing how its market structure appears to influence profit levels, prices and efficiency.

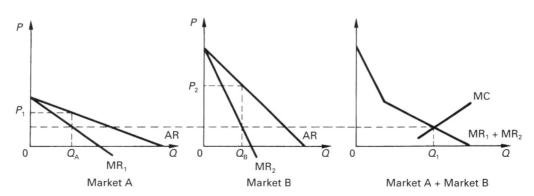

Figure 9.4 Price discrimination in two markets

9.3 Data response

Example 9.2

Food/Cut Throat Competition
Supermarket 'real bread' ruins the small bakers

THE SMELL of fresh bread, once on every British high street, is now more common in the supermarket as scores of local bakeries – unable to compete with mass-produced loaves – close each month.

There are now only 3,500 family bakeries left in Britain. In the past five years, 1,500 have closed. Fifty years ago, small bakeries produced 83 per cent of British bread. Today, with the advent of the sliced loaf and the supermarket bakery, they sell only 8 per cent.

Over the past 10 years, supermarkets such as Tesco, Sainsbury and Safeway have sought to reproduce the ambience of the high-street bakery to attract customers. Most loaves are baked overnight and the assistants wear bakers' hats and aprons. The choice of bread is wider than in a local bakery, ranging from ordinary white sliced loaves to Italian ciabatta.

The National Association of Master Bakers is alarmed by the speed of closures. It fears that supermarkets may be trying to drive bakeries out of business and has asked the Office of Fair Trading to intervene.

"Bakers haven't been able to keep up with competition," said Mary Rance, Director of the NAMB. "They have tried vigorously, but supermarkets have been selling bread below its market price as a loss leader for some years. The family bakeries are really fighting against very adverse trading conditions. They are closing every day."

But the OFT, although it said it sympathised with the small bakeries' plight, concluded that supermarkets were not trying to drive them out of the market and refused to act.

Source: Extract from an article by Marie Woolf, *Independent on Sunday*, 19 March 1995.

(a) Under what market structure do family bakeries produce? Explain your answer. **(5 marks)**

(b) Explain what is meant by a loss leader. **(3 marks)**

(c) Apart from loss leaders, how else have supermarkets attracted customers away from family bakeries? **(5 marks)**

(d) What advantages do supermarkets have over family bakeries in the sale of bread? **(6 marks)**

(e) What disadvantages would consumers experience as a result of more bakeries closing? **(6 marks)**

Solution 9.2

(a) Family bakeries operate under conditions of monopolistic competition. Although declining, there is still a large number of them. They produce a slightly differentiated product, do not make high profits and it is relatively easy to enter the market.

(b) A loss leader is a product sold at cost or below cost with the aim of attracting consumers into the shop. Once in, it is hoped that they will buy a range of other products.

(c) Supermarkets have attracted customers by copying the personal approach of family bakeries. Bread and related items are frequently sold in a separate section of the shop by people dressed as bakers. The supermarkets also offer a greater range of loaves, including more exotic items. In addition they advertise on a large and national scale.

(d) Supermarkets have significant advantages over small bakeries. They spread their overheads over a large number of items and they can take advantage of a number of forms of internal economies of scale, including financial, risk bearing, technical and staff facilities. As well as offering staff canteen facilities, for example, they offer higher pay and greater promotion prospects. They can sell bread at a loss, if they so choose, because they can cross-subsidise it with other items on sale. They also have a national reputation and so attract passing as well as local trade.

(e) The closure of more bakeries will reduce consumer choice and competition. Family bakeries may be conveniently situated and may provide a personal service as the baker will have a small enough customer base to get to know them all. The baker may also be willing to meet any specific requirements they have. Shopping in a family bakery is a more leisurely and less pressurised experience than shopping in some supermarkets. With fewer family bakeries, supermarkets will be faced with less competition and may be tempted to reduce choice and raise price.

9.4 Objective questions

Example 9.3

The following details are known about the long-run cost and revenue position of a firm:

- Marginal cost = £5
- Average cost = £8
- Marginal revenue = £5
- Average revenue = £8

Which of the following markets cannot be consistent with this information?

A monopoly   B oligopoly

C perfect competition   D monopolistic competition

Example 9.4

Two firms are making supernormal profits. One is monopoly and the other is operating under conditions of perfect competition. Only in the former case will:

A average revenue be equal to average cost

B marginal revenue be equal to marginal cost

C average revenue be greater than marginal revenue

D marginal revenue be greater than marginal cost

Example 9.5

Which of the following diagrams illustrates the total revenue curve of a firm operating under conditions of imperfect competition?

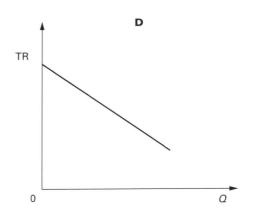

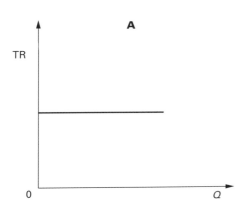

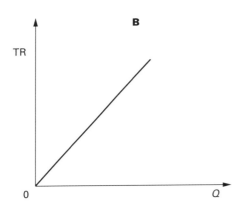

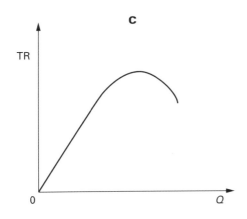

Example 9.6

The diagram below shows the short-run costs and revenue of a profit-maximising monopolist. This monopolist is worried about potential competition and believes that engaging in limit pricing and setting a price of P_X will prevent the entry of new competitors.

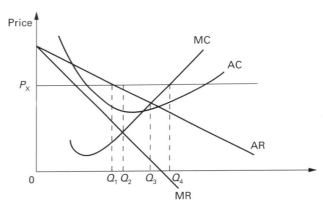

Which level of output will ensure that the monopolist achieves maximum profit compatible with preventing the entry of new competitors?

A $0Q_1$ **B** $0Q_2$ **C** $0Q_3$ **D** $0Q_4$

Example 9.7

The diagram below illustrates the output of a profit-maximising firm.

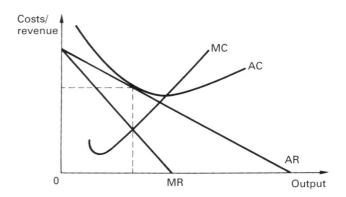

Is the firm producing under conditions of:

A   perfect competition and earning normal profits

B   imperfect competition and earning normal profits

C   perfect competition and earning supernormal profits

D   imperfect competition and earning supernormal profits

Example 9.8

A firm operating under conditions of perfect competition will achieve allocative efficiency when it earns:

	Subnormal profit:	Normal profit:	Supernormal profit:
A	yes	yes	yes
B	no	yes	no
C	yes	no	yes
D	no	yes	yes

Example 9.9

In the diagram below, $0P$ represents the price that would be charged by a perfectly competitive industry and $0Q$ is its output. $0P_X$ and $0Q_X$ represent the price and output, respectively, of a monopolist.

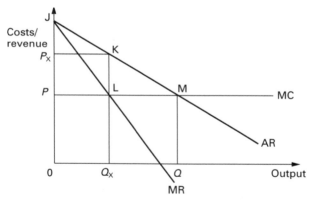

Which area represents the dead weight loss that would occur if a perfectly competitive industry was replaced by a monopoly?

A P_XJK   B PP_XKM   C PP_XKL   D KLM

Example 9.10

In which market structures may supernormal profits be earned in the long run?

A Perfect competition and monopoly

B Perfect competition and monopolistic competition

C Monopolistic competition and oligopoly

D Oligopoly and monopoly

Example 9.11

The diagram below shows the cost and revenue curves of a monopolist.

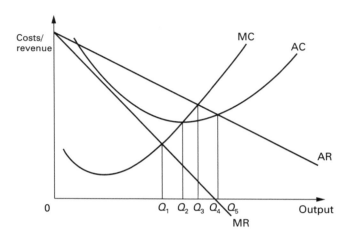

If the monopolist changes her or his objective from making normal profits to achieving sales revenue maximisation he will alter her or his output from:

A Q_1 to Q_2 B Q_2 to Q_4 C Q_3 to Q_1 D Q_5 to Q_4

Example 9.12

In which type of market structure are there no barriers to entry and exit?

A Duopoly   B Monopoly

C Oligopoly   D Contestable

9.5 Solutions to objective questions

Solution 9.3   Answer: **C**

The information shows that the firm is producing at the point where MC = MR, and hence is maximising profits, and where AC = AR, and so is making normal profits. The firm cannot be producing under conditions of perfect competition since perfectly competitive firms are price takers and thus their average revenue is equal to their marginal revenue.

A, B and **D** ⇒ In all these cases AR > MR and it is possible that firms producing either these market structures could earn normal profits.

Solution 9.4   Answer: **C**

A monopolist is a price maker and his AR > MR. As stated in Solution 9.3 a firm producing under conditions of perfect competition is a price taker and its average revenue equals its marginal revenue.

A $\Rightarrow$ If supernormal profits are earned, average revenue will exceed average cost.

B and **D** $\Rightarrow$ In both cases the firms are likely to be profit maximisers and hence be producing where marginal cost equals marginal revenue.

Solution 9.5   Answer: **C**

Under imperfect competition, total revenue rises when demand is elastic and marginal revenue is positive. It reaches its peak when elasticity of demand is unity and marginal revenue is zero, and falls when demand is inelastic and marginal revenue is negative.

B $\Rightarrow$ shows the total revenue curve of a firm producing under conditions of perfect competition.

Solution 9.6   Answer: **A**

To ensure a price of P_X the monopolist will have to sell the output at the point where quantity intersects the average revenue (demand) line.

Solution 9.7   Answer: **B**

The firm is producing under conditions of imperfect competition as AR >MR. It is making normal profits as it is producing at the point where AC = AR.

Solution 9.8   Answer: **A**

Allocative efficiency is achieved at the point where P(AR) = MC. Firms producing under conditions of perfect competition always produce where P = MC since they produce where MC = MR and in this market structure P = MR.

Solution 9.9   Answer: **D**

Under perfect competition consumer surplus is PJM. Under monopoly it would be P_XJK, which is a reduction of PP_XKM. Of this fall in consumer surplus, PP_XKL is converted into producer surplus and KLM is lost to both parties, i.e. is a deadweight loss.

Solution 9.10   Answer: **D**

Supernormal profits can be earned in market structures where there are barriers to entry and exit – these exist under oligopoly and monopoly.

B $\Rightarrow$ Firms producing under conditions of both perfect competition and monopolistic competition earn normal profits in the long run due to the absence of barriers to entry and exit.

Solution 9.11   Answer: **D**

Normal profits are earned at the point where AR = AC, i.e. at an output of QS. Sales revenue is maximised where MR = 0, i.e. at an output of Q_4. Q_1 is the maximum profit output, Q_2 the productively efficient output and Q_3 the allocatively efficient output.

Solution 9.12   Answer: **D**

A market is perfectly contestable when there are no entry or exit costs.

A, **B** and **C** $\Rightarrow$ In each case there are barriers to entry and exit.

9.6 Essays

Example 9.13

(a)   Explain why a firm's profits are maximised when marginal cost equals marginal revenue.
(10 marks)

(b)   Do firms always use profit maximisation for determining prices?   **(15 marks)**

•   Demonstrate profit maximisation, assuming either perfect or imperfect competition.

•   The second part of the question asks you why firms use non-profit-maximising pricing strategies.

Solution 9.13

(a)   There are three types of profit in economics. Normal profit is a return that is sufficient to keep the firm in the industry. Normal profit is seen as a cost of production and is therefore included in the firm's cost curves. Any return above normal profit is called supernormal (or abnormal) profit. It is also possible that a firm may make a subnormal profit (i.e. produce) when average cost exceeds average revenue.

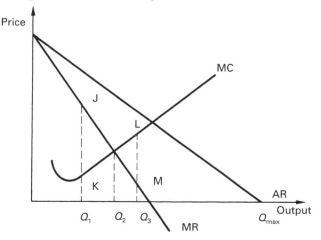

The diagram shows the short-run unit cost and revenue curves of an imperfectly competitive firm. Assume that the firm can produce any level of output between 0 and Q_{max}. The marginal cost curve, MC, tells the firm the cost of making the extra unit. The marginal revenue curve, MR, tells the firm the revenue received from the sale of the extra unit. At Q_1, the difference between MR and MC (J − K) is greatest. However there is an incentive for the profit-maximising firm to increase output beyond this point. The revenue received from the sale of each additional unit up to Q_2 is greater than the cost of making that extra unit. Any firm that fixed output at Q_1 would be forgoing a profit on each of Q_2 and Q_1. A normal profit is made on the sale of the Q_2 unit. Above output level Q_2, a loss is made on the sale of each extra unit, because marginal cost exceeds marginal revenue. For example, at Q_3 a loss of L − M is made on the sale of that unit alone. Profits are therefore maximised when marginal cost equals marginal revenue.

(b) Economic theory assumes that individuals and firms are 'rational', acting in a manner that maximises their own satisfaction. In the case of the firm, the maximisation of profits guarantees the largest possible income for the owners of a company. A profit-maximising pricing policy is likely to be used by sole traders and partnerships.

However the emergence of limited companies means that ownership and control of the most important firms are now separated. In general, shareholders expect the firm to maximise profits and therefore to set its output so that marginal cost equals marginal revenue. Managers may have different objectives.

New 'managerial' theories of the firm suggest that companies use pricing criteria that improve the welfare of managers. For example salaries and 'fringe benefits' are more likely to be linked to sales than to profits. Bonuses may be paid for achieving sales targets. It follows that manager-controlled firms will try to maximise sales revenue rather than profit and to fix output so that average cost equals average revenue.

Managers may decide that setting a price that maximises the firm's rate of growth is in their own best interest. An expanding company increases a manager's salary and status. Moreover the resulting increase in the value of the company's shares is in the interest of the owners.

Large businesses are highly complex, with different departments taking responsibility for specialised functions such as production, sales and finance. Each department has a different objective, so that the maximisation of one goal – profits – is inappropriate. Instead, satisficing occurs when each department is set minimum acceptable levels of performance – for example asking the sales department to obtain a given market share.

The firm may feel that the cost of collecting information about marginal cost and revenue is too high and therefore managers use a cost-plus pricing strategy. The firm fixes output and then estimates unit cost. Adding a profit margin to average cost gives the final selling price.

Nationalised industries aim to operate in the public interest. Profit maximisation results in an inefficient allocation of resources. Instead, state-owned firms adopt a marginal cost pricing strategy and increase output to the point where, including externalities, marginal cost equals price.

Example 9.14

Compare and contrast oligopoly and monopolistic competition. **(25 marks)**

- Discuss the similarities and differences between the two market structures.
- Concentrate on how firms behave in the two market structures.

Solution 9.14

Monopolistic competition and oligopoly are both forms of imperfect competition. In both cases firms are price makers. A change in their output will affect price and their average revenue will exceed their marginal revenue. In monopolistic competition and oligopoly, productive and allocative efficiency are unlikely to be achieved. The firms are likely to produce at the point where average cost exceeds marginal cost (and hence not at the bottom of the average cost curve) and where price exceeds marginal cost. In both market structures the firms will engage in non-price competition and product differentiation may occur.

Monopolistically competitive firms produce a good that is only slightly different from that of all other sellers. Buyers can therefore tell the difference between the output of different firms. The output of oligopolies can be homogeneous (perfect oligopoly) or differentiated (imperfect oligopoly).

In monopolistic competition there are a large number of small producers selling to a large number of buyers. In oligopolistic industries a small number of large producers dominate the market.

The large number of firms in monopolistic competition means that the actions of one firm have little effect on competitors. In an oligopoly the actions of one of the dominant firms can have a significant effect on its competitors.

The independence of monopolistically competitive firms means that pricing policy is influenced only by cost and revenue considerations. Interdependence means that oligopolistic pricing decisions take into account the likely response of other firms. The theory behind the kinked demand curve (Figure 1) argues that if an oligopolistic firm increases its price, other firms will not raise theirs and customers are lost. Reducing price has no effect on market share, because other firms will follow suit. Oligopolies therefore tend to exhibit price rigidity.

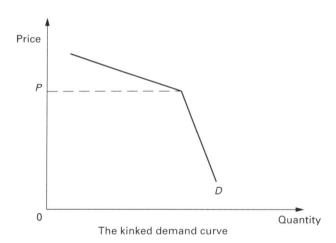

Figure 1

Economies of scale are more significant in an oligopoly than in monopolistic competition. When economies of scale are available, those firms able to increase their plant size acquire a cost advantage over smaller competitors. Small firms are uncompetitive, and the industry becomes oligopolistic. In industries offering little or no scope for scale economies, firms are unable to reduce unit costs or are unable to reduce them significantly by increasing their size. Such industries tend to be perfectly or monopolistically competitive.

Non-price competition is used in both market structures but the scale differs. Indeed UK advertising is dominated by oligopolies trying to increase consumer loyalty to their product.

In monopolistic competition, new firms are free to enter and leave the industry. However there are barriers to entry into oligopolistic markets. This difference affects the types of profit that firms in the different market structures can earn in the long run. Figure 2 shows a representative firm in monopolistic competition. Supernormal profits attract new firms into the industry, reducing market share and thereby reducing demand for the individual firm. In Figure 3 the demand curve shifts to the left until price equals average cost. Monopolistically competitive firms earn only normal profits in the long run.

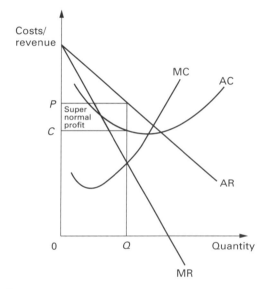

Figure 2

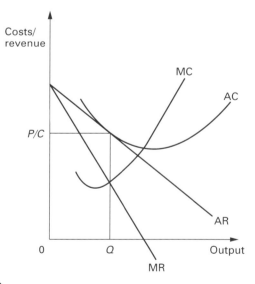

Figure 3

The ability of oligopolists to exclude competition allows them to continue earning supernormal profits in the long run.

PART III

Market Failure and Government Intervention

AEB	NEAB	OCSEB	UCLES	ULE	UODLE	Topic	Date begun	Date completed	Self-assessment
✓	✓	✓	✓	✓	✓	**Fact sheets**			
✓					✓	**Investigative study**			
✓	✓	✓	✓	✓	✓	**Data response**			
✓	✓	✓	✓	✓	✓	**Objective questions**			
✓	✓	✓	✓	✓	✓	**Essays**			

Competition Policy

10.1 Fact sheet

(a) Measures of UK competitiveness

The competitiveness of UK industry can be measured in terms of:

(1) Profitability
(2) Return on capital employed
(3) Productivity
(4) Export performance
(5) Import penetration
(6) Employment levels

(b) Competition policy

UK competition policy seeks to encourage and enhance the competitive process. It is based on a case-by-case examination. It does not assume that possession of market power is in itself against the public interest, but that certain uses of it may be. Consumers would be disadvantaged by, for example:

(1) Excessive prices
(2) Restrictions on output
(3) Decline in the levels of service
(4) Unfair restrictions on entry into the market

Key Competition Acts are:

(1) The Fair Trading Act 1973, which is concerned with monopolies and mergers.

(2) The Restrictive Trade Practices Act 1976, which deals with uncompetitive practices.
(3) The Resale Prices Act 1976, which concerns attempts to set minimum prices at which goods can be sold.
(4) The Competition Act 1980, which covers anti-competitive practices.

(c) Monopoly and merger policy

This is implemented by:

(1) The Office of Fair Trading (OFT)
(2) The Monopolies and Mergers Commission (MMC)

- A merger can be investigated when:
  (a) the total assets of the company to be taken over exceed £70 million in value;
  (b) the new merged company will have 25% or more of the supply or purchase of goods.
- The MMC decides whether a merger will operate against the public interest and have anti-competitive effects.
- The OFT can refer a monopoly to the MMC if it thinks it is acting against the public interest.
- In practice few monopolies and mergers are investigated.

(d) Restrictive practices policy

- This is designed to take action against practices that reduce competition and harm the public interest, including:

(a) cartels;

(b) resale price maintenance.

- Collective agreements that include restrictive practices must be registered with the OFT.
- The Restrictive Practices Court was established in 1956 to consider exemptions for individual cases. To obtain exemption an agreement must pass through at least one of eight so-called gateways, e.g. that it helps to protect jobs and on balance operates in the public interest.

(e)   Anti-competitive practices policy

- The Competition Act 1980 defines an anti-competitive practice as one that restricts, distorts or prevents competition.
- If, after a preliminary investigation, a practice is found to be anti-competitive the Director General of Fair Trading can refer it to the MMC.

(f)   The role of the European Union

UK competition policy is influenced by EU competition rules, as contained in Articles 85 and 86 of the Treaty of Rome.

- Article 85 prohibits restrictive practices, including price fixing and discriminatory terms of supply, within the EU.
- Article 86 prohibits the abuse of monopoly and oligopoly power insofar as it may affect trade between member states.
- Since 1990 the European Commission has had the power to control mergers that have a union-wide dimension. Mergers where the parties have an aggregate exceeding 5 billion ECUs, at least two of the companies have an EU turnover above 250 million ECUs and the companies do not conduct more than two thirds of their ECU-wide business in one member country must be notified to the European Commission.

(g)   Privatisation

Privatisation covers:

(1) Denationalisation.

(2) The sale of government shares in private sector companies.

(3) The sale of council houses to sitting tenants.

(4) The contracting out of services by central and local government.

(5) Deregulation, i.e. the removal of government regulations that restrict entry and exit of firms and competition.

- Arguments for privatisation:
  raises revenue;
  may promote efficiency;
  exposes firms to market forces;
  may open up firms to competition in the goods market;
  firms are obliged to compete for finance;
  increases share ownership.
- Arguments against privatisation:
  may reduce revenue in the long run;
  private sector firms may not be efficient;
  public sector assets may be sold off too cheaply;
  competition may not be increased;
  private sector firms may not take externalities into account;
  reduction in government control over the economy.

10.2 Investigative study

Example 10.1

A critical analysis of the role and success of one of the regulatory agencies, e.g. OFLOT, which regulates the National Lottery.

10.3 Data response

Example 10.2

PRIVATISATION and liberalisation are in fashion, even in the once-straitjacketed economies of Latin America and Eastern Europe. And rightly so: as a rule, the best thing a government can do with an industry is to let businessmen, not bureaucrats, run it. Ordinarily, competition forces firms to keep prices and costs low. But many utility industries (such as electricity, telecommunications and water) are largely monopolies. When the discipline of competition is absent, governments cannot afford to abandon all controls when they give up ownership. Regulation is needed to stop the monopolists fleecing their customers.

Source: Extract from 'The regulatory experiment', *The Economist*, 28 January 1995.

(a)   Explain the thinking behind the statement 'the best thing is to let businessmen, not bureaucrats, run it'.   **(5 marks)**

(b)   Why does competition keep prices and costs low?   **(4 marks)**

(c) What is the government definition of a monopoly and how does this definition differ from the definition of a pure monopoly? **(2 marks)**

(d) In what sense may a monopoly 'fleece' its customers? **(7 marks)**

(e) What forms does government regulation of privatised monopolies take? **(7 marks)**

Solution 10.2

(a) Supporters of free-market forces argue that government intervention reduces efficiency. They argue that entrepreneurs are better informed about what consumers want and about changes in demand. Entrepreneurs, it is claimed, are responsive to changes in consumer demand because they have a financial incentive to be so. If consumers demand more of a product they will bid up its price. The opportunity to increase profits will encourage firms to make more of the product.

(b) If an industry consists of a large number of similar sized firms making products with a high degree of positive cross-elasticity of demand there will be a high level of competition. In this situation, if one firm fails to keep down its costs and prices it will lose all, or a substantial number, of its customers to more efficient companies.

(c) Government competition policy defines a monopoly as a firm whose share of the market is 25% or more. In contrast a pure monopoly is a firm that has a 100% share of the market.

(d) A monopoly, because of its market power, can reduce output and thereby raise price. This means that it may fleece its customers in the sense of charging a price above, and producing an output below the socially optimum level. The diagram below contrasts the socially optimum price and output (P_X and Q_X) with the output of a private sector monopolist (P and Q).

(e) Monopolies, whether privatised or not, can be referred by the Director General of the Office of Fair Trading or the President of the Board of Trade for investigation to the Monopolies and Mergers Commission if it engages in harmful anticompetitive practices. Monopolies, other than pure monopolies, may engage in restrictive practices with other firms in the industry, and thus are subject to restrictive practices legislation. Privatised utilities have regulators who limit the annual price increases to the

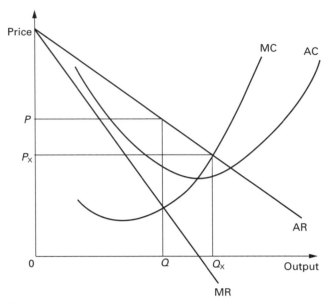

Figure 1

change in the retail price index plus or minus a certain, specified amount each year, known as 'X'. This encourages the utilities to cut their costs as they gain from any increase in cost efficiency.

10.4 Objective questions

Example 10.3

What is the most likely reason for the Monopolies and Mergers Commission to prevent a proposed merger from going ahead?

A The aim of the merger is found to be to asset strip

B The merger will result in significant economies of scale

C The proposed merger is of a vertical rather than a horizontal nature

D The new merged company will control more than 40% of the market

Example 10.4

A government policy of deregulation is intended to:

A increase government control

B improve the supply-side performance of the economy

C reduce the size of the manufacturing sector

D reduce the prices charged by nationalised industries

Example 10.5

According to the government definition, a monopoly is a firm that has:
A 25% or more of the market
B $33\frac{1}{3}$% or more of the market
C 50% or more of the market
D 100% of the market

Example 10.6

Which of the following is the best definition of privatisation?
A Denationalisation
B The transfer of assets from the public to the private sector
C The sale of government held shares in private sector companies
D The sale of government-owned assets, compulsory competitive tendering and deregulation

Example 10.7

A firm controls the supply of a raw material used in the production of a good. It is also involved in all stages of the productive process of the product. It sells the raw material to competitors at such a high price that its competitors are unable to compete with it in selling the finished product. This action is known as:
A price discrimination
B predatory pricing
C selective distribution
D vertical price squeezing

Example 10.8

When may price discrimination be beneficial for consumers? If it:
A reduces consumer surplus
B increases industrial concentration
C enables a foreign firm to eliminate domestic producers
D turns a loss-making monopoly into a profitable one

Example 10.9

Which government body decides if a monopoly should be referred to the Monopolies and Mergers Commission?
A OFT
B OFTEL

C The Bank of England
D The Restrictive Practices Court

Example 10.10

When may the imposition of a government tax on a good enable a market to work more effectively?
A When social costs exceed private costs
B When there is too much competition in the market
C When production costs in the industry are falling
D When short-run supernormal profits are being earned

Example 10.11

In relation to which products is resale price maintenance legal?
A Cars   B Houses
C Televisions   D Pharmaceuticals

Example 10.12

A merger will qualify for possible investigation by the Monopolies and Mergers Commission in terms of assets if it has total gross assets over:
A £30 million   B £50 million
C £70 million   D £100 million

10.5 Solutions to objective questions

Solution 10.3 Answer: **A**

Asset stripping is when a company buys another company (usually one which it believes is undervalued), breaks it up, sells the parts to other companies and usually closes down the remainder. The aim is profit, and whilst the asset stripper will benefit, consumers are likely to suffer from the fall in output and choice and the workers made redundant will obviously suffer.

B ⇒ Consumers are likely to benefit if the costs of production fall since this may result in lower prices. The economy will also benefit from the firm becoming more internationally competitive.

C and **D** ⇒ The Monopolies and Mergers Commission judges each proposed merger on its own merits or otherwise. A vertical nature and control of more than 40% of the market do not in themselves imply that the proposed merger will be against the public interest.

Solution 10.4   Answer: **B**

Deregulation is the removal of regulations on the activities of the business sector, e.g. ending the legal monopoly that qualified opticians had over the sale of spectacles. The prime aim behind deregulation is to enable market forces to operate more effectively, free of government intervention. Supporters of deregulation argue that this will increase firms' efficiency and make them more responsive to changes in consumer demand. The supply side of the economy will improve.

Solution 10.5   Answer: **A**

The minimum-market-share criterion for a monopoly subject to investigation by the Monopolies and Mergers Commission was given as 25% in the 1973 Fair Trading Act.

$\mathbf{D} \Rightarrow$ This is a pure monopoly where the firm is the industry, i.e. the sole supplier.

Solution 10.6   Answer: **D**

Privatisation has a broad meaning. Options **A**, **B** and **C** all describe forms of privatisation, but the most complete definition is option **D**.

Solution 10.7   Answer: **D**

In this case the firm is making its finished product more price competitive by charging its rivals a high price for the raw materials. What enables the firm to do this is its monopoly of the raw material source and the fact that the firm is vertically integrated.

$\mathbf{A} \Rightarrow$ Price discrimination is charging different prices to different groups of consumers.

$\mathbf{B} \Rightarrow$ Predatory pricing is charging low prices, sometimes below cost, with the intention of drawing out existing competitors or preventing the entry of new competitors into the industry.

$\mathbf{C} \Rightarrow$ Selective distribution is when a producer will only sell to outlets that meet certain requirements.

Solution 10.8   Answer: **D**

Price discrimination may enable a firm to stay in business. If that firm confers positive externalities this will benefit society.

A and **B** $\Rightarrow$ are potential disadvantages of price discrimination from a consumers' point of view.

$\mathbf{C} \Rightarrow$ The elimination of domestic producers will reduce competition and is likely to lead to higher prices and less choice.

Solution 10.9   Answer: **A**

A monopoly can be referred for investigation by the President of the Board of Trade and by the Director General for the Office of Fair Trading (OFT).

$\mathbf{B} \Rightarrow$ OFTEL is the Office of Telecommunications, which regulates the telecommunications industry.

$\mathbf{C} \Rightarrow$ The Bank of England regulates the banking sector.

$\mathbf{D} \Rightarrow$ The Restrictive Practices Court decides whether agreements between firms are against the public interest.

Solution 10.10   Answer: **A**

If social costs exceed private costs there are external costs (negative externalities) that do not go through the market. If the tax is placed on the good is equal to the external costs, social costs will equal private costs and resource allocation will be improved.

Solution 10.11   Answer: **D**

Currently, resale price maintenance is permitted in the case of certain medicines. Resale price maintenance is when a producer can legally insist that retailers charge a set price for its products.

Solution 10.12   Answer: **C**

There are two tests to determine whether a particular merger is liable to investigation. One is the market-share test, i.e. 25% plus, and the other is the assets test. In the latter case mergers can be investigated if the companies' joint assets exceed £70 million.

10.6 Essays

Example 10.13

Examine the economic arguments for and against privatisation.   **(25 marks)**

- Define privatisation
- Give some examples

Solution 10.13

Privatisation is a broad term. It includes the sale of nationalised industries, the sale of part of nationalised industries, the sale of government shares in public limited companies and the contracting out of work by local authorities.

Since 1979 the UK government has privatised a significant proportion of the public sector. This policy has been adopted by many other countries, including France, Italy, New Zealand and former command economies.

The sale of nationalised industries in whole or part and the sale of government shares in public limited companies raises revenue and reduces the PSBR. This was a significant consideration in the early 1980s, when the government was keen to reduce the PSBR. Revenue, in the form of corporation tax, will also be increased if privatisation results in a rise in efficiency and profitability. This may occur because private sector industries may be more subject to market discipline in both the goods and the financial market – if they are not efficient they will go out of business due to their inability to sell their products and raise revenue. Depending on how the privatisation is organised, the new private sector firms may become subject to greater competition, e.g. British Telecom is now facing increasing competition from Mercury.

Those in favour of privatisation also argue that private sector firms are more responsive to changes in consumer demand, as reduced government intervention results in greater flexibility and speed of response. This may in turn bring about the more efficient allocation of resources.

Privatisation can promote shareholding among the population, and indeed shareholding is now higher than in 1979. However many of the new shareholders have shares in only one privatised company and these are often purchased with the intention of selling them quickly in the hope of making a capital gain.

Privatisation may provide increased opportunities for raising investment finance as nationalised industries can have limits placed on their external funds.

Whilst privatisation has been a major movement, there are nevertheless a number of arguments against it. One concerns the process of privatisation. It has been claimed that a number of industries have been sold off at artificially low prices, thereby involving a loss of potential income for the government. For example share prices in the regional electricity companies that were sold off in 1990 quickly rose, indicating that the initial share prices could have been higher. The sale of profitable industries, for example gas and electricity, also results in a long-term loss of government revenue and could cause a long-term rise in the PSBR.

The sale may also divert funds from other organisations, including banks and building societies.

A private sector firm may be less concerned with externalities and base its pricing and output decisions on private costs and benefits. For this reason the government has established a number of regulatory bodies, including OFFER (electricity) and OFGAS (gas), to monitor price and output decisions.

Privatisation can also make it more difficult to implement government policy. With fewer industries under direct government control a prices and incomes policy or a new training initiative may have less chance of success.

Example 10.14

How may the government promote competition?

(25 marks)

- Recognise that competition can take various forms.
- Comment on UK competition policy.

Solution 10.14

Competition may be in the form of price or non-price competition. Non-price competition includes advertising, free gifts, brand names, competitions, after sales service, guarantees.

Government competition policy mainly seeks to promote price competition. This can be achieved in a number of ways. To discourage monopolists from charging high prices a tax can be placed on supernormal profits. This occurred in the mid 1980s in the UK when the government placed a windfall tax on the high profits earned by retail banks.

A government could also nationalise the industry to ensure that the monopolist charges a price equal to marginal cost. However in the 1980s and 1990s the UK government used privatisation rather than nationalisation to promote competition. The thinking behind this approach is that private sector firms are more subject to market forces. If they do not supply what consumers want they will go out of business – they will not be 'bailed out' by the government.

A government could also break up a monopoly into separate competing units. This approach has been followed in the USA but the main thrust of UK policy is to regulate monopolies. This is achieved through the Monopolies and Mergers Commission, which investigates existing and potential monopoly situations. The MMC and the Office of Fair Trading act on the assumption that possession of market power is not in itself harmful, but that how it is used may be – so a case-by-case approach is followed.

The privatisation of public utilities resulted in a number of specialised regulators being set up to regulate industries. These include OFTEL (which regulates the telecommunications industry), OFGAS (the gas industry), OFFER (electricity), OFWAT (water) and OFLOT (the lottery). The regulator checks the output and price decisions of the industry and can, if it thinks it appropriate, refer to the MMC.

Competition can also be promoted via merger policy. A government can investigate proposed mergers and prevent those which act against the public interest from going ahead. The MMC can investigate mergers that will result in the new company controlling 25% or more of the market or has assets of £30 million or above.

Restrictive practice agreements concerning prices, output and production process have to be registered with the Office of Fair Trading. To be allowed to continue they have to be able to prove that the benefits outweigh the disadvantages of such agreements, and they have to satisfy at least one of a number of 'gateways', e.g. to protect the public against injury.

The primary aim of the 1980 Competition Act was to promote greater competition. It identified a number of anticompetitive practices, including predatory pricing and price discrimination. The OFT can investigate such anticompetitive practices if the firms concerned are monopolies (as defined in terms of a market share of 25% or more).

Competition may also be promoted by reducing barriers to entry into industries and occupations. Deregulation has been used in the 1980s and 1990s to increase the role of market forces. For example bus services were deregulated in 1986 and a number of routes were opened up to greater competition from different bus companies.

The government has also sought to promote competition in the National Health Service by developing an internal market, and in a range of other areas by contracting out services to the most competitive bidder. These areas include schools career services, schools canteen services and refuse collection.

Regional Economics

11.1 Fact sheet

(a) Influences on industrial location

A profit-maximising firm expands in a location that minimises unit costs. The firm takes account of:

(1) *Natural advantages*, including:
    (a) the area's proximity to raw materials;
    (b) the physical features of the area;
    (c) the climate of the area.
(2) Nearness to markets.
(3) *Acquired advantages* from other firms having located in the area. (The resulting external economies of scale are described in Table 6.4.)
(4) Government regulations and financial incentives (regional policy).

- *Weight-losing industries* use bulky raw materials to produce a compact finished product, and tend to locate near a major source of raw materials.
- *Weight-gaining industries* use compact raw materials to produce a bulky finished product, and tend to locate near a major market for the good.
- A *footloose industry* gains no cost advantage from any one particular site and therefore can set up anywhere.
- Improved transport and power networks (e.g. motorways and the national grid) have made many industries footloose.

- *Industrial inertia* occurs when a firm remains in its original location even after the initial advantages have disappeared.

(b) Location of industry in the UK

See Table 11.1 on page 100.

(c) Deindustrialisation

Deindustrialisation refers to a continuing reduction in the share of manufacturing in national output. Deindustrialisation may cause:

(1) Unemployment if there is no corresponding increase in service-industry employment.
(2) Economic decline in regions with a high concentration of manufacturing industries.
(3) A reduction in the rate of economic growth.
(4) A deterioration in the balance of payments if the import of manufacturers increases while the export of goods falls.

(d) The regional problem

The *regional problem* refers to an uneven spread of living standards and employment levels between different areas of the UK. A region may be in relative decline because:

(1) Factory and office closures result in a regional multiplier effect.

Table 11.1 Structure of UK industry by region

Standard regions	Major industries
North	Traditional heavy industry concentrated around Tyneside and Teeside; public administration; vehicles
North-west	Heavy engineering; cotton; clothing; glass; chemicals; vehicles
Yorkshire and Humberside	Iron and steel; textiles and clothing; fishing; agriculture
East Midlands	Diverse industry, including hosiery, footwear and clothing
West Midlands	Mechanical and electrical engineering; vehicles; iron and steel; potteries.
South-west	Agriculture and food processing; tourism; aerospace; tobacco.
East Anglia	Agriculture and food processing; footwear; tourism; micro-technology
South-east	Financial and commercial centre; technological and light engineering; public administration
Wales	Iron and steel; agriculture; light engineering.
Scotland	North Sea oil; agriculture; tourism; construction
Northern Ireland	Textiles; agriculture; construction; public administration

(2) Net migration from the area reduces:
  (a) the local demand for products;
  (b) the local supply of skilled labour.
(3) Local authorities have insufficient income to provide an adequate infrastructure and services.
(4) A contracting industrial base reduces the external economies of scale of an area.

(e) Regional policy approaches

- Interventionist economists believe that market forces will not remove regional differences and that government policies are required.
- Supply-side economists favour removing restrictions on free-market forces so that the unemployed can move to prosperous regions and firms can move to areas where inputs are cheaper.

(f) Regional policy measures

- Government regional policy aims to reduce high levels of regional unemployment and to reduce congestion in prosperous areas.
- Assisted areas qualify for special government aid including:
  (a) *regional selective assistance* (RSA), which covers financial aid for projects that either create new jobs or preserve existing ones;
  (b) *regional enterprise grants* (REGs), which are grants to help small firms in assisted areas.

- Government measures have been mainly geared towards moving jobs to workers rather than workers to jobs.
- The *European Regional Development Fund* is used to provide financial assistance to declining regions.

(g) The urban problem

Since 1945 there has been a significant movement in employment and population from conurbations to rural areas because:

(1) there is little urban land for expansion;
(2) urban rents, rates and wages are high;
(3) more industries have become footloose.

- The most serious decline has occurred in inner-city areas. The population has a high proportion of semi-skilled, low-income and ethnic minorities who cannot afford to move elsewhere.

(h) Urban policy

Government urban policy instruments include the following:

(1) Restricting the growth of urban areas through green-belt legislation.
(2) Encouraging firms to locate in derelict inner-city *enterprise zones* and *simplified planning zones* by

Table 11.2 Multinationals

Advantages of MNCs for the host country	Disadvantages of MNCs for the host country
MNCs provide domestic employment opportunities	MNCs may force competing local firms out of business
Investment improves the current account of the balance of payments	Returned profits worsens future balance of payments
Investment increases the domestic growth rate	MNCs may exploit monopsony (sole buyer) power in wage negotiations
Imports replaced by home-produced MNC-made goods	MNCs may deplete local natural resources too quickly
Technology and production techniques are transferred.	Transfer pricing may be used to minimise tax payments.

offering rate and tax rebates, and exemption from many planning restrictions.

(3) Encouraging investment in declining areas by allowing 'free ports', where goods can be processed for re-exportation without incurring customs duties.

(4) Establishing *urban development corporations* (UDCs) to buy up and improve derelict land with the involvement of local private sector firms.

(i) Multinationals

A *multinational corporation* (MNC) is a company that produces in more than one country.

- The largest MNCs have turnovers in excess of the GNP of most countries, and account for the bulk of world trade in manufactures.
- MNCs reduce unit costs by locating different production processes in different countries.

11.2 Investigative study

Example 11.1

A study of what influences local firms to base themselves in the area, or a study of the performance of a multinational company and the influences on and results of its locational decision.

11.3 Data response

(a) How many regions had below-average GDP per head? **(2 marks)**

(b) How many regions had above-average unemployment? **(2 marks)**

(c) The regions of the UK are sometimes classified in terms of North and South. Four regions are grouped as the South, i.e. the East Midlands, East Anglia, the South East and the South West. Do the data support the view that living standards are higher in the South? **(9 marks)**

(d) Name three other indicators of living standards that could be used to make a comparison between regions. **(6 marks)**

(e) Give three reasons why unemployed workers do not move from regions of low income and high unemployment to regions of high income and low unemployment? **(6 marks)**

Example 11.2

	1993	
Region	*GDP (index per head) (UK = 100)*	*Unemployment (per cent) (UK average = 10.4)*
North	89	12.0
Yorkshire & Humberside	91	10.4
East Midlands	96	9.6
East Anglia	102	8.2
South East	116	10.2
South West	97	9.5
West Midlands	93	10.9
North West	91	10.8
Wales	85	10.4
Scotland	98	9.9
Northern Ireland	82	14.1

Sources: CSO, *Social Trends*, 1995; *Monthly Digest of Statistics*, March 1995

Solution 11.2

(a) Nine of the eleven regions had below-average GDP per head. These were the North, Yorkshire and Humberside, the East Midlands, the South West, the West Midlands, the North West, Wales, Scotland and Northern Ireland. In other words, all regions except East Anglia and the South East.

(b) Four regions had above-average unemployment. These were the North, the West Midlands, the North West and Northern Ireland. Two regions – Yorkshire and Humberside and Wales – had unemployment that equalled the national average.

(c) The data does not provide conclusive evidence of higher living standards in the South. All four Southern regions did have unemployment levels that were below the national average. However the unemployment rate in Scotland, a Northern region was below that in the South East. Two of the Southern regions (the East Midlands and the South West) also had below-average income per head and Scotland had a higher rate than these two regions.

　The three areas with the lowest income per head (Northern Ireland, Wales and the North) were all in the North. Similarly the three regions with the highest unemployment were in the North (Northern Ireland, the North and the West Midlands).

(d) There are number of possible additional indicators of living standards that could be studied. These include average life spans, net migration inwards or outwards, number of cars per head or number of a particular type of consumer durable per head, e.g. washing machines.

(e) Unemployed workers may not move to regions of greater prosperity and lower unemployment because of family ties, the difficulty of obtaining accommodation in another region or lack of qualifications and training for the jobs on offer there. It is also possible that, whilst other regions have lower unemployment, they may not necessarily have many unfilled vacancies, suitable or otherwise.

11.4 Objective questions

Example 11.3

Industrial inertia occurs when:
A labour is geographically immobile
B firms fail to exploit economies of scale
C the initial reasons for location have disappeared
D the share of manufacturing in national output declines

Example 11.4

Weight-gaining industries tend to locate:
A in assisted areas
B close to major markets
C close to the source of raw materials
D close to important transport networks

Example 11.5

Which one of the following industries is the least dispersed throughout the UK?
A Retailing　　　　　　B Agriculture
C Tourism　　　　　　D Car manufacturing

Example 11.6

Multinational corporations are firms that:
A invest overseas
B export and import goods
C have shareholders in many countries
D produce goods in more than one country

Example 11.7

Which of the following is not used by the UK government to solve regional unemployment?
A Enterprise zones
B Direction of labour
C Regional enterprise grants
D Regional selective assistance

Example 11.8

Which of the following is an example of infrastructure improvement in the assisted areas of the UK?
A Development grants
B Low-interest loans
C Expenditure on road improvements
D Grants towards the cost of training labour

Example 11.9

An example of an acquired locational advantage is:
A flat land
B coal deposits
C a mild climate
D an international airport

Example 11.10

Which of the following industries is market orientated?

A Banking   B Fishing
C Sugar-beet   D Iron and steel

Example 11.11

Which of the following is an external economy?
A Increased bureaucracy
B Employment of specialist staff
C Bulk buying of raw materials
D The development of ancillary industries

Example 11.12

A host country that allows a multinational company to undertake direct foreign investment generally benefits from:

A transfer pricing
B technology transfer
C rapid depletion of natural resources
D the multinational company gaining a monopsony position

11.5 Solutions to objective questions

Solution 11.3   Answer: C

Once the natural advantages of a site have disappeared, the firm may still find it cheaper to expand at its current location. This is because it is expensive to move plant to a new site. Hence steel plants are found in areas where the local supply of coal has long been exhausted.
   D ⇒ refers to deindustrialisation.

Solution 11.4   Answer: B

As the finished product of a weight-gaining industry tends to be relatively bulky in comparison with its raw materials, it is likely to locate near to its main markets.

Solution 11.5   Answer: D

A dispersed industry is one spread throughout the country. In all counties there are, for example, shops, farms and tourist organisations and companies. There are a number of car companies in the UK but these are less widely spread than business units in the agricultural, retailing and tourist industries.

Solution 11.6   Answer: D

A multinational corporation is a firm with production capacity located in two or more countries.

Solution 11.7   Answer: B

Direction of labour has been used in the UK only under conditions of war and then its aim was not to solve the regional problem.
   A, C and D ⇒ are currently being used to reduce regional unemployment.

Solution 11.8   Answer: C

Infrastructure includes roads, bridges, sewers etc. It particularly covers transportation and communications – the services that support industry.

Solution 11.9   Answer: D

An acquired locational advantage is an advantage that has developed over time as a result of the deliberate action of firms and/or the government.
   A, B and C ⇒ are natural advantages.

Solution 11.10   Answer: A

A market orientated industry is one based near to its customers.
   B, C and D ⇒ are raw material orientated industries.

Solution 11.11   Answer: D

An external economy is an advantage of an industry growing in size which is available to the firms in the industry. The development of ancillary industries, i.e. industries that produce raw materials, components and services for the industry concerned, is a major external economy.
   A ⇒ is an internal diseconomy of scale.
   B and C ⇒ are internal economies of scale.

Solution 11.12   Answer: **B**

A host country may be able to pick up information about developments in technology from multinational companies setting up plants in the country.

A, C and D ⇒ are potential disadvantages.

11.6 Essays

Example 11.13

To what extent is the location of industry determined by government regional policy?   **(25 marks)**

- Avoid simply describing the theory of location and the regional problem.
- Explain how government industrial policy affects industrial location decisions.
- Consider the likely impact of other factors on location.

Solution 11.13

The UK is divided into eleven standard economic regions. Income per capita tends to be higher and unemployment lower in the south than in the north. In theory, market forces should eliminate regional disparities over time. The low wages and rents of depressed areas influence location decisions and attract new firms. However, capital and labour can be geographically immobile.

To offset these market imperfections, a number of controls and incentives have operated since 1945 to influence the location decisions of firms. Currently firms that locate in assisted areas may be able to gain regional selective assistance and, in the case of small firms, regional enterprise grants.

Firms, then, have to compare the cost advantage of sites in development and non-development areas. Companies take into account the natural advantages of an area, including the physical features and climate of a region. The acquired advantages of an area, such as transport network, labour force and proximity to markets, are also important factors.

However it is difficult to isolate the impact of government regional policy on location decisions since 1945. Detailed regional statistics have only recently become available, and the areas actually qualifying for assistance have been changed frequently. Let us consider the evidence.

New firms may ignore offers of assistance and be reluctant to locate in declining regions because the younger members of the local workforce have moved to areas of high employment. The negative regional multiplier reduces the size of the market, thereby reducing the area's external economies of scale. Firms that suffer industrial inertia expand at their current site and their location decision is unaffected by regional policy.

Regional policy is likely to be more successful in a period of economic expansion. During a recession firms will not open up new factories and offices and may be more concerned about the risks of relocating.

Firms where government financial incentives make up a large proportion of locations costs are most likely to take account of regional policy. For example capital-intensive firms such as ICI have been attracted into assisted areas. Multinational enterprises considering direct foreign investment in UK greenfield sites have accepted grants and located in development areas. The Nissan plant at Washington in Tyne and Wear is an example. However other multinationals have emphasised different location factors, such as proximity to markets and transport networks, in their location decision. Honda have sited their engine plant in Swindon without any government assistance.

Microtechnology is a footloose industry where no one site offers a cost advantage. Transport costs are only a small proportion of total costs. Despite the allowances on offer elsewhere, many 'sunrise' information technology firms have decided to locate along the M4 corridor between London and Bristol. However government assistance has helped to create a high concentration of silicon chip firms in Scotland's glens.

In conclusion, it has been demonstrated that the financial assistance given by postwar regional policy is an important but not overriding consideration in the location decision of the firm.

Example 11.14

(a)   What has caused the economic decline of inner-city areas of the UK?   **(15 marks)**
(b)   Discuss possible remedies for this decline.
          (10 marks)

- Explain what is meant by inner-city decline.
- Include examples of recent government policies and their effects.
- (1) Discuss the negative multiplier effect.

Solution 11.14

(a) The decline in inner-city areas can be measured in terms of falling output, increased unemployment and below-average income levels. Two major factors have contributed to this trend: (1) the movement of labour-intensive firms away from inner areas and (2) the flight of well-paid employees to outer-urban and rural areas.

One reason for the migration of inner-urban firms is the introduction of modern production techniques, which have increased the demand for floor space. Greenbelt restrictions and the active use of Industrial Development Certificates in the 1960s and 1970s made it difficult for firms seeking expansion to locate in inner-city areas. Footloose firms faced with high rents and the availability of selective financial assistance in assisted areas have left some inner-city areas. In the service sector, many companies have relocated their offices, with a subsequent loss of inner-city office jobs. The continuous flight of firms generates a negative inner-city multiplier effect, causing even further decline. The negative multiplier effect is shown in the diagram.

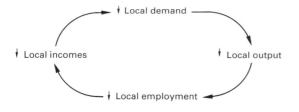

The type of external economy of scale available in inner-city areas has changed. Transport economies gained by locating weight-gaining industries close to the market have been eroded by diseconomies caused by traffic congestion. Inner-city decline has left local authorities with insufficient income to maintain an adequate social infrastructure.

Demographic trends also account for the decline of inner-city areas. Many workers have used increased real incomes to move to suburban and rural areas where improved communications allow them to commute to work. Many of the jobs left to inner-city residents are low-skilled low-income ones. As a result, average earnings in outer areas have risen while inner-city earnings have declined. The resultant negative local multiplier effect has further reduced income output and employment in inner cities.

(b) Many argue that inner-city decline can only be arrested by government intervention. One possible remedy is to offer firms incentives to locate in inner cities. Since 1981 a number of enterprise zones in the most derelict inner-urban areas have been established, which give firms tax allowances and exemption from rates and certain planning regulations. Special agencies for urban renewal (urban development corporations) have been given resources to acquire land, improve social and industrial infrastructure, and involve private-sector firms. Urban development grants are available to encourage investment in inner-city areas that would not otherwise take place.

In 1990 simplified planning zones were introduced to encourage firms to set up in deprived inner-city areas. They do not provide financial incentives but they do simplify planning regulations. 1991 saw the introduction of the City Challenge scheme. This involves local authorities drawing up plans to improve particular inner-city areas. The Department of the Environment then selects the best proposals.

Incentive schemes that are successful in generating new investment have a spin-off multiplier effect. Local businesses experience an increase in the demand for their products. Yet there is no guarantee that the employment created by new investment will automatically reduce unemployment in inner-city areas. New jobs may be filled by workers from other areas. Moreover incentives can have the effect of simply diverting investment from one region to another. Increased employment in inner-urban areas would have taken place elsewhere. Government intervention can lead to a misallocation of resources. Siting production in inappropriate inner-urban areas is justified on the basis of the resulting social benefits. However these must be weighed against the costs of not producing at the least-cost site.

Income and Wealth

12.1 Fact sheet

(a) Factor incomes

The demand for all factors of production (inputs) is a *derived demand* – i.e. the demand for factors of production depends on the demand for the products they produce. In return for providing their services, land, labour, capital and entrepreneurs receive factor incomes.

(b) Marginal revenue productivity

- The demand for a factor of production is based on its *marginal revenue productivity*.
- Marginal revenue product is *marginal physical product* multiplied by marginal revenue:
  MRP = MPP × MR
- MRP will increase if either MPP and/or MR rise.
- An increase in MRP will increase the payment the factor receives, as shown in Figure 12.1

(c) Profit

- *Profit* is the reward for bearing uninsurable risks associated with production. The types of profit are explained in Table 8.2. Note that profit is uncertain and may even be negative. Profit has the following functions:
  (a) rewards those who bear uncertain risks;

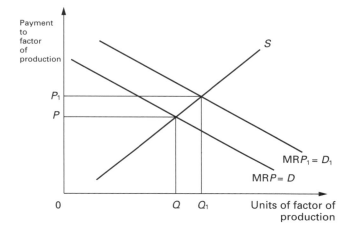

Figure 12.1 An increase in marginal revenue productivity

(b) encourages invention and innovation;
(c) indicates efficiency;
(d) encourages firms to switch resources from loss-making to profit-making operations;
(e) provides a source of finance for investment.

(d) Economic rent

- *Rent* is a payment made for the use of an asset owned by someone else.
- *Economic rent* is a surplus paid to any factor of production over its supply price.
- *Transfer earnings* is the minimum payment needed to keep the factor in its present occupation. This can also be defined as the payment that can

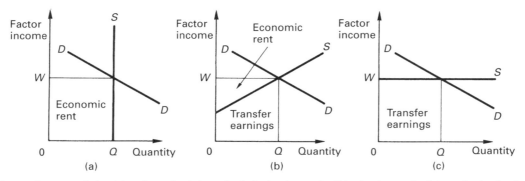

Figure 12.2 Economic rent and elasticity of supply: (a) perfectly inelastic supply; (b) elastic supply; (c) perfectly elastic supply

be earned in the factor's next-best-paid occupation (opportunity cost):

present earnings less transfer earnings = economic rent.

(lawyers pay £40 000) less (teacher's pay £22 000) = £18 000.

- *Quasi-rent* is short-term economic rent arising from a temporary inelasticity of supply.
- *Pure economic rent* is the reward to any factor that is in completely inelastic supply.
- The proportion of a factor's earnings made up of economic rent increases as supply becomes more inelastic.

(e) Interest

- *Interest* is the reward for forgoing *liquidity*, and is an amount paid to a lender over and above the original sum borrowed.

- The *loanable funds (classical) theory* states that the rate of interest is determined by the demand for loanable funds (largely for investment) and the supply of loanable funds (savings) (Figure 12.3).
- Keynesian theory states that the rate of interest is determined by the demand for and supply of money. For simplification, the supply of money is presumed to be largely government-determined and to be perfectly interest-inelastic. Keynes identified three motives for demanding money (*liquidity preference*) – that is, for holding wealth in the form of money:
  (a) the *transactions motive* is the desire to keep money to make everyday purchases.
  (b) The *precautionary motive* is the desire to hold money to meet unexpected expenses and take advantage of bargains.
  (c) The *speculative motive* is the desire to hold idle balances to take advantage of changes in the price of bonds.
- In Figure 12.4 the *liquidity trap* occurs after point A, when the rate of interest is so low (and the price of bonds is so high) that everyone anticipates a future fall in the price of bonds. If the money

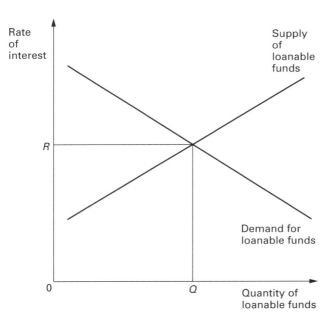

Figure 12.3 The determination of the rate of interest according to the loanable funds theory

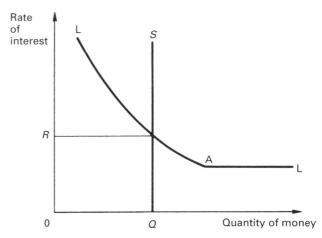

Figure 12.4 Determination of the rate of interest according to the liquidity preference theory and the liquidity trap

Table 12.1 Functional distribution of income in the UK, 1993

Source (factor of production)	Share of total earnings (£m)	(%)
Income from employment	352 896	64.6
Income from self-employment	61 360	11.2
Profit	74 733	13.7
Rent	52 872	9.7
Other	4 259	0.8
Total domestic income	546 120	100.0

Source: Adapted from *Blue Book*, 1994 edition, UK National Accounts (CSO)

supply increases, people will hold all the extra money for fear of making a capital loss from holding bonds. Hence the demand for money becomes perfectly interest-elastic.

(f)   Wages

Wages are a payment to labour. A number of factors help determine wage rates:

(1) Demand for, and supply of, labour. The marginal productivity theory suggests that any factor of production will receive a payment equal to the value of its marginal product. So in the case of labour: wage rate = marginal revenue product.

(2) Government action in the form of incomes policies, arbitration and conciliation, and as an employer.

(3) Trade unions and professional organisations.

(g)   Income distribution

- *Income* is a flow of earnings. The *functional distribution of income* is the distribution of income between factors of production.

- The *size distribution of income* is concerned with the proportion of income received by different proportions of the population. The degree of income inequality can be represented by *Lorenz curves* and Gini *coefficients*.

The Gini coefficient is the ratio between the area between a Lorenz curve and the 45° line and the area below the 45° line:

$$\frac{\text{area } a}{\text{area } a + b} \times \frac{100}{1}$$

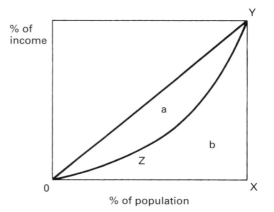

Figure 12.5 The Lorenz curve. 0Y = complete equality; 0XY = complete inequality, with the last person having all the income; 0ZY = degree of inequality

The Gini coefficient has a range from 0 (complete equality) to 1 (complete inequality).

- Income has become more unevenly distributed since 1979. In 1979 the top fifth of individuals received 35% of disposable income. By 1992 this had risen to 41%.

(h)   Wealth distribution

- *Wealth* is a stock of all those assets capable of earning an income.
- Wealth can be human (e.g. skills, qualifications) or material (e.g. time deposits, shares, property).
- Inheritances, capital gains, pensions and savings are the major sources of wealth.
- Note that wealth is more unequally distributed than income in the UK.

Table 12.2 Distribution of wealth in the UK in 1992

% of wealth owned by	Marketable wealth (%)	Marketable wealth less value of dwellings
Most wealthy 1%	18	29
Most wealthy 5%	37	53
Most wealthy 10%	49	65
Most wealthy 25%	72	82
Most wealthy 50%	92	94

Source: *Social Trends 1995* (CSO)

12.2 Investigative study

Example 12.1

An assessment of the effect of profit sharing of schemes on, for example, labour productivity, labour turnover and profitability.

12.3 Data response

Example 12.2

The poor get poorer

THE gap between the incomes of the rich and poor in Britain grew rapidly between the late 1970s and the early 1990s, ending a process of increasing equality that stretches back for several centuries.

A report earlier this month by the Joseph Rowntree Foundation, which funds research into economic and social issues, said that between 1979 and 1992 the poorest 20–30 per cent of the population failed to benefit from economic growth. It warned that the way in which the living standards of a sizeable minority of people had lagged behind over the past 15 years was not only a problem for those affected directly, but also damaged "the social fabric and so affects us all".

The Rowntree report found that there had been a sharp increase in the number of people living on incomes less than half the level of the national average. The number fell from 10 per cent in the 1960s to a low of 6 per cent in 1977 but has since risen to over 20 per cent.

Government ministers dispute that the growing divide between high and low incomes has left poorer people worse off than when the Conservative Party came to power in 1979. Both the Prime Minister and the Social Security secretary, Peter Lilley, said last week that all groups in society had seen their standards of living rise, even though the Department of Social Security's own figures show that the poorest 10 per cent of the population saw their incomes fall by more than 15 per cent between 1979 and 1992, once the cost of housing was taken into account.

Source: Extract from the *Guardian*, 21 February 1995.

(a) What happened to income distribution between the late 1970s and the early 1990s? **(2 marks)**

(b) Distinguish between absolute and relative poverty. **(5 marks)**

(c) Was the Social Security Secretary denying a rise in absolute or relative poverty? Explain your answer. **(5 marks)**

(d) Which groups of the poor would benefit from the introduction of a minimum wage? **(4 marks)**

(e) Identify two other measures to reduce poverty. **(4 marks)**

(f) How would the reduction in poverty benefit those not directly affected by poverty? **(5 marks)**

Solution 12.2

(a) The report by the Joseph Rowntree committee found that the distribution of income became more uneven between the late 1970s and early 1990s. The gap between rich and poor widened. This is in contrast to previous recent periods, when income became more evenly distributed.

(b) Absolute poverty has to be related to a level of living standards considered necessary for human health and existence. Those living below this level can be said to be experiencing absolute poverty. Relative poverty is experienced by those who are poorer than other members of the community. The extract refers to 20% of the British population living on incomes less than half the level of the national average. This 20% forms the lowest quintile group of income recipients.

(c) The Social Security Secretary, Peter Lilley, was denying a rise in absolute poverty. He claimed that all groups had experienced a rise in living standards. His view was that whilst the gap between rich and poor had increased, the greater distance was between those who had become substantially richer and those who had become richer by small amounts.

(d) Single people of working age, one-parent families, and working-age couples with and without children would benefit if they are in employment, initially receiving less than the national minimum wage, and if they remain in employment after its introduction. Pensioners and the unemployed would not benefit directly.

(e) Among other suggested measures to reduce poverty are:

(1) increasing benefits and pensions;
(2) increasing tax thresholds and lowering the standard rate of taxation;
(3) retraining, training and education;
(4) increasing employment by increasing demand and/or incentives.

(f) A reduction in poverty would benefit society in a number of ways. Demand and output are likely to rise. Tax revenue would rise and the need for government expenditure on social security and health care associated with illnesses related to poverty would fall. The education performance and future productivity of the children of previously poor families is likely to increase. The stock of housing would be better maintained and the circle of poverty could be broken.

12.4 Objective questions

Example 12.3

Normal profit is:
A the positive difference between total revenue and total cost
B the level of profit earned where marginal cost equals marginal revenue
C the average level of profit made by the firms in the industry
D the level of profit necessary to keep the firms in the industry in the long run.

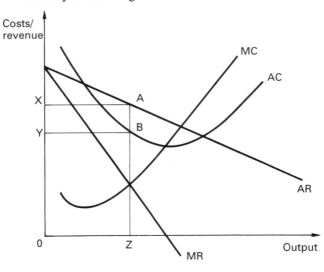

Example 12.4

The diagram at the foot of the previous column shows a firm producing under conditions of monopoly. 0YBZ contains:

A supernormal profit   B normal profit
C economic rent   D quasi-economic rent?

Example 12.5

An acre of land could receive a yearly rental of £5000 in its least remunerative occupation. It is currently earning £7600 in its present use. Which of the following statements is correct?
A Transfer earnings are £2600
B Economic rent is £2600
C Economic rent is £5000
D Economic rent cannot be determined from the information given.

Example 12.6

The following diagram shows the demand for and supply of a group of workers.

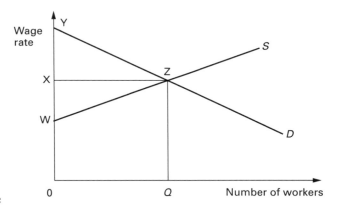

If 0Q workers are employed, what are the total transfer earnings received by the labour force?
A 0WZQ   B WXZ   C XYZ   D 0XZQ

Example 12.7

Which of the following is an example of quasi-rent?
A Normal profits earned under conditions of perfect competition
B Supernormal profits earned under conditions of perfect competition
C Normal profits earned under conditions of monopoly
D Monopoly profits

Example 12.8

If the market rate of interest is 12%, what will a bond paying £18 interest sell for now?

A £88   **B** £112   **C** £150   **D** £168

Example 12.9

The liquidity trap is said to occur when:

A a change in the rate of interest has no effect on the price of bonds
B a change in the price of bonds has no effect on the rate of interest
C demand for money becomes perfectly elastic as people expect the rate of interest to rise in the future
D demand for money becomes perfectly inelastic at high rates of interest as people expect the rate of interest to fall in the future.

Example 12.10

	Year 1	Year 2
Hourly wage rate	£6	£11
Price index	120	150

The above table shows that between years 1 and 2 the hourly wage rate in real terms changed by approximately:

A 126%   **B** 83%   **C** 47%   **D** $33\frac{1}{3}$%

Example 12.11

Demand for a factor of production will be more elastic:

A the less elastic the demand for the final product
B the greater the level of employment of factors in the economy
C the greater the ease with which the factor input can be substituted by other inputs
D the lower the proportion of the cost of the factor in the total cost of production

Example 12.12

A firm operating under conditions of perfect competition in both the labour and product markets is faced with the following output schedule:

Number of workers	Total output
2	560
3	640
4	740
5	810
6	850

The price of the product is £4 and the wage rate is £280. How many workers should the firm employ to maximise profits?

A 3   **B** 4   **C** 5   **D** 6

12.5 Solutions to objective questions

Solution 12.3   Answer: **D**

Normal profit is the supply price of entrepreneurship – i.e. the minimum that needs to be paid to entrepreneurs for them to supply their services and keep their firms in the industry. This can also be referred to as transfer earnings.

    A $\Rightarrow$ refers to supernormal profit.

    B $\Rightarrow$ A firm that produces where MC = MR is producing at the equilibrium output, and this may be where normal profits are earned. However it may also be where supernormal profits or losses are earned.

    C $\Rightarrow$ In the short run, under any market structure the average level of profit may be supernormal, normal or subnormal. In the long run, under conditions of perfect competition and monopolistic competition the average level of profit will be normal profit but under conditions of oliopoly and monopoly it may be supernormal profit.

Solution 12.4   Answer: **B**

0YBZ represents the cost of producing 0Z quantity. Normal profits are included in costs of production, so costs of production include the return to all the factors of production – i.e. wages, interest, rent and normal profit. In this case the firm is producing at the point where total revenue is greater than total cost, and hence it is earning more than normal profits. The area of supernormal profits is shown by YXAB.

Solution 12.5   Answer: **D**

If an acre of land can earn £5000 in its least remunerative occupation, the word 'least' implies that the land has more than two uses. Economic rent is a surplus above what can be earned in its next best paid occupation – i.e. above transfer earnings. In this case it is not known what can be earned in the next best paid occupation – just what can be earned in the least most profitable use. So it is not possible to calculate economic rent or transfer earnings.

Solution 12.6   Answer: **A**

Transfer earnings is the minimum that must be paid to keep a factor in its present occupation. It is shown by the area below the supply curve.

  B ⇒ WXZ represents economic rent.

  C ⇒ XYZ is consumer surplus.

  D ⇒ 0XZ*Q* represents total earnings, consisting of both economic rent and transfer earnings.

Solution 12.7   Answer: **B**

Quasi-rent is short-run economic rent. In the long run it is usually competed away by an increase in the supply of the factor concerned.

  Supernormal profits are a surplus over what is necessary to keep the firm in the industry. In perfect competition these will last only in the short run, since in the long run new firms will be attracted into the industry, which will lower price and return output to the normal profit level.

  A and **C** ⇒ Normal profits represent transfer earnings.

  D ⇒ Monopolists may produce at the point where AR > AC in the long run, and so in these cases supernormal (monopoly) profits may be regarded as economic rent.

Solution 12.8   Answer: **C**

If the market rate of interest is 12%, a bond paying £18 interest will sell for a figure that means that £18 is 12% of it:

$$\frac{18}{12} \times 100 = 150$$

The bond will sell for £150, earning £18 interest, i.e. 12% interest.

Solution 12.9   Answer: **C**

Keynes believed that, at a low interest rate, demand for money could become perfectly elastic. If the rate

of interest is very low (and hence the price of bonds is very high), everyone might expect that the price of bonds will fall and the rate of interest will rise in the future. They will hold any increase in the money supply, since they will not want to buy bonds now for fear of making a capital loss if and when their price falls.

Solution 12.10   Answer: **C**

To calculate rises in real income it is first necessary to remove the effects of price changes by use of a price deflator. In this case money wages rose to £11 when the price index increased from 120 to 150. Thus in year 2 the real wage changed to:

$$£11 \times \frac{\text{price index in base year}}{\text{price index in current year}} = £11 \times \frac{120}{150}$$

$$= £8.80$$

So in real terms the wage has risen by £2.80, which in percentage terms is:

$$\frac{2.80}{6.00} \times 100 = 47\%$$

Solution 12.11   Answer: **C**

Demand for a factor of production will be elastic when a rise in the price of the factor causes a greater percentage fall in demand for the factor. If a factor can be easily substituted by another factor, if it rises in cost the employer will switch to using more of the other factors.

  A, **B** and **D** ⇒ In each case demand will be inelastic and a rise in price of the factor would cause a smaller percentage fall in demand for the factor.

Solution 12.12   Answer: **C**

In theory, a firm will employ the number of workers where the wage rate equals the marginal revenue product of labour. To calculate MRP it is necessary to work out marginal product (change in total output as a result of employing one more workers) and multiply it by MR (which, under conditions of perfect competition, equals price). So in this case:

Number of workers	Total output	Marginal × product (£)	Marginal revenue	= MRP (£)
1	500			
2	560	60	4	240
3	640	80	4	320
4	740	100	4	400
5	810	70	4	280
6	850	40	4	160

Thus the wage rate of £280 equals MRP when five workers are employed.

12.6 Essays

Example 12.13

(a) What is meant by economic rent? **(10 marks)**

(b) Why do some economists argue that taxes should be imposed on economic rent? **(15 marks)**

- Define economic rent and give examples.
- Explain the main determinants of economic rent.
- Discuss the effect on resource allocation of a tax on economic rent.

Solution 12.13

(a) Economic rent can be earned by any factor of production. It is a surplus paid above the income needed to keep that factor in its present occupation.

For instance, a football player earning £6000 a week may have as his next best paid occupation bricklaying, for a wage of £300 a week. So the football player will be receiving an economic rent of £5700 and the opportunity cost of his present job will be the £300 (transfer earnings) he is forgoing as a result of being a professional sportsman. Similarly, an area of land that is used for industrial purposes may receive a rent of £1000 per week, whereas if it were to be used for residential purposes it might receive a rent of £800. So the land will be receiving an economic rent of £200. If a piece of machinery has no alternative use, then all of its earnings will be economic rent.

Indeed one of the main determinants of the economic rent a factor receives is that factor's elasticity of supply. If supply is perfectly inelastic, then all of the factor's earnings will constitute economic rent, whereas if the supply is perfectly

elastic no economic rent will be received and all of the earnings will represent transfer earnings. In practice, for most factors supply will be neither perfectly elastic nor perfectly inelastic. Figure 1 shows that in a case where supply is relatively elastic some of the payment received will represent economic rent, while the rest will represent transfer earnings.

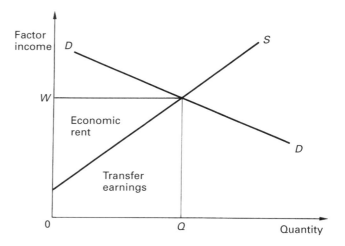

Figure 1

(b) It is sometimes suggested that a tax should be placed on economic rent, as it is a surplus. If some but not all of this surplus is taken by the government in tax, then the factors are unlikely to transfer to other uses. For instance, if a model is being paid £4000 per week when her next best paid occupation is as a shop assistant earning £170 per week, then taxing the economic rent of £3830 at 90% is unlikely to result in her giving up her modelling job.

Monopoly profits are a form of economic rent, and a tax on monopoly profits (provided that it is less than 100%) will not result in a change in the output or

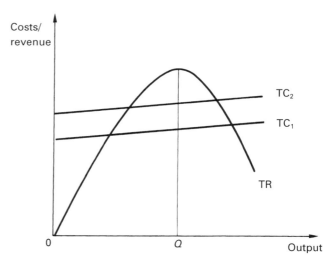

Figure 2

pricing policy of the monopolist. Figure 2 shows the total revenue and total cost curves of a monopolist. Prior to the imposition of a tax, maximum profits are earned at $0Q$ output. The imposition of a tax causes the total cost curve to shift from TC_1 to TC_2, but the maximum profit output remains at $0Q$. Some economists argue that at least part of monopoly profits should be taxed away on grounds of equity.

The economic rent on land can also be taxed without affecting the allocation of resources. If all land, irrespective of use, is taxed at the same rate, the relative profitability of different uses will be unaffected. As supply will be unaffected, prices will not change and the burden of the tax will fall entirely on landlords. In addition, some economists argue that the economic rent earned on land should be taxed, because a high return from land may result partially from public spending on the infrastructure.

However, in practice it is not always easy to identify economic rent, particularly as it may be difficult to ascertain what a factor's transfer earnings are. For instance, at any particular time few workers will know with certainty what employment they would be able to gain if they left their present jobs.

So economic rent is a payment in excess of transfer earnings that may be earned by any factor of production that is not in perfectly elastic supply. It has been suggested that economic rent could be taxed without affecting the allocation of resources, but in practice it can be difficult to isolate that part of a factor's payment which represents economic rent.

Example 12.14

(a) What determines the demand for money?
(15 marks)

(b) What effect will an increase in the supply of money have on the rate of interest? **(10 marks)**

- Explain what is meant by the demand for money.
- Cover the transactions, precautionary and speculative motives.
- Include diagrams.
- Bring out the difference between Keynesian and monetarist view points.

Solution 12.14

(a) The demand for money means the demand to hold wealth in the form of notes, coins and sight deposits rather than in the form of, for example, government

bonds, shares, antiques etc. It is referred to as liquidity preference.

There are thought to be three main reasons why economic agents hold their wealth in a money form. One is the transactions motive. People hold money in order to buy goods and services. Influences on how much they hold include income levels, price levels and how frequently they are paid. Another motive is the precautionary motive. This refers to money held to meet unexpected expenses and take advantage of unexpected bargains and opportunities.

It is thought that both the transactions and precautionary motives are interest inelastic as a change in the interest rate will not have a significant effect on the amount of money held.

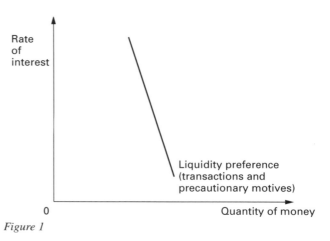

Figure 1

The speculative demand for money is much more sensitive to interest rate changes. This motive is concerned with money held, mainly by those who deal in financial markets, to take advantage of changes in the price of bonds. If the price of bonds is low and hence the rate of interest is high (since the price of bonds and the rate of interest move in opposite directions), people will wish to buy bonds. This is because they will expect the price of bonds to rise in the future, when they will make a capital gain, and because meanwhile they will be enjoying a high rate of interest. Figure 2 shows the speculative demand for money.

Some economists include a fourth motive. This is the assets motive, which sees money being held as one of a range of assets, including shares. The amount of each type of asset held will depend on the significance of their returns to the holder. Shares provide dividends, bonds provide interest and money liquidity.

The overall shape of the liquidity preference curve will depend on which motive is dominant. Keynesians

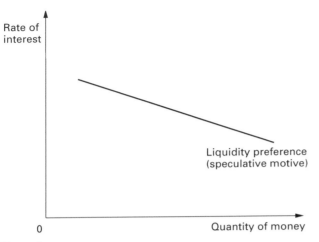

Figure 2

believe that the speculative motive is the most important one and so think that demand for money is interest elastic. In contrast monetarists believe that the transactions motive is the most dominant one and so demand for money is more interest inelastic. Figure 3 contrasts the Keynesian view (a) and the monetarist view (b).

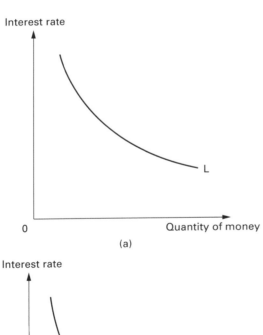

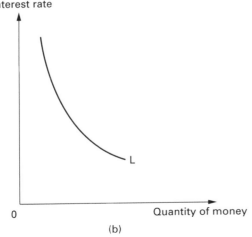

Figure 3

(b) An increase in the money supply will cause the money supply curve to shift to the right and the interest rate to fall.

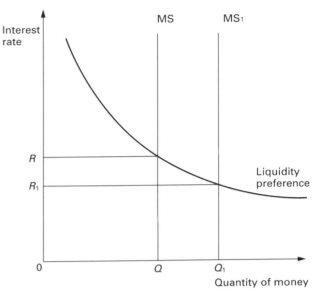

Figure 4

When the money supply increases, people will be holding more money than they desire. They will use at least some of their increase in money balances to buy bonds. This higher demand for bonds will increase the price of bonds and lower the interest rate. How much the interest rate falls will depend on the size of the change in the money supply and how elastic the demand for money is. As Keynesians believe that demand for money is more elastic than monetarists do, they think the fall will be smaller. Indeed at very low interest rates Keynesians believe that demand for money may

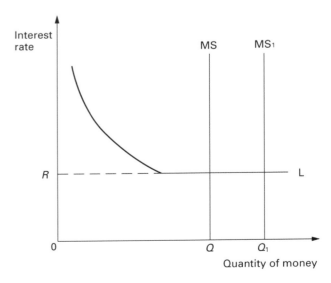

Figure 5

become completely interest elastic. In this case (often referred to as the liquidity trap) an increase in the money supply will have no effect on the demand for money.

When the interest rate is very low, and hence the price of bonds is very high, people may believe that the price of bonds will fall in the future and therefore will hold on to any extra money balances.

Market Failure

13.1 Fact sheet

(a) Optimal resource allocation

Economic systems have to choose between alternative allocations (uses) of land, labour and capital. *Welfare economics* provides a framework for deciding on the *optimal (best) use* of scarce resources. A particular resource allocation is assessed by using:

(1) *Efficiency criteria* (rules) first developed by Pareto, whereby the economy should have:
   (a) *Technical or productive efficiency.* This occurs when resources are fully employed and all firms are producing at minimum average cost. It is then impossible to increase the output of any one good without reducing the output of some other good.
   (b) *Consumption or allocative efficiency.* This occurs when it is impossible to redistribute products to increase the welfare of any one consumer without reducing the welfare of some other consumer.
(2) *Equity (fairness) criteria*, which judge the 'desirability' of a particular resource allocation.

- Using *Pareto criteria*, a reallocation of resources is desirable only if someone gains and no one loses.
- A *Pareto optimal allocation of resources* exists when no one can be made better off without someone else being made worse off, following a reorganisation of production or distribution.

- *Pareto efficiency criteria* cannot be used in resource decisions where someone gains and someone loses as this requires the use of equity criteria.
- Equity judgements can be made by using the *Kaldor–Hicks test*. A change in production or distribution is desirable only if those who gain can compensate those who lose, and still be better off. Note that compensation does not necessarily take place.

(b) Social costs and social benefits

Analysis of a resource allocation requires an accurate valuation of the true costs and benefits involved in economic activity, including *externalities*. Externalities are the spillover effects of production or consumption, for which no compensation is paid.

Externalities can be *positive* (e.g. beekeepers indirectly provide a source of pollination to market gardeners).

Social benefit = private benefit + positive
externalities
(benefit to the individual) +
(benefits to third parties)

Externalities can also be *negative* (e.g. pollution from a power station may damage the health of local residents).

Social cost = private cost + negative externalities
(cost to the individual) + (costs to
third parties)

Figures 13.1 and 13.2 show the effect of externalities on social cost and social benefit.

Where *social marginal cost* exceeds *private marginal cost* there is an *external marginal cost*.

Where *social marginal benefit* exceeds *private marginal benefit* there is an *external marginal benefit*.

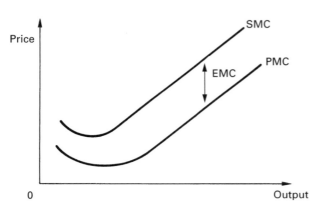

Figure 13.1 Social marginal cost

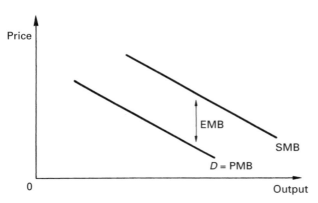

Figure 13.2 Social marginal benefit

(c)   Market failure

Market failure occurs when the price mechanism results in an inefficient allocation of resources.

An efficient allocation of resources occurs in a market where the opportunity cost of the extra unit (SMC) equals the value placed by society on its consumption (SMB) – i.e. where SMC = SMB.

(d)   Market failure through externalities

Figures 13.3 and 13.4 show market failure caused by negative and positive externalities.

In Figure 13.3, Q is the *socially efficient level of output* where SMC = SMB. Q_1 is supplied by the industry. The resulting *overproduction* results in a *welfare loss triangle* of ABC.

In Figure 13.4, Q is the socially efficient level of output where SMC = SMB. Only Q_1 is supplied by the industry. The resulting *underproduction* results in a welfare loss triangle of JKL.

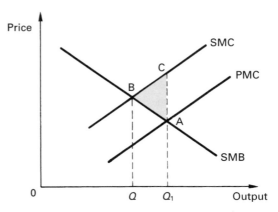

Figure 13.3 Negative externalities

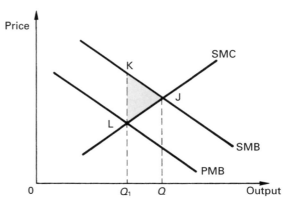

Figure 13.4 Positive externalities

(d)   Market failure through public goods, merit goods and demerit goods

- A *public good* is a product such as defence that is:
  - (a) non-rival – i.e. an individual's consumption of a public good does not reduce its benefit to others;
  - (b) non-excludable – i.e. once a public good is provided, others cannot be stopped from consuming it.
- The non-excludability of a public good encourages some consumers to avoid payment and become free riders.
- A *merit good* is a product that consumers may undervalue but the government believes is 'good' for consumers, e.g. education. Unlike public goods, merit goods can be bought and sold.

- A *demerit good* is a product that consumers may overvalue but the government believes may be harmful to consumers, e.g. alcohol.
- Market failure occurs because profit-maximising firms underproduce public and merit goods and overproduce demerit goods.

(e) Market failure through imperfect competition

Assuming no externalities, marginal cost (MC) equals social marginal cost (SMC) and price (P) accurately measures social marginal benefit (SMB). Figure 13.5 and Table 13.1 indicate that, unless a firm sets output at the point where the cost of making the last unit equals its price (marginal cost pricing), market failure results.

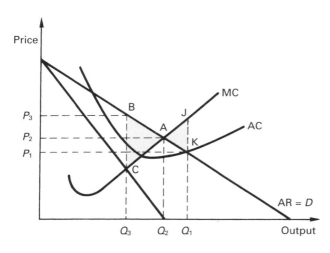

Figure 13.5 Alternative pricing policies in imperfect competition

- Nationalised industries generally use a marginal cost pricing policy. Following privatisation the same firm will underproduce if it uses a profit-maximisation pricing policy.

(f) Measures to correct market failure

There are a number of measures a government can take to correct market failure. These include:

(1) Regulating companies, e.g. requiring car companies to fit antipollution exhaust systems.
(2) Extending property rights so that, for example, people affected by air pollution can sue.
(3) Subsidising goods that create positive externalities.
(4) Taxing or banning demerit goods.
(5) Providing information about merit goods and demerit goods.
(6) Producing the goods itself or contracting private sector companies to produce the goods.
(7) Redistributing income by means of direct taxes and benefits.

(g) Cost–benefit analysis

Cost–benefit analysis (CBA) is a method of assessing the social costs and benefits of an investment project. This involves comparing the private costs and negative externalities of a scheme with its private benefits and positive externalities, using money as a measure of value. Problems involved in CBA occur because:

(1) Externalities are difficult to measure:
  (a) negative externalities are valued by calculating how much those who suffer need to be compensated;
  (b) positive externalities are valued by estimating the change in consumer surplus of those affected by the project.
(2) Future costs and benefits are difficult to measure. The present value (P) of future net social benefits (social benefits less social costs) is found by *discounting*. For example £500 lent for two years earning 10% interest per annum is worth: £500 (loan) + £50 interest (in year 1) + £55 interest (in year 2) = £605 (total). Therefore the PV of £605 in two years' time, discounted at 10% per annum, is £500.

- A scheme is worth undertaking only if the present value of net social benefits is positive.

Table 13.1 Consequences of pricing policies

Pricing policy	Condition		Price	Output	Result	Welfare loss
Average cost	P	$= AC$	P_1	Q_1	Overproduction	Triangle AJK
Profit maximisation	MC	$= MR$	P_3	Q_3	Overproduction	Triangle ABC
Marginal cost	P	$= MC$	P_2	Q_2	Efficient production	None

(h)   Green economics

Green economics, which can also be called *environmental economics*, is the study of environmental issues, including the depletion of non-renewable resources, the recycling of paper and other materials, and pollution.

*   *Green taxes* are taxes imposed with the objective of improving the environment.

13.2 Investigative study

Example 13.1

A cost–benefit analysis carried out on a local issue, e.g. assessing the costs and benefits of widening a local road.

13.3 Data response

Example 13.2

'It is a criminal offence to leave litter in any public place in the open air or to dump rubbish except in designated places. The maximum penalty was raised in 1992 to £2,500. The Act also introduced new duties on local authorities to keep their public land as free of litter and refuse (including dog faeces) as practicable and new powers for the public to take action against those who fail to comply with their responsibilities.

To help counteract the problem of litter, financial support – totalling £2.9 million in 1994–95 – is given to the Tidy Britain Group, which is recognised as the national agency for litter abatement. It provides a comprehensive litter abatement programme in collaboration with local authorities and the private sector. The Group secures sponsorship from industry to undertake litter abatement promotions and programmes such as its Neighbourhood Care Scheme.'

(*Britain 1995: An Official Handbook*, London: HMSO)

(a)   Explain why litter is a negative externality.

(4 marks)

(b)   Identify two other forms of pollution. **(2 marks)**

(c)   Discuss the ways in which the government seeks to reduce the problem of litter.   **(6 marks)**

(d)   Explain why the optimum level of pollution is not zero.   **(13 marks)**

Solution 13.2

(a) A negative externality is a cost on third parties resulting from the activity of others. A person who drops litter reduces the quality of the environment for others. Some forms of litter may, in addition, pose a health threat, e.g. broken bottles and dog faeces.

(b) There are a number of other forms of pollution, including water and noise.

(c) The extract mentions four government measures. One is fining those who leave litter in a public place or who dump it away from designated areas, e.g. council rubbish tips. It will also take legal action, including fining local authorities that fail to keep public places as litter-free as practically possible. It gives financial support to the Tidy Britain Group and runs anti-litter advertising campaigns.

In addition to these measures outlined in the extract, the government promotes the recycling of waste materials by requiring local authorities to make plans for the recycling of waste.

(d) Many people might think that the optimum level of pollution would be zero. However to achieve an entirely and permanently litter free environment would require the use of a vast number of resources. For instance, even in a small town 600 workers and 60 machines may be needed. Society would view the opportunity cost as too high as the quantity of other goods and services produced would have to fall to release the resources for eliminating pollution. Figure 1 illustrates the optimum level of pollution which is $0Q$.

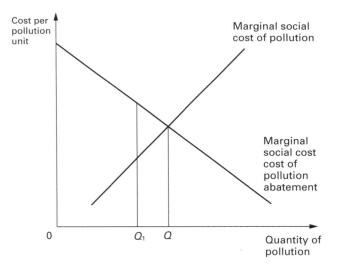

Figure 1

Reducing pollution to $0Q_1$ would involve a welfare loss. This is because the marginal social cost of reducing pollution would exceed the benefit people would receive. The resources that would have to be employed to reduce the quantity of pollution from $0Q$ to $0Q_1$, could be used to greater benefit producing other products.

13.4 Objective questions

Example 13.13

Market failure occurs when there is an imperfectly competitive market because:

A price exceeds marginal cost
B all firms are profit maximisers
C marginal cost exceeds marginal revenue
D firms overproduce merit goods and underproduce demerit goods

Example 13.4

The following data refer to a cost–benefit analysis of three possible investment projects

	Project J	Project K	Project L
Private benefits (£000s)	125	140	50
Private costs (£000s)	115	150	90
External benefits (£000s)	75	50	200
External costs (£000s)	100	10	150

It can be deduced that economic welfare would be improved by undertaking:

A project J only
B projects J and K
C projects K and L
D projects J, K and L

Example 13.5

The government decides to fit filters to reduce the amount of sulphur dioxide discharged into the atmosphere by power stations. To maximise net social benefit, the government should fit extra filters up to the point where:

A total social benefit is maximised
B marginal social benefit is maximised
C total social benefit minus total social cost is zero
D marginal social benefit minus marginal social cost is zero

Example 13.6

The private costs of a firm do not equal its social costs. All other things being equal, which one of the following government actions improves welfare?

A Tax the firm if social costs are less than its private costs
B Tax the firm if social costs are more than its private costs
C Subsidise the firm if social costs are more than its private costs
D Close the firm down if social benefits minus social costs are positive.

Example 13.7

The data below refer to a chemical factory that creates a spillover effect in the form of river pollution:

Output (units)	1	2	3	4	5	6
Average revenue (£)	14	12	10	8	6	2
Marginal private cost (£)	2	4	6	8	10	14
Marginal external cost (£)	2	3	4	5	6	8

Assuming no external benefits, the socially efficient level of output is:

A 2   B 3   C 4   D 5

Example 13.8

Goods that could be provided by the market mechanism, that have positive externalities and are often supplied by the government are known as:

A merit goods   B public goods
C Veblen goods   D inferior goods

Example 13.9

A government taxes a firm by an amount equivalent to the external costs it imposes on the rest of society by its productive activity. What will be the results?

A The firm will increase its output in order to cover its higher costs
B Production and resource allocation will not change
C The tax will increase the gap between the firm's social and private costs
D There will be an improvement in resource allocation as prices will move accurately to reflect costs and benefits.

Example 13.10

Which of the following comes closest to being a pure public good?

A Education   B Flood control
C Medical care   D Postal services

Example 13.11

The most common use of cost–benefit analysis has been for planning:

A the budget position
B public sector investment schemes
C the pricing policy of private sector firms
D the level of government

Example 13.12

Demerit goods are products that:

A create positive externalities
B can only be bought in a black market
C are likely to be overconsumed in a market economy
D involve no external costs in production or consumption

13.5 Solutions to objective questions

Solution 13.3   Answer: **A**

Market failure occurs when a free market economy fails to reach a Pareto optimal allocation of resources. If the price of a good exceeds its marginal cost, underproduction occurs. In the Figure below, the area BAC illustrates market failure from setting output below the point where marginal cost equals price.

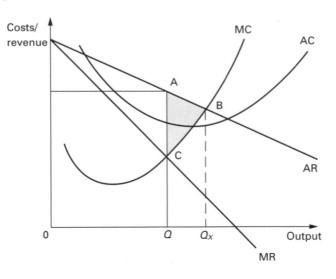

Solution 13.4   Answer: **C**

Adding together private and external benefits gives social benefits. Adding together private and external costs gives social costs. Subtracting social costs from social benefits gives net social benefits. If net social benefits are positive, general welfare can be increased by undertaking the project.

	Project J	Project K	Project L
Social benefit (£)	200	190	250
Social cost (£)	215	160	240
Net social benefit (£)	−15	30	10

Solution 13.5   Answer: **D**

Welfare is improved by fitting an extra filter, provided that the social benefit from the extra filter is greater than or equal to the social cost of installation.

   A and **B** ⇒ ignore the social costs of installation.

   C ⇒ The decision to install extra filters requires a marginal and not total method of analysis.

Solution 13.6   Answer: **B**

If a firm has costs that do not pass through the market (e.g. pollution), then the government should tax the enterprise so that the firm internalises the externality and incurs its true total costs.

   A ⇒ If social costs are less than private costs the firm's production must be providing external benefits to third parties. In this case the output of the firm should be encouraged.

   C ⇒ A subsidy would only encourage the firm to produce more, and hence increase negative externalities.

   D ⇒ Net social benefits are positive and therefore the firm should be allowed to carry on producing.

Solution 13.7   Answer: **B**

Adding together private marginal cost (PMC) and external marginal cost (EMC) gives social marginal cost (SMC). The price consumers are willing to pay for an extra unit of a good is given by average revenue (AR) – remember that average revenue always equals price. The socially efficient level of output occurs when SMC = AR. At output level 3,
SMC = PMC + EMC = 6 + 4 = 10 = AR.

Solution 13.8   Answer: **A**

Merit goods are goods that can be provided by the market mechanism but would be underproduced when left to market forces. This is because market forces only take into account private costs and benefits. The social benefit of merit goods exceeds the private benefit as merit goods have positive externalities.

B ⟹ Public goods are non-rival and non-excludable. They will not be provided by the market mechanism

C ⟹ Veblen goods are goods with 'snob value' and positive price elasticity of demand

D ⟹ Inferior goods are goods with negative income elasticity of demand

Solution 13.9   Answer: **D**

The tax will internalise the external costs and will mean that the firm will produce at the point where marginal revenue (reflecting marginal benefit) equals marginal social cost, since marginal social cost will now equal marginal private cost.

Solution 13.10   Answer: **B**

It is difficult, if not impossible, to make consumption of flood control dependent on prior payment. One person benefiting from flood control will also not reduce another person's benefit.

A and **C** ⟹ are examples of merit goods, which are rival and excludable products.

Solution 13.11   Answer: **B**

Cost–benefit analysis (CBA) is a method of evaluating investment projects to include all costs and benefits, i.e. social costs and benefits. It is usually used in the evaluation of public sector investment projects but there is no reason why it could not be applied to private sector schemes.

Solution 13.12   Answer: **C**

Demerit goods, such as cigarettes, harm consumers and impose costs on society in general, for example the cost of treating lung cancer caused by smoking. Demerit goods are consumed in quantities above that which is socially desirable.

A ⟹ Demerit goods create negative rather than positive externalities.

B ⟹ Some demerit goods, such as alcohol, are not illegal and are readily available in the market.

D ⟹ Demerit goods do create external costs in their consumption.

13.6 Essays

Example 13.13

A large chemical company decides to reduce its costs by discharging waste products into rivers and lakes.

(a)   Explain why such discharges may constitute a negative externality.   **(5 marks)**
(b)   On what grounds may the level of output of the chemical company be regarded as excessive?   **(10 marks)**
(c)   What government policy could be implemented to achieve a socially more efficient level of chemical production.   **(10 marks)**

• This question focuses on a particular example of market failure through negative externalities.
• Use social cost and benefit curves to illustrate the welfare loss of overproducing chemicals that cause negative externalities.
• Be careful to concentrate your analysis on the specific example of a chemical firm.

Solution 13.13

(a) An externality occurs whenever the production or consumption decision of an individual or firm directly affects others, other than through market prices. That is, an externality is a spillover effect from economic activity that affects third parties but for which no compensation is paid. The discharge of waste products into rivers and lakes is an example of a negative externality. The private cost to the firm of waste disposal is the cost of transportation. Society at large has to bear, without compensation by the firm, the external costs that arise from the resulting destruction of the environment, reduced leisure facilities and other inconveniences.

(b) The diagram illustrates the amount of welfare loss from the overproduction of chemicals.

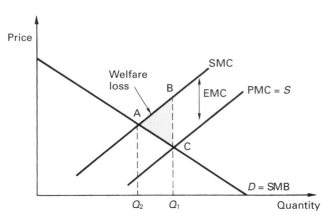

Figure 1

Assuming no positive externalities, the demand curve, *D*, shows the money value placed by society on the consumption of each extra unit of chemicals – i.e., social marginal benefit (SMB).

Assuming perfect competition, the industry's supply curve, *S*, is the addition of each firm's marginal cost curve. The private costs of producing each extra unit of chemicals is given by the private marginal cost curve (PMC). In a market economy, profit-maximising chemical firms ignore the wider social costs of their activity. If any one company were to incur the cost of treating its waste product it would become uncompetitive and unable to match the price of rivals. The interaction of supply and demand results in quantity *Q*1 being produced.

In the diagram, external marginal cost, EMC, is the amount consumers would be prepared to pay to avoid the pollution associated with the manufacture of extra units of chemicals. Adding EMC to PMC gives the social marginal cost, SMC, of producing extra units of chemicals. The socially efficient level of output occurs at Q_2. Profit-maximising firms produce Q_1. Chemical production at levels above Q_2 is excessive because social cost exceeds social benefit. Total loss from overproduction is given by the triangle ABC.

(c) The government can achieve a socially more efficient level of chemical production by imposing a specific tax equal to EMC at each level of output. Firms include the amount of the tax as a private cost and reduce their level of activity to the desired level of Q_2. However a socially efficient level of output is achieved only if the government is accurate in calculating the monetary cost to society of pollution.

Alternatively the government could introduce legislation banning the discharge of waste products into the environment. Firms would then have to include waste treatment as a private cost. However the PMC of chemicals, including treatment might then exceed SMC, excluding treatment, so legislation would only achieve a socially efficient level of production if combined with a subsidy to chemical firms.

Finally, the government may consider a policy of banning chemical production altogether. This would result in a loss of welfare. Even after taking into account the pollution chemicals cause, consumers still value extra units up to Q_2, more than the social cost of manufacture. Government policy would be more successful if a quota restricting output to Q_2 were introduced.

Example 13.14

How do public sector investment decisions differ from private sector investment decisions? **(25 marks)**

- Use either the discounted cash flow or internal rate of return method to explain investment decisions.
- Private firms only calculate private costs and benefits. Public bodies include private and social costs and benefits in a cost–benefit analysis of investment decisions.
- The bulk of the essay should consider the difficulties involved in such a cost–benefit analysis.

Solution 13.14

Profit-maximising private firms only take into account the effect on their own costs and revenues of buying capital. The spillover effects of investment are of no concern. Social-welfare-maximising public agencies, on the other hand, take full account of the social implications of buying capital. Public bodies have to include in their investment calculations any indirect effects on third parties.

The calculation of private costs is a relatively simple matter for the private firm. The cost of the machine can be found in a catalogue. There may be an element of uncertainty in estimating the probable net yield from the project in times of inflation or changing market conditions, but usually the firm can predict future private benefits. The business then buys new plant or machinery, provided that the return on the investment exceeds its cost.

Public bodies have to undertake a more detailed and involved cost–benefit analysis. For instance a local authority considering building a bypass around a town has first to identify and then value the likely social costs and benefits that arise in each year of the project. Private costs and benefits from building the bypass are included at their market price. However, if market prices are distorted and do not accurately reflect true opportunity cost, alternative 'shadow' prices will have to be calculated.

Money is also used as a unit of account for valuing external costs and benefits. For instance the bypass is likely to benefit motorists by reducing travel time. Multiplying the number of minutes saved by the average wage rate gives an estimated value of the resulting social benefit. If the scheme reduces the number of road accidents, reduced expenditure on medical treatment is included in the calculations. The benefit the bypass brings to new travellers is another positive externality, which is included by estimating the increase in consumer surplus.

The wages of anyone unemployed before working on the bridge should not be included as a social cost, because they would not otherwise have produced anything. On the other hand a monetary value is placed on the loss of landscape. If noise from the bypass affects local residents, a sum is deducted in the cost–benefit analysis that represents that damage. The authority must be particularly careful not to include irrelevant changes. For example reduced travel time may increase the value of local houses but this is not a true benefit of the scheme.

All investment decisions have to calculate the present value of future net benefits. Benefits received in the future are worth less than the same benefit received now. Firms resolve this problem by discounting future benefits at a given rate of interest. For example, at an interest rate of 10% per annum, £550 in one year's time is worth only £500 now. Private firms use the current market rate of interest in their calculations. Public bodies have to calculate a social rate of discount that states the true opportunity cost of future benefits.

Finally, private investment decisions typically involve schemes with only a short life. Machines are expected to last only a few years before being replaced by an improved model. Public projects have a lifespan measured in decades. Estimates of future supply and demand patterns, and demographic trends over a period of 20 years, make public sector investment decision peculiarly difficult and complex.

Labour markets

14.1 Fact sheet

(a)   Population structure

Demography is the study of population. Population size is a *stock value* (an amount at a given moment in time). Population size is affected by inflows (births and immigration) and outflows (deaths and emigration) over time.

- The *birth rate* is the number of live births per thousand of the population in a year.
- The *death rate* is the number of deaths per thousand of the population in a year.
- The *natural change* in population is the difference between the number of births and deaths in a year.
- *Net migration* is the difference between immigration and emigration in a year.

- The *activity (or participation) rate* is the percentage of the population of working age in the labour force.
- An *ageing population* occurs when the average age of the population is rising.
- *Malthus* argued that, since population has a tendency to grow geometrically (i.e. as the series 1, 2, 4, 8, 16) while agricultural output rises arithmetically (i.e. as the series 1, 2, 3, 4, 5), economies may eventually operate at a subsistence level. Unless people raise small families, famine, war and disease would be the only checks on population growth.
- Agricultural innovations, international trade and a low birth rate have enabled the UK to avoid Malthus's prediction.
- *Optimum population* occurs when productivity (output per person) is highest.

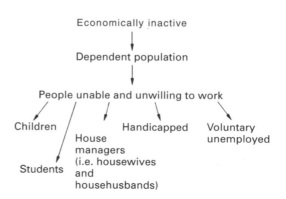

Figure 14.1 Economic activity and inactivity

- *Population pyramids* show the age and gender distribution of a country at a particular moment in time.

(b) Supply of labour

The total supply of labour depends on:

(1) the size and age structure of the population;
(2) the activity rate;
(3) social acceptance of women working;
(4) wage levels;
(5) the level of income tax and of the job seekers' allowance;
(6) the length of the working week and of holidays;
(7) industrial relations record.

(c) Demand for labour

The total demand for labour depends on:

(1) the level of economic activity;
(2) the productivity of labour;
(3) wage levels;
(4) productivity and price of substitute and complementary factors of production.

- *Elasticity of demand* for labour measures the responsiveness of demand for labour to changes in the wage rate. Demand for labour is elastic when:
  (a) demand for the finished product is elastic;
  (b) labour costs form a high proportion of total costs;
  (c) labour can be easily substituted by other factors of production;
  (d) the time period is long.

(d) Occupational distribution of labour

Table 14.1 shows that there has been a relative decline in the share of agricultural and manufacturing employment in total employment. The service sector of the economy has expanded.

Table 14.1 Distribution of employment in the UK (%)

	1964	1984	1994
Primary sector	5	3	1
Secondary sector	47	32	28
Tertiary sector	48	65	71

(e) Wage differentials

Wage differentials are the difference in wages between workers in different occupations, age groups, industrials, areas etc. Wage differentials arise through:

(1) *occupational immobility* due to non-monetary advantages and disadvantages of jobs;
(2) occupational immobility because of age, physical skills and qualifications;
(3) *geographical immobility* due to family ties, housing shortages etc.;
(4) *economic rent* arising from high demand for special talents;
(5) differences in the strengths of trade unions and professional organisations;
(6) social convention and public opinion influencing wage claims and settlements.

14.2 Investigative study

Example 14.1

A study of the extent and causes of differences in the amount paid to students undertaking part-time jobs.

14.3 Data response

Example 14.2

Real gross weekly earnings by selected occupation

Great Britain	£ per week at April 1994 prices	
	1981	1994
Cleaner	169	180
Bricklayer	225	252
Medical Practitioner	550	746
Nurse	188	316
Secondary Teacher	314	427
Solicitor	367	569

Source: Adapted from CSO Social Trends 1995

(a) Explain what is meant by real gross weekly earnings **(2 marks)**
(b) Calculate and comment on the percentage increase in earnings experienced by the three occupations shown. **(7 marks)**
(c) Give three reasons why cleaners receive relatively low pay. **(6 marks)**
(d) Give three reasons why medical practitioners receive relatively high pay. **(6 marks)**
(e) Given the size of the wage differential why do bricklayers not become solicitors? **(4 marks)**

Solution 14.2

(a) Real gross weekly earnings is the pay a worker receives inclusive of overtime and bonus payments and adjusted for inflation. In this case earnings have been adjusted to April 1994 prices.

(b)

Occupation	%Δ real gross weekly earnings 1981–94
Cleaner	6.5
Bricklayer	12.0
Medical practitioner	35.6
Nurse	68.1
Secondary teacher	36.0
Solicitor	55.0

All the occupational groups received an increase in real gross weekly earnings but at markedly different rates. The earnings of cleaners and bricklayers rose relatively slowly. It was nurses and solicitors who experienced the most rapid rise in earnings. Nurses have been required to carry out more highly skilled tasks and the qualifications necessary to become a nurse have risen. There are now a number of graduate entrants to the nursing profession. There is also a high proportion of male nurses now than in the 1980s and this has tended to raise the status of nursing as a profession. Increased recourse to law, both criminal and civil, and the increase in fees that can be charged for the services of solicitors, has increased the marginal revenue product of solicitors.

(c) Cleaners receive low pay because their supply is relatively high. It takes no or few qualifications to become a cleaner. Demand is relatively low and elastic, as with improved cleaning machines fewer cleaners are needed. They can also be replaced easily by currently unemployed workers. Cleaners are not highly unionised and many are part-timers.

(d) Medical practitioners are highly paid because they are in short supply and high demand. It takes a high level of education and training to become a doctor. It is also difficult to replace a doctor by machinery. Doctors belong to a powerful professional body, the British Medical Association (BMA), and are held in high social esteem.

(e) Bricklayers do not become solicitors, primarily because they lack the necessary qualifications. This lack of qualifications acts as a barrier to the market for solicitors. Some bricklayers may have the ability to become solicitors but may not seek to enter the labour market for solicitors because they are unaware of the pay and conditions of solicitors or because they believe that the non-monetary advantages of being a bricklayer, e.g. working outside, exceed those of being a solicitor.

14.4 Objective questions

Example 14.3

Optimum population occurs when, with current resources:
A   productivity is rising
B   productivity is constant
C   productivity is highest
D   the largest population possible is supported

Example 14.4

An ageing population will be most likely to result in:
A   an increase in labour mobility
B   a reduction in transfer payments
C   a constant pattern of consumption
D   increase in the dependent population

Example 14.5

Which of the following factors will increase the average age of the population?
A   A rise in the birth rate
B   A rise in net immigration
C   A decline in the death rate
D   A decline in the infant mortality rate

Example 14.6

Which of the following may cause an increase in the labour force in the short run and a decline in the long run?
A   Net emigration
B   A fall in the birth rate
C   A fall in the retirement age
D   A fall in the school leaving age

Example 14.7

The next diagram shows the offer curve (S) for labour:

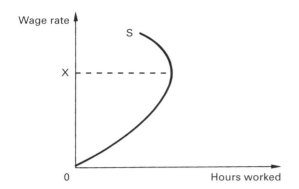

Beyond point 0X:

A the wage rate rises more rapidly

B workers substitute work for leisure

C workers are unresponsive to changes in the wage rate

D the income effect of a rise in wages is greater than the substitution effect

For Examples 14.8–14.10 use the diagram below, where DD is the original demand curve for bricklayers and SS the original supply curve. S is the initial equilibrium position.

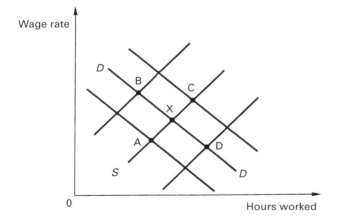

Example 14.8

An increase in the productivity of bricklayers.

Example 14.9

A reduction in the apprenticeship period for bricklayers.

Example 14.10

A significant increase in interest rates.

Example 14.11

As an economy develops, the proportion of the labour force in which sector (*S*) usually declines?

A Primary

B Primary and secondary

C Primary and tertiary

D Secondary and tertiary

Example 14.12

Which of the following will increase occupational wage differentials?

A A reduction in labour mobility

B A decline in labour market discrimination

C An increase in information about job opportunities

D A decline in the differences in non-monetary advantages between jobs.

14.5 Solutions to objective questions

Solution 14.3   Answer: **C**

Optimum population occurs when productivity (output per person) from a given amount of resources is highest.

Solution 14.4   Answer: **D**

An ageing population is likely to cause an increase in the number of retired people. People who have retired are economically inactive and are classified as dependents.

　A ⇒ As people get older they tend to become less occupationally and geographically mobile.

　B ⇒ More pensions will increase transfer payments as more pensions will be paid.

　C ⇒ There will be an increase in demand for products required by the elderly, e.g. bungalows.

Solution 14.5   Answer: **C**

A decline in the death rate will mean that people are living longer, which will increase the average age of the population.

　A and **D** ⇒ will increase the number of very young children and will lower the average age of the population.

　B ⇒ This will tend to lower the average age as most immigrants are relatively young, aged between 20 and 40.

Solution 14.6   Answer: **B**

A fall in the birth rate will reduce the number who leave the labour force to raise children. However in the long run a fall in the birth rate will result in fewer people entering the labour force.

A and **C** $\Rightarrow$ would decrease the labour force – net emigration for as long as it continues as most emigrants are aged between 20 and 40 – and a fall in the retirement age for as long as the legislation remains in place.

D $\Rightarrow$ would increase the labour force as people will become potential workers earlier.

Solution 14.7   Answer: **D**

Up to point 0X a rise in wages would cause an expansion in the supply of labour. Workers respond to higher wages by substituting work for leisure. However after point 0X workers would work fewer hours, as with higher incomes they would choose to 'buy' more leisure.

Solution 14.8   Answer: **C**

An increase in productivity raises the marginal revenue product of bricklayers, which, in turn, increases the demand for their labour. The demand curve for bricklayers shifts to the right.

Solution 14.9   Answer: **D**

A reduction in the apprenticeship period means that more people are likely to be willing to become bricklayers and these people will become bricklayers more quickly. The supply of bricklayers will increase.

Solution 14.10   Answer: **A**

An increase in interest rates reduces aggregate demand and increases the cost of mortgages. A consequent decrease in the demand for houses reduces the derived demand for workers involved in construction, such as bricklayers.

Solution 14.11   Answer: **B**

As an economy develops, the proportion of the labour force employed in the primary and secondary sectors tends to decline whilst the proportion employed in the tertiary sector increases.

Solution 14.12   Answer: **A**

A decline in labour mobility will mean that differences in wages for different jobs are likely to increase as workers become less able to move from low-paying jobs to high-paying jobs.

B, **C** and **D** $\Rightarrow$ will reduce occupational differentials.

14.6 Essays

Example 14.13

Why are pilots paid more than shop assistants?

- Make use of marginal revenue productivity theory and demand and supply analysis.
- Avoid value judgements.

Solution 14.13

The wage rate operating in any particular labour market is influenced by the demand for labour, the supply of labour, the activities of trade unions and professional bodies, government policy and social convention.

Wages will be higher in occupations where demand for labour is high and supply is low, and where demand and supply are inelastic.

Demand for labour is a derived demand. Marginal revenue productivity (MRP) is concerned with the demand for labour. The higher the price (and hence MR) that can be obtained for the output of labour and the greater the output (marginal physical product) that labour can produce, the higher the wage rate that will be earned. Pilots have a high MRP. The price that can be charged for air travel is relatively high and pilots can fly planes that carry a large number of passengers. Demand for pilots is also inelastic as it is not possible to provide air travel without pilots.

In contrast, demand for shop assistants is relatively elastic. Reorganisation of shops and the introduction of new technology means that shop owners may have the opportunity to reduce quite significantly the number of shop assistants if their wage rises. Shop assistants may work hard but the products they sell do not always command a high price and their MRP tends to be low.

The supply of shop assistants is also high and elastic because it is a job that requires few qualifications and little training, whereas the supply of pilots is lower and more inelastic. To become a pilot a person needs to have both relatively high academic qualifications and good health. This limits the number of people who can become pilots.

Figure 1 shows the demand and supply of pilots (a) and the demand and supply of shop assistants (b).

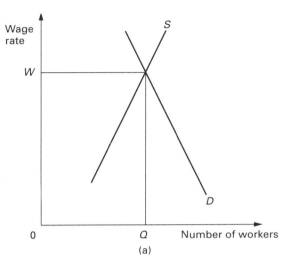

(a)

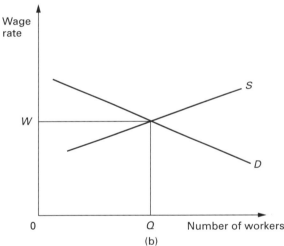

(b)

Figure 1

The British Air Line Pilots Association is a powerful trade union. It supports limited entry into the profession by requiring artificially high qualifications. This has the effect of reducing supply and thereby raising wages.

In contrast shop assistants have weak bargaining power. The union that represents shop assistants is USDAW (The Union of Shop, Distributive and Allied Workers). However not all shop assistants are in the union and those who are, are widely dispersed throughout the country and employed by different employers. They are therefore difficult to get together and organise.

A variety of government policies have contributed to high wages for pilots. For instance deregulation has

increased the number of airlines that can operate on routes. This has increased the demand for pilots, whereas the requirement for health checks has reduced the supply of pilots. Social convention also favours pilots. Most are white, middle-class men, and society tends to value work undertaken by this group more highly than that done by working-class women. Most shop assistants are in fact women. Views on the value of different jobs will influence the wage claims workers advance and the offers employers make.

Example 14.14

(a) Explain what is meant by the elasticity of demand for labour. **(4 marks)**

(b) What may cause the demand for bank clerks to become more elastic? **(14 marks)**

(c) What effect would an increase in the elasticity of demand for bank clerks have on the power of any trade union representing them to raise their wage rate? **(17 marks)**

- Give the formula for elasticity of demand for labour.
- Explain elastic demand for labour.
- Bring out the main determinants of elasticity of demand for labour.
- Although given below, it is not necessary to know the name of the union representing bank clerks.
- Consider more than one way of raising the wage rate.

Solution 14.14

(a) Elasticity of demand for labour measures the responsiveness of demand for labour to a change in the wage rate. The formula is:

$$\frac{\text{\% change in quantity of labour demanded}}{\text{\% change in wage rate}}$$

Demand for labour is elastic when a given change in the wage rate, e.g. a 10% rise, causes a greater percentage change in demand for labour, e.g. a fall of 12% (giving an elasticity of 1.2).

(b) A number of factors could cause demand for bank clerks to become more elastic. If the required period of training is shortened, demand will become more elastic. This is because if the existing trained workers press for a wage rise, their employers will be more willing to make them redundant as it will take less time to train new workers. Employers will also ʳ easier to attract new staff in periods of high unemployment and will find it cheaper when the costs of recruiting new staff (e.g. advertising, interviewing time) fall.

A rise in the wage rate will have a more significant impact if it becomes easier to substitute capital for labour or if the relative prices of capital and labour change to favour capital. This has been a significant factor in the case of bank clerks. The introduction of modern technology, including the electronic transfer of funds, has considerably reduced the demand for bank clerks.

A related influence is the proportion of labour costs in total costs. The greater the proportion the more significant any wage rise would be on firms' total costs, and so the more elastic demand will be. Whether the cost of labour in banks' total costs increases or falls will depend not just on the number of workers and machines employed but also on their relative costs.

Over time, with increasing competition in the financial sector, the demand for bank services may become more price elastic. Consumers may be more willing and able to switch away from those banks that charge relatively high interest rates on loans and pay relatively low interest rates on saving deposits. This will mean that banks will have to keep their costs low

and will become more reluctant to see their total wage bill rise.

The longer the time period under consideration the more elastic demand will be, as it will be possible to reorganise production to make less use of labour and more of other factors of production if wages rise. There will also be time to give workers legally adequate periods of notice.

(c) The main union representing bank clerks is the Banking Insurance and Finance Union (BIFU). An increase in the elasticity of demand for bank clerks would make it more difficult for BIFU to push the wage rate above the equilibrium level. Figure 1 shows that when demand is elastic this action will cause a greater fall in employment than when demand is inelastic.

A union is unlikely to be prepared to accept a large fall in the employment of its members. However the increase in elasticity of demand does not prevent the union employing other approaches to raise wages. It may support measures to raise the marginal revenue productivity of bank clerks. Indeed bank clerks do, on occasion, appear in television advertisements to promote banking services. The BIFU can also support measures to restrict the supply of bank clerks, e.g. by pressing for an increase in the qualifications or training needed.

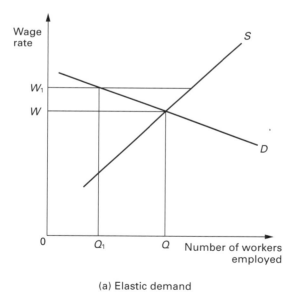

(a) Elastic demand

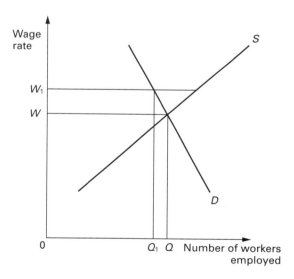

(b) Inelastic demand

Figure 1

Labour Market Failure

15.1 Fact sheet

(a) Definition

Labour market failure occurs when labour markets fail to clear at the going wage rates, when wage rates are distorted and when the most efficient use of labour resources is not achieved.

The main causes of labour market failure are immobility of labour, discrimination, concentrated market power in the buying and selling of labour and lack of information.

(b) Immobility of labour

There are a number of barriers to the movement of workers and these may cause shortages of workers in certain jobs, industries and areas, but surpluses in others.

- Workers may be prevented from changing jobs (*occupational immobility of labour*), e.g. due to:
  (a) unwillingness, lack of opportunity or inability to retrain;
  (b) employment barriers placed by unions and professional bodies.
- Workers may experience difficulty in moving between jobs requiring the same skills (*industrial immobility*). Workers in declining industries tend to be industrially immobile.
- Workers may be prevented from moving to different regions (*geographical immobility*), e.g. due to:

(a) regional variations in house prices;
(b) lack of rented accommodation;
(c) existing family and social ties.

(c) Discrimination

Discrimination arises when one group of workers is treated differently from others in terms of wages paid, and employment and promotion opportunities. Discrimination may be on the basis of:

(1) gender
(2) ethnicity
(3) sexual orientation
(4) social background
(5) age
(6) height
(7) appearance

- *Negative discrimination* will result in a group having lower pay and lower employment and promotion opportunities than other groups. Figure 15.1 shows the effects of demand for black workers being below the MRP. The wage rate ($0W$) and the number employed ($0L$) are below the efficient levels of $0W_X$ and $0L_X$.

(d) Concentrated market power

- A *monopoly trade union* may cause unemployment by using its bargaining power to push the wage rate above the market equilibrium

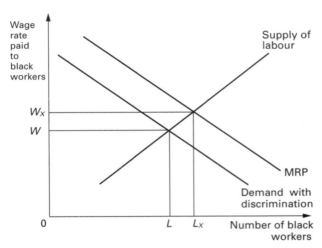

Figure 15.1 The effects of discrimination

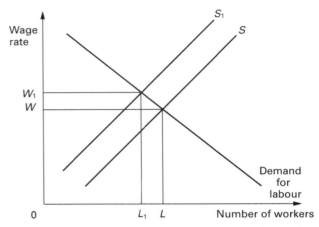

Figure 15.3 The effect of union action in restricting the supply of labour

level. This is shown in Figure 15.2, where union action raises the wage rate to $0W$ but lowers the number of workers employed to $0L_1$. A monopoly trade union may also seek to raise the wage rate by restricting the supply of labour, e.g. by insisting on artificially high qualifications (Figure 15.3).

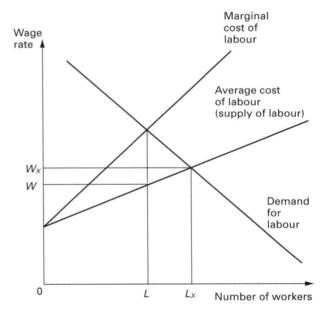

Figure 15.4 A monopsonist employer. With a monopsonist employer, wage rate = $0W$, number of workers employed = $0L$. In a competitive labour market wage rate = $0W_x$, number of workers employed = $0L_x$.

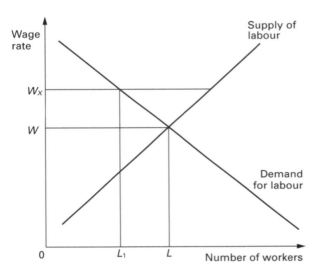

Figure 15.2 The effect of union action in raising the wage rate

- A monopsonist employer is a sole buyer of labour and one that is likely to pay a wage below the MRP and below that which would operate in a competitive labour market (Figure 15.4).

(e) Lack of information

Participants in labour markets do not have perfect knowledge. This often results in *suboptimal decisions* being made.

- Workers may not be in the best paid and most appropriate jobs because they lack information or have incorrect information about pay, promotion structure and working conditions in alternative jobs, industries and areas.
- Employers may not employ the most skilled workers at the most cost-effective wage rates because they lack information or have incorrect information about the number of people willing and able to work for them, the skills of potential workers, the cost and quality of training courses and the wage rates rival companies are paying.

(f) Government measures to correct labour market failure

These include:

(1) providing education and training to increase labour mobility;
(2) trade union reform;
(3) antidiscrimination legislation;
(4) provision of labour market information, e.g. through government training centres;
(5) *labour market reforms*, e.g. ending the legal monopoly of solicitors in the conveyancing of house property.

15.2 Investigative study

Example 15.1

An analysis of the extent of one form of discrimination in a local labour market.

15.3 Data response

Example 15.2

Year	Working days lost in industrial disputes (million)	Unemployment (%)	Trade union membership (million)
1988	1.64	8.4	10.4
1989	0.75	6.3	10.2
1990	1.10	5.8	9.9
1991	0.22	8.0	9.7
1992	0.09	9.8	9.2
1993	0.11	10.4	8.7

Sources: *Annual Abstract of Statistics*, 1994, *Social Trends*, 1995; *Monthly Digest of Statistics*, March 1995; *Employment Gazette*, March 1995.

(a) Comment on the relationship between unemployment and the number of working days lost in industrial disputes. **(8 marks)**
(b) What are the other two main measures of strike-proneness? **(2 marks)**
(c) Comment on the relationship between unemployment and trade union membership. **(8 marks)**
(d) Why do you think the number of trade unions declined in the 1980s and early 1990s? **(4 marks)**
(e) What is the TUC and what are its functions? **(3 marks)**

Solution 15.2

(a) Unemployment fell from 1988 to 1990 and then rose from 1990 to 1993. The number of days lost through strikes fell from 1988 to 1989, then rose in 1990, fell from 1990 to 1992 and then rose very slightly in 1993. This does not produce a consistent pattern and indeed the number of days lost due to industrial disputes fluctuates widely from year to year. Nevertheless this period does show that the number of days lost are highest in the period 1988 to 1990, when unemployment was falling, and lowest in the period 1990 to 1993, when unemployment was rising. Higher unemployment means that the number of workers declines, so there are fewer people to go on strike. It is also likely to make workers more wary of going on strike for fear of losing their jobs.

(b) The other two main measures of strike-proneness are the number of stoppages and the number of workers involved.

(c) As mentioned above, unemployment fell between 1988 to 1990 and then rose from 1990 to 1993. Trade union membership fell throughout the period. Indeed now only approximately 35% of the civilian labour force in employment belong to a trade union. One cause of the decline in union membership has been the relatively high levels of unemployment. However this is not the sole cause. As the data here shows, membership fell even when unemployment declined. Other causes include a decline in the strength of trade unions as a result of legislation passed by the government, a decline in the manufacturing and public service sectors (both of which have a higher than average membership) and a rise in part-time employment as fewer part-time workers join unions.

(d) The number of trade unions declined for two main reasons. One was the fall in membership of trade unions and the other was the mergers that occurred between trade unions. For instance the UK's largest union, UNISON, was formed in 1993 from a merger between the Confederation of Health Service Employees (COHSE), the National Union of Public Employees (NUPE) and the National and Local Government Officers' Association (NALGO).

(e) The Trade Union Congress is the national body of UK trade unions. It seeks to promote the interests of the trade unions that belong to it, to improve the economic and social conditions of working people and to campaign for higher employment and job security.

15.4 Objective questions

Examples 15.3 to 15.5 are based on the following diagram, which shows a monopsony employer in a labour market.

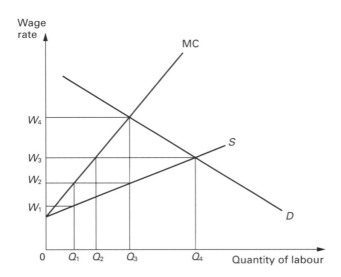

Example 15.3

What will be the number of workers hired by the monopsonist?

A Q_1 **B** Q_2 **C** Q_3 **D** Q_4

Example 15.4

What would be the level of employment if this labour market had been perfectly competitive?

A Q_1 **B** Q_2 **C** Q_3 **D** Q_4

Example 15.5

What will be the wage rate paid by the monopsonist?

A W_1 **B** W_2 **C** W_3 **D** W_4

Example 15.6

Which of the following would increase the ability of a trade union to increase the wages of its members without significantly affecting employment?

A A reduction in demand for the finished product

B A reduction in the national level of employment

C An increase in the cost of an alternative, automated manufacturing process

D An increase in the proportion of labour costs in total costs of production.

Example 15.7

If a government introduces equal pay legislation that raises the wages of women workers, what is the most likely outcome?

A A fall in the wages of male workers

B A decline in female participation in the labour force

C An expansion in the supply of women workers

D The replacement of male workers by women workers

Example 15.8

Under which of the following conditions would a labour market be described as oligopsonistic?

A There are many employers

B There is a single employer

C There are a few dominant employers

D There are an equal number of employers and employees

Example 15.9

The government raises the wages of teachers to encourage more people to train as teachers. The effect of this on the economic rent and transfer earnings of those already employed as teachers will be to:

	Economic rent:	*Transfer earnings:*
A	increase	leave unchanged
B	leave unchanged	increase
C	leave unchanged	leave unchanged
D	increase	increase

Example 15.10

It has been suggested that a cut in money wages would stimulate economic activity. However this may not occur if:

A the aggregate level of demand falls

B the fall in wages reduces firms' costs of production

C the lower prices increase spending by higher income groups

D the lower prices reduce the transactions demand for money and thereby reduce the rate of interest

Example 15.11

In a particular area workers can gain employment in one of two firms, X and Y. If firm X starts to discriminate, in terms of pay and employment opportunities, against women workers, what effect will this have on the wage rate paid to women workers by firm X and firm Y?

	Firm X:	Firm Y:
A	reduce	reduce
B	reduce	leave unchanged
C	leave unchanged	increase
D	reduce	increase

Example 15.12

If the entry qualifications to an occupation are reduced, what effect is this likely to have on the wage rate paid and the economic rent enjoyed by employees?

	Wage rate:	Economic rent:
A	increase	increase
B	increase	reduce
C	reduce	reduce
D	reduce	increase

15.5 Solutions to objective questions

Solution 15.3   Answer: **C**

A monopsonist is a sole purchaser of labour and will hire the number of workers where the demand for labour (based on marginal revenue product) equals the marginal cost of labour, i.e. at Q_3.

Solution 15.4   Answer: **D**

If the labour market had been perfectly competitive the employer would not have altered the wage rate when employing more workers. So the average cost of labour (the supply of labour) would have equalled the marginal cost of labour. The firm would have employed the number of workers where the average cost of labour (the supply of labour) equalled demand, i.e. Q_4.

Solution 15.5   Answer: **B**

As determined in Solution 15.3, the monopsonist will employ Q_3 number of workers. The wage rate is found

from the average cost of labour (supply curve). The marginal cost curve shows the change in the total cost of employing labour and not the wage rate paid. This is illustrated in the example below.

No. of workers	Wage rate (ACL)	Total cost of labour	Marginal cost
1	200	200	200
2	240	480	280
3	290	870	390
4	360	1440	570

Solution 15.6   Answer: **C**

A trade union will be in a stronger position to raise wages without significantly affecting the employment of its members if demand for the labour of its members is inelastic. If an alternative automated manufacturing process becomes more expensive, employers are unlikely to make many workers redundant following a wage rise, provided machinery remains relatively more expensive.

A, **B** and **D** ⟹ would all reduce the ability of the trade union to raise wages without causing a significant rise in unemployment among its members. If demand for the finished product is falling, fewer workers will be needed anyway. A reduction in the national level of employment would make it easier for employers to replace existing workers with previously unemployed workers, and if labour costs form a higher proportion of total production costs the demand for labour will become more elastic as any wage rise will have a significant effect on the costs and price of and demand for the finished product.

Solution 15.7   Answer: **C**

Higher pay for women will encourage more women to participate in the labour force, resulting in an expansion in the supply of women workers.

Solution 15.8   Answer: **C**

An oligopsonistic market is one in which there are a few dominant buyers. In the case of a labour market there will be a few dominant buyers of labour, i.e. a few dominant employers.

B ⟹ is a monopsonist.

Solution 15.9   Answer: **A**

People already employed as teachers will receive a wage rate that is above, or even well above, what is required to keep them working as teachers. Hence their economic rent will rise.

Transfer earnings are what workers can earn in their next paid jobs, and therefore the minimum necessary to keep them in their present job. Transfer earnings will be influenced by the rate of pay in alternative occupations.

Solution 15.10   Answer: **A**

If lower money wages reduce aggregate demand, then output and employment are likely to fall.

B, **C** and **D** ⇒ could all stimulate economic activity, *ceteris paribus*.

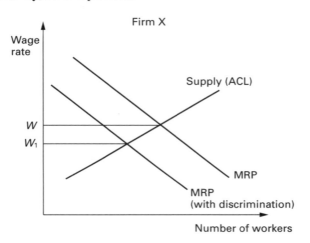

Solution 15.11   Answer: **A**

If firm X discriminates against women it will pay them a wage rate below the point where their true marginal revenue product equals the supply of

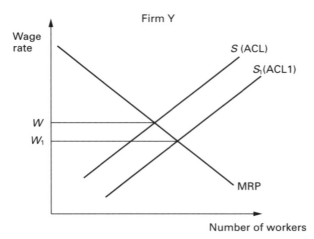

labour. The low wage will encourage women to seek employment with firm Y. The increase in the supply of women workers to firm Y will lower the wage rate. These effects are shown in the diagram at the bottom of the previous column.

Solution 15.12   Answer: **C**

If the entry qualifications to an occupation are reduced, the supply of potential workers will increase, which will lower the wage rate. Supply will also become more elastic, which will reduce economic rent.

15.6 Essays

Example 15.13

Assess the arguments for and against the introduction of a national minimum wage.   **(25 marks)**

- Explain how minimum wage legislation works.
- Concentrate on a minimum wage set above the existing level.
- Discuss the impact on wages and poverty.
- Discuss the impact on employment.

Example 15.13

The effects of introducing a national minimum wage will depend mainly on the level at which it is set and how workers and employers respond. The main motive is likely to be to reduce poverty, while the main argument against the introduction of a minimum wage is that it may result in a rise in unemployment.

If a minimum wage is set below the existing level, then there will be little or no effect. For instance, if an employer is paying a wage rate of £150 and legislation is introduced stating that workers have to be paid at least £180, it is unlikely that there will be a change in the wage paid to existing workers. However there is a possibility, particularly during times of high unemployment, that new workers may be recruited at lower wages, although existing workers are likely to resist any cut in money wages.

However it is more likely that the minimum wage will be set above the existing wage level in some industries. The introduction of a national minimum wage is sometimes urged as a measure to reduce income inequality and, in particular, poverty. A national minimum wage can be imposed to raise the wage level of the lowest-paid and possibly reduce the number of people who decide not to work, even though there are vacancies, because the wages they would receive are below the benefits they are currently receiving.

Another argument for setting a minimum wage is to protect workers in industries dominated by monopsonists. In the case of a monopsonist, the marginal cost of hiring additional labour (MCL) will be greater than the average cost of labour (wage per employee). Figure 1 shows that the employer initially equates the marginal cost of labour with his/her demand for labour (DL) and employs $0L_1$ amount of labour at wage of W_1. The establishment of a government minimum wage of W_2 (where DL equals the average cost of labour) raises both the wage rate and employment.

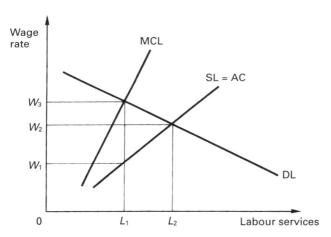

Figure 1

However in most industries a minimum wage set above the equilibrium level, while raising wages, is likely to result, at least in the short term, in the supply of workers exceeding the demand for workers and a fall in employment. Figure 2 shows the minimum wage (W_2) being set above the equilibrium wage (W_1). This causes a fall in employment from $0L_1$ to $0L_2$.

The groups of workers who are most likely to be made redundant or who are less likely to be taken on include the elderly, the disabled and the less skilled workers. These may be the very groups that a national minimum wage may be designed to help. Raising the wage rate will also increase the cost of training workers, which may result in higher unemployment among school leavers and in the longer term may lead to a shortage of skilled workers.

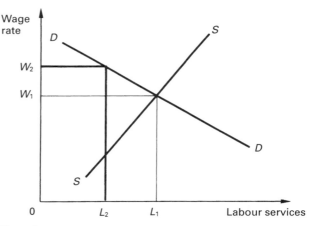

Figure 2

The extent to which unemployment will occur in different industries will depend on a number of factors. These include the profitability of the industry, the proportion of total costs accounted for by wages, the type of market structure and the elasticity of demand for the product.

Another influence will be the extent to which labour can be substituted. As labour becomes more expensive, there may be some substitution of capital for labour. The extent to which this occurs will depend on the nature of the product being produced, and the relative productivities and prices of the factors.

New classical economists believe that a government-imposed national minimum wage will interfere with free market forces and thereby reduce the efficiency of the labour market. This could result in a decrease in aggregate supply and a fall in output and employment.

However some Keynesians argue that if a national minimum wage is imposed, then demand for most industries' products will rise. So although costs will rise, the level of employment may remain constant or possibly rise.

Nevertheless the response of workers to the policy may result in a further rise in production costs, inflation and unemployment. Workers may press for wage rises to restore their wage differentials. If successful and if productivity does not rise, this will increase the costs of production and possible cost-push inflation. Rising prices may reduce domestic competitiveness, and hence domestic employment. If unsuccessful, the narrowing of wage differentials may reduce labour mobility and result in a shortage of skilled workers. The effectiveness of a national minimum wage in reducing poverty will be affected by the fact that a large number of poor people will not be helped by the legislation, including those past retirement age, the unemployed and some single parents.

Example 15.14

(a) Why may a worker stay in a less well paid job when there is a vacancy in a better paid job?

(15 marks)

(b) How may a government promote labour mobility? **(10 marks)**

- Discuss both monetary and non-monetary advantages and disadvantages of jobs.
- Mention some relevant labour market imperfections.
- Cover both occupational and geographical mobility.

Solution 15.14

(a) A worker may stay in a less well paid job because she believes its overall benefits outweigh those in other, albeit better paid, jobs, because she is unaware of suitable better paid vacancies or because she is unable to change jobs.

A less well paid job may be more attractive because it may offer better promotion chances, greater job security, better working hours and conditions, so a person may not be tempted by higher wages if the job on offer is, for example, dangerous, involves working unsocial hours or working in a noisy, unpleasant environment.

People do take into account both monetary and non-monetary advantages. However, in practice many jobs with pleasant working conditions and good promotion chances are well paid and those with unpleasant working conditions and poor promotion chances are badly paid. This is because the supply of workers for the less pleasant jobs is higher than those for pleasant jobs because fewer qualifications are needed.

Lack of qualifications, training or skills are significant reasons why a worker may be unable to transfer into better paid jobs. Many people might be attracted by the wages paid to barristers, but few have the necessary training and qualifications. A number of people would also like the pay and life style achieved by top film stars, but again few have the talent required. A person may also be too old, too young or lack a physical requirement to gain entry into the job. For example pilots need to have good eyesight! Another requirement may be the need to join a union

or professional organisation. In the UK people who wish to become actors first have to gain an equity card.

A person may have the qualifications and other requirements for a better paid job, indeed it may be the same occupation as she is currently working in, but she may be unable to take it because it is in a different part of the country. Geographical immobility arises mainly because of family ties and differences in the availability and cost of housing in different parts of the country.

For workers to be able to move easily from one job to another there would have to be perfect competition in the labour market. This obviously is not the case. Labour is not homogeneous. In practice there are a number of separate labour markets that have barriers to entry, including qualifications. Some of these labour markets are closer than others. For example it is easier for a teacher to become a civil servant than it is for a bricklayer to become a brain surgeon.

One example of labour market imperfection is imperfect knowledge – people may be unaware of job vacancies for which they are suitable.

(b) A government can seek to promote labour mobility in a number of ways. If successful this will mean that workers will find it easier to switch jobs and the labour market will become more flexible, allowing successful firms to expand and declining firms to contract.

One measure is to increase information about job vacancies. At present the government does this primarily through job centres.

The government can promote geographical mobility by giving grants to workers transferring from one part of the country, making it easier for people to change council and housing association accommodation and encouraging the development of the private rented sector. Improvements in infrastructure and social capital in depressed areas of the country may also make workers more prepared to move.

Occupational mobility can be improved by more and higher quality education and training and by removing unnecessary entry barriers to particular occupations. The government may itself provide this education and training, or it may encourage private sector provision of education and training, e.g. by giving tax incentives to firms that spend a given amount on training. The government may also remove artificial restrictions on entry to occupations, e.g. by breaking down the distinction between barristers and solicitors.

Key Markets

16.1 Fact sheet

(a) Education

- Education is a *merit good*, some people underestimate its private benefits and it confers benefits on third parties, e.g. higher output resulting from a better educated workforce.
- Education is both a *consumption* and an *investment good*. It both provides enjoyment and increases earning potential.
- The *opportunity cost* to society of providing higher education is the alternative uses to which the resources could have been put, e.g. health care.
- The opportunity cost to a student of attending higher education may include lost leisure time, lost earnings and lost opportunity to attend an alternative course.
- In 1991 the UK government introduced a student loans scheme.

(b) Health

- *Health care* is a merit good, some people underestimate its private benefits and it confers benefits on third parties, e.g. people will benefit from others being inoculated.
- Health care is both a consumption and an investment good. It improves the quality of people's lives and increases earning potential by reducing the number of days sickness and increasing average lifespan.

- The demand for health care exceeds supply. NHS treatment is rationed by means of waiting lists.
- Demand for health care treatment is increasingly due to:
  - (a) an increase in the average age of the population;
  - (b) advances in medical technology that enable more illnesses to be treated;
  - (c) a decline in willingness to put up with minor medical complaints.
- The 1990 National Health Service and Community Care Act introduced an internal market with fundholding GPs purchasing services from hospitals.
- In the UK the average life span is increasing by two years every decade.
- Half the men and two fifths of the women in the UK are overweight.
- The greatest cause of preventable death in the UK is smoking.

(c) Housing

- Housing used to be seen as both a consumption and an investment good. It provides accommodation and it used to rise in value by more than the rate of inflation. However the recent falls in house prices have resulted in housing being perceived more as a consumption good.
- *Negative equity* occurs when a house is worth less than the loan (mortgage) on it.

- The housing market is volatile due to:
  - (a) inelastic demand in the short run – no close substitutes and consumers respond slowly to house price changes as they take other costs into account, including estate agents' fees, solicitors' fees, removal expenses and the stress involved in moving;
  - (b) inelastic supply in the short run – it is difficult to adjust supply quickly;
  - (c) people take changes in house prices as indicators of future price changes.
- A fall in house prices:
  - (a) causes some building firms to go out of business;
  - (b) makes it difficult for people to sell their homes and so reduces labour mobility;
  - (c) reduces demand for consumer goods as the value of people's main asset falls and because, for example, curtains, washing machines etc. are often purchased when people move into a new home.
- The government promotes home ownership by:
  - (a) tax relief on mortgage interest payments – although this is being reduced;
  - (b) exemption from capital gains tax;
  - (c) sales of council houses to sitting tenants.
- Houses are provided by the private sector, housing associations and local authorities.
- There is a continuing rise in the number of dwellings occupied by one person.

(d) Transport

- Transport can be by air, rail, road or water.
- The main method of transport is by road.
- Road transport imposes a number of negative externalities including:
  - (a) air, noise and visual pollution;
  - (b) congestion;
  - (c) damage to buildings;
  - (d) accidents.
- Government action to reduce road transport may include:
  - (a) taxing road transport, e.g. petrol tax;
  - (b) subsidising rail transport;
  - (c) road pricing, e.g. tolls on motorways;
  - (d) providing information to the public about the relative costs and benefits of different forms of transport.
- In 1995 more than 80% of UK households had a car.

16.2 Investigative study

Example 16.1

An investigation into how the introduction of student loans for higher education has affected peoples' decisions to proceed on to higher education, their choice of course, their staying-on rates and the implications any changes have for society.

16.3 Data response

Example 16.2

Roads policy

Much of Britain's road system is snarled with congestion; so is government transport policy. Bolder men would risk the radical solution: to price, and then privatise, almost every road in the land

As road traffic grows, so do the indirect costs it inflicts on everyone, motorist and non-motorist alike. In London, for example, traffic congestion causes more air pollution today than existed before the Clean Air Act banned the burning of coal in 1956. Consumers pay for gas, electricity and water. Rail fares include a return on the capital costs of the track. It is difficult to see, at least in terms of economic rationality and equity, why drivers should not pay for road use if some way can be found to charge them for it.

Current transport policies, based on free access to roads, are unsustainable. At a time when the roads are becoming more and more congested and the railway's tiny share of the passenger and freight market continues to diminish, total public spending on transport is being cut. Official forecasts that road traffic will double over the next 30 years have produced a near-universal agreement that the supply of road space cannot be increased to meet demand. Even if annual spending on road building were raised by half, congestion would still get worse, according to a British Road Federation study published last year.

The most direct and efficient way to restrain traffic is by charging for the use of roads. It should be an attractive option for a government which believes in market forces. Yet ministers are approaching the introduction of road pricing as though it were a short cut to political suicide.

A three-year study of the feasibility of restraining traffic in London by road pricing is due to be published by the Department of Transport this spring. But even before the study's publication, ministers are backing away, claiming that the technical difficulties of introducing charging in such a large city with the technology currently available are insurmountable.

Source: Extract from *The Economist*, 1 April 1995.

(a) On what grounds can it be argued that UK road space is increasingly fitting into the category of a private rather than a public good? **(5 marks)**

(b) What is the current relationship between the demand for and supply of UK road space? **(4 marks)**

(c) Explain why increasing road space is unlikely to be a solution to road congestion. **(4 marks)**

(d) What difficulties would be involved in direct road pricing? **(6 marks)**

(e) Outline two other methods of reducing the demand for road space. **(4 marks)**

(f) Identify a negative externality caused by road use not mentioned in the extract. **(2 marks)**

Solution 16.2

(a) A private good is one that is rival and that non-payers can be excluded from enjoying. Increasing use of UK roads meant that one more car on the road will, in most cases, reduce the enjoyment of other drivers, e.g. by adding to congestion. It has always been possible to put tolls on roads but these can add to traffic delays. However advances in modern technology will make it increasingly easy to charge for the use of roads.

(b) Currently, demand for road use exceeds supply. With no price for the use of most roads, demand is greater than supply. Figure 1 shows the resulting shortage of QQ_X.

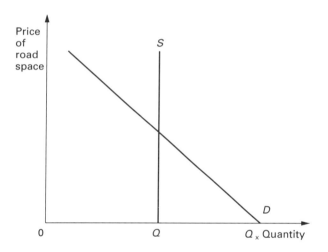

Figure 1

(c) Increasing road space involves an opportunity cost. With few open spaces this opportunity cost is increasing. There is also increasing evidence that building more roads, far from easing road congestion, actually generates more road use. The higher the quality and the more initial space on roads, the more people will be tempted to drive and the more each person is likely to drive.

(d) There are a number of potential problems with direct road pricing. The technology is still relatively expensive for most forms of direct road pricing. However it is developing quickly, including satellites to deduct charges via smart cards installed in cars. For some time relatively high-technology methods have been used to control the speed at which people drive, e.g. speed cameras, and now these methods are

being applied to the question of road pricing.

Imposing tolls or using some other form of road pricing on some roads only, e.g. motorways, may cause diversion of traffic away from these roads to other roads. If this is the case, overall congestion will not be reduced. This may mean that some form of charge may have to be made on most roads. Differential pricing could be used, with a higher price being charged for congested roads at peak times.

Road pricing may also be regressive, i.e. take up a higher proportion of the income of the poor. Many of the poor do not have a car, but those that do may live in areas that suffer from congestion and could be assisted to pay any extra costs by increased benefits.

(e) Demand for road space could be reduced by increasing fuel tax. This would increase the cost of using a car but would not discriminate between use on congested and uncongested roads. The government could also use direct regulation, limiting the use of vehicles at particular times or banning them from, for example, city centres.

(f) Road use imposes a number of costs on third parties, i.e. negative externalities. The extract mentions air pollution, but cars, lorries and buses also cause noise pollution, damage to buildings and accidents, and prevent children from playing in the streets.

16.4 Objective questions

Example 16.3

Investment in education is investment in:
A fixed capital
B human capital
C financial capital
D the primary sector

Example 16.4

A rise in house prices could be caused by an increase in the:
A rate of interest
B level of disposable income
C level of investment in new housing
D supply of trained building workers

Example 16.5

A government decides to replace a student grant system by a scheme of student loans that have to be repaid by the students from their future incomes. The most likely outcome is:

A an increase in government expenditure on higher education

B an increase in the number of students applying for higher education

C an increase in the private rate of return on investment in higher education

D a switch in demand by students towards job-related courses

Example 16.6

What is the most likely effect of a fall in mortgage interest rates on house prices and house building?

	House prices:	*House building:*
A	decrease	decrease
B	decrease	increase
C	increase	increase
D	increase	decrease

Example 16.7

A government decides to introduce an urban road tax. If this is set at the socially efficient level this will:

A maximise road use

B eliminate road congestion

C maximise government revenue

D reduce congestion to an optimal level

Example 16.8

Which of the following arguments provides support for a government policy of subsidising higher education?

A Higher education is a public good

B The social benefit of higher education exceeds the private benefit

C The provision of higher education helps to increase the size of the labour force

D Higher education helps to redistribute income as the poor participate in higher education to a greater extent than middle- and high-income groups

Example 16.9

In a cost–benefit analysis of a proposed motorway, which of the following is unlikely to be included among the prospective benefits?

A Reduced operating costs of public transport

B A saving in the time experienced by commuters

C A reduction in the running costs incurred by private motorists

D An increase in the quality of the environment near the motorway

Example 16.10

A government introduces a grant of £5000 for people wishing to buy a house costing less than £80 000. The effect of this will be to:

A benefit first-time borrowers only

B increase the demand for houses across the price range

C increase the demand for houses costing less than £80 000 only

D result in a reduction in the resources committed to house building

Example 16.11

If the government decides to provide free higher education to students, it follows that higher education:

A is available to all

B has no opportunity cost

C cannot be provided by the private sector

D is likely to be allocated by some form of direct rationing

Example 16.12

Which of the following is an external benefit of rail transport?

A The revenue from rail fares

B Reduced road congestion

C The comfort of rail travel

D The sale of refreshments on trains

16.5 Solutions to objective questions

Solution 16.3   Answer: **B**

Human capital is the accumulated skill, knowledge and expertise of workers. Education and training increase the value of human capital, thereby raising workers' productivity.

Solution 16.4   Answer: **B**

The price of houses can rise as a result of an increase in demand or a decrease in supply. Higher disposable income will result in an increase in the demand for houses, which have positive income elasticity of demand.

A ⇒ A rise in the rate of interest will increase the mortgage interest rate, which will in turn reduce the demand for houses

C and **D** ⇒ will increase the supply of houses and reduce price.

Solution 16.5   Answer: **D**

Knowing that they will have to repay the loans, some students are likely to reject courses that are not directly job related in favour of, for example, degree courses in accountancy and medicine.

A ⇒ Replacing student grants with loans will reduce government expenditure on higher education, *ceteris paribus*.

B ⇒ The introduction of a student loan scheme is likely to discourage some potential students from undertaking higher education courses.

C ⇒ The private rate of return on investment in higher education will fall as students will have to pay back the loans out of their future income.

Solution 16.6   Answer: **C**

A fall in mortgage interest rates will increase the demand for houses, thereby raising their price and leading to an expansion in house building.

Solution 16.7   Answer: **D**

A socially efficient urban road tax would ensure that the level of road congestion is reduced to the point where the marginal benefit of congestion reduction equals the marginal cost of congestion reduction. The benefit that people are likely to derive from using a large number of resources to eliminate all road congestion is likely to be less than if some of these resources are put to alternative uses.

Solution 16.8   Answer: **B**

Education has positive externalities. It is not only the students themselves who benefit from education. Society also benefits from having a better informed and skilled population. When making their

consumption choices people take into account private benefit rather than social benefit. Left to market forces, higher education is likely to be underprovided.

A ⇒ Higher education is a merit rather than a public good.

C ⇒ The provision of a higher education reduces the size of the labour force but raises its quality.

D ⇒ The middle- and high-income groups participate in higher education to a greater extent than the poor.

Solution 16.9   Answer: **D**

There is likely to be a deterioration in the quality of the environment near a motorway.

A, **B** and **C** ⇒ are all likely to occur and would be taken into account in a CBA.

Solution 16.10   Answer: **B**

A grant of £5000 to buy a house costing less than £80 000 will increase demand for houses in that price range. This will raise the price of those houses and make them easier to sell. People selling these houses will be able to 'trade up' and buy more expensive houses. This process will continue upwards through the price range.

Solution 16.11   Answer: **D**

Unless unlimited resources are devoted to higher education (a very unlikely event!) demand for free higher education will exceed supply and will therefore have to be rationed in some way. In practice this is likely to be by requiring students to gain a certain level of qualifications.

A ⇒ This does not necessarily follow and is an unlikely proposition.

B ⇒ Higher education has an opportunity cost as the resources used to provide it could be put to alternative uses.

C ⇒ Higher education can, and is, provided by the private sector. Students can be excluded from enjoying higher education unless they pay.

Solution 16.12   Answer: **B**

An external benefit is a benefit from the production or consumption of a good or service experienced by people who are not involved in the production of the good and are not consumers of it, i.e. third parties.

Road users can benefit from other people travelling by rail.

A, **C** and **D** ⇒ are private benefits.

16.6 Essays

Example 16.13

(a)   Define public, private and merit goods.

(15 marks)

(b)   What type of goods are education and health?

(10 marks)

- Give clear definitions, bringing out the characteristics of the examples.
- Give examples.

Solution 16.13

(a) A public good is one that is non-rival and non-excludable. This means that one person's enjoyment of the good does not reduce another person's, and that those who are not willing to pay for the good cannot be excluded from consuming it – they can be free riders. These are the two defining characteristics of a public good, which may also have other characteristics. The marginal cost of providing the good to one more individual is often zero and it may be non-rejectable in the sense that individuals may not be able to abstain from consuming it even if they want to. Examples of public goods include defence, public drainage, flood control dams and street lighting. The market mechanism will not provide public goods. They have to be financed by the state, through taxation or borrowing, and are provided directly or by giving contracts to private sector firms.

A private good is one that is both rival and excludable. One person's consumption will mean that the good is not available for another person to consume it. The enjoyment of the good can also be made dependent on payment. Most goods are private goods. Examples include books, cars, televisions and yachts. Private goods can be provided through the market mechanism.

A merit good is one that is underprovided by the market mechanism as individuals do not appreciate its true benefits. It is also likely to have positive externalities. A state can encourage the consumption of merit goods by providing them free to consumers, by subsidising them, by providing information about their benefits or by passing legislation, for example

requiring car manufacturers to fit, and drivers and their passengers to use, seat belts. Other examples of merit goods include training and inoculation.

(b) In the UK education and health are both private and merit goods. To benefit from private medical care people have to pay and those who are willing or able to do so are excluded. Similarly if people do not pay school fees for their children, those children will not be able to receive private education (unless they gain a scholarship).

However in the UK most people receive medical care under the National Health Service and most children receive state education. In these cases the services are financed by taxation and provided free to consumers because the state views them as merit goods. The consumers may lack knowledge about the true benefits of these services, may take short-term views on them and may just make mistakes. So both these services would be underconsumed if left entirely to market forces.

Education and health also provide both private and external benefits. Education provides enjoyment and increases the potential earning power of the consumers. It also creates a better educated workforce, which benefits third parties by increasing the quantity and quality of output. Consumers of health care receive the private benefit of improved quality of life and others gain from increased output and reduced risk of catching contagious illnesses.

Example 16.14

Discuss the effects on the housing market of:

(a)   the abolition of tax relief on mortgage interest payments   **(9 marks)**

(b)   a rise in real income   **(8 marks)**

(c)   an increase in the wage rates of building workers   **(8 marks)**

- Include diagrams.
- Concentrate on the short run.
- Consider the effects on demand, supply and price.

Solution 16.14

(a) Most people buy houses with the use of a loan – a mortgage. If tax relief on mortgage interest payments were to be abolished, this would increase the amount of interest house buyers would have to pay on their mortgage loans. This is likely to discourage some first-time buyers and some people who had been seeking to sell their existing property and to purchase more expensive accommodation. The demand for mortgage loans would decrease. Mortgage loans and houses are in effect, complements. The decrease in demand for mortgage loans would cause a decrease in the demand for houses, which in turn would cause prices to fall and supply to contract.

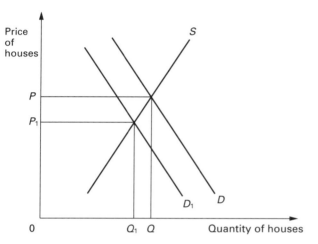

Figure 1

A change in demand could have a significant effect on price as both demand for and supply of houses are relatively price inelastic. A gradual withdrawal of mortgage interest tax relief is planned by both major UK political parties.

(b) A rise in real income would increase the demand for houses, thereby raising their price and causing supply to expand.

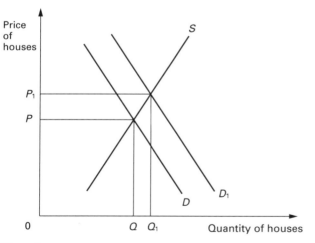

Figure 2

Houses are normal goods with positive income elasticity of demand. So income and demand move in the same direction. Demand for houses is relatively income elastic. A rise in real income means that people's purchasing power also rises. They are able to borrow more and purchase more expensive houses. Higher incomes also promote house purchase via expectations and the 'feel good factor'. When incomes are rising and the economy is expanding people feel optimistic and may be more confident that they will be able to pay off a larger loan. Changes in income and economic activity can have a significant effect on the housing market.

(c) An increase in the wage rates of building workers that is not offset by an equal rise in productivity will cause building costs to rise. This in turn will cause supply to decrease, prices to rise and demand to contract.

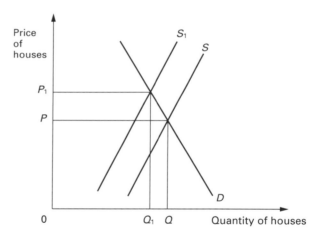

Figure 3

A rise in wage rates may cause a relatively large decrease in supply as house building is still a labour-intensive industry where wage costs make up a significant proportion of total costs. The rise in wage rates may stimulate the building industry to become more capital-intensive.

PART IV The National Economy

AEB	NEAB	OCSEB	UCLES	ULE	UODLE	Topic	Date begun	Date completed	Self-assessment
✓	✓	✓	✓	✓	✓	**Fact sheets**			
✓					✓	**Investigative study**			
✓	✓	✓	✓	✓	✓	**Data response**			
✓	✓	✓	✓	✓	✓	**Objective questions**			
✓	✓	✓	✓	✓	✓	**Essays**			

Measures of Living Standards

17.1 Fact sheet

(a) Indicators of living standards

A number of indicators of living standards are used, including:

(1) national income figures;
(2) measurable economic welfare (MEW);
(3) the human development index (HDI);
(4) consumer durables per head;
(5) mortality rates;
(6) the amount of time taken to earn sufficient money to buy given products.

See also Section 27.1 (a).

(b) Uses of national income figures

National income figures have a number of functions. They provide data for:

(1) showing the current allocation of resources;
(2) government economic planning;
(3) calculating trends within the economy;
(4) measuring a country's standard of living;
(5) comparing standards of living between different countries.

(c) Calculating national income

National income is the money value of the goods and services produced by a country in one year. There are three methods of calculating national income.

(i) The income method

First calculate *total domestic income* by adding up all the money earned by people and firms in producing this year's output. Include:

(1) income from employment;
(2) income from self-employment;
(3) rent;
(4) gross trading profits of companies;
(5) gross trading surpluses of nationalised industries;
(6) an imputed charge for the consumption of non-traded capital.

Then proceed as in Figure 17.1

*   GDP refers to *gross domestic product* and is a measure of economic activity within a country.
*   GNP refers to *gross national product* and is a measure of the activity of the country's citizens all over the world.
*   NNP refers to *net national product* and is the technical term for national income.
*   NDP refers to Net Domestic Product and is NNP minus property income from abroad.
*   *Stock appreciation* is the increase in the value of inventories brought about by inflation.
*   *Statistical discrepancy* occurs because income and expenditure data are collected from different sources. The two statistical discrepancies used in the income and expenditure methods are jointly known as the *residual error*. They are amounts used to balance up the difference between the two estimates.

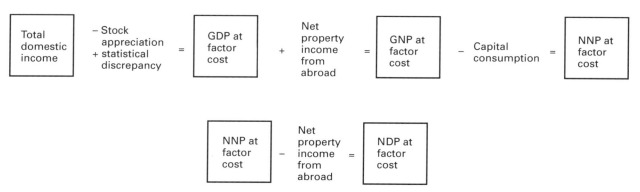

Figure 17.1 The income method

(ii) The expenditure method

First calculate *total domestic expenditure* by adding up all the money spent buying up this year's output. Include:

(1) consumer expenditure (*C*);
(2) general government final consumption (*G*);
(3) investment expenditure (*I*) on:
   (a) gross domestic fixed capital formation (e.g. machinery, vehicles);
   (b) physical increase in stocks and work in progress.

Then proceed as in Figure 17.2.

(iii) The output method

The economy is divided into industrial sectors (e.g. construction etc.). The value of *inputs* (purchases) is then deducted from the value of *outputs* (sales) to find each industrial sector's value added. For example:

Sales − purchases = value added
£60b − £50b = £10b

* Adding up each sector's value added, and including an imputed (estimated) value for the ownership of dwellings, gives GDP at factor cost.

The relationship between the different measures of national income is shown in Table 17.1.

(d) Problems in calculating national income figures

Difficulties arise in the calculation of national income figures because of:

(1) *double counting* if transfer payments (e.g. pensions), intermediate expenditures or outputs (e.g. components) and stock appreciation are included;
(2) unrecorded production in the *black economy*;
(3) *arbitrary definitions*:
   (a) the imputed value of services from owner-occupied houses is included in national figures, while the imputed value of services of consumer durables (e.g. cars) is not;
   (b) paid production (e.g. a decorator) is included in national income figures, while unpaid production (e.g. DIY) is not.

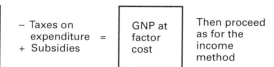

Figure 17.2 The expenditure method

Table 17.1 National income accounting equations

National income	=	national expenditure = national output
GNP	=	GDP + net property income from abroad
NNP	=	GNP − capital consumption
NDP	=	NNP − net property income from abroad
Gross investment	=	net investment + capital consumption
Factor cost	=	market prices − expenditure taxes + subsidies

(e) Real and money national income

- *Money (or nominal) national income* (MNY) is the value of this year's output at current prices.
- A *price deflator* is an index used to eliminate the effect of inflation. There are two main price indices in the UK:
  - (a) the *retail price index* (RPI), covering only consumer goods and services;
  - (b) the *GDP deflator*, covering both consumer and capital goods.
- *Real national income* (RNY) is the value of this year's output at constant prices and is calculated by using either of the following equations:

$$RNY = \frac{NNY}{GDP\ deflator} \times 100$$

$$RNY = MNY \times \frac{price\ index\ of\ base\ year}{price\ index\ of\ current\ year}$$

(f) Using national income figures as a measure of a country's standard of living

In assessing standard of living it is appropriate to use real national income per capita (per person). This is calculated by using the equation:

$$Standard\ of\ living = \frac{RNY}{population}$$

Table 17.2 gives examples of calculating changes in a country's standard of living, over time.

An increase in the value of RNY per capita implies an increase in economic welfare, unless:

(1) only a small fraction of the population receive the benefits because of an unequal distribution of income;
(2) additional output results in negative externalities such as pollution;

(3) additional output is on non-consumer items such as defence and capital goods;
(4) increased output is the result of harder conditions of work or reduced leisure time;
(5) quality of output declines

(g) Comparing living standards in different countries

Using per capita RNY to compare standards of living between countries is difficult because:

(1) the distribution of income varies between countries;
(2) the extent of the black economy varies between nations;
(3) the proportion of capital and defence goods differs between countries;
(4) working hours and conditions vary between countries;
(5) different statistical procedures are used to calculate national income in different countries;
(6) the extent of externalities varies between countries;
(7) the amount of home-produced goods and services varies between countries.

- Changes in the exchange rate can affect the relative value of each country's national income. For this reason national income figures are increasingly being compared with the use of *purchasing power parities* – e.g. if a basket of goods costs £40 in the UK and $60 in the USA, then national income should be converted at an exchange rate of £1 = $1.5.

(h) Measurable economic welfare (MEW)

MEW (devised by Nordhaus and Tobin) adjusts GDP by adding the value of, for example, leisure time, DIY and unpaid housework and deducting expenditure on, for example, defence, police and road maintenance and negative externalities.

Table 17.2 Calculating the standard of living

Year	MNY (£m)	RPI (deflator)	RNY (£m)	Population (m)	SOL (£)
1989	£20 000	100	£20 000	5.0	£4000
1990	£22 000	105	£20 952	5.0	£4190
1991	£24 000	110	£21 818	5.5	£4970

(i) Human development index (HDI)

The *HDI* was introduced by the UN in 1990. It is based on three sets of indicators:

(1) Real GDP
(2) Mean years of schooling and adult literacy
(3) Life expectancy

These take into account not only the goods and services produced but also the ability of a population to use them and the time they have to enjoy them.

17.2 Investigative study

Example 17.1

A comparative study of living standards in two countries.

17.3 Data response

Example 17.2

BRITAIN's black economy – income and spending that evades the taxman – may have topped £50 billion, according to Inland Revenue estimates. Data for cash in circulation and employment suggest the black economy is growing faster than the officially recorded economy, probably because, with taxes going up, there is a greater incentive to avoid them.

The black economy ranges from criminal activities such as drug-dealing and theft to unde-clared self-employment income by plumbers, builders and decora-tors. It can include selling by pro-fessional traders at car-boot sales and the re-sale in Britain of alco-hol and tobacco bought at low duty in France.

The Inland Revenue, drawing on research last year by the Insti-tute for Fiscal Studies (IFS), esti-mates the black economy is worth 6%–8% of gross domestic prod-uct – or between £41 billion and £54 billion for 1994–95. If taxed at the same rate as the rest of the economy, it would bring in £14.5 billion–£19 billion in extra rev-enue, enough to wipe out the tax increases announced last year by Kenneth Clarke, the chancellor, and his predecessor, Norman Lamont.

The IFS researched household spending and compared it with the declared incomes of the self-employed. It concluded that their true incomes were up to $1\frac{1}{2}$ times those declared for tax purposes. Taken with a rise of more than 1m in self-employment since the late 1970s, this points to a substantial increase in the black economy.

Source: Extract from 'Missing Billions that Dwarf Government Spending', by David Smith, *The Sunday Times*, 13 February 1995

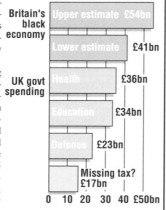

(a) What is the black economy? **(5 marks)**
(b) How can the size of the black economy be estimated? **(3 marks)**
(c) What factors influence the size of the black economy? **(8 marks)**
(d) What are the disadvantages of the black economy? **(6 marks)**
(e) Mention one of the benefits of the black economy. **(3 marks)**

Solution 17.2

(a) The black economy covers undeclared and hence unrecorded economic activity. The output of goods and services may not be declared in order to avoid paying tax on the resulting income. For instance a roof tiler may repair a roof damaged in a storm. He may ask to be paid in cash and not include the figure in his earnings when completing his tax return. The other reason for not declaring economic activity is because the activity is illegal, e.g. the sale of unlicensed guns.

(b) The size of the black economy can be estimated, as the extract mentions, by comparing the amount people spend and the incomes they declare to the tax authorities. The gap between expenditure and income can give an indication of undeclared economic activity.

(c) The size of the black economy is influenced by a number of factors. One is the tax rate. The higher taxes are, the more people may be tempted to evade them. Their decision as to whether or not to take this action will also be influenced by the detection rate of tax evasion and the penalties imposed.

Tax evasion is also affected by how many people are self-employed. The larger the size of the self-employed sector, the greater the amount of tax evasion that tends to occur. This is because tax evasion is easier when people are responsible for paying their own tax than when it is deducted at source.

The size of the black economy is also influenced by the public attitude to law-breaking, both in terms of tax evasion and in terms of, for example, selling drugs and crime detection rates and penalties.

(d) The black economy results in a loss of government tax revenue. As the extract indicates, this could be above £50 billion. This amount exceeds expenditure on, for example, education. If the tax were to be collected it would enable spending on education or another area to rise or tax rates to be reduced.

The existence of the black economy can also make government planning difficult. Using official national income figures the government may underestimate economic activity and may inject extra spending into the economy when activity is already high.

(e) The black economy may enable certain goods and services to be produced that would otherwise not be provided. For example a plumber may not be prepared to mend a leaking pipe for a pensioner if the return is too low.

17.4 Objective questions

Example 17.3

Which one of the following is not a reason for a country collecting national income statistics?
A To calculate changes in the cost of living
B To estimate the rate of economic growth
C To calculate changes in the standard of living
D To compare standards of living between countries

Example 17.4

On reaching 65, a builder earning £30 000 per year sells his firm for £200 000 but stays on as a consultant for a fee of £8000 per year. He receives an annual occupational pension of £9000. One of two assistants, each earning £12 000, loses his job and is not eligible for state benefits. As a result national income:
A rises by £175 000
B rises by £166 000
C falls by £25 000
D falls by £34 000

Example 17.5

Gross national product exceeds gross domestic product by the amount of:
A transfer payments
B capital consumption
C subsidies less expenditure taxes
D net property income from abroad

Example 17.6

Which of the following is the most accurate measure of a country's standard of living?

A Real national income
B Nominal national income
C Per capita real national income
D Per capita nominal national income

Example 17.7

The following table gives information about a country in 1995, 1996 and 1997. In 1994 real GDP per capita was £8200

	GDP (£ millions)	GDP deflator index (1990 = 100)	Population (millions)
1995	440 000	110	50
1996	450 000	120	50
1997	480 000	120	51

From the data, it can be deducted that real GDP per capita:
A has increased in all three years
B has decreased in all three years
C increased in 1995 and 1996 only
D decreased in 1995 and 1996 only

Example 17.8

If, over the last twelve months, prices have gone up by 6%, the population has increased by 2% and nominal national income has risen by 6%, then:
A real national income has increased
B real national income has decreased
C real income per capita has increased
D real income per capita has decreased

Example 17.9

All other things being equal, which of the following would increase the average standard of living of a country?
A A fall in population and no change in national product
B No change in population and a decrease in national product
C A rise in population and a proportionately smaller increase in national product
D A fall in population and a proportionately greater decrease in national product

Example 17.10

The difference between gross national product at factor cost and net national product at factor cost is:

A imports
B depreciation
C taxes on expenditure
D net property income from abroad

Example 17.11

Which of the following is included in the measure of measurable economic welfare but not GDP?

A Exports
B The value of leisure time
C The output of consumer goods industries
D Government expenditure on goods and services

Example 17.12

Which of the following must increase the quality of a person's life?

A A more even distribution of income
B An increase in negative externalities
C An increase in expenditure on the police force
D None of the above

17.5 Solutions to objective questions

Solution 17.3   Answer: **A**

Change in the cost of living is calculated by use of the retail price index.

B, C and D $\Rightarrow$ are all reasons for a country collecting national income statistics.

Solution 17.4   Answer: **D**

The pension of the builder (a transfer payment) and the money received from the sale of the firm (a transfer of ownership) are not included in national income. The fall in national income is £22 000 (the builder's reductions in earnings) + £12 000 (the loss of the assistant's salary) = £34 000.

Solution 17.5   Answer: **D**

Gross national product is a measure of incomes earned by UK residents in whichever countries they earn them, whereas gross domestic product is a

measure of incomes generated within the UK, irrespective of the nationality of the people who have earned them. So GNP is GDP plus net property income from abroad.

Solution 17.6   Answer: **C**

Per capita real national income is national income adjusted for changes in the price level and changes in population. A rise in per capita real national income will indicate a rise in the material standard of living of the population, whereas a rise in national income may not mean a rise in the number of goods and services available per head of population. It is possible that the same number of goods and services have been produced but at a higher price, or that changes in output have merely kept pace with changes in population – there are more goods and services to share among a larger population.

Solution 17.7   Answer: **D**

There are two stages in calculating real GDP per capita:

(1) divide GDP by the GDP deflator to find real GDP;
(2) divide real GDP by population

In 1995 real GDP = (£440 000/110) = £400 000, so real GDP per capita = £4000 000/50 = £8000.
   In 1996 real GDP = (£450 000/120) $\times$ 100 = £375 000, so real GDP per capita = £375 000/120 = £7500.
   In 1997 real GDP = (480 000/120) $\times$ 100 = £400 000, so real GDP capita = £400 000/51 = £7843.

Solution 17.8   Answer: **D**

A and B $\Rightarrow$ Equal percentage increases in nominal (money) national income and prices mean that real national income is unchanged.
   C $\Rightarrow$ A 2% population increase with constant real national income means that real income per capita has decreased.

Solution 17.9   Answer: **A**

The question states all other things being equal, so it can be assumed that there has been no change in the general price level. So when it states in option A that national product has remained constant, it can be taken that real national product is unchanged. The same real national product to be shared among a smaller population will mean a rise in real national income per capita.

B, **C** and **D** ⇒ would all result in a fall in the average standard of living of a country.

Solution 17.10   Answer: **B**

Gross national product includes all investment, i.e. both net investment and replacement investment (which can also be called capital consumption or depreciation), whereas net national product only includes net investment. So GNP minus depreciation equals NNP.

Solution 17.11   Answer: **B**

MEW takes the value of leisure time into account whereas GDP does not.

A and **C** ⇒ are included in both MEW and GDP.

D ⇒ Government expenditure on goods and services is included in GDP and most is included in MEW, although spending on certain items, e.g. defence, are omitted.

Solution 17.12   Answer: **D**

A ⇒ This will benefit some people, particularly the poor, but not necessarily everyone.

B ⇒ although owners of some of the companies creating externalities may benefit from a fall in their costs of production, negative externalities will reduce the quality of most people's lives.

C ⇒ The quality of people's lives will improve if the expenditure on the police force reduces crime and the fear of crime. However if the expenditure is undertaken in order to keep pace with rising crime, people will suffer a deterioration in their living standards.

17.6 Essays

Example 17.13

(a)   Distinguish between wealth and welfare
                                                        (5 marks)
(b)   Does an increase in national income mean an improvement in welfare?   **(20 marks)**

- Material welfare is the satisfaction derived from the consumption of wealth.
- National income is a narrow measure of a nation's wealth creation in a given time period.
- Include a discussion of the circumstances in which an increase in national income does and does not improve welfare.
- A detailed discussion of how national income accounts are calculated is not required.

Solution 17.13

(a)   Any asset that can be exchanged for money can be regarded as an item of wealth. There are two main types:

(1)   Material wealth consists of financial assets such as shares, and real assets such as property and consumer durables.
(2)   Human wealth consists of the skills, training and education of individuals.

The consumption of material wealth satisfies the wants and needs of individuals. The higher an individual's rate of consumption the higher his or her material welfare. Hence wealth and material welfare are interlinked.

(b)   A nation's stock of wealth allows it to produce an enormous variety of goods and services, which can then be used to satisfy material wants and needs. National income is simply the money value of all final products provided during a year that flow through the markets. Hence national income is an indicator of economic welfare.

However an increase in national income does not automatically raise living standards. For instance an increase in national income may be the result of an increase in the price level, with output held constant, or an increase in output, with prices held constant. Only the latter suggests an increase in material well-being. To measure changes in real as opposed to money national income, output is valued at constant prices by dividing current money national income by a general index of all prices, called the GDP deflator.

Yet an increase in real national income is still no guarantee that average living standards have improved. Any improvement in material standards could be negated by a proportionately larger increase in population. The actual standard of living of a nation is found by dividing real national income by the total population. Material well-being, then, increases only if per capita real national income increases.

It can be argued that per capita real national income is a restrictive, narrow welfare indicator. Official statistics only count final products sold in markets and ignore the value of non-market activities such as the output of unpaid housekeepers. The value of leisure time finds no place in national income accounts. Official statistics fail to take into account the impact of intangibles such as the quality of the environment on overall social welfare. The presence of negative externalities may cause the material and social welfare of a nation to diverge.

William Nordhaus and James Tobin (1972) have devised an alternative measure of social welfare: measurable economic welfare. Here real national income is adjusted to include an allowance for non-marketed output and leisure time, while expenditure on 'regrettable necessities', including defence, and the effects of negative externalities such as pollution are deducted. An improvement in measurable economic welfare indicates an improvement in social welfare.

Similarly an increase in human development index, which takes into account income levels, years of schooling and average lifespan, would indicate an improvement in welfare over time. The United Nations publishes data on the infant mortality rates, suicides and road accidents of various countries. A fall in these figures implies an improvement in a nation's quality of life. Similarly an increase in the proportion of the population owning various types of consumer durable such as video recorders, or a reduction in the time taken to earn sufficient money to buy given products, implies improved social welfare.

In conclusion, it has been shown that a country's stock of wealth helps to determine the quantity of goods available for the satisfaction of material wants and needs. Increases in real per capita national income are a suitable indication of improvements in material welfare. However a simultaneous and larger increase in negative externalities or reduced leisure would lower overall social welfare.

Example 17.14

Discuss the difficulties involved in comparing the standards of living of different countries.

(25 marks)

- Discuss various methods of measuring living standards.

- Detailed knowledge of other countries' economic systems is not required.
- Place the emphasis of the essay on the problems of comparing the living standards of different countries.

Solution 17.14

Standards of living can be compared in a number of ways, however they are often defined in terms of real per capita income. Hence international comparisons are usually made by referring to national income statistics. However great care should be taken when using raw national income figures. Money national income states the value of this year's final marketed output at current prices. An increase in one country's nominal national income may be the result of inflation rather than an increase in total output. Therefore national income divided by an index of all prices – e.g. the GDP deflator – provides a better basis for comparison. Even then, real GDP alone is not an accurate guide to a country's standard of living. The real GDP of China is obviously higher than the real GDP of Luxembourg. So it is necessary to divide GDP by total population. This will show that the real GDP per capita of Luxembourg is higher than that of China.

A further adjustment is also often made to convert the figures of each country to the same currency. This can cause problems if the market rate of exchange of one country does not reflect different costs of living. For example the amount of roubles exchanged for £1 at the official rate may buy fewer goods in Russia than can be bought with £1 in the UK. Converting Russian national income into sterling at the official exchange rate would result in an overvaluation. Moreover a number of countries have floating exchange rates, and the resulting continual changes in the relative value of currencies make a direct comparison difficult. It is for these reasons that increasing use is being made in international comparisons of GDP and other national income figures of purchasing power parities. This involves converting the GDP figures not in terms of the official exchange rate, but in terms of how much of the domestic currency is needed in each country to buy a given basket of goods. For instance if it takes 270 roubles and £90 to buy the basket the GDP of Russia would be converted on the basis of 3 roubles = £1, even if the official exchange rate was 2 roubles = £1.

Countries vary in terms of what proportion of

economic activities are recorded. Intensive specialisation means that most UK citizens use markets to buy the goods and services they do not have time to make or carry out themselves. Hence UK national income figures include most of the economic activity that took place in the previous year. Unmarketed and undeclared activity (the black economy) is only likely to account for a small percentage of total output. For example the tax returns of a UK farmer are usually an accurate indicator for national income accountants of the value added by a farmer in any one year. By way of contrast, markets are less developed in, for example, Mali because communities are more self-sufficient and practice less specialisation and exchange. The output of a Mali farmer will not be officially recorded if a crop is either consumed by the farmer or exchanged for other goods, or if the income from it is not declared to the authorities.

Problems arise when different countries use different statistical procedures when calculating national income figures. For instance Cuba is a planned economy where resources are allocated by the state. Official prices are used to value output, but these may not reflect the relative value of goods and services consumed in Cuba.

Physical conditions vary widely between countries. The climate of Finland is severe in winter; the climate of Brazil is not. Thus the national income of Finland includes expenditure on heating, which Brazil does not have to undertake to the same extent, and the value of the resources used to heat buildings is included in Finland's national income.

Working conditions, working hours, the distribution of income and the quality of goods produced will differ between countries. The extent of negative externalities, e.g. pollution, and the proportion of national income spent on 'regrettable necessities' also vary between countries. For example defence spending in the UK accounts for a larger percentage of GDP than in Switzerland. Measurable economic welfare, developed by Nordhaus and Tobin, adjusts GDP figures by deducting expenditure on 'regrettable necessities', negative externalities and expenditure on consumer durables and adding services given by consumer durables, the value of non-marketed work, including DIY, and the value of leisure time.

A number of other measures of welfare are used to make international comparisons of standards of living. The country where least time is taken by a worker to earn sufficient income to buy a given basket of goods is likely to enjoy the highest standard of living. Low suicide rates and low infant mortality rates also indicate a good quality of life. The human development index takes into account not only income levels but also access to education and average life span.

Aggregate Demand

18.1 Fact sheet

(a) The aggregate demand curve

- *Aggregate demand* (AD) is the total of all planned expenditure at each level of prices. It is composed of consumption C), investment (*I*), government spending (*G*) and exports minus imports (*X* − *M*):

  AD = *C* + *I* + *G* + (*X* − *M*)

- The *aggregate demand curve* slopes down from left to right because:
  (a) the lower the price level the lower the interest rate and hence the greater the demand for interest-sensitive investment and consumer goods;
  (b) as prices fall, people's wealth buys more products;
  (c) as UK prices fall, UK and overseas consumers substitute UK goods for goods produced overseas.

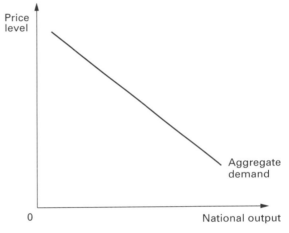

Figure 18.1 Aggregate demand

(b) Movements along and shifts in aggregate demand

- A movement along the aggregate demand curve is caused by a change in the price level.
- The AD curve shifts to the right if there is an increase in aggregate demand at each price level. This may be the result of an increase in planned:
  (a) consumption due to, for example, a fall in tax rates;

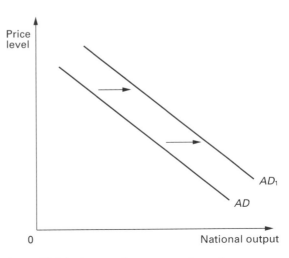

Figure 18.2 An increase in aggregate demand

(b) investment due to, for example, a rise in optimism;

(c) government spending due to, for example, a rise in the government's desire to promote training;

(d) exports due to, for example, an improvement in the quality of UK goods and services.

(c) Consumption

Consumption is expenditure by households on goods and services that satisfy current wants.

* The *consumption function* in Figure 18.3 shows how much will be spent at different levels of disposable income and is given by the equation:

$C = a + bY$

where C = consumption, a = *autonomous consumption* (what is spent when income is zero and does not vary with income), b = the marginal propensity to consume and Y = disposable income. bY is income-induced consumption.

* As disposable income rises the amount spent rises, depending on the value of the marginal propensity to consume. As disposable income rises, the proportion spent usually declines.

* The *average propensity to consume* (APC) is the proportion of disposable income spent:
  APC = C/Y

* The *marginal propensity to consume* (MPC) is the proportion of each extra pound of disposable income spent by households and is the change in consumption resulting from a change in disposable income: MPC = $\Delta C/\Delta Y$.

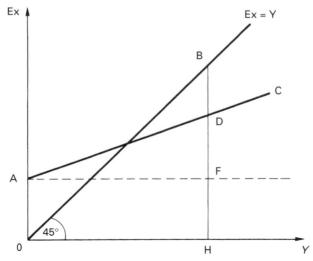

Figure 18.3 Autonomous and induced consumption: 0A or HF = autonomous consumption = a; DH/BH = APC

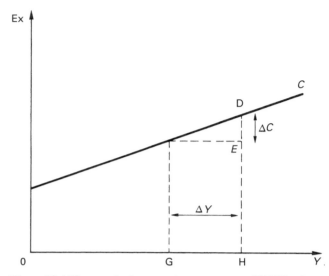

Figure 18.4 The marginal propensity to consume: DE/GH = b

Influences on consumption include level of disposable income, credit facilities, distribution of income, the population's age structure, quality and availability of consumer goods, amount and distribution of wealth and expectations of inflation.

It is important to remember that there is more than one theory of consumption. Most economists agree that the main influence on consumption is income. However there are three main theories as to which particular form of consumption is most important:

(1) *Absolute income hypothesis:* this is the Keynesian view that consumption depends on current disposable income.

(2) *Relative income hypothesis:* this is the theory put forward by Duesenberry that people's consumption is influenced by the spending pattern of others.

(3) *Permanent income hypothesis:* this is the view put forward by Milton Friedman that spending is based on average lifetime income.

(d) Saving

Saving is that part of disposable income (income less direct taxes plus state benefits) not spent on goods and services.

* The *saving function* shows how much will be saved at different levels of disposable income and is given by the equation:

$S = -a + SY$

where S = saving; $-a$ = *autonomous dissaving* (the amount of S when Y = 0); s = the marginal propensity to save, Y = disposable income and sy = induced saving. As income rises, both the amount saved and the proportion saved usually increase.

- The *average propensity to save* (APS) is the proportion of disposable income saved: APS = S/Y
- The *marginal propensity to save* (s or MPS) is the proportion of each extra pound of disposable income not spent and is the change in saving resulting from a change in income: $s = \Delta S/\Delta Y$

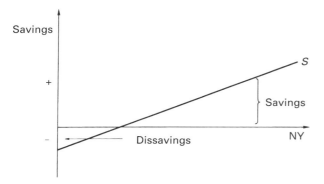

Figure 18.5 The savings function

Influences on saving include level of income, rate of interest, rate of inflation, quality of financial institutions, general attitudes to the virtue of saving, government policies (e.g. tax concessions), expectations of inflation, and advertising.

(e) Investment

Investment is expenditure on capital goods and changes in stock.

- The *marginal efficiency of capital* is the expected rate of return on investment.
- The *accelerator theory* states that a given change in the demand for consumer goods will cause a greater percentage change in the demand for capital goods. So the level of planned investment is a function of changes in income:

$I = (F)\Delta Y$

The level of investment is also influenced by:
(a) the rate of interest;
(b) the relative prices of capital and labour;
(c) corporation tax;
(d) technological change and innovation;
(e) business expectations;
(f) profits.

(f) Government

Government spending (G) adds to aggregate demand and taxation (T) reduces it.

- The *marginal rate of tax* (MRT) which is also called the marginal propensity to tax (MPT) is the proportion of each extra pound of income taken by the government, and is the change in tax resulting from a change in income: $\Delta T/\Delta Y$.
- The *average rate of tax* (ART) is the proportion of total income taken in tax: T/Y.

(g) The international sector

Exports (X) add to income and demand in the home economy whereas imports (M) result in income leaving the domestic economy and aggregate demand falling.

- The *marginal propensity to import* (MPM) is the proportion of each extra pound of disposable income spent on foreign-made goods and is the change in expenditure on imports resulting from a change in disposable income: $\Delta M/\Delta Y$.

18.2 Investigative study

Example 18.1

An investigation into changes in the savings ratio, their causes and effects.

18.3 Data response

Example 18.2

(£ million, 1990 prices)

Year	GDP at factor cost	Gross domestic fixed capital formation	Treasury bill rate
1988	465 746	105 164	12.91
1989	476 228	111 470	15.02
1990	478 886	107 577	13.50
1991	468 913	94 403	10.45
1992	466 564	96 280	6.44
1993	475 889	96 611	4.98

Sources: CSO, *Economic Trends*, Annual Supplement, 1995; *Monthly Digest of Statistics*, February 1995.

(a) Define:
    (1) GDP at factor cost;
    (2) gross domestic fixed capital formation;
    (3) treasury bill rate. **(3 marks)**

(b) Do the data indicate a relationship between changes in GDP at factor cost and changes in gross domestic fixed capital formation? **(5 marks)**

(c) Do your findings in (b) reflect the relationship that economic theory would lead you to expect? **(6 marks)**

(d) Do the data indicate a relationship between changes in the treasury bill rate and changes in gross domestic fixed capital formation? **(5 marks)**

(e) Do your findings in (d) reflect the relationship economic theory would lead you to expect? **(6 marks)**

Solution 18.2

(a)(1) GDP at factor cost is gross domestic product at factor cost. It is a measure of output, income and expenditure generated in a country in the period of one year. It is net of indirect taxes and subsidies.

(2) Gross domestic fixed capital formation is total spending on fixed capital goods, e.g. plant and machines, in the UK.

(3) The treasury bill rate is the rate of interest paid on treasury bills, which are short-term loans to the government. It influences other interest rates in the economy.

(b)

Year	%Δ GDP at factor cost	%Δ gross domestic fixed capital formation
1989	2.2	6.0
1990	0.6	3.5
1991	−2.1	−12.2
1992	−0.5	2.0
1993	2.0	0.3

The data shows that in three of the five years GDP and investment change in the same direction and that in four of the five years the change in investment exceeded the change in GDP in percentage terms.

(c) The accelerator theory states that variations in the rate of change in income cause greater percentage changes in investment. The accelerator theory is actually concerned with net investment. Nevertheless it can be expected that if income starts to rise more quickly firms will wish to expand their productive capacity and hence buy more capital goods. Similarly if income starts to grow more slowly firms may become reluctant to expand.

The data shows, with one exception, that investment fluctuated more than income. The fall in GDP in 1991 was probably a reaction to the slowdown in economic activity and reflected entrepreneurs' pessimism about the future. Positive growth in investment may have resulted in entrepreneurs becoming more optimistic as the economy moved out of recession. The unusual relationship shown in 1993, with GDP growing more rapidly than investment, may be explained by other influences on investment.

(d)

Year	%Δ gross domestic fixed capital formation	%Δ treasury bill rate
1989	6.0	16.3
1990	−3.5	−10.1
1991	−12.2	−12.1
1992	2.0	−38.4
1993	0.3	−22.7

The treasury bill rate fell from 1990 to 1993, whereas investment fell from 1990 to 1991 and then rose from 1991 to 1993. In 1989 both investment and the treasury bill rate rose. In three of the five years the variables moved in the same direction.

(e) It would be expected that investment and the interest rate would move in opposite directions. A fall in the interest rate might increase investment as it will become cheaper to borrow to finance investment, and if – as in most cases – retained profits are used, marginal investment projects become viable. Figure 1 shows a fall in the interest rate, causing planned investment to rise.

The data do not bear out this expected relationship. At the start of the period investment rose despite a large increase in the interest rate. In 1990 and 1991 falls in the interest rate did not cause investment to rise. In 1992 and 1993 large falls in the interest rate only caused small rises in investment.

It would be useful to know the real interest rate, i.e.

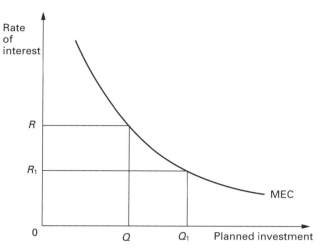

Figure 1

nominal interest minus inflation rate. With this reservation, the data do suggest that in this period other influences on investment were more significant than the interest rate.

18.4 Objective questions

Example 18.3

A man has a rise in income from £25 000 to £27 000. As a result, his saving rises from £900 to £1300. His MPC is

A 0.2 **B** 0.3 **C** 0.6 **D** 0.8

Example 18.4

The following table shows a country's consumption schedule:

Income (£m)	Consumption (£m)
0	60
100	130
200	200
300	270
400	340

C is consumption and *Y* is national income. Which of the following represents the consumption function:

A $C = -£60m + 0.3Y$
B $C = £60m + 0.3Y$
C $C = £60m + 0.7Y$
D $C = £130m + 0.7Y$

Example 18.5

An economy has a saving function (*S*), which is given by the equation $S = -£500 + 0.2Y$ (where *Y* is national income). If the level of national income is £5000m, what is the average propensity to save?

A 0.1 **B** 0.2 **C** 0.8 **D** 0.9

Example 18.6

In the diagram below, as income increases from £15 000m to £17 000m, what is the marginal propensity to consume?

A 0.8 **B** 0.6 **C** 0.4 **D** 0.2

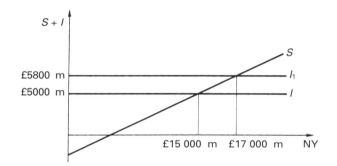

Example 18.7

A firm makes 10 000 goods using 20 machines. Each year two machines wear out. If demand for the good rises to 12 000, gross investment will increase by:

A 50% **B** 100% **C** 200% **D** 300%

Example 18.8

In an economy, *Y* (national income) = *C* (consumption) + *I* (investment). If consumption = £50m + 0.75*Y*, planned investment = £80m and national income = £800m, realised investment will be:

A £50m **B** £100m **C** £150m **D** £200m

Example 18.9

According to Keynesian analysis, consumption is a function of:

A permanent income
B current income
C estimated lifetime income
D previous income

Example 18.10

Which of the following is concerned with how capital expenditure responds to a change in consumer expenditure?

A The multiplier
B The accelerator
C The consumption function
D The savings function

Example 18.11

The largest component of UK aggregate demand is:

A net exports
B investment
C consumption
D government expenditure

Example 18.12

Which of the following would cause a movement along an aggregate demand curve? A change in:

A business expectations
B the money supply
C the exchange rate
D the general price level

18.5 Solutions to objective questions

Solution 18.3   Answer: **D**

The man's savings rise by £400 when his income rises by £2000. So his MPS is
400/2000 = 0.2. 1 − MPS = MPC, so
MPC = 1 − 0.2 = 0.8.

Solution 18.4   Answer: **C**

The consumption function shows the relationship between income and consumption, i.e. $C = a + bY$. In this case, autonomous consumption (a) is £60m and MPC is 70/100 = 0.7. So the consumption function is $C = £60m + 0.7Y$.

Solution 18.5   Answer: **A**

If the savings function is $S = −£500m + 0.2Y$, then, when NY is £5000m, total savings will be
$−£500m + 0.2 × £5000m = £500m$. So
APS = £500m/£5000m = 0.1.

Solution 18.6   Answer: **B**

When income rises by £2000m, savings rise by £800m, so MPS = £800m/£2000m = 0.4. So MPC is
1 − 0.4 = 0.6.

Solution 18.7   Answer: **C**

Each machine makes 10 000/2 = 500 goods, and the firm originally buys two machines. To produce an extra output of 2000 it will need additional machines of 2000/500 = 4. So the firm will purchase a total of six machines – two replacement and four to expand output (net investment). Thus gross investment (depreciation + net investment) rises from 2 to 6 – i.e. an increase of 4/2 × 100 = 200%.

Solution 18.8   Answer: **C**

Realised investment is actual investment and includes both planned investment and changes in stock.
$C = £50m + 0.75 × £800m = £650m$. So
savings = $Y − £650m = £150m$. Since actual investment = actual savings, actual investment will be £150m. This consists of £80m (planned investment) + £70m unsold stock (£720m consumer goods made but only £650m sold).

Solution 18.9   Answer: **B**

According to Keynesian analysis, the main determinant of consumption is current income.

A ⟹ Milton Friedman and other supporters of the permanent income hypothesis suggest that consumption depends on permanent income. Therefore, if people experience what they expect to be a short-term change in income, they may not alter their consumption.

C ⟹ Franco Modigliani and Albert Ando developed the life cycle hypothesis, which states that people estimate the income they are likely to earn over their lifetime and upon this base a lifetime consumption plan.

Solution 18.10   Answer: **B**

The accelerator theory states that a given change in demand for consumer goods will cause demand for capital goods to change by a greater percentage.

A ⟹ The multiplier is concerned with how NY changes as a result of a change in an injection, e.g. investment.

Solution 18.11   Answer: **C**

Consumption is the largest single component of aggregate demand and accounts for approximately half of total final expenditure.

Solution 18.12   Answer: **D**

A rise in the general price level would cause a contraction in aggregate demand, and a fall in the general price level would cause an expansion in aggregate demand. The one thing that can cause a movement along the aggregate demand curve is a change in the general price level.

A, **B** and **C** ⇒ would all cause a shift in the aggregate demand curve.

18.6 Essays

Example 18.13

Describe the interrelationships between consumption, investment and income, and discuss how a change in each one will affect the other two.   **(25 marks)**

- Stress the interrelationships between the three variables in Keynesian analysis.
- Make use of the multiplier and accelerator concepts.
- Discuss how an increase in one variable will cause the other two to increase.

Solution 18.13

Income, consumption and investment are all interrelated and are important variables in Keynesian analysis.

Income equals consumption plus investment. If investment and/or consumption rise, income will increase. Keynes used Kahn's concept of the multiplier to show that not only will income increase, but also it will rise by a multiple amount.

A rise in investment and a rise in autonomous consumption are injections into the circular flow of income, which will result in a multiple rise in NY. For instance, if investment increases by £50m and MPC is 0.8, the final rise in NY will be £50m × 5 = £250m. The diagram shows that a rise in investment from I to I_1 causes NY to increase from Y to Y_1.

Just as a rise in investment will result in a rise in income, so an increase in income will cause a rise in private-sector investment. The accelerator theory,

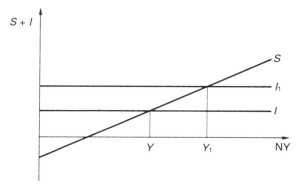

Figure 1

incorporated by Keynes into his analysis, states that a given percentage rise in the demand for consumer goods will induce a greater percentage rise in the demand for investment goods. For instance, if 100 goods are usually produced by 10 machines and one machine wears out each year, then the demand for capital goods will be one per annum. Should consumption rise by 50% to 150 goods, the demand for capital goods will rise by 500% to six machines, one of which will be to replace a worn-out machine and five will represent net investment. However if income is increasing, government investment may be reduced. Part of government investment may be undertaken to influence the level of aggregate demand in the economy. When private-sector demand is low, the government may inject investment into the economy to raise aggregate demand. Conversely if private-sector demand is high, the government may reduce investment in order to offset inflationary pressures.

A rise in income will induce a rise in consumption. Income is the main influence on consumption. While investment is likely to increase by a greater percentage than the rise in income that has brought it about, consumption is likely to rise by a smaller percentage than income. Keynes pointed out that, when income rises, a person's or a society's spending is also likely to rise. However the proportion of total income spent (the average propensity to consume) and the proportion spent out of extra income (the marginal propensity to consume) are likely to decline. When people or a society are poor, the whole of their or its income is likely to be spent. Indeed there may be dissaving – i.e. spending more than income by borrowing or drawing in past savings. However as income rises there will be increased opportunities for saving and therefore, while both saving and spending will rise, the proportion devoted to consumption is likely to decline.

Consumption and investment are not only components of national income, they are also influences on the level of that income and are in turn influenced by income.

Example 18.14

(a) What might cause an increase in aggregate demand? **(10 marks)**

(b) What effect will an increase in aggregate demand have on long-run output and the price level? **(15 marks)**

- Define aggregate demand.
- Bring out the components of aggregate demand.
- Consider the effect of an increase in aggregate demand from a Keynesian and a new classical viewpoint.
- Include diagrams.

Solution 18.14

(a) Aggregate demand is the total of all planned expenditure in an economy and consists of consumption, investment, government spending and net exports. An aggregate demand curve plots equilibrium national income (output) against the price level. A movement along an aggregate demand (AD) curve is caused by a change in the price level. However an increase in AD will occur if any of the components of desired expenditure rise for a reason other than a change in the price level. Now more will be demanded at any combination of price level and real income. For example consumers may decide to spend more and firms to increase their investment if they feel more optimistic. A government may raise its expenditure in a bid to improve educational standards and net exports may rise due to a rise in incomes abroad.

An increase in AD is represented by a shift in the AD curve, as illustrated in Figure 1.

(b) All economists agree that if an increase in aggregate demand occurs when the economy is operating at full employment its only effect will be to increase the price level. It will not be possible to raise output and the higher demand will bid up prices. So at this level of real national income an increase in AD will result in demand-pull inflation.

New classical economists believe that in the long run the economy will operate with the labour market

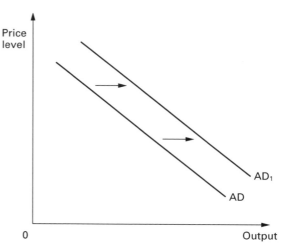

Figure 1

in equilibrium so they believe the long-run aggregate supply curve (LRAS) is vertical and the economy will operate at the full employment level (the non-accelerating inflation rate of unemployment). Hence they think that changes in aggregate demand will affect only the price level.

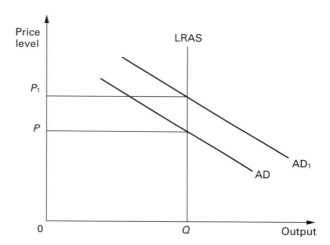

Figure 2

In contrast Keynesians believe that the economy may operate at any level of employment as the labour market will not automatically clear and AD may be below that required to achieve full employment.

Figure 3 shows that at low levels of output when unemployment is high and there is spare capacity in the economy, an increase in AD will increase output and have no effect on the price level. When the economy approaches full employment and some supply constraints are experienced, e.g. shortages of skilled workers, the aggregate supply becomes upward sloping. If AD increases at this point, both prices and output will rise.

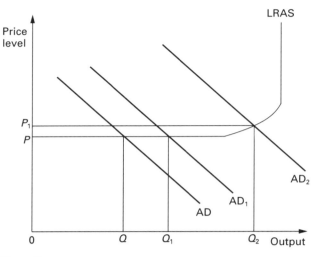

Figure 3

So Keynesians believe that the effect of an increase in AD will depend on the level of economic activity in the economy, and that when unemployment is high the main impact will be on output. New classical economists believe that the impact will be entirely on the price level, as in the long run the economy will be operating at the full employment level.

19 Aggregate Supply and Income Determination

19.1 Fact sheet

(a) Aggregate supply

Aggregate supply is the total of all planned production in a period at each price level. A change in the price level will cause a movement along the existing *aggregate supply curve*, whereas any other influence on aggregate supply will cause a shift.

(b) Short-run aggregate supply curve

- The *short-run aggregate supply curve* (SRAS) slopes up from left to right because, whilst it is assumed that the prices of all factors of production are fixed, an increase in output will raise unit costs. This is because to raise output in the short run a less efficient combination of resources may have to be used and overtime paid.
- The SRAS is relatively elastic because, whilst unit costs rise with output, they rise by small amounts.

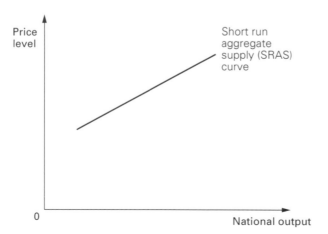

Figure 19.1 Short run aggregate supply curve

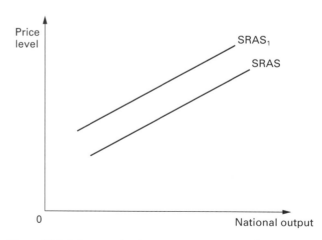

Figure 19.2 A decrease in short-run aggregate supply

(c) Shifts in the short-run aggregate supply curve

The possible causes of a decrease in the SRAS, as shown in Figure 19.2, include:

(1) a rise in corporation tax;

(2) a rise in wage rates;

(3) a rise in raw material costs.

(d) The long-run aggregate supply curve

There are two main views on the *long-run aggregate supply curve* (LRAS):

(1) The *new classical view* is that the LRAS is vertical as the economy will operate at the full employment level. This is shown in Figure 19.3.

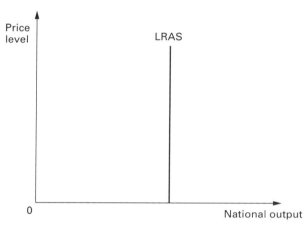

Figure 19.3 New classical view of the LRAS

(2) The *Keynesian view* is that the LRAS is horizontal at low levels of output (and high

unemployment), rises as supply constraints are experienced and becomes vertical when full employment is experienced. This is shown in Figure 19.4.

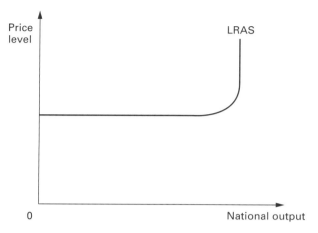

Figure 19.4 Keynesian view of the LRAS

• The LRAS will shift to the right if the quantity and/or quality of factors of production increase.

(e) Determination of output and prices

• *Equilibrium output* and the *price level* occur when aggregate demand equals aggregate supply.

• Figure 19.6 shows short-run equilibrium output.

• New classical economists believe that in the long run aggregate demand will equal aggregate supply at the full employment level (Figure 19.7a)

• Keynesians believe that the long-run equilibrium output can occur at any level of employment (Figure 19.7b).

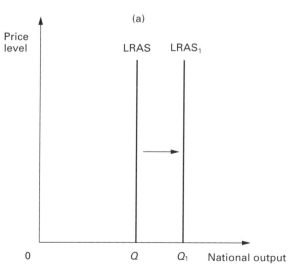

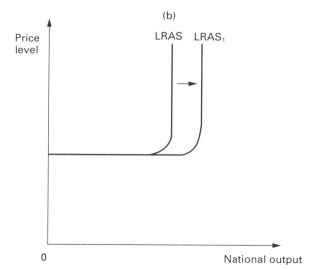

Figure 19.5 New classical view (a) and Keynesian view (b) of an increase in aggregate supply

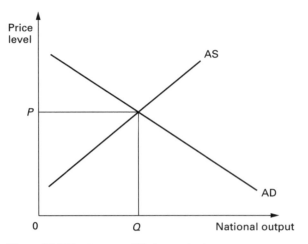

Figure 19.6 Short-run equilibrium output

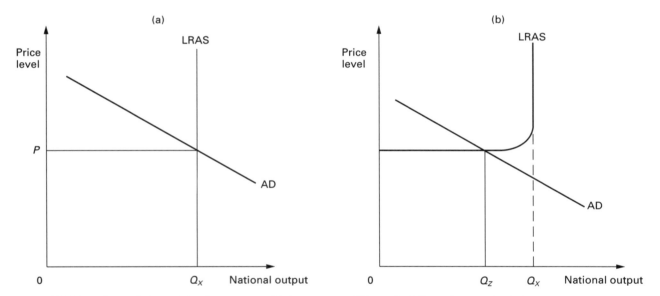

Figure 19.7 New classical view (a) that long-run equilibrium output will be at the full employment level of $0Q_X$. Keynesian view (b) that long-run equilibrium output may be at less than the full employment level of $0Q_X$ – in this case at $0Q_Z$.

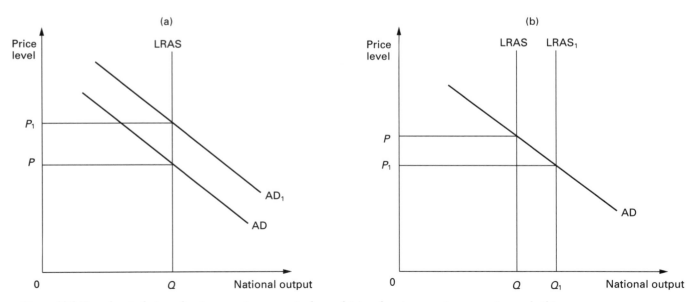

Figure 19.8 New classical view of an increase in aggregate demand (a) and an increase in aggregate supply (b)

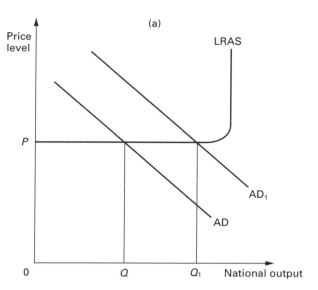
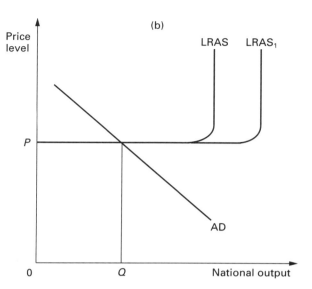

Figure 19.9 Keynesian view of an increase in aggregate demand (a) and an increase in aggregate supply (b)

- Equilibrium output also occurs when planned national expenditure equals national income. At this equilibrium output, injections will equal withdrawals.
- *Injections* (*J*) are additions to the income of firms that do not normally arise from the expenditure of domestic households. There are three types: investment, government spending and exports. Injections cause a rise in spending in the economy.
- *Withdrawals* (*W*) or *leakages* is any income not passed on in the circular flow of income. There are three types: saving, taxation and imports. Withdrawals reduce spending in the economy.

(f) Changes in national output

- Output may rise in the short run if there is an increase in either aggregate demand or aggregate supply.
- New classical economists argue that output can only be increased in the long run by an increase in aggregate supply. Figure 19.8 shows the contrasting effects of an increase in aggregate demand and an increase in aggregate supply.
- Keynesians believe that if the economy is operating at a high level of unemployment, an increase in aggregate demand will raise output without increasing the price level, whereas an increase in aggregate supply will have no impact on output.

(g) The multiplier

The multiplier (*k*) shows by how much income changes as a result of a change in an injection. The value of the multiplier is given by

$$k = \frac{\Delta Y}{\Delta J} \text{ or } \frac{1}{W}$$

Where *W* is the *marginal propensity to withdraw*, i.e. the proportion of each extra pound withdrawn from the circular flow.

To calculate the effect of changes in an injection on national income, use the equation:

$$\Delta Y = k \times \Delta J$$

For example, assume an economy where $W = 0.2$. An increase of £50m in government spending results in an increase in national income of $1/0.2 \times £50m = 5 \times £50m = £250m$. Note that:

(1) $W = s$ in a two-sector closed economy (i.e. one with households and firms).
(2) $W = s + t$ in a three-sector economy (i.e. one with households, firms and the government), where *t* is the *marginal rate of tax* (also called the *marginal propensity to tax*)
(3) $W = s + t + m$ in a four-sector economy (i.e. one with households, firms, government and international trade sector), where *m* is the *marginal propensity to import*.

- The *multiplier effect* is the series of consumer incomes and expenditures generated by an initial change in an injection.

19.2 Investigative study

Example 19.1

An investigation into the causes of changes in GDP.

19.3 Data response

Example 19.2

The capacity crunch

THAT interest rates will have to rise again soon to dampen inflationary pressures became even more certain this week. Despite last year's rate increases, the economy continues to go full steam ahead. According to statistics published on January 23rd, in the fourth quarter of last year, GDP grew more sharply than most economists had forecast. It was up by 0.8% on the third quarter, and by 4% compared with the fourth quarter of 1993. A word of caution is in order, however; these growth figures are estimates and, on past form, are likely to be revised sharply one way or the other.

One of the biggest questions facing the chancellor of the exchequer and the governor of the Bank of England when they next meet on February 2nd is how much longer the economy can go on growing at the current rate before firms start to run out of productive capacity. When that happens, supply will not be able to keep pace with demand and prices will start to rise quickly.

The Confederation of British Industry's latest quarterly survey of industrial trends, pub-lished on January 24th, showed that spare manufacturing capacity is shrinking fast. The percentage of firms working below capacity fell to 49% in the fourth quarter of 1994, down from 57% a year earlier. This is the lowest figure since July 1990. The proportion of firms believing that their plant capacity will limit growth in their output over the next four months rose to 24%, the highest since October 1988.

Intriguingly, bigger firms (those with more than 5,000 staff) have more spare capacity than smaller ones. Those manufacturers sell-ing unfinished goods to others have least capacity, but they have found it hard to pass on price rises.

The puzzle is that, despite the fact that spare capacity is rapidly disappearing, firms remain reluctant to invest in new capacity. The CBI survey found that, compared with October's survey, fewer firms plan to invest over the coming 12 months. Apparently, firms have become less confident that demand will remain strong. This may become a self-fulfill-ing prophecy: the shrinkage of spare manu-facturing capacity is one reason why interest rates are likely to be raised, which will in turn curb demand.

Source: *The Economist*, 28 January 1995.

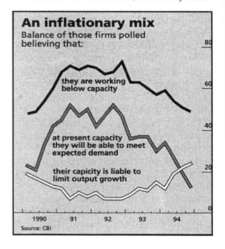

(a) Explain what is meant by spare capacity.
(3 marks)

(b) Draw and explain an aggregate demand and supply diagram to illustrate the fact that the economy is experiencing a capacity constraint.
(8 marks)

(c) What was causing spare capacity to disappear?
(4 marks)

(d) Why were a number of firms reluctant to expand their capacity? **(4 marks)**

(e) What effect would an increase in investment have on the long-run aggregate supply curve? Illustrate your answer. **(6 marks)**

(b)

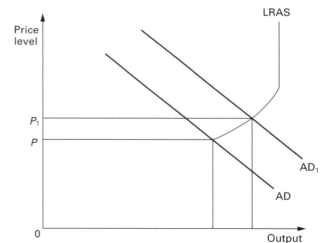

Figure 1

Solution 19.2

(a) Spare capacity occurs when a firm is not making full use of its plant, equipment and workers. When there is spare capacity a firm is able to produce more with its existing resources.

Figure 1 shows that when demand increases from AD to AD₁ both output and prices rise. The economy is capable of producing more but it is beginning to experience shortage of some factors of production, e.g. skilled workers. This results in the price of factors of production and the products they make being bid up.

(c) Spare capacity was disappearing because of the increase in economic activity. The higher level of demand was causing firms to increase their output by making use of previously underutilised machines in particular, but also factory space and workers.

(d) A number of firms were reluctant to expand their capacity for fear that the rise in demand would not last. If firms purchase more machines and factory space and they then lie idle, this proves expensive and threatens profit levels.

(e) An increase in investment, if it is net investment or replacement investment that embodies new technology, would increase the productive capacity of the economy. This would cause the long-run aggregate supply curve to shift to the right, as illustrated in Figure 2.

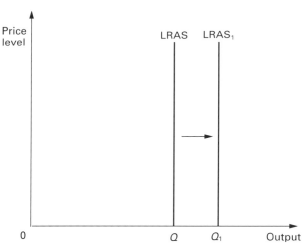

Figure 2

19.4 Objective questions

Example 19.3

According to supply-side economics, which of the following could have caused the short-run aggregate supply curve to shift to the right?

A An increase in demand for consumer goods

B A reduction in marginal tax rates

C An increase in government spending

D A reduction in the differential between earnings from employment and job seekers' allowance

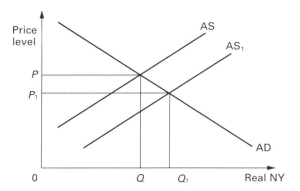

Example 19.4

If, in an economy, out of every additional £100 of national income, £20 is taxed, £20 is saved and £10 is spent on imports, the value of the multiplier is

A 2 **B** 2.5 **C** 3.3 **D** 5

Example 19.5

A closed economy has a national income of £65m, a marginal propensity to save of 0.3 and a marginal propensity to tax of 0.1. If the government wishes to achieve the full employment level of NY of £75m, it will have to increase government expenditure by:

A £1m **B** £3.3m **C** £4m **D** £10m

Example 19.6

A shift to the left of the long-run aggregate supply curve indicates:

A improvements in technology

B an increase in wage rates

C the discovery of new materials

D a decrease in the productive potential of the economy

Example 19.7

Which of the following represents a leakage from the circular flow?

A Exports

B Investment

C Interest paid on bank loans

D National insurance contributions

Example 19.8

$C = 40 + bY$, $I = 30$, $X = 50$, $M = 60$ and $b = 0.8$ (where C = consumption, Y = income, I = investment,

X = exports, M = imports and b = the marginal propensity to consume). The equilibrium level of Y will be:

A 275   **B** 300   **C** 400   **D** 550

	Unemployment:	The price level:
A	increase	leave unchanged
B	leave unchanged	increase
C	increase	reduce
D	reduce	leave unchanged

Example 19.9

The table below refers to a closed economy:

Income (£m)	Investment (£m)	Savings (£m)	Government spending (£m)	Taxation (£m)
100	60	20	40	50
200	70	20	30	60
300	80	20	20	70
400	90	20	10	80

The equilibrium level of national income is:

A £100m   **B** £200m   **C** £300m   **D** £400m

Example 19.10

If the marginal propensity to consume of all members of a closed economy is equal, than a rise in taxation of £5000m and of government expenditure of £5000m will cause national income to:

A remain constant
B rise by £5000m
C rise by £5000m
D rise by less than £5000

Example 19.11

An increase in government spending is likely to have a large impact on the level of employment when there is:

A a high marginal propensity to save
B a high marginal propensity to import
C a high marginal propensity to consume
D a high marginal rate of taxation

Example 19.12

If the long-run aggregate supply curve is vertical, what will be the effect, in the long run, of an increase in aggregate demand on unemployment and the price level?

19.5 Solutions to objective questions

Solution 19.3   Answer: **B**

The aggregate supply curve will shift to the right if the productivity of the factors of production increases. Supporters of supply-side economics urge tax cuts to increase the attractiveness of paid employment and the productivity of workers.

    A and **C** $\Rightarrow$ would initially influence demand rather than supply.

    D $\Rightarrow$ Supply-side supporters argue that, if the differential between earnings from employment and the job seekers' allowance is narrowed, this will reduce the incentive for workers to increase productivity.

Solution 19.4   Answer: **A**

In this case, the multiplier is:

$$1/(MPT + MPS + MPM) = 1/(0.2 + 0.2 + 0.1)$$
$$= 1/0.5 = 2$$

Solution 19.5   Answer: **C**

If MPS is 0.3 and MPT is 0.1 the multiplier is: $1/(MPS + MPT) = 1/0.4 = 2.5$. The gap between present and desired NY is £10m. To achieve this the government will have to increase its spending by £10m/2.5 = £4m.

Solution 19.6   Answer: **D**

The long-run aggregate supply curve shows the full employment level of output and productive capacity. A fall in potential output is shown by a leftward shift in the long-run aggregate supply curve.

    A and **C** $\Rightarrow$ would increase aggregate supply.

    B $\Rightarrow$ would cause a shift in the short-term aggregate supply curve to the left.

Solution 19.7   Answer: **D**

National insurance contributions are a tax and therefore reduce the amount of income passed round the economy.

A and **B** $\Rightarrow$ Exports and investment are injections into the circular flow.

C $\Rightarrow$ Interest is an income earned within the economy and forms part of the circular flow.

Solution 19.8   Answer: **B**

The equilibrium level of Y will be where:

$$Y = C + I + (X - M)$$
$$Y = 40 + 0.8Y + 30 + (50 - 60)$$
$$0.2Y = 40 + 30 - 10$$
$$Y = 300$$

Solution 19.9   Answer: **D**

The equilibrium level NY is where planned injections equal planned withdrawals. In a closed economy this will be where: investment + government spending = savings + taxation, i.e. $90 + 10 = 20 + 80$, which occurs when NY is £400m.

Solution 19.10   Answer: **C**

According to the balanced budget multiplier theorem, if the MPCs of taxpayers and recipients of government spending are equal then a rise in government spending and taxation of equal amounts will cause NY to rise by the amount of the change. For instance, if MPC is 0.8, a rise in taxation of £5000m will cause private spending to fall by £5000m $\times$ 0.8 = £4000m. Public spending increases by £5000m, so the net injection of spending is £5000m $-$ £4000m = £1000m. MPS is 0.2, so the multiplier is 1/0.2 = 5. Thus NY will rise by £1000m $\times$ 5 = £5000m.

Solution 19.11   Answer: **C**

A high MPC will mean a high multiplier, i.e. if MPC is 0.9 the multiplier will be 10. Thus a rise in government spending of £50m will cause NY to rise by £50m $\times$ 10 = £500m. The larger the rise in NY the greater the likely increase in employment.

A, **B** and **D** $\Rightarrow$ A high MPS, a high MPM and a high MRT will all reduce the size of the multiplier.

Solution 19.12   Answer: **B**

If the long-run aggregate supply curve is vertical an increase in aggregate demand will cause inflation but will not alter the level of output and employment. This is shown in the diagram below.

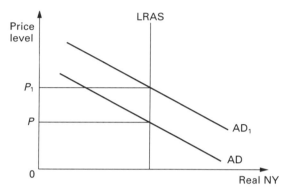

19.6 Essays

Example 19.13

(a)   What could cause:
   (1) the short-run aggregate supply curve to shift to the right;
   (2) the long-run aggregate supply curve to shift to the right?   **(10 marks)**

(b)   What effect will an increase in long-run aggregate supply have on output and employment?   **(15 marks)**

- Distinguish between short- and long-run aggregate supply.
- Compare Keynesian and new classical views on the effects of a shift in the LRAS.
- Include diagrams.

Solution 19.13

(a)(1) The short-run aggregate supply curve shows how much all firms in the economy wish, and are able, to supply at each price level. In the short run it is

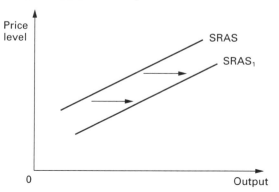

Figure 1

assumed that the prices of all factors of production are fixed, e.g. money wage rates, as output changes.

A shift to the right of the short-run aggregate supply curve (SRAS) means that more is being supplied at each price level.

The SRAS will move to the right and supply will increase if firms' costs of production fall. This could be caused by, for example, a fall in wage costs per unit, a decline in raw material costs or a fall in taxes on firms.

(2) The long-run aggregate supply curve is drawn on the assumption that costs of production have adjusted to changing market conditions. A shift to the right of the long-run aggregate supply curve (LRAS) means that the potential output of the economy has increased. This can be caused by anything that increases the quantity and/or quality of factors of production in the economy, e.g. an increase in the labour force and/or an increase in training. More investment and improvements in technology would increase productive capacity. It is also likely, but not certain, that increased incentives for entrepreneurs and workers would increase long-run aggregate supply.

(b) New classical economists believe that an increase in long-run aggregate supply will have a beneficial effect on the economy, raising output and employment and lowering, or at least putting downward pressure on prices. They believe that the LRAS is vertical, as in the long run the economy will operate at full employment defined in terms of NAIRU (the non-accelerating inflation rate of unemployment).

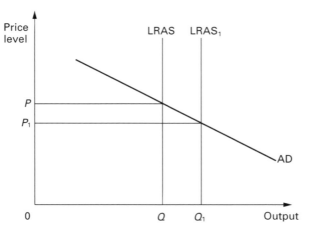

Figure 2

An increase in investment, in technological advances or in those actually willing and able to work will increase the economy's productive potential. Whilst new classical economists believe that

increasing the LRAS has a good effect on the economy, they think an increase in aggregate demand will raise the price level but fail to have any impact on output and employment in the long run. They therefore favour supply-side policies to promote increases in output.

Keynesians agree that, if the economy is operating at full employment, an increase in the LRAS will raise output and lower prices. However they believe that the economy can operate at any level of employment as labour markets may not clear. They think that there can be disequilibrium unemployment with supply of labour exceeding demand and with actual output being below potential output. This leads them to conclude that the LRAS will have a different shape from that envisaged by new classical economists. Keynesians believe that the LRAS is horizontal at low levels of output (and hence high unemployment), slopes up as supply constraints are experienced and only becomes vertical at the full employment level of output.

The shape of the LRAS implies that an increase in the LRAS will increase potential output, but not actual output when output is low. Figure 3 shows an increase in the LRAS occurring when output and employment are low, leaving output and the price level unchanged.

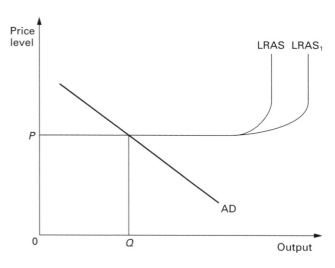

Figure 3

This leads Keynesians to believe that supply-side policies, implemented on their own, will not succeed in raising output and reducing unemployment when the economy is operating at a low capacity.

Example 19.14

Discuss the likely effect on national output of:

(a) a cut in the rate of job seekers' allowance;
(**12 marks**)
(b) an increase in government spending. (**13 marks**)

- Consider both Keynesian and new classical viewpoints.
- Include diagrams.

Solution 19.14

(a) Economists disagree about the likely effect of a cut in the job seekers' allowance. Some supply-side economists think that it will increase national output. This is because they believe that, by reducing the gap between paid and unpaid employment, it will make the unemployed seek work more actively. Reducing frictional unemployment, in particular search unemployment, will lower the non-accelerating inflation rate of unemployment (also sometimes known as the natural rate), which in turn will shift the long-run aggregate supply curve (LRAS) to the right, thereby increasing output.

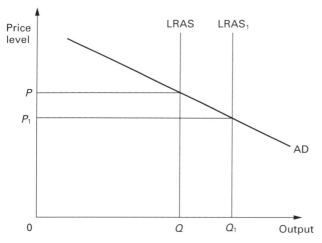

Figure 1

However Keynesians argue that the reason most people are out of work is not an unwillingness on their part to look for work but a lack of vacancies. They think that reducing the job seekers' allowance will make the situation worse. Those receiving the job seekers' allowance are likely to be poor and have a high marginal propensity to consume. Providing them with less income will reduce their purchasing power, which will in turn lower aggregate demand. Keynesians believe that the fall in spending on

benefits will have a multiplier effect on output. For example the unemployed will be able to buy fewer clothes for their children, so the shops selling clothes will receive less revenue and their owners and staff will be able to spend less. A fall in benefits of £10 million may actually cause output to fall by, say, £20 million. Hence Keynesians believe a cut in the job seekers' allowance will reduce national output.

(b) Keynesians believe an increase in government spending will increase national output unless the economy is already at full employment. Government spending is an injection into the circular flow and will cause national output to rise by a multiple amount. For example, if the multiplier is 3 a rise in government spending of £20 million will cause national income to rise by £60m. Figure 2 shows aggregate demand increasing as a result of a rise in government spending.

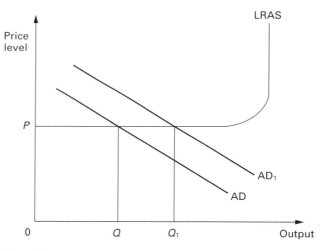

Figure 2

A crucial determinant of the impact of government spending on aggregate demand is what it is spent on. If the extra spending goes on benefits to the poor it is likely to have a relatively large impact on aggregate demand, as the poor have a high marginal propensity to consume.

Some new classical economists believe that an increase in government spending is unlikely to increase output, although the outcome will be influenced by what it is spent on and how it is financed. Monetarists in particular argue that a rise in government spending financed by borrowing will succeed in raising inflation but will leave unemployment and output, in the long run, unchanged. To illustrate this view they make use of the expectations-augmented Phillips curve.

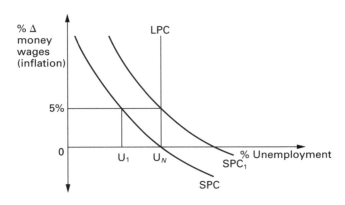

Figure 3

A rise in government spending succeeds in reducing unemployment in the short run to U_1, but in the longer run the economy will return to U_N unemployment, with 5% inflation and the expectation of inflation built into the economy.

Government expenditure on training might succeed in raising output by shifting the LRAS to the right. However some new classical economists argue that resources work more effectively when in the control of the private sector. Government spending on training would have to be financed by either borrowing or taxation, both of which would involve a transfer of resources from the private to the public sector.

20.1 Fact sheet

(a) Economic growth

Economic growth typically refers to an increase in a country's output of goods and services. It is usually measured by changes in real GDP.

(b) Causes of economic growth

A rise in output can occur following:
(1) An increase in resources through:
    (a) net investment;
    (b) the discovery of natural resources;
    (c) an increase in the labour force.
(2) Better use of existing resources through:
    (a) using previously unemployed factors;
    (b) training the labour force;
    (c) innovations that increase productivity;
    (d) a reallocation of factors from low-productivity (e.g. agricultural) to high-productivity (e.g. manufacturing) sectors.

(c) Benefits and costs of economic growth

Economic growth provides benefits but may also impose costs. Some of these are outlined in Table 20.1.

(d) Business cycles

A *business* or *trade cycle* is a fluctuation in economic activity and occurs when real GDP moves away from its trend path.

(e) Causes of business cycles

A number of explanations are put forward to explain business cycles. These include:

(1) Bursts of technological innovation, e.g. development of the microchip.

Table 20.1 The effects of economic growth

Potential benefits of economic growth	Potential costs of economic growth
Improved standard of living	The opportunity cost of additional investment
Poverty can be reduced	Resulting externalities, including pollution
Opportunities for more leisure time	The depletion of non-renewable resources
A rise in people's expected lifespan	Alienation and stress among the labour force

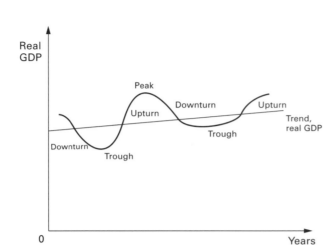

Figure 20.1 Business cycle

(2) Changes in the money supply.

(3) *Stop–go cycles.* A government may seek to increase economic activity prior to a general election and take harsher, deflationary measures after an election.

(4) *Multiplier–accelerator interaction.* An injection of extra spending will cause national income to rise by a multiple amount. This will cause investment to rise, which will further increase national income. Once shortages are experienced, costs rise and other difficulties are encountered, national income and investment will fall.

20.2 Investigative study

Example 20.1

A study on the extent, causes and effects of the black economy among students.

20.3 Data response

Example 20.2

'One of the most fateful errors of our time is the belief that "the problem of production" has been solved. Not only is this belief firmly held by people remote from production and therefore professionally unacquainted with the facts – it is held by virtually all the experts, the captains of industry, the economic managers in the governments of the world, the academic and not-so-academic economists, not to mention the economic journalists. For the rich countries, they say, the most important task now is "education for leisure" and, for poor countries, the "transfer of technology".

Modern man does not experience himself as part of nature but as an outside force destined to dominate and conquer it. He even talks of battle with nature, forgetting that, if he won the battle, he would find himself on the losing side.

The illusion of power is based on the failure to distinguish between income and capital where this distinction matters most. Every economist and businessman is familiar with the distinction and applies it conscientiously and with considerable subtlety to all economic affairs – except where it really matters; namely the irreplaceable capital which man has not made, but simply found, and without which he can do nothing.

A businessman would not consider a firm to have solved its problems of production if he saw it was rapidly consuming its capital. How, then, could we overlook this vital fact when it comes to that very big firm, the economy of Spaceship Earth and, in particular, the economies of its rich passengers?' (E. F. Schumacher, *Small is Beautiful – A Study of Economics As If People Mattered*, London, Abacus, 1974, pp. 10–11).

(a) From the above passage, distinguish between income and capital. **(6 marks)**

(b) Explain the major problems that the author identifies as being faced by nations. **(9 marks)**

(c) What are the implications of the passage for government policies promoting economic growth? **(10 marks)**

Solution 20.2

(a) Income is a flow value, and is the amount of money, goods or services received by an individual, firm or economy in a given period, usually one year. Capital is a stock value, is one of the four factors of production and refers to producer goods used to manufacture other goods. However the author is using a broader definition of capital than is generally employed by economists by his inclusion of the Earth's natural resources. Traditional economists count natural resources as land.

(b) The passage advances two points of view concerning the problems facing rich nations. Most traditional economists argue that great advances in technology have allowed rich countries to produce such a surplus of goods and services that the bulk of human wants and needs can now be satisfied. The problem is not so much one of scarcity as of knowing what to do with the large number of workers now no longer needed in the manufacturing process and who require training in the use of free time. Schumacher argues that the major problem facing rich nations is the over-rapid consumption of irreplaceable natural resources such as metals and minerals. Hence economic growth is only achieved by running down our 'capital' – that is, our stock of finite natural resource.

Poor countries, it is argued, do not have sufficient infrastructure to allow for capital accumulation through net investment, either because there is no surplus after output has been used to satisfy basic needs or because the nation lacks the technology to generate such surpluses. A transfer of 'production know-how' from rich to poor nations would overcome this last problem.

(c) Economic growth is typically taken to mean an increase in a country's output of goods and services, and occurs through either an increase in the amount of resources available or the better use of existing resources. Measures that encourage increases in production have been advanced by successive governments because output increases allow more wants and needs to be satisfied. Measures to encourage economic growth through net investment include subsidies to firms building new factories, particularly in depressed areas, and tax incentives to firms buying new machinery.

The passage highlights the concern of some economists for what they see as an unpleasant side-effect of economic growth: the unacceptably high level of consumption of resources that are gifts of nature and that, once used, cannot be replaced. Sustained economic growth implies an accelerating rate of consumption for non-renewable natural resources. Governments may be concerned to ensure that the system of resource allocation used takes full account of such negative externalities, as well as any pollution generated by high growth.

For instance the price mechanism does not immediately take account of the depletion of finite resources such as oil. As the world's resources begin to reach exhaustion, restricted supply will result in higher prices. But in the immediate term governments might want consumers and producers to pay some penalty for using irreplaceable resources, e.g. by imposing an indirect tax on their consumption. For example substantially taxing petrol reduces consumption and encourages conservation.

Alternatively the government might want to

encourage conservation of scarce gifts of nature by offering subsidies to firms that recycle waste products. For example some local authorities convert refuse collected from households into electricity by burning waste at plants.

Finally, government energy policy can be adjusted. One man-made source of energy is nuclear power, the use of which avoids the depletion of finite resources such as oil, coal and gas. The government might want to achieve economic growth in the energy sector by building more nuclear power stations. However this in itself creates more problems because of the high, long-term economic and social costs of disposing of radioactive waste.

20.4 Objective questions

Example 20.3

The most common measure of economic growth is changes in:
A real GDP
B the output of consumer goods
C the productivity of labour
D the share of capital goods in total output

Example 20.4

Which of the following is an advantage of economic growth?
A An increase in negative externalities
B An increase in the standard of living
C A decline in non-renewable resources
D A reduction in the capital stock

Example 20.5

If GDP has risen by 4%, population by 2% and prices by 3%, then:
A real and nominal GDP per capita have risen
B real and nominal GDP per capita have fallen
C real GDP per capita has risen but nominal GDP per capita has fallen
D real GDP per capita has fallen but nominal GDP per capita has risen

Example 20.6

How would an increase in the productive capacity of the economy be illustrated on a production possibility diagram?

A A movement along the production possibility frontier

B A shift of the production possibility frontier to the left

C A shift of the production possibility frontier to the right

D A movement from with inside the production possibility frontier to on it.

Example 20.7

Which government policy would be most likely to stimulate economic growth?

A An increase in income tax

B An increase in education and training

C An increase in the rate of interest

D An increase in the exchange rate

Example 20.8

What is the main, short-run opportunity cost of economic growth?

A A reduction in capital goods

B A reduction in consumer goods

C A reduction in non-renewable economic resources

D A reduction in the government's ability to alleviate poverty

Example 20.9

Which of the following is a potential cost of economic growth?

A An increase in capital deepening

B An increase in positive externalities

C An increase in the capital/labour ratio

D An increase in the number of workers whose skills are made obsolete by changes in rapid economic change

Example 20.10

Which of the following is a characteristic of the downturn of a business cycle?

A Increasing inflationary pressure

B Increasing stocks of unsold goods

C Falling government expenditure on benefits

D A reduction in the number of companies going into liquidation

Example 20.11

Which of the following is a lagging indicator of changes in economic activity?

A Profits

B Real GDP

C Unemployment

D Building of new houses

Example 20.12

A recession is:

A a slowdown in economic growth

B a rise in unemployment accompanied by a rise in inflation

C a decline in real GDP for two or more successive quarters

D a period of rapidly declining inventories and increasing capital utilisation

20.5 Solutions to objective questions

Solution 20.3   Answer: **A**

Economic growth is usually measured in terms of a change in real GNP or, more commonly, a change in real GDP.

Solution 20.4   Answer: **B**

One of the main benefits of economic growth is a rise in the goods and services that the population can consume.

A and **C** ⇒ are potential disadvantages of economic growth.

D ⇒ The capital stock is likely to increase with economic growth.

Solution 20.5   Answer: **D**

If GDP has risen by 4% and prices by 3%, then real GDP has risen by approximately 1%. If the population has increased by 2% the increase in real GDP has not kept pace with the increase in population and real GDP per capita has fallen. Nominal GDP has increased by more than population (4% compared with 2%) so nominal GDP per capita has risen.

Solution 20.6   Answer: **C**

An increase in the productive capacity of the economy will mean that the country will be able to produce more goods and services. This is illustrated by a shift to the right of the production possibility curve.

A ⇒ This is a change in the combination of goods produced with productive capacity remaining unchanged.

B ⇒ This would illustrate a decrease in the productive capacity of the economy.

D ⇒ This would result in an increase in production. However the maximum potential output of the economy has not changed. When the economy was producing inside the curve it was not making as much as it was capable of, now it is.

Solution 20.7   Answer: **B**

Increases in education and training will raise the productivity levels of workers, thereby raising the productive capacity of the economy.

A ⇒ An increase in income tax is likely to reduce aggregate demand, may discourage entrepreneurial effort and dissuade some people from entering the labour force.

C ⇒ This may lower investment.

D ⇒ An increase in the exchange rate will raise the price of exports and lower the price of imports. This may reduce domestic output.

Solution 20.8   Answer: **B**

If a country is producing at or near full capacity it may have to reduce the output of consumer goods in the short run, so that the freed resources can be switched to producing capital goods. The extra capital goods made will, in the longer run, produce more capital and consumer goods.

Solution 20.9   Answer: **D**

Economic growth requires workers to be mobile and flexible. Workers will have to cope with new technology and change jobs. Not everyone will be able to manage rapid change.

A, B and **C** ⇒ are advantages of growth.

Solution 20.10   Answer: **B**

During the downturn of a business cycle the pace of economic activity declines. Demand falls, so not all the goods produced are sold and stocks rise.

A ⇒ Falling demand and declining wage claims reduce inflationary pressure.

C ⇒ Rising unemployment will increase government expenditure on unemployment-related benefits.

D ⇒ More companies will go into liquidation.

Solution 20.11   Answer: **C**

A lagging indicator is one that reacts after the change in the business cycle. If there is a downturn in economic activity firms will not immediately lay off workers – they will wait to see whether the fall in demand will last, just as when the economy is coming out of recession firms will not immediately take on more workers – they have to be certain that the rise in demand will last. Thus many changes in unemployment occur after changes in output.

A and **D** ⇒ are leading indicators, i.e. indicators that point to changes in economic activity.

B ⇒ is a coincident indicator as it forms the basis of the business cycle itself.

Solution 20.12   Answer: **C**

A recession is usually defined as a fall in real gross domestic product (GDP) over two or more successive quarters.

A ⇒ A slowdown in economic growth still implies positive growth, although it may indicate that the economy is moving towards a recession.

B ⇒ This is a definition of stagflation.

D ⇒ This indicates increasing economic activity. Declining inventories means that stocks of goods are falling and increasing capital utilisation means that firms are making more use of their machines and factories.

20.6 Essays

Example 20.13

(a)   What is meant by economic growth?   **(5 marks)**
(b)   Discuss the benefits and costs of economic growth.   **(20 marks)**

*   Distinguish between actual and potential growth.
*   Consider the impact not just on material living standards but also on the quality of life.
*   Cover the opportunity cost of growth.

Solution 20.13

(a) Economic growth refers to changes in actual and/or potential growth. Actual growth is a rise in the amount of goods and services provided. Potential growth is a rise in the productive potential of the economy and is represented by a rightward shift of the country's production possibility curve.

In the short run actual growth can be achieved by a movement from within a production possibility curve towards the curve. This will involve making fuller and more efficient use of existing resources.

However in the long run actual growth can only be sustained by a shift of the production possibility curve to the right following an increase in the quantity and/or quality of resources. Figure 1 shows an increase in actual output from point X to point Y (actual growth) and a shift in the production possibility curve from AB to CD (potential growth).

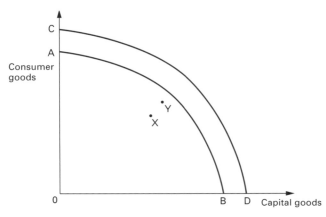

Figure 1

(b) Actual economic growth is usually measured by changes in real GDP. A rise in real GDP will mean that more goods and services are being produced. The main benefit of economic growth is a rise in the material living standards of the population. If real GDP rises by more than the population, real GDP per capita will increase. Over time the number and range of goods and services available to people have increased. Now more than 90% of UK households have a television and a significant proportion have at least one car and go on a foreign holiday at least once a year.

Economic growth can make it easier to alleviate poverty. This is because at least some of the rise in income can be distributed to the poor. In the absence of growth the income of the poor could only be increased by reducing the income of the rich.

Economic growth may improve a country's

international status and its ability to influence international organisations, including the IMF, WTO and EU. Economic growth also increases an economy's ability to improve the environment. Some of the extra goods and services produced can be devoted to improving the quality of the environment.

Indeed what economic growth does is to provide an economy with more choice. The extra goods and services produced can be put to a variety of uses. Some may be used to help the poor, some to reduce pollution whilst others may be used, for example, to improve a state-financed health service.

In a poor country extra goods and services are likely to be used primarily to reduce malnutrition, improve the quality of drinking water and provide basic housing. In such a country economic growth is likely to be viewed as a necessity. However in more affluent countries the desirability of economic growth is a more debatable issue. As well as conferring benefits, economic growth also imposes costs.

In the short run economic growth is likely to involve an opportunity cost of forgone consumer goods. This is because some resources may have to be diverted from producing consumer goods to producing capital goods. The extent of this opportunity cost will depend on the current degree of utilisation of resources and how mobile they are.

Economic growth may result in a longer-term opportunity cost in terms of forgone non-renewable resources and environmental quality. The production of extra goods and services may involve the use of, for example, trees from the rainforests of Brazil and may create air, noise and water pollution.

Producing more goods and services may put extra stress on people, leading to increases in the divorce rate, mental illness and other problems that reduce the quality of people's lives. It is also questionable to what extent the consumption of goods and services makes people happier. The increase in car ownership has resulted in more congestion, more accidents and reduced opportunities for children to play in the street and cycle and walk to school. Some claim that what economic growth does is to generate demand for even more goods and services. The greater availability of, for example, TVs, compact disc players and dishwashers in the UK has not necessarily increased people's happiness significantly. What it has done is to increase the dissatisfaction of those who do not possess these goods or who do not possess the quantity of goods they aspire to. So perhaps, rather than reducing the gap between current and desired consumption, economic growth may increase it or keep it constant.

A connected aspect is that economic growth may increase the uneven nature of income distribution. As the economy grows the demand for some factors of production will rise whilst the demand for others will fall. Some people may be unable, or less able, to cope with the need to learn new skills and to move to new industries.

Example 20.14

(a)   What may cause a consumer boom? **(12 marks)**
(b)   What are the advantages and disadvantages of a consumer boom?   **(13 marks)**

- Define a consumer boom.
- Consider causes of changes in autonomous consumption.
- Consider the effects on output, inflation and the balance of payments position.

Solution 20.14

(a) A consumer boom is a rise in economic activity generated by extra consumer spending. It is consumption-led growth.

A rise in GDP stimulated by a rise in consumer spending implies that autonomous consumption (i.e. spending independent of changes in income) has increased.

There are a number of reasons why people may choose to spend a higher proportion of their income. One is expectation. If people feel more optimistic about economic prospects in terms not just of future income levels but also of job security, they may spend more now.

An increase in the availability of credit and a reduction in its cost, via a fall in the real interest rate, may increase spending, particularly on consumer durables and housing. More people will be able to borrow and each person who does borrow is likely to borrow and spend more.

A rise in wealth is another reason for higher consumer spending. The main asset of many people is their own home. If house prices rise more than the retail price index, people will experience a rise in the real value of this asset and this may encourage them to spend more. The effect of a change in real wealth on consumer spending is known as the wealth effect.

A change in social attitudes may also result in a consumer boom. If people value thrift less highly they will spend more.

(b) A consumer boom is likely to stimulate economic activity. The higher aggregate demand, at least in the short run, will encourage firms to increase their output. In turn this is likely to raise employment. Figure 1 shows a rise in consumer spending increasing natural income. The rise in the quantity of consumer goods and services will increase the material standard of living people enjoy.

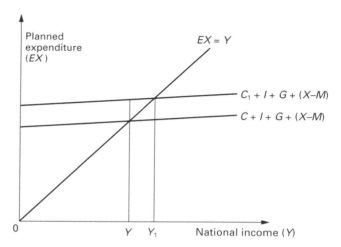

Figure 1

However a consumer boom may not be self-sustaining and may involve a number of disadvantages. Higher consumer spending may cause demand-pull inflation if aggregate demand rises at a faster rate than aggregate supply. This will occur if supply constraints are experienced and when full employment is reached.

Higher consumer spending may result in the use of previously idle resources. However at least part of the extra consumer goods are likely to be produced by resources that have been switched from producing capital goods. If more consumer goods are produced at the expense of capital goods this will reduce future growth potential.

A rise in consumer spending may lead to a deterioration in the country's balance of payments. The higher demand in the home market will result in more goods and services being purchased, some of which will be imports and some of which may have been originally intended for the export market. So a consumer boom tends to increase imports and divert goods from the export to the home market.

If the rise in consumer spending is based on borrowing, people will experience difficulties if real interest rates rise above what is anticipated or if incomes and job prospects improve less than anticipated.

Money, Banking and Monetary Policy

MV=PT

21.1 Fact sheet

(a) Functions and characteristics of money

- *Money* is any item that is widely accepted as payment for products. Money has the following functions:

  (a) *Medium of exchange*: money is used to buy goods.

  (b) *Measure of value (unit of account)*: money is used to compare the value of goods, services and factor rewards.

  (c) *Store of value*: money is used to hold wealth (savings).

  (d) *Standard for deferred payments*: money is used to enable people to borrow and lend agreed amounts.

- The most important characteristic of money is *general acceptability*. If a commodity ceases to be acceptable, it will cease to act as money.

- Other characteristics include portability, divisibility, durability, homogeneity and limited supply.

(b) Measures of the money supply

Two of the most important measures of the money supply in the UK are:

(1) *M0*, which consists of notes, coins and retail banks' balances at the Bank of England. It is a *narrow measure*, which means it concentrates on money that is used mainly as a medium of exchange.

(2) *M4*, which consists of notes, coins and all deposits with banks and building societies denominated in sterling. It is a *broad measure*, which means it concentrates on money kept as a store of value and on which interest is paid.

(c) Financial intermediaries

Financial intermediaries are institutions that channel funds from people and institutions wishing to lend to those wishing to borrow.

(d) The Bank of England

The *Bank of England* (BoE) is the central bank. Its functions include:

Table 21.1 Examples of financial intermediaries

Institution	Functions
Retail banks	Also called commercial banks, high street banks and clearing banks. They provide customers with three traditional services – accepting deposits, acting as agents for payment, and lending – plus a wide range of other services.
Building societies	Accept deposits, lend to house buyers and, since the 1986 Building Societies Act, offer a wide range of banking services.
Discount houses	Borrow from the retail banks and other institutions at short notice and use this money to buy treasury bills, commercial bills and other financial assets.
Merchant banks	Accept bills of exchange, arrange and underwrite the issuing of new shares, provide credit and advice to companies.

(1) Issuing bank notes. The BoE has sole responsibility in England and Wales for the printing, issuing and distribution of notes.
(2) Issuing and managing the national debt.
(3) Acting as the government's bank. Tax revenues and current government expenditure are recorded in the Exchequer's account.
(4) Acting as banker to the monetary sector.
(5) Acting as *leader of last resort*. The BoE will always lend to the banking sector, thereby ensuring sufficient liquidity in the monetary sector to maintain confidence.
(6) Supervising the monetary sector, checking that banks follow prudent policies and maintain adequate liquidity ratios.
(7) Carrying out monetary policy.
(8) Managing the *Exchange Equalisation Account*, which is a Treasury account operated by the BoE to buy and sell sterling to influence the exchange rate.

(e)   Credit creation

- *Liabilities* are the money owed by retail banks and consist mainly of deposits (accounts). Assets are the various resources owned by the bank. The profitability of assets tends to increase as their liquidity is reduced. Banks seek to maximise the amount of profitable but illiquid assets held, while maintaining sufficient liquid assets to meet their customers' demand for cash.

Items (4)–(8) of the balance sheet are the *liquid* or *reserve assets* of the bank.

The liquid asset ratio is the proportion of overall deposits held in liquid form.
- The *bank, money or credit multiplier* shows by how much total liabilities (deposits or low-powered money) can increase as a result of a rise in *liquid assets* (high-powered money) deposited in the bank system.
- Using the equation $D = 100/\text{liquidity ratio} \times R$, it is possible to calculate the change in deposits (D) following a change in liquid assets (*R*). Assume that the liquidity ratio is 12.5% and a bank's liquid assets increase by £2m:

$D = 100/\text{liquidity ratio} \times R = 100/12.5 \times £2m = 8$ (the bank multiplier) $\times £2m = £16m$

- The change in bank lending (i.e. the credit created) is $D - R = £16m - £2m = £14m$.

(f)   Monetary policy

Monetary policy covers measures that seek to change the supply of money or the price of money (the interest rate). Among *monetary policy targets* are:

(1) growth of the money supply;
(2) the level and structure of interest rates;
(3) the exchange rate;
(4) the inflation rate.

(g)   Control of credit creation

The Bank of England can use a number of measures to restrict the ability of banks to create credit, although some have not been used recently:

Table 21.2 Balance sheet of a retail bank

Liabilities (D)	Assets (A)
(1) Sight deposits	(4) Cash in till
(2) Time deposits	(5) Balances at the BoE
	(6) Money at call and short notice
	(7) Treasury and other bills
	(8) Short-term investments
	(9) Investments
	(10 Advances
	(11) Property
(3) Total liabilities	(12) Total assets

(1) Customers' current accounts.
(2) Customers' deposit accounts.
(3) Total amount of money owed by the bank to customers.
(4) Cash in till held on the premises.
(5) Operational accounts used to settle interbank debts at clearing and to draw out cash when necessary.
(6) Money lent at call or short notice (seven days) to the discount houses.
(7) Short-term (91 days) loans to the government or companies.
(8) Government and local authority stocks (securities or bonds) with less than a year to run.
(9) Government securities, etc. with more than one year to run.
(10) Loans to customers.
(11) The value of bank premises etc.
(12) Total amount of bank claims on other people.

(1) *Open market operations*, where the BoE sells short-term government securities and bills, thereby reducing retail banks' liquid assets and raising interest rates.
(2) *Funding*, where the BoE issues more long-term securities and fewer short-term securities, thereby reducing the banks' liquid assets.
(3) *The minimum lending rate* (MLR) is the rate, announced in advance, at which the BoE lends to the discount houses. The MLR influences other market interest rates.
(4) *Interest rate policy*. The BoE may operate a number of undisclosed interest rate bands at which it will discount bills, raising or lowering these bands to influence the structure of interest rates in the money market.
(5) *Special deposits* are the compulsory loans that the BoE can demand from the retail banks, thereby reducing their liquid assets.
(6) An increase in the *liquid asset ratio requirement* reduces the amount of liabilities a retail bank can have from a given volume of liquid assets.
(7) *Quantitative controls* on lending involve the BoE setting an upper limit on the volume of bank lending.
(8) *Qualitative lending* guidelines involve requesting banks to direct lending to particular groups and/or restrict lending to other groups.
(9) *Moral (suasion)*. The BoE can informally try to persuade retail banks to change their lending policy.
(10) *Monetary base control* involves the BoE regulating base money.

(h) Effects of interest rate changes

A rise in interest rates is likely to:

(1) reduce bank lending;
(2) increase the savings ratio;
(3) reduce consumer spending;
(4) reduce investment;
(5) increase the external value of the pound sterling.

(i) The public-sector borrowing requirement

The *public sector borrowing requirement* (PSBR) is the positive difference between the total income and expenditure of the public sector. This borrowing can be financed by:

(1) Borrowing from the BoE, which is likely to increase the money supply via a rise in the high-powered monetary base.

(2) Borrowing from the banking sector by selling treasury bills, which is likely to increase the money supply via a rise in banks' liquid assets.

(3) Borrowing from the non-bank private sector by selling government securities, which some argue may crowd out private investment.

(4) Borrowing from overseas residents, which results in a rise in interest payments on national debt going abroad.

• A negative PSBR means that the income of the public sector exceeds its expenditure and there is a *public sector debt repayment* (PSDR).

21.2 Investigative study

Example 21.1

An analysis of the effects of a change in interest rates on local businesses.

21.3 Data response

Example 21.2

Pressure for a rise in interest rates eased slightly yesterday after the Bank of England said M0, the narrowest measure of money supply, fell back in January.

M0 fell a seasonally adjusted 0.3 per cent in January compared with the previous month, the Bank said.

Measured without the volatile bankers' deposits, the level of notes and coins in circulation – which account for 99 per cent of M0 – fell 0.1 per cent in the month.

In the year to January, M0 grew a seasonally adjusted 6.4 per cent.

This is still outside the government's target range for M0 of zero to 4 per cent. However, January was the third month in which the annual growth rate of M0 fell after growing 7.3 per cent in October.

M0 has traditionally been regarded as a good indication of the level of retail sales, and some economists yesterday suggested that the drop may indicate that high street sales had fallen sharply in January.

Source: Extract from an article by Gillian Tett, *Financial Times*, 31 January 1995.

(a) What is the difference between narrow and broad measures of the money supply? **(6 marks)**

(b) What does the M0 measure of the money supply include? **(3 marks)**

(c) What are the advantages of a government announcing a target for the change in M0? **(6 marks)**

(d) Why is M0 seen as 'a good indication of the level of retail sales'? **(4 marks)**

(e) How may a rise in interest rate reduce inflationary pressure? **(6 marks)**

Solution 21.2

(a) Narrow money measures include assets that represent immediate purchasing power, i.e. assets used mainly as a medium of exchange. Broad money measures include not only assets used as a medium of exchange, but also those used as a temporary store of value, i.e. immediate and potential purchasing power.

(b) The M0 measure of the money supply includes banks' operational balances at the Bank of England, notes and coins. It is a narrow measure of the money supply and focuses on the monetary base.

(c) Two main advantages are claimed for announcing a target for the growth of a monetary aggregate. One is that it imposes discipline on the government's monetary policy. The other is that it reduces expectations of inflation. Announcing a target range for M0 of 0–4 per cent makes it possible to assess whether the government has achieved its objective. In addition, if people believe that a government is determined to control the money supply it may convince them that inflation will fall. The expectation of lower inflation may result in a fall in wage claims and price increases.

(d) If M0 rises the monetary base increases. This enables bank lending to rise. More money in circulation and increased bank lending is likely to result in an increase in spending, so shops are likely to experience increased sales. Similarly a fall in M0 is likely to reduce retail sales.

(e) A rise in the interest rate, specifically the real interest rate, may reduce demand-pull inflation. This is because it will reduce demand for consumer durables purchased with borrowed money since borrowing will become more expensive. A rise in the mortgage interest rate will reduce people's discretionary income, thereby lowering their ability to buy goods and services. A rise in the interest rate may also reduce spending by encouraging people to save more.

21.4 Objective questions

Example 21.3

The essential condition for an item to act as money is that:
A it is homogeneous
B it is legal tender
C it is backed by gold
D it is generally acceptable

Example 21.4

Which financial institution underwrites the weekly treasury bill tender?
A Discount houses
B Market banks
C Retail banks
D The Bank of England

Examples 21.5–21.7 refer to three assets and one liability of a retail bank:
A Operational balances at the Bank of England
B Treasury bills
C Advances to customers
D Customers' sight deposits

Example 21.5

Which of the items **A** to **D** constitutes the largest figure on the assets side of a retail bank's balance sheet?

Example 21.6

Which of **A** to **D** is a liability of a retail bank?

Example 21.7

Which of the assets in **A** to **D** is the most liquid?

Example 21.8

A bank keeping a liquidity ratio of 10% receives a cash deposit of £240m. On the basis of this additional cash, the maximum additional deposits it could create would be:
A £1200m   B £2160m   C £2400m   D £2640m

Example 21.9

A bank that keeps a 12.5% liquidity ratio experiences a reduction in liquid assets of £90m. If the bank's holdings of liquid assets was previously just meeting its liquidity ratio, the withdrawal of cash will cause a total decrease of liabilities of:
A £11.25m B £90m   C £720m   D £1125m

Example 21.10

The Bank of England sells government securities to the non-bank general public. This will tend to:
A reduce the money supply and raise interest rates
B reduce the money supply and lower interest rates
C increase the money supply and raise interest rates
D increase the money supply and lower interest rates

Example 21.11

If government's prime objective is to reduce unemployment by increasing demand, the monetary policy it is most likely to adopt is to:
A call in special deposits
B lower the interest rate
C sell government securities to the non-bank private sector
D sell fewer treasury bills and more long-term government securities

Example 21.12

Which of the following means of financing government spending is likely to lead to the greatest increase in the money supply?
A An increase in direct taxation
B An increase in indirect taxation
C The sale of treasury bills to the banking sector
D The sale of national savings certificates to the general public

21.5 Solutions to objective questions

Solution 21.3   Answer: **D**

An item may possess many of the desirable characteristics of money, but if it ceases to be generally acceptable, it will cease to act as money and people will use another item.

 A $\Rightarrow$ is regarded as an important quality for money to possess but is not as significant as acceptability.

 B $\Rightarrow$ The main form of money in the UK is bank deposits, which are not legal tender.

C ⇒ The vast majority of money – i.e. all bank and building society deposits and cash – is not backed by gold and therefore is fiduciary issue

Solution 21.4   Answer: **A**

A number of financial institutions and individuals buy treasury bills. However it is only the discount houses that are committed to purchasing any treasury bills not taken up through the competitive bidding process. In return for carrying out this function, the discount houses are able to use the Bank of England's 'lender of last resort' facility.

Solution 21.5   Answer: **C**

Retail banks hold a range of current and fixed assets. However their most profitable activity is lending, and advances account for the largest single item in their assets, usually in excess of 60%.

Solution 21.6   Answer: **D**

Customers' sight deposits are liabilities, as a retail bank has an obligation to pay these out to its customers on demand.

A, **B** and **C** ⇒ are all assets, items that the bank possesses.

Solution 21.7   Answer: **A**

A retail bank can draw out money from its operational balances at very short notice. Operational balances are regarded as very liquid assets, usually the next most liquid after cash in till.

Solution 21.8   Answer: **B**

A bank with a liquidity ratio of 10% has a bank multiplier of 100/10 = 10. A cash deposit of £240m will enable total liabilities to increase by £240m × 10 = £2400m. This includes the deposit given to the customer who deposited the £240m. As a result, additional loans of £2400m minus the initial deposit could be created, i.e. £2400m − £240m = £2160m.

Solution 21.9   Answer: **C**

The bank multiplier works in reverse. A liquidity ratio of 12.5% will mean a bank multiplier of

100/12.5 = 8. Thus a reduction in liquid assets of £90m will cause a fall in total liabilities of £90m × 8 = £720m.

Solution 21.10   Answer: **A**

The sale of government securities will reduce the money supply. The increase in the supply of government securities will also reduce their price. The price of government securities and interest rates vary inversely. Thus a fall in the price of government securities will be accompanied by a rise in interest rates.

Solution 21.11   Answer: **B**

Lowering the interest rate is likely to stimulate borrowing and spending.

A, **C** and **D** ⇒ are all likely to reduce bank lending and demand.

Solution 21.12   Answer: **C**

The sale of treasury bills to the banking sector will increase banks' supply of liquid assets, which will enable an increase in bank lending to occur.

A, **B** and **D** ⇒ are likely to have a neutral effect on the money supply. This is because the increase in bank deposits resulting from the injection to government spending is likely to be offset by a fall in bank deposits arising from increased taxation or the purchase of government securities.

21.6 Essays

Example 21.13

What effect will an increase in the real UK interest rate have on the level of:

(a)	consumer spending;	**(8 marks)**
(b)	capital investment;	**(8 marks)**
(c)	the sterling exchange rate?	**(9 marks)**

- Distinguish between nominal and real interest rates.
- Consider the effects on both spending and saving.
- Cover MEC.
- Consider the effects under both a fixed and a floating exchange rate system.
- Include a diagram in parts (b) and (c).

Solution 21.13

(a) The real interest rate is the rate of interest adjusted for inflation. It is the nominal interest rate minus the inflation rate. For example if the nominal interest rate is 10% and the inflation rate is 4%, the real interest rate is 6%.

A rise in the real interest rate is likely to reduce consumer spending, for a number of related reasons. The higher interest rate charges will discourage borrowing, which in turn will reduce expenditure on, for example, cars, foreign holidays, washing machines and other consumer durables, which are often purchased with borrowed money.

The higher interest rate will also mean that people who have borrowed in the past at a variable interest rate will have less discretionary income. A high proportion of the population have taken out a mortgage loan on their homes and a rise in the interest rate will reduce their purchasing power. Those net savers who hold interest-bearing deposits will experience an increase in their unearned income and these people may spend more. However those who hold their wealth in the form of houses, government bonds or shares are likely to see their value fall and so may reduce their spending.

Consumer spending may also fall because a rise in the real interest rate will make saving more attractive. People will save a higher proportion of their income and hence spend a smaller proportion.

(b) A rise in the real interest rate is also likely to reduce capital investment, i.e. expenditure on goods that are used to produce other goods, such as machinery. Firms invest when the expected yield from the investment, which is referred to as the marginal efficiency of capital, exceeds the cost. The cost of investment is the interest rate. This is because when firms borrow to buy capital goods they have to pay interest. In practice most firms use retained profits to finance investment. In this case the interest rate is the opportunity cost of investment. When deciding whether to use at least some of its retained profits to buy capital goods a firm has to consider the return from alternative uses, for example placing the money in an interest-bearing deposit account. Figure 1 shows the relationship between the interest rate and planned investment. A rise in the interest rate from R to R_1 reduces planned investment from Q to Q_1.

(c) A rise in the real UK interest rate, if not matched by a rise in other countries' real interest rates, is likely

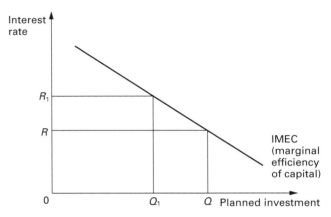

Figure 1

to result in a net capital inflow into the UK. This is because the return on deposits in UK financial institutions will increase, which in turn will encourage foreigners to place money with these financial institutions.

The higher demand for sterling from foreign financial investors will put upward pressure on the pound. If the UK is operating a floating exchange rate, this will raise the exchange rate, as illustrated in Figure 2.

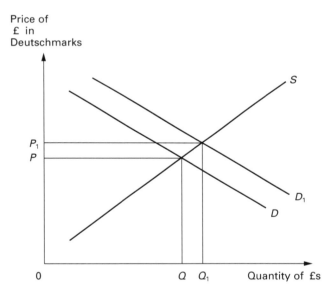

Figure 2

If the UK is operating an adjustable peg system it may raise the exchange rate towards the top of the upper margin. If it threatened to go above this, the government would have to stop this trend by selling the currency. Similarly if the government wishes to maintain a fixed exchange rate it would have to take similar appropriate measures to offset the upward pressure caused by the rise in the interest rate.

Example 21.14

(a) What is meant by the money supply? **(5 marks)**
(b) Why does the government measure the money supply? **(5 marks)**
(c) Why may a government seek to control the growth of the money supply? **(15 marks)**

- Define money and discuss what is included in the main two measures of money.
- Concentrate on the relationship between changes in the money supply and inflation, but also consider how changes in the money supply will affect other objectives.

Solution 21.14

(a) The money supply is a measure of the items that fulfil the functions of money, i.e. act as a medium of exchange, unit of account, store of value and standard for deferred payments. An item that fulfils these functions will have a number of characteristics, the most important of which is to be generally acceptable.

The main components of the UK money supply are notes, coins and bank and building society deposits. There are a number of official measures of the money supply, each of which includes different items. At any one time the government is likely to concentrate on one or two measures. In recent years M0 (essentially notes, coins and banks' operational balances at the Bank of England) and M4 (notes, coins, banks' sight and time deposits and building society deposits) have received the greatest attention.

(b) One reason why the government measures the money supply is as an indicator of economic trends and the state of financial markets. For instance a rapid growth of base money (M0) will indicate a future rise in bank deposits.

Another reason is that the government may wish to use changes in the money supply as a policy instrument or objective, to influence one of its four main macroeconomic objectives. These are low inflation, balance of payments equilibrium, full employment and growth. To achieve the last two objectives the government may wish to increase the money supply, perhaps by encouraging bank lending. However to achieve the first two objectives it may seek to reduce the growth of the money supply and the level of demand.

(c) A government whose main objective is to reduce inflation, and which believes that inflation is caused by the money supply growing too rapidly at a rate exceeding the growth of output, will place considerable emphasis on controlling the growth of the money supply.

Monetarists argue that a rise in the money supply will increase people's money balances, some of which will be used to purchase goods and services. The rise in demand will, after a period of time, cause producers to raise their prices. To illustrate this analysis, monetarists make use of the quantity theory. They suggest that if V (velocity of circulation) and T (transactions) are presumed to be constant, then a rise in M (money supply) will cause a percentage rise in P (prices).

Monetarists wishing to see a reduction in the growth of the money supply may urge a decrease in the PSBR (public sector borrowing requirement) and possibly control of bank lending.

Some monetarists favour announcing targets for the growth of monetary aggregates. They argue that this may help to convince people that the government is taking steps to control prices and thereby reduce expectations of inflation, which can affect wage claims and price rises. They also suggest that this will also impose discipline on the government, which will not want to be seen to be failing to meet its targets.

If the banks increase their lending, this may not only contribute to inflation but also worsen a current account deficit. People borrowing from the banks may purchase imports, and the rising home demand may cause some producers to divert goods from the export to the home market.

In contrast some economists argue that a failure of bank lending to keep pace with the demand for loans can cause problems. During times of inflation entrepreneurs face rising costs and are likely to try to borrow more from the financial sector. If they are unable to raise sufficient funds they may go out of business, thereby causing unemployment.

The money supply may be regarded as an indicator, a target and a policy instrument, and it plays a particularly important role in monetarist analysis and policy. However it is difficult to know which measure(s) of the money supply to use, and economists have found that, once one measure is under control, others start to move in undesired directions.

Unemployment

22.1 Fact sheet

(a) Definition of unemployment

Unemployment is a stock, the size of which is influenced by inflows and outflows and the duration of unemployment experienced.

- *Disequilibruium unemployment* occurs when the aggregate demand for labour is less than the aggregate supply of labour at the current real wage rate.
- *Equilibrium unemployment* occurs when the aggregate demand for and the supply of labour at the current wage rate are equal. Those who are unemployed are unemployed because they are unable or unwilling to take up vacancies.
- *Full employment* does not mean that everyone is employed. In a dynamic economy there will always be some workers changing jobs and some people choosing not to take up paid employment.
- Over-full employment occurs when the number of vacancies exceed the number of unemployed.

(b) Measuring unemployment

In the UK, official unemployment figures include those claiming unemployment-related benefits, principally the job seekers' allowance.

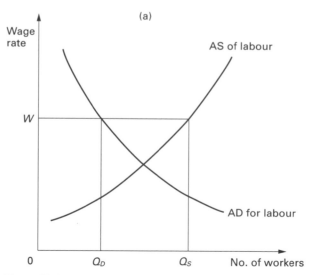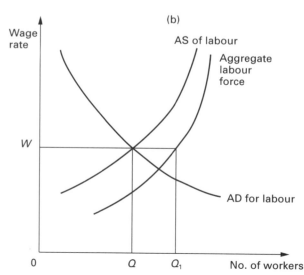

Figure 22.1(a) Disequilibrium unemployment of QD – QS; (b) Equilibrium unemployment of Q – Q₁.

- *Seasonally adjusted unemployment figures* take out the effects of seasonal factors such as weather, which results in unemployment being unusually high or low in certain months.

Table 22.1 gives examples of adjustments that some suggest should be made to the official figures.

The unemployment rate is: registered unemployment/labour force $\times$ 100.

(c) Types and causes of unemployment

Figure 22.2 illustrates Keynes' explanation of unemployment caused by insufficient aggregate demand. At the full employment level of national income (Y_{fe}), output is J, while aggregate demand is only K. The deflationary gap of $J - K$ causes cyclical unemployment.

Table 22.1 Measuring unemployment

Some economists/politicians believe the following should be included	Some economists/politicians believe the following should be omitted
Unemployed over-60s	Severely disabled people
Discouraged workers	Claimants working in the 'black' economy
Those in government special employment measures	Claimants who are not looking for work
Unemployed not entitled to benefits	Mentally and physically handicapped people
Those on short-time working	Those in between jobs
Those who choose not to register	
Students on vacation	

Table 22.2 Types and causes of unemployment

Type of unemployment	Description
Frictional, or *transitional*	Occurs when workers are temporarily unemployed while moving from one job to another
Search	A form of frictional unemployment when workers do not accept the first job offered but remain unemployed while searching for a better job
Casual	Another form of frictional unemployment when workers are unemployed in between short periods of employment
Seasonal	Those who are unemployed as a result of seasonal fluctuations in demand and/or changes in weather conditions
Structural	Those out of work because of a permanent decline in the demand for an industry's products
Regional	Those out of work are disproportionately concentrated in particular regions, largely as a result of these areas being dependent on declining industries
Technological	A form of structural unemployment due to the introduction of new automated methods of production
International	Those out of work due to a fall in demand for domestically produced goods
Cyclical, or *mass* or *demand-deficient*	Those out of work because of a lack of aggregate demand
Involuntary	Workers without a job who are willing and able to work at current wage rates
Voluntary	Workers without a job who prefer to live on benefits

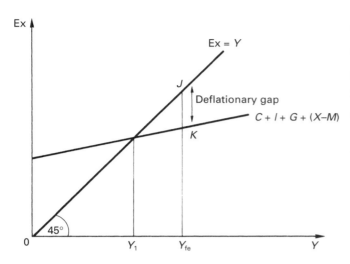

Figure 22.2 A deflationary gap

(d) The non-accelerating inflation rate of unemployment (NAIRU)

NAIRU can also be called the *natural rate of unemployment*. It is the level of unemployment that is associated with a constant rate of inflation. At NAIRU the demand for labour is equal to the number of people prepared to supply their labour for the prevailing wage rate. Any unemployment is equilibrium unemployment and arises from labour market imperfections.

(e) The costs of unemployment

The costs are influenced by the numbers unemployed and the length of time they are unemployed. They include:

(1) Cost to the economy from lost production that can never be regained.
(2) Cost to the government in the form of:
    (a) lost revenue from, for example, income tax, National Insurance contributions, VAT;
    (b) increased expenditure on the job seekers' allowance and other benefits, special employment schemes, redundancy payments in the public sector.
(3) Cost to the individual, usually in the form of:
    (a) decreased income;
    (b) loss of status, alienation and frustration;
    (c) reduced chance of regaining employment the longer unemployed.

(f) Remedies for unemployment

22.2 Investigative study

Example 22.1

A study of the impact of changes in the rate of, or conditions needed to be fulfilled to receive, job seekers' allowance.

Table 22.3 Remedies for unemployment

Type	Remedy
Frictional and search	May be reduced by improved vacancy information services and retraining
Casual and seasonal	Finding other activities during slack periods; employ students, retired people or work overtime during peak employment periods
Structural	Improve occupational mobility through retraining; import protection for declining industries
Regional and technological	Regional policies; retraining and import protection for particular industries
International	Lowering the exchange rate; imposing import controls
Cyclical	Increasing aggregate demand by expansionary fiscal and/or monetary policy. In addition, the Cambridge Economic Policy Group believe in imposing general import controls to ensure that rising demand goes on domestic goods and providing protection while UK industry is restructured
NAIRU	Monetarists suggest supply-side policies to widen the gap between unemployment and employment income by reducing direct taxes and unemployment-related benefits; reducing trade union power; improving the mobility of labour

22.3 Data response

Example 22.2

Year	% change in RPI	% UK unemployment (thousands)	UK unemployment (thousands)	Unfilled vacancies (thousands)
1988	4.9	8.4	2370.4	247.8
1989	7.8	6.3	1798.7	218.4
1990	9.4	5.8	1664.4	172.5
1991	5.9	8.0	2291.9	116.6
1992	3.8	9.8	2778.6	116.0
1993	1.6	10.4	2919.2	126.6
1994	2.5	9.4	2636.5	175.8

Sources: Employment Gazette, March 1995; CSO *Economic Trends*, Annual Trends, annual supplement, 1995.

It is estimated that only about one third of all vacancies are notified to job centres and that approximately one quarter of all appointments are made through job centres.

In any period, some of the vacancies may be in different areas of the country from the areas in which the unemployed live, may require different skills and qualifications from those possessed by the unemployed, or may be for jobs that the unemployed are unwilling to do.

(a) Do the figures support the relationship between inflation and unemployment indicated by the Phillips curve? **(6 marks)**

(b) Explain how a fall in the inflation rate can reduce unemployment. **(6 marks)**

(c) Discuss the relationships between vacancies and unemployment from 1988 to 1994. **(5 marks)**

(d) Why might the proportion of vacancies notified to job centres (i) increase or (ii) decrease during times of high unemployment? **(5 marks)**

(e) '... some of the vacancies ... may be for jobs that the unemployed are unwilling to do': what types of unemployment may this describe? **(3 marks)**

Solution 22.2

(a) The Phillips curve suggests that high inflation will be associated with low unemployment, and vice versa. It implies a trade-off relationship between inflation and unemployment.

The figures do support the relationship suggested by the Phillips curve. From 1988 to 1990 inflation rose and unemployment fell. From 1990 to 1993 inflation fell and unemployment rose. Then from 1993 inflation rose and unemployment fell. So throughout the period inflation and unemployment moved in the directions predicted by the Phillips curve.

(b) A fall in the inflation rate could make UK goods more competitive at home and abroad. If the UK inflation rate were to fall below that of the UK's main competitors, then the demand for exports would rise, while the demand for imports would fall. The extent to which unemployment will fall will depend on the original level of unemployment, how much output rises, the relative costs of labour and capital and changes in technology.

(c) Between 1988 and 1990 both unemployment and vacancies fell, but at different rates. Unemployment

Year	Number of unemployed per unfilled vacancy
1988	9.6
1989	8.2
1990	9.6
1991	19.7
1992	24.0
1993	23.1
1994	15.0

rose between 1990 and 1993 and then fell in 1994. Vacancies fell from 1990 to 1992 and then rose. The number of unemployed per unfilled vacancy fluctuated throughout the period.

(d) During times of high unemployment, employers may be keener to notify vacancies to job centres as they believe that people possessing higher skills and qualifications will be registered there. However it is possible that a smaller proportion of vacancies may be notified, since employers may be able to fill vacancies relatively easily and quickly through, for example, word of mouth, 'in-house' publications and newspaper advertisements.

(e) A situation where jobs are available but the unemployed do not take them up may describe voluntary or search unemployment. The former occurs when people are unwilling to work, and the latter occurs when people do not accept the first job offered but remain unemployed while seeking a better job.

22.4 Objective questions

Example 22.3

Which group of workers is most likely to experience casual unemployment?
A Accountants
B Actors
C Chiropodists
D Undertakers

Example 22.4

As a result of a decrease in the demand for blankets, several blanket mills are closed down and the workers are made redundant. This is a result of:
A demand deficiency unemployment
B seasonal unemployment
C residual unemployment
D structural unemployment

Example 22.5

The natural rate of unemployment is the rate:
A at which unemployment is zero
B at which inflation is constant
C at which all unemployment is involuntary
D below which it is impossible to lower unemployment, in both the short and the long term, by increasing aggregate demand

Example 22.6

The government attempts to reduce cyclical unemployment by means of an expansionary fiscal policy. The impact of the policy in lowering unemployment would be reduced by:
A a low interest rate
B a high marginal propensity to import
C a low marginal propensity to save
D a high marginal propensity to consume

Example 22.7

Which of the following would increase a deflationary gap?
A An increase in savings
B An increase in investment
C An increase in export revenue
D An increase in government spending

Example 22.8

Which of the following conditions will ensure full employment in an economy?
A A balanced budget
B Planned savings equalling planned investment
C Total leakages from the circular flow of income equalling total injections
D None of the above

Example 22.9

Search unemployment is a form of:
A frictional unemployment
B structural unemployment
C regional unemployment
D cyclical unemployment

Example 22.10

An increase in which of the following would reduce the NAIRU?
A Income tax
B Labour mobility
C Government expenditure
D Job seekers' allowance

Example 22.11

Which of the following groups is included in the government's official unemployment figures?

A Unemployed men aged 60-plus
B People on government training schemes for the unemployed
C Students looking for jobs in vacation periods
D People who are claiming the job seekers' allowance while working in the 'black economy'

Example 22.12

What will be the effect, *certeris paribus*, of an increase in unemployment?

	Government expenditure:	Taxation revenue:
A	increase	increase
B	increase	decrease
C	decrease	decrease
D	decrease	increase

22.5 Solutions to objective questions

Solution 22.3   Answer: B

Casual unemployment occurs when workers who are usually employed on a short-term basis are laid off. Actors are frequently 'resting', i.e. are unemployed between roles. Accountants, chiropodists and undertakers are usually employed on a more regular and long-term basis than actors.

Solution 22.4   Answer: D

This is an example of unemployment arising from an industry experiencing a decline in demand for its products.

A ⇒ Demand deficiency unemployment arises as a result of a lack of aggregate demand.

B ⇒ Seasonal unemployment results from changes in demand occurring in particular times of the year and when weather conditions prevent production.

C ⇒ Residual unemployment refers to those people who would be likely to be unemployed even when demand is high.

Solution 22.5   Answer: B

According to monetarists the natural rate of unemployment (which can also be referred to as the non-accelerating inflation rate of unemployment) is when inflation is stable but not necessarily zero.

A ⇒ At the natural rate there is likely to be some unemployment in the form of those who are not

prepared to work at that wage rate and people in between jobs.

C ⇒ Monetarists argue that unemployment above the natural rate is voluntary and not involuntary.

D ⇒ Monetarists believe that, while it is not possible to reduce unemployment below the natural rate in the long term by increasing demand, it is possible to do so in the short term but only at the expense of accelerating inflation.

Solution 22.6   Answer: B

Cyclical unemployment arises from a lack of aggregate demand. Expansionary fiscal policy will increase demand. However a high MPM will mean that a significant proportion of the extra demand will create increased employment abroad rather than at home.

A, C and D ⇒ are all likely to mean that a high proportion of the extra demand will be spent, much of it on domestic output.

Solution 22.7   Answer: A

A deflationary gap exists when aggregate monetary demand is below the level required to ensure full employment –people demand fewer goods and services than the labour force can produce. An increase in savings would reduce demand and hence increase the gap.

B, C and D ⇒ would all tend to increase the demand for domestic goods and services and hence reduce the gap.

Solution 22.8   Answer: D

None of the conditions will ensure full employment.

A and B ⇒ consider only some of the potential injections and leakages and neither condition will guarantee full employment.

C ⇒ will mean that the economy is in equilibrium, but Keynes argued that an economy can be in equilibrium at any level of employment and not necessarily at the full-employment level. Indeed, without planning it would be very unlikely to be at this level.

Solution 22.9   Answer: A

Search unemployment arises when unemployed workers do not accept the first jobs on offer but seek better pay and/or conditions. The unemployed, in this case, are in between jobs and hence search unemployment is a form of frictional unemployment. The length of time people are unemployed in this case will be influenced by, for example, the level of the job seekers' allowance and the amount of information about job opportunities.

Solution 22.10   Answer: **B**

The non-accelerating inflation rate of unemployment (NAIRU) can be reduced, according to new classical economists, by supply-side measures, including increasing labour mobility.

A ⇒ An increase in income tax will lower disposable income and may discourage some people from seeking paid employment.

C ⇒ will increase demand, but according to new classical economists will not reduce NAIRU in the long term.

D ⇒ New classical economists argue that an increase in the job seekers' allowance is likely to increase NAIRU by raising voluntary unemployment.

Solution 22.11   Answer: **D**

While many would agree that those who are working in the 'black economy' are not really unemployed, if they are receiving the job seekers' allowance they will be counted. Indeed it is difficult to assess which claimants are looking for work and which are illegally claiming benefit.

A, B and **C** ⇒ These groups have been included in official unemployment figures in the past and some economists believe they still should be, but they are not currently included.

Solution 22.12   Answer: **B**

A rise in unemployment will mean that the government will pay out more in unemployment-related benefits, including the job seekers' allowance, whilst the more people are unemployed the lower expenditure (and hence, for example, VAT revenue) will be and the lower income (and hence, for example, income tax) will be.

22.6 Essays

Example 22.13

(a) Distinguish between disequilibrium unemployment and equilibrium unemployment.
        (15 marks)

(b) What measures may be used to reduce equilibrium unemployment.   **(10 marks)**

*   Define equilibrium and disequilibrium unemployment and discuss their causes.
*   Include diagrams.
*   In part (b) concentrate on supply side measures.

Solution 22.13

(a) Disequilibrium unemployment occurs, as its name suggests, when the labour market is not in equilibrium. It arises when the aggregate supply of labour exceeds the aggregate demand for labour at the going wage rate. It represents involuntary unemployment – potential workers who are willing to work at the going wage rate but who are unable to find jobs. It is assumed that money wages are sticky downwards, with workers resisting cuts in money wages. So labour markets will not clear. If aggregate supply exceeds the aggregate demand for labour, the wage rate will not fall to restore equilibrium. Figure 1 shows disequilibrium unemployment of QQ_1.

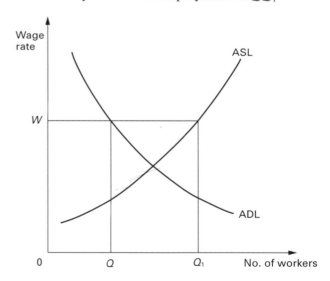

Figure 1

There are three main causes of disequilibrium unemployment. One is trade unions pushing up the wage rate above the equilibrium level. Another is an increase in the labour supply with no corresponding fall in the wage rate. However the cause that receives the most attention is a fall in demand with no corresponding fall in wages. The lack of aggregate demand at the going wage rate results in disequilibrium unemployment.

Equilibrium unemployment occurs when, in contrast to disequilibrium unemployment, there is equilibrium in the labour market. The labour market is in equilibrium when the aggregate demand for labour and the aggregate supply of labour are equal at the going wage rate. At this point there can still be unemployed workers. Not all of those in the aggregate labour force will be in employment. Figure 2 shows equilibrium unemployment of QQ_1.

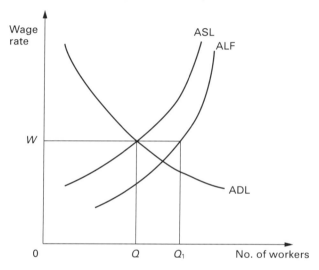

Figure 2

As the wage rate rises the gap between the aggregate labour force and the aggregate supply of labour (those willing to work at the going wage rate) becomes narrower. This is because people become more willing to accept jobs the higher the wages on offer.

Equilibrium unemployment represents those in the labour force who are unwilling or unable to find employment at the going wage rate or who are unaware of job opportunities. Some unemployed workers may be seeking higher wages, some may be occupationally immobile because they lack suitable skills, training and qualifications, some may be geographically immobile and some may lack information about vacancies. So whilst there can be macroeconomic equilibrium in the labour market, there can also be microeconomic disequilibrium with frictional, structural and seasonal unemployment.

Equilibrium unemployment is also referred to as the natural rate of unemployment or the non-accelerating inflation rate of unemployment.

(b) There are a number of measures that supply-side economists advocate to reduce equilibrium unemployment.

To reduce unemployment arising from a lack of willingness to accept jobs at the going wage rate (voluntary unemployment) they suggest increasing the gap between earnings from paid employments and the benefits that can be received by the unemployed. This can be achieved in one of two main ways. Direct taxes in the form of income tax and national insurance contributions can be cut to increase the return from employment and effort. The return from unemployment can be reduced by cutting the job seekers' allowance and other benefits the unemployed can receive, such as housing benefit.

To increase the ability of the unemployed to obtain employment, the government could promote training and education. Mobility could also be encouraged by, for example, removing rent controls and promoting flexible pension schemes.

Supply-side economists also favour trade union legislation to reduce the ability of trade unions to place artificial restrictions on entry to, and flexibility of, labour markets. They also advocate cutting corporation tax to encourage enterprise, output and employment. Other measures that they suggest would increase employment via improvements in the efficiency of markets include deregulation and privatisation, as they believe resources work more efficiently in the private sector.

Example 22.14

(a) What are the costs of unemployment?

(15 marks)

(b) Are there any benefits arising from unemployment? **(10 marks)**

- Include costs and benefits to different groups.
- Include a production possibility curve to illustrate the loss of potential output.

Solution 22.14

(a) Unemployment imposes costs on the unemployed, taxpayers and the wider society.

The main cost to society is forgone output. This output is lost for all time. People will consume fewer goods and services than the economy is capable of producing. Hence actual living standards are below potential living standards. Figure 1 shows that the economy is capable of producing, for example, 0B consumer goods and 0D capital goods, or any other combination on the production possibility curve. However with unemployed workers it only produces 0A of consumer goods and 0C of capital goods, and produces at point X inside the production possibility curve.

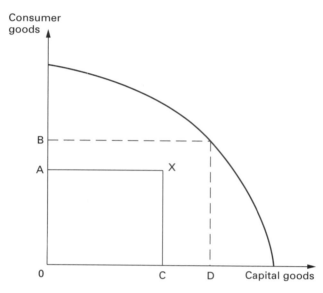

Figure 1

There is increasing evidence of a link between unemployment and crime, particularly between unemployed young men and crime. The costs of crime are obviously high and include the costs of prevention and detection, imprisonment of those found guilty of committing crimes, national health care of victims, damage to property and fear of crime. National Health Service costs can also rise as a result of increased mental illness due to depression and increased physical illness due to the poor living conditions that occur because of higher unemployment.

Unemployment imposes a financial cost on taxpayers for two main reasons. Because fewer are in work the government will receive less tax revenue, both direct and indirect. It will also have to pay out more in unemployment-related benefits such as the job seekers' allowance. Hence those paying tax will have to pay more to make up both the shortfall and the need for extra expenditure.

The unemployed themselves will experience financial, psychological and reduced employment opportunity costs. Most of the unemployed experience a loss of real disposable income as a result of unemployment. This reduces their material living standards. Being unemployed can lower a person's self-esteem and can lead to depression, suicide and divorce. In addition, when people are out of work they lose out on promotion and training, and experiencing the routine of work. The longer people are out of work, the harder it is for them to find another job. Some employers are reluctant to interview, for example, anyone who has been out of work for more than a year. The costs of unemployment are not evenly spread as certain groups are more likely to experience unemployment. These include the disabled, the young and those from ethnic minorities.

(b) Whilst the costs of unemployment exceed the benefits, there are some potential benefits. Having a pool of unemployed workers provides some flexibility in the economy. Those firms wishing to expand should find it relatively easy to do so, provided the unemployed possess the right skills and are in, or are able to move to, the right areas of the country. During times of high unemployment recruitment costs may be lowered. It may not be necessary to advertise jobs –word of mouth may be sufficient.

Firms may also benefit from the existence of unemployed workers if their presence keeps the pressure for wage rises low and stimulates increased productivity among workers in fear of losing their jobs. The existence of unemployed workers also allows firms to take on staff on a temporary basis to cope with short-term rises in demand.

Unemployment by lowering aggregate demand and wage claims may reduce inflationary pressure in the economy. It may also reduce a deficit on the current account of the balance of payments. Spending on all goods, including imports, is likely to fall and some goods may be diverted from the home to the export market. Firms, unable to sell at home, will have to work harder in terms of marketing, quality of goods and after sales service to find gaps in the export market.

The unemployed have more time, but less money, to spend on leisure activities – unless they are on government training schemes. They also have more time to spend in search of jobs. If they find jobs to which they are well suited, both they and society are likely to gain. Those gaining employment may enjoy higher earnings and more satisfaction in their new jobs than if they had taken the first job on offer. Society will benefit if their productivity is higher in the jobs they eventually accept.

23

Inflation

23.1 Fact Sheet

(a) Definition of inflation

Inflation is a persistent rise in the general price level, and hence a sustained fall in the value of money.

- *Creeping inflation* is a low rate of inflation.
- *Hyperinflation* is a very high rate of inflation that can cause major economic problems and political instability.
- *Stagflation* is a situation of high inflation and high unemployment.
- *Slumpflation* occurs when there is high inflation, high unemployment and negative growth.

(b) Measuring inflation

(1) *The retail price index* (RPI) is the most widely used index of general consumer prices. *RPIX* is the RPI minus mortgage interest payments and is the government's target measure. *RPIY* is the RPIX minus indirect and local authority taxes and is known as the *underlying rate of inflation*.

(2) *The tax and price index* (TPI) measures average household purchasing power, including the effects of changes in direct taxes as well as prices.

(3) *Producer price indices* (PPI) measure changes in material and product prices, and give an indication of the future trend of retail prices.

(4) The *pensioners' retail price index* (PRPI) indicates price changes in goods and services purchased by the retired.

(5) The *GDP deflator* measures changes in the price of consumer goods, capital goods and exports. It is used to convert national income figures at current prices to national income at constant prices (i.e. real NY).

- These measures are weighted indices, which means that particular importance is attached to items that form a large proportion of expenditure or output.

(c) Cost-push

Cost-push inflation occurs when a cost of production (e.g. wages) increases and firms put up prices to maintain profits. Causes of cost-push inflation include:

(1) Wage increases, which may result from:
  (a) *a wage–price spiral*, when wage increases raise prices, thereby encouraging further wage demand etc.;
  (b) *a wage–wage spiral*, when a wage increase in one industry sets off a series of wage claims in other industries so as to maintain differentials.

(2) *Imported inflation* from overseas increases in the price of goods imported into the UK.

(3) An increase in the price of imports as a result of a depreciation of sterling.

(4) An increase in profit margins.

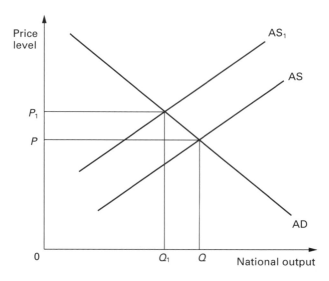

23.1 Cost-push inflation

(d)   Demand-pull inflation

Demand-pull inflation occurs when aggregate demand exceeds aggregate supply. In Figure 23.2 an increase in a component of aggregate demand means that aggregate demand exceeds the full employment value of output. An *inflationary gap* of J−K results.

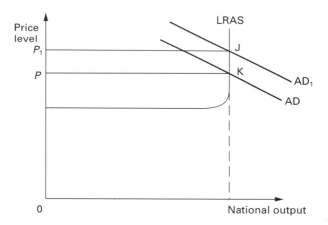

Figure 23.2 Demand-pull inflation

(e)   Monetary inflation

Monetarists argue that, if the growth of the money supply exceeds the growth of output, prices will eventually rise. *The quantity theory of money* states:

$$MV = PT$$

where M is the money supply; V is the *velocity of circulation* (i.e. the number of times one unity of currency changes hands): P is average prices; and T is the number of transactions (goods bought).

- Monetarists assert that V and T are constant in the short term. Any increase in M must necessarily increase P.
- However Keynesians argue that at less than full employment an increase in M causes an increase in T, as more output is made, and may leave prices unchanged. V rises in times of boom and falls during recessions.

(f)   The benefits of inflation

A low level of inflation may confer a number of advantages, including:

(1) Stimulating output if prices are increased before wages rise.
(2) Increased efficiency. Inflation may enable prices and wages to respond more quickly to changes in market forces. It is easier, for example, to reduce real wages than nominal wages.
(3) Increased demand if negative real interest rates reduce the debt burdens of households and firms.

(g)   The costs of inflation

The costs of inflation include:

(1) *Shoe leather costs*: the high opportunity cost of holding money means people hold lower money balances and make frequent journeys to banks, building societies etc.
(2) *Menu costs*, as a result of changing price tags, slot machines etc.
(3) *Fiscal drag* occurs when people's money income rises, dragging them into higher tax brackets. A higher percentage of real income is paid in tax.
(4) Uncertainty may reduce investment and increase the resources devoted to planning.
(5) The balance of payments will be adversely affected if the country's inflation rate is higher than that of competitors and there are no offsetting exchange rate changes.
(6) Labour unrest may occur as workers seek wage rises to maintain real income.
(7) Expectations of inflation may arise, further fuelling inflation.
(8) *Money illusion* may occur when people confuse changes in nominal balances with changes in real balances.
(9) Arbitrary redistribution of income and wealth may occur, as shown in Table 23.1.

Table 23.1 Redistribution of income through inflation

From	To
Taxpayers	The government
Holders of the national debt	The government
Savers	Borrowers
Creditors	Debtors
Workers in weak trade unions, non-unionised labour and those on fixed incomes	Those who can raise their incomes by more than the rate of inflation
Domestic producers	Foreign producers with lower inflation rates

(h)   Remedies for inflation

The measures taken to cure inflation depend on its perceived cause.

(i) Cost-push inflation remedies

(1) Imposing *prices and incomes policies* in order to freeze price and income increases breaks the wage–price and wage–wage spirals.
(2) Subsidising production in order to reduce costs.
(3) Reducing indirect taxes in order to reduce the cost of imported materials and components and to force domestic producers and exporters to remain competitive with foreign producers.

(ii) Demand-pull inflation remedies

(1) *Deflationary fiscal policy*, where increased taxes and/or reduced government spending lowers aggregate demand.
(2) *Deflationary monetary policy*, where reducing the growth of the money supply and/or raising the rate of interest lowers demand.
(3) Stimulating output by improved productivity, labour relations, etc.

(iii) Monetary inflation remedies

(1) Implementing measures to restrict bank lending.
(2) Reducing the PSBR.

(i) Inflation and unemployment

* *The Phillips curve* implies a trade-off relationship between inflation and unemployment. For instance in Figure 23.2 the percentage change in money wages is high when unemployment is low.

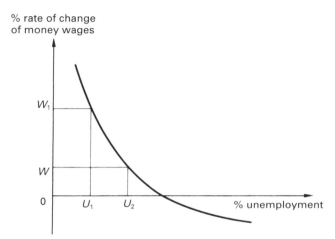

Figure 23.3 The Phillips curve

* *The expectations-augmented Phillips curve* reflects the monetarist view that there is no long-term inflation–unemployment trade-off. Any attempt to reduce unemployment below the natural rate will only succeed in accelerating the rate of inflation.

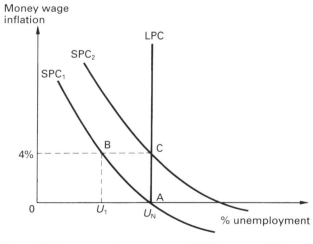

Figure 23.4 An expectations-augmented Phillips curve. SPC_1 and SPC_2 are short-term Phillips curves. LPC is the long-term Phillips curve at the NRU. Economy initially on SPC_1 curve at U_N at point A. Government reduces unemployment to U_1 by increasing demand. This causes prices and wages to rise. Move to point B. Higher wages and costs result in a rise in unemployment to U_N but at a higher expected rate of inflation on SPC_2. Move to point C.

• *The rational expectations hypothesis* suggests that there is no long-term or short-term trade-off. Supporters argue that people base their actions on past experiences of inflation and their expectations of current and future government policies. On average, they correctly forecast the results of current economic events and policies, and do not suffer from money illusion.

23.2 Investigative study

Example 23.1

An investigation into what influences people's expectations of inflation and how those expectations affect their behaviour.

23.3 Data response

Example 23.2

A warning

"DISAPPOINT-ING" was Kenneth Clarke's verdict on December's inflation figures, released on January 18th. This was an understatement. The chancellor's hope that he might avoid, at least until the spring, the next inflation-curbing rise in interest rates have been dashed. Mr Clarke next meets Eddie George, the governor of the Bank of England, on February 2nd to discuss interest-rate policy. Another rise may not be far behind.

The inflation numbers were well above expectations. Retail prices jumped by 0.5% in December, on both the headline and underlying (excluding changes in mortgage-interest payments) measures. The annual headline rate of inflation was 2.9%, and the underlying rate 2.5%. Firms may finally be passing on to customers the much-discussed increases in factory-gate prices.

That December's inflationary rise is unlikely to prove a blip is underlined by that month's surprisingly buoyant retail-sales figures, released on January 19th. These showed a monthly rise of 0.5%, in volume terms, and a yearly one of 3.8%.

Inflationary fears were further fuelled by December's unemployment statistics, also released this week. These revealed an unexpectedly large fall of almost 55,000 in the jobless total, compared with November, to just over 2.4m. In this economic recovery, changes in unemployment have coincided with changes in output; on that basis, December's jobless numbers suggest that the economy is still growing rapidly.

Mr Clarke will take comfort that, amidst so many worrying numbers, November's growth in average earnings was the same as October's, at 3.75% year-on-year. The consensus forecast was for it to edge up to 4%.

Source: The Economist, 21 January 1995, p. 30.

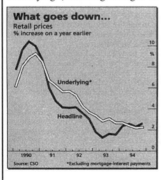

(a) What happened to retail prices over the period 1990–94? **(5 marks)**

(b) What is meant by the headline rate of inflation? **(1 mark)**

(c) What evidence is there in the passage of:
(1) cost-push inflationary pressures? **(2 marks)**
(2) demand pull inflationary pressures? **(3 marks)**

(d) Why would Mr Clarke have taken comfort in the November 1994 average earnings figure? **(3 marks)**

(e) How could a rise in interest rates curb inflation? **(4 marks)**

(f) Discuss other policies that might be adopted to cure inflation. **(7 marks)**

Solution 23.2

(a) Retail prices, as measured both in terms of headline and underlying inflation, rose throughout the period but at varying rates.

The headline rate of inflation peaked at approximately 11% in spring 1990. Then prices rose more slowly until autumn 1992, when inflation reached its lowest point of approximately 1%.

The underlying rate of inflation followed a similar pattern to the headline rate in the first part of the period. It peaked at approximately 9% in late spring 1990 and then the inflation rate fell (as retail prices rose more slowly). Unlike the headline rate, the underlying rate continued a downward trend throughout the period after early 1990. It started and finished below the headline rate, but for most of the period was above it.

(b) The headline rate of inflation is a measure of changes in the retail price index, RPI. It includes mortgage interest payments.

(c) (1) The extract mentions increases in factory-gate prices, which implies that costs of production had risen.

(2) The extract mentions buoyant retail sales, which increased – in volume terms – by 3.8% on a yearly basis. This suggests that consumer demand was increasing. The extract also mentions falling unemployment, which would have increased consumer demand. People would have experienced higher incomes and increased confidence, leading them to spend more.

(d) The growth of average earnings was less than had been anticipated. This means that firms' costs of production rose more slowly than expected. Indeed if average earnings had risen in line with productivity increases, costs would not have risen. Rises in earnings above productivity increases would have had a significant impact on firms' costs.

(e) A rise in interest rates may reduce demand-pull inflation. The higher cost of borrowing is likely to reduce consumer demand for items purchased with borrowed money. Demand for other products will fall as consumers' income, after paying higher mortgage interest charges, decline. The greater return from saving may also cause some people to spend less and save more.

(f) The policies that may be adopted to cure inflation will depend on what is believed to be the cause of inflation and views on the effectiveness of the policies. Economists who consider that inflation results from increases in costs of production may urge the implementation of a prices and incomes policy. They argue that this will reduce price rises while avoiding the adverse effects of deflationary policies – in particular, rises in unemployment. Economists who consider that inflation has resulted from demand exceeding supply (demand-pull inflation) may urge a reduction in demand. This could be achieved by deflationary fiscal policy, i.e. reducing government spending and/or increasing taxation. An alternative to reducing demand is increasing output by, for example, giving subsidies to producers. This will only be a viable policy if the economy is below the full employment level.

A rise in the exchange rate may also be employed to reduce inflationary pressures. The resulting fall in import prices will lower the cost of finished imported goods, some UK producers' costs of production and possible wage claims. The lower import prices may also increase pressure on domestic producers to keep their prices low in order to remain competitive at home and abroad.

23.4 Objective questions

Example 23.3

The weights in the retail price index indicate:
A seasonal fluctuations in price
B by how much the prices of goods have changed
C the relative amount spent on each category of good
D which goods have risen by more than the average rise in prices

Example 23.4

The following information shows a country's consumer expenditure pattern on four goods and the price indices of these commodities for two years.

Commodity	Index of prices in year 1	Index of prices in year 2	Consumers' expenditure (£ million) in year 1
W	100	80	300
X	100	110	200
Y	100	120	100
Z	100	150	400

Between years 1 and 2 the general level of prices has:
A remained the same
B risen by 4.5%
C risen by 12%
D risen by 18%

Example 23.5

Which of the following groups is most likely to benefit from a period of higher than anticipated inflation?
A Creditors
B Non-unionised labour
C The government
D The unemployed

Example 23.6

Demand-pull inflation may initially be caused by:
A an increase in wages
B an increase in bank credit
C an increase in profit margins
D an increase in the price of imported raw materials

Example 23.7

An inflationary gap is said to exist when:
A government spending exceeds government revenue
B leakages exceed injections at the full employment level of national income
C aggregate demand is greater than the full-employment level of national income
D the full-employment level of national income exceeds the equilibrium level of national income

Example 23.8

In conditions of full employment, which of the following would be most likely to lead to inflation?
A   An increase in income tax
B   An increase in the demand for exports
C   An increase in labour productivity
D   An increase in expenditure on imports

Example 23.9

If a government believes that inflation is the result of cost-push factors and it wishes to reduce inflation, which of the following measures is it likely to adopt?
A   A rise in interest rates
B   An increase in income tax
C   The imposition of a prices and incomes policy
D   A reduction in the growth of the money supply

Example 23.10

In year 1, an economy has a money supply of £400 and a velocity of circulation of 6, and it produces 800 goods. In year 2 the velocity of circulation and the level of output remain constant, but the money supply increases to £600. According to the quantity theory, this will cause the price level to rise by:
A   £1.5   B   £3   C   £4.5   D   £6

Example 23.11

In the diagram below U_N is the natural rate of unemployment, SPC_1, SPC_2, SPC_3, and SPC_4 are short-run Phillips curves associated with successively higher levels of inflationary expectations, and LPC is the long-run, vertical Phillips curve. If inflationary expectations are at 6% and a government wishes to eliminate wage inflation, it would have to permit unemployment in the short run to change to:
A U_1 B U_2 C U_3 D U_4

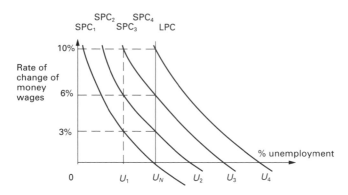

Example 23.12

Which of the following must occur as a result of inflation?
A   Fiscal drag will take place
B   Debtors will gain and creditors will lose
C   The volume of exports will decline
D   The domestic purchasing power of the currency will decline

23.5 Solutions to objective questions

Solution 23.3 Answer: C

The index of retail prices is a weighted price index. This means that the price changes of different categories of goods and services are multiplied by weights. These weights indicate what proportion of consumer expenditure is devoted to the different categories. For instance if, out of a total expenditure of £100m, £30m is spent on food, then food will receive a weighting of 3/10.

Solution 23.4 Answer: D

To determine the change in the general price level it is necessary to multiply the price change of each commodity by its weighting. The total of the weighted price changes gives the answer.

Commodity	Weight	Price change	Weighted price change
W	(3/10) ×	20%	= −6%
X	(2/10) ×	10%	= 2%
Y	(1/10) ×	20%	= 2%
Z	(4/10) ×	50%	= 20%
			18%

Solution 23.5 Answer: C

The government is a net debtor and therefore is likely to have to pay lower real interest. The government may also raise more revenue if fiscal drag occurs. Other options are incorrect.
   A ⇒ Creditors are likely to lose during a period of higher than anticipated inflation, since the real rate of interest is likely to fall.
   B ⇒ Non-unionised labour is likely to suffer, since it will be in a weak position to maintain real wages.

D ⇒ The unemployed may experience a fall in living standards if benefits are not adjusted in line with inflation or if there is a lagged response.

Solution 23.6 Answer: **B**

An increase is bank credit will mean that firms and consumers will have more to spend and the resulting increase in demand may result in demand-pull inflation.

A, **C** and **D** ⇒ are likely to increase the costs of production, which might result in cost-push inflation.

Solution 23.7 Answer: **C**

An inflationary gap occurs when aggregate demand is greater than the output that can be produced when there is full employment.

A ⇒ Describes a budget deficit.

B and **D** ⇒ describe a deflationary gap.

Solution 23.8 Answer: **B**

An increase in the demand for exports will mean more money coming into the country while goods are going out. Thus there will be more money but fewer goods to spend it on. With full employment it will be difficult to produce more goods and an inflationary gap is likely to develop, with demand exceeding supply.

A and **D** ⇒ would be likely to reduce demand, and hence inflationary pressure.

C: ⇒ would result in more goods being available and, assuming no increase in wages, a fall in the inflation rate.

Solution 23.9 Answer: **C**

Cost-push inflation arises when prices are pushed up by increases in the costs of production, such as wages. One possible solution is a prices and incomes policy that aims to limit rises in prices and incomes while avoiding deflation. All the other measures mentioned are designed to reduce demand and/or the money supply – **A** and **D** by monetary measures and **B** by a fiscal measure – and are likely to be implemented if it is believed that inflation is being caused by demand-pull or monetary factors.

Solution 23.10 Answer: **A**

The quantity theory is represented by the formula $MV = PT$, or $P = MV/T$. In year 1 the price level is:
$P = MV/T = 400 \times 6/800 = 2400/800 = £3$

In year 2 the price level is:
$P = MV/T = 600 \times 6/800 = 3600/800 = £4.5$

Therefore the price level has risen from £3 to £4.5, i.e. by £1.5. The money supply has increased by 50%, causing a 50% rise in the price level.

Solution 23.11 Answer: **C**

If inflationary expectations are at 6%, the economy is on the short-run Phillips curve SPC_3. On this curve, U_3 is the rate of unemployment that will reduce the rate of change of money wages, since U_3 is where SPC_3 cuts the zero percentage of change of money wages line. In the long term, when the expected rate of inflation equals the actual rate of inflation, unemployment will return to the natural rate of U_N.

Solution 23.12 Answer: **D**

If prices rise, each unit of currency (e.g. each £1) will be able to buy fewer goods and services.

A B and **C** ⇒ May occur, but not necessarily. Fiscal drag will only take place if tax rates are not adjusted in line with inflation. Debtors will gain and creditors will lose if the inflation rate rises more rapidly than the interest rate. However the interest rate may rise in line with inflation, and possibly at a faster rate. Whether or not the volume of exports decreases will depend on a number of factors, including the inflation rate experienced in other countries. Indeed if the home country's inflation rate is below that of rival countries, its exports will become more and not less competitive.

23.6 Essays

Example 23.13

Is inflation only harmful if it is at a rate above that prevailing in other countries? **(25 marks)**

• Consider the effects of inflation on a country's external position.
• Also consider the effects on a country's internal position.

Solution 23.13

Inflation, which is a persistent rise in the general price level, may have detrimental effects, not only externally but also internally. The internal effects can occur even if the country has a lower inflation rate than that of other countries.

If the UK's inflation rate is higher than that of other countries, then the UK's products will become less competitive both at home and abroad. This is likely to result in a fall in export revenue and a rise in import expenditure. Investment in the UK may be discouraged. So there is likely to be an adverse effect on the UK's balance of payments position and employment. It may also result in a fall in the exchange rate, which will accelerate inflation.

Inflation, especially if it is above a creeping level, will also probably be undesirable, because of the internal effects. Inflation will affect the distribution of income, and this can create social tension. For instance unions will have to press for wage rises merely to keep pace with inflation, i.e. to maintain real wages. Members of weak unions – e.g. USDAW – are more likely to suffer a decline in real wages than are members of strong unions.

The effects of inflation can be alleviated by index linking wages and/or benefits. However if, for example, the job seekers' allowance is not raised in line with inflation the unemployed will experience a fall in their living standards. In contrast house owners may benefit as the value of their property is likely to rise by more than the rate of inflation, while the real cost of their mortgage payments is likely to fall.

Creditors may suffer and debtors may gain if the interest rate does not rise in line with inflation. Fiscal drag may occur, although the government could eliminate this effect by adjusting tax brackets in line with inflation.

There are costs involved in living with inflation. Firms will incur menu costs and will have to adjust prices regularly, and time and effort may have to be taken to estimate future inflation. Firms and individuals may also experience shoe leather costs.

Government measures to reduce inflation may have an adverse effect on other economic objectives, particularly growth and full employment. Deflationary monetary policy and fiscal policy reduce demand and hence tend to result in lower output and employment, at least in the short term.

One possible advantage of inflation may arise if it is at a low level and is of a demand-pull nature. This is because a situation where demand exceeds supply may make entrepreneurs optimistic about the potential returns that can be earned by expanding output.

However inflation, particularly if it is high, has effects within a country as well as on its competitive position abroad. While it is possible to alleviate some of the internal effects, some may cause inconvenience or disruption, and possible hardship. For a number of countries, including the UK, a reduction in international competitiveness would be significantly detrimental, but it is not the only adverse effect the country may suffer as a result of inflation.

Example 23.14

(a) Explain what is meant by cost-push inflation.

(10 marks)

(b) Discuss the policies that may be used to reduce cost-push inflation. **(15 marks)**

- Discuss the main causes of cost-push inflation.
- Assess some of the policy measures that may be implemented.

Solution 23.14

(a) Cost-push inflation is a sustained rise in the general price level caused by increases in the costs of production. Higher costs of production cause the aggregate supply curve to shift to the left – 'a supply shock'. The decrease in aggregate supply causes the price level to rise, as illustrated in the diagram.

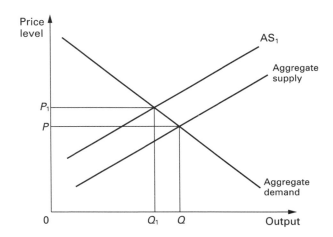

Higher costs of production can arise as a result of wage increases in excess of rises in productivity. Wage rises may be a significant factor as wages form the highest proportion of factor incomes – approximately 70% – so any change in wage rates is likely to have a relatively large impact on costs and prices. Wage rises may also result in a wage–wage spiral and a wage–price spiral. If one group of workers receives a wage rise this may stimulate other groups of workers to press for a wage rise to restore wage differentials. Higher wages may push up prices, which in turn may cause workers to press for wage rises to restore real pay.

An increase in the price of imported raw materials will also increase the costs of production. For example if the price of oil rises, firms, transport, heating and manufacturing process costs will increase and they are likely to pass at least some of these higher costs on to the consumer in the form of higher prices.

Cost-push inflation can also be caused by firms increasing their profit margins and the government increasing indirect taxes or decreasing subsidies to firms.

(b) A number of policy measures may be implemented to reduce cost-push inflation. To counter inflationary wage and profit margin rises a government may impose a prices and incomes policy. This is a direct way of seeking to reduce inflation without creating unemployment. Limits or freezes can be placed on wage and price rises. However this policy approach has a number of drawbacks. Percentage pay limits will benefit the highly paid whereas fixed-sum limits will benefit the lowly paid, so whichever form is used it will tend to cause dissatisfaction among one group of workers. Other problems of this policy include the fact that workers and employers will seek to get round any limits or freezes and the inflexibility it creates in markets. For

example if employers wish to raise the prices of their products or raise the wages of their workers above a limit set by the government they can, for example, change the weight of their goods and promote their staff to newly created posts.

To offset the effects of higher imported raw material costs a government could raise the exchange rate. This would lower import prices and reduce cost-push inflation by reducing the costs of production and placing increased pressure on domestic producers to keep their costs and prices low in order to remain competitive in the home and overseas markets. However, a higher exchange rate may result in lower domestic output and higher unemployment if domestic producers are unable to improve their competitiveness.

A government could also seek to reduce cost-push inflation by cutting indirect taxes and increasing subsidies. This approach should increase aggregate supply. However the effectiveness of the measures have to be assessed carefully. For instance a subsidy to promote training will not only immediately lower firms' costs, assuming they are already undertaking some training, but should also reduce costs in the long run by increasing productivity.

A government could also lower firms' costs by reducing real interest rates. Firms may have borrowed in the past, so a cut in interest rates will reduce their interest rate payments. However, lower real interest rates may contribute to demand-pull inflation by stimulating a rise in consumer expenditure.

There are a number of other measures that some economists would advocate to increase the cost efficiency of firms, including deregulation and privatisation.

International Trade and Government Policy

PART V

AEB	NEAB	OCSEB	UCLES	ULE	UODLE	Topic	Date begun	Date completed	Self-assessment
✓	✓	✓	✓	✓	✓	**Fact sheets**			
✓					✓	**Investigative study**			
✓	✓	✓	✓	✓	✓	**Data response**			
✓	✓	✓	✓	✓	✓	**Objective questions**			
✓	✓	✓	✓	✓	✓	**Essays**			

International Trade

24.1 Fact sheet

(a) Problems of international trade

International trade is the exchange of goods and services between countries. Problems arise over:

(1) currencies;
(2) language;
(3) distance;
(4) customs/tastes;
(5) foreign competition;
(6) import restrictions;
(7) legal and technical regulations;
(8) possible delays in payment.

(b) Benefits of international trade

(1) A greater variety of goods for consumers.
(2) A larger market allows domestic producers greater scope for economies of scale.
(3) An opportunity to obtain goods that the country cannot produce itself. This accounts for a very small percentage of the goods the UK imports.
(4) Consumers' welfare may increase as a result of lower prices resulting from international competition.
(5) Trade with other countries may lead to the spread of technology, management techniques and ideas.
(6) International specialisation raises output.

(c) Absolute and comparative advantage

The main advantage claimed from international trade is higher world output. The theories of absolute advantage and comparative advantage explain how output may be increased by specialisation and trade.

- *Absolute advantage* exists when a country can produce more of a product per resource unit than another country.
- *Comparative advantage* exists when a country can produce a product at a lower opportunity cost than its trading partners.

Table 24.1 An example of comparative advantage

Country	Daily output per resource unit	
	Cars	Boats
A	2	4
B	4	10

While country B has an absolute advantage in the production of both goods, A has a comparative advantage in the production of cars. A sacrifices only two boats for one extra car (four boats/two cars), while B has to forgo 2.5 cars (ten boats/four cars).

(d) Costs of international trade

(1) *Infant industries* (also called *sunrise industries*) may not be able to become established if faced

with competition from foreign companies with lower costs due to greater economies of scale.

(2) *Declining industries* (also called *sunset industries*) may decline rapidly, causing a significant rise in unemployment.

(3) Foreign producers may engage in dumping (i.e. selling surplus output at a low price, even sometimes below average cost) in the home market.

(4) A country may become dependent on other nations for products – e.g. weapons, food – which may be cut off during periods of dispute or war.

(5) A country may experience the disadvantage of overspecialisation, including diseconomies of scale, vulnerability to sudden changes in demand and unemployment.

(e) Pattern of UK international trade

The UK is a major trading country, importing and exporting mainly manufactured goods from and to mainly developing countries.

(f) Protectionism

Protectionism is the restriction of international trade by means of tariffs, quotas and non-tariff barriers. The main forms of restriction are:

(1) *Tariffs* (also called *customs duties*), which are a tax on imported goods. This is the most common form of restriction. In addition to protecting domestic industries, tariffs may be imposed to raise revenue.

(2) *Quotas* are limits on the quantity of a commodity that is allowed to enter the country.

(3) *Exchange control* occurs when a government controls the availability of foreign currency. This often involves a limit on the foreign exchange available to importers.

(4) *Physical control (embargo)* occurs when a ban is placed on the export or import of a certain good or on trade with a particular country or countries.

(5) *Purchasing policy* is when a government places orders with domestic producers in preference to more competitive importers.

(6) *Administrative restrictions* may cover lengthy paperwork to be completed by importers in connection with artificially high health and safety regulations.

(7) *Import deposit schemes* require importers to deposit a sum of money before they can bring in goods from abroad.

(8) *Voluntary export restraint* is an agreement between two countries where the exporter agrees to limit the volume of its exports.

(9) *Subsidies* are an indirect measure designed to reduce imports by making domestic products more price competitive.

• A government may seek to protect particular industries or industries in general.

(g) Trading blocs

There are four main types of trading bloc:

(1) A *free trade area* is a group of countries that

Table 24.2 The UK's main trading partners in 1993

	Most important sources of UK imports	Most important recipients of UK exports
1.	Germany	Germany
2.	USA	USA
3.	France	France
4.	Netherlands	Netherlands
5.	Japan	Belgium and Luxembourg
6.	Italy	Irish Republic
7.	Belgium and Luxembourg	Italy
8.	Irish Republic	Spain
9.	Switzerland	Sweden
10.	Norway	Japan

Source: *Monthly Digest of Statistics*, February 1995 (CSO).

Table 24.3 Arguments for protectionism

Arguments for selective controls	Arguments for general controls
Help infant industries	Improve terms of trade
Help declining industries	Raise revenue
Protect strategic industries	Correct current account deficit
Prevent dumping	Avoid overspecialisation
Further political objectives	Promote growth

removes tariff barriers between member countries but allows each member to decide its own tariff policy towards non-members.

(2) A *customs union*, in addition to removing tariffs between members, also imposes common external tariffs on non-members.

(3) A *common market* is a customs union that permits the free movement of capital and labour between member states.

(4) An *economic union* is a common market whose members follow common economic policies.

(h)　The European Union

The *European Union* (EU) currently has fifteen member countries.

- The *Common Agricultural Policy* (CAP) seeks to increase agricultural productivity, ensure a fair standard of living for the agricultural community, stabilise markets and ensure the availability of supplies. The high support prices have resulted in large surpluses and considerable expenditure.
- The UK is a net contributor to the EU budget.
- The *Maastricht Treaty*, signed in 1992 and ratified in 1993, sets out a common foreign and social policy and a timetable for economic and monetary union.

24.2 Investigative study

Example 24.1

A study of the impact the move towards economic and monetary union is having on UK firms.

24.3 Data response

Example 24.2

(a)　What is meant by the UK's trade gap? **(2 marks)**

(b)　What can cause a growth in exports?　**(6 marks)**

(c)　What is the difference between the value and the volume of exports?　**(2 marks)**

(d)　Why may imports increase at a faster rate than exports during an economic recovery? **(5 marks)**

(e)　Why does a fall in the value of sterling give UK goods a competitive advantage?　**(4 marks)**

(f)　What measures can be taken to reduce a trade deficit?　**(6 marks)**

Leap in imports widens UK's world trade gap

Surging imports widened the UK's trade gap with the rest of the world in November, according to the latest government figures, and City economists believe that it has since widened further.

The trade deficit for November was £640 million, after a revised £553 million shortfall in October, bringing the deficit for the first 11 months of last year to £8.2 billion, down from £12 billion at the same stage in 1993.

The Budget forecast for the whole of 1994 is an £11 billion deficit. Previously published figures for trade with the European Union (EU) revealed a sharp widening of the deficit in December, to £1.05 billion, which points to a full-year global deficit of below £10 billion, against 13.3 billion the year before.

Export growth remained impressive. A 3 per cent rise from October took exports to £12.1 billion in November. Richard Needham, the Trade Minister, said that exports were at record levels in both volume and value terms.

However, imports rose faster than exports, climbing 3.5 per cent to £12.7 billion, reflecting continued economic recovery. Most forecasters expect import growth to run ahead of export growth, as the competitive edge derived from lower sterling fades.

The latest three-month figures, which provide a guide to the trend in visible trade, showed exports up by 3.5 per cent in value terms and imports up by 3 per cent.

In volume terms, excluding oil and erratic items, such as aircraft and gems, exports increased by 5 per cent, while imports gained 3 per cent, suggesting a core improvement in the trade balance.

In November, however, volume exports rose by only 2 per cent, against a 3 per cent increase for imports. Excluding oil and erratics, the November deficit widened to £940 million, for £899 million.

Source: Article by Colin Narbrough, *The Times*, 10 February 1995.

Solution 24.2

(a)　The UK's trade gap is the negative difference between UK visible exports and UK visible imports. It is a visible trade deficit. The article states that in November 1994 the trade gap was £640 million, i.e. the UK imported £640 million more in value of imports than it exported.

(b)　There are a number of causes of an increase in exports. More exports are likely to be sold if they become more price competitive. This may be because of a fall in unit costs or because of a reduction in the value of the currency. An improvement in the quality of exports, their marketing and, in some cases, after sales service will also tend to increase demand and sales. Other possible causes are an increase in incomes abroad, a fall in income at home and the removal of import restrictions abroad.

(c)　The value of exports is the quantity of exports multiplied by price, i.e. the amount earned from the sale of exports. The volume of exports is the quantity of exports.

(d)　During an economic recovery incomes will rise and so will spending. More imports will be purchased.

Some countries, including the UK, have a high marginal propensity to import. This means that a significant proportion of extra income is spent on imports. Most imports purchased are finished manufactured goods, but imported raw materials are also purchased and these are likely to be brought in larger quantities as domestic firms increase their output. However exports may rise more slowly because the buoyant home market may cause goods to be diverted from the export to the home market.

(e) A fall in the value of sterling relative to other currencies lowers the price of exports in terms of foreign currencies. For example, if initially £1 = $2, a UK good priced £10 would sell in America for $20. If the value of the pound were to fall to £1 = $1.5 the same good would sell for $15. The lower price abroad should enable a large share of the overseas market to be captured. If demand is elastic the rise in quantity demanded will be of a higher percentage than the fall in price, and total revenue will rise.

(f) There are three main immediate measures that can be taken to reduce a trade deficit. One is to devalue the currency, which will not only lower the price of exports in terms of foreign currency but also raise the price of imports in terms of the home currency. For devaluation to be successful a number of conditions have to be met, including elastic demand for exports and imports.

The government could also deflate the economy in the hope that the resulting lower demand will reduce expenditure on imports and divert some goods from the home to the export market. However deflation may have an adverse effect on domestic output and employment.

Another possible measure is to impose or increase import restrictions. For example a quota could be placed on the number of cars allowed into the country from overseas. However membership of international organisations may restrict a country's ability to impose import restrictions.

In the longer run a government may seek to reduce a long-lasting trade deficit by introducing measures to increase the quality and price competitiveness of domestic goods, e.g. by increasing expenditure on training.

24.4 Objective questions

Example 24.3

A country is said to have a comparative advantage in the production of a good when:

A it can produce more of it than any other country

B it can produce it at a lower opportunity cost than its trading partners

C it has captured a larger percentage share of the world market than any other country

D it accounts for a greater percentage of total world sales in the product than in any other product it produces

Example 24.4

With respect to the table below, which of the following statements is correct?

Units of resources required to	Country A	Country B
Produce one TV	30	60
Produce one radio	10	40

A Country B has an absolute advantage in the production of both products

B Country B has a comparative advantage in the production of radios

C Country A has a comparative advantage in the production of TVs

D None of the above statements is correct

Examples 24.5 and 24.6 are based on the following information

	Cuba	USA
Output of cigar units per factor input	30	10
Output of sugar units per factor input	90	50

Example 24.5

Which of the following is true of the situation above?

A Cuba has a comparative advantage in the production of sugar

B Cuba has an absolute advantage in the production of both sugar and cigars

C The USA has an absolute advantage in the production of both sugar and cigars

D The USA has an absolute advantage in the production of sugar and Cuba has an absolute advantage in the production of cigars

Example 24.6

Which of the following exchange rates will benefit both Cuba and the USA?

A 1 cigar for 6 sugar
B 1 cigar for 4 sugar
C 1 sugar for 8 cigars
D 1 sugar for 6 cigars

Example 24.7

The following table shows the output per factor input in two products

	UK	Nigeria
Units of iron	240	48
Units of steel	80	16

If there are no trade barriers and no transport costs, which of the following is most likely to occur?

A Nigeria will import iron and steel from the UK
B The UK will export iron to Nigeria and import steel from Nigeria
C Nigeria will export iron to the UK and import steel from the UK
D There will be no trade between the two countries in the products concerned

Example 24.8

Figure 1 shows the production possibility curve of country X and Figure 2 shows the production possibility curve of country Y. In this case, which of the following is most likely to occur?

A Country X will tend to export wheat to country Y
B Country Y will tend to export wheat to country X
C No trade, since country Y is better at making both products

D No trade, since the opportunity cost ratios are identical

Example 24.9

Which of the following would reduce the level of protection faced by domestic producers in the home market?

A An increase in VAT
B The introduction of exchange control
C A reduction in the level of import quotas
D An agreement to implement reciprocal tariff concessions proposed by WTO

Example 24.10

Before the imposition of a tariff, the domestic price of good T is P_X and domestic producers supply DS. Domestic demand is represented by DD. When the country engages in free international trade, the world supply is represented by WS and the price is P_Y. The imposition of a tariff on the product causes price to rise to P_Z. The tariff will result in domestic producers increasing their output by:

A 0C   B CD   C DF   D FG

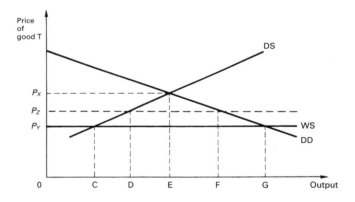

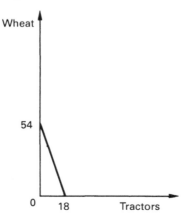

Example 24.11

Which of the following is the main feature distinguishing customs unions from free-trade areas?

A Only free-trade areas have no tariff barriers between members

B Only customs unions maintain tariffs between member countries

C Only customs unions require members to adopt a common external tariff with non-members

D Only free-trade areas require members to adopt a common external tariff with non-members

Example 24.12

What is the main argument for protecting sunset industries?

A To enable them to develop economies of scale

B To prevent a rapid increase in unemployment

C To offset the effects of dumping by overseas producers

D To ensure that there is a basis of production if imports are cut off during a war

24.5 Solutions to objective questions

Solution 24.3 Answer: B

The law of comparative advantage states that international trade is beneficial to two or more countries, provided that there are differences in their opportunity cost ratios. For instance, in the example below the two countries with one resource unit can produce:

	UK	France
Cars	20	2
Steel	5	1

France has the comparative advantage, or lesser disadvantage, in producing steel. In France the opportunity cost of producing one unit of steel is two cars, whereas in the UK it is four cars.

Solution 24.4 Answer: D

In this question it is important to remember that the figures given relate not to the output per resource unit, as is most commonly the case, but to the number of resource units required to produce one TV and to produce one radio. Country A can produce both goods

more efficiently (i.e. with fewer resources) and so it has an absolute advantage in the production of both goods. Option **A** is incorrect.

Country A is even better at producing radios, since it requires only one quarter of the resources that country B does to produce radios, whereas it requires one half of the resources that B does to make one TV. So country A has the comparative advantage in producing radios, and hence option **C** is incorrect.

Country B has the comparative advantage in producing TVs, since it requires twice the resources to make TVs but four times the resources to make radios. Thus option **B** is also incorrect.

Solution 24.5 Answer: B

Cuba can produce more of both products per factor input and therefore has an absolute advantage in the production of both goods. Hence option **B** is correct and options **C** and **D** can easily be rejected.

Cuba has the comparative advantage in producing cigars, since it has a lower opportunity cost in the production of the good than the USA has. In Cuba the opportunity cost of one cigar equals three units of sugar, whereas in the USA it is five units of sugar. Thus, after due consideration, option **A** can be rejected.

Solution 24.6 Answer: B

An exchange rate that will be beneficial to both trading countries must be between their internal opportunity cost ratios. In Cuba one cigar equals three units of sugar and in the USA one cigar equals five units of sugar. In terms of sugar, in Cuba one unit of sugar equals one third of a cigar and in the USA one unit of sugar equals one fifth of a cigar, so the only exchange rate that will benefit both countries must lie in the range: 1 cigar = 3–5 units of sugar.

Solution 24.7 Answer: D

The UK has the absolute advantage in both products. However, as the opportunity cost ratios are the same, a situation of comparative advantage does not exist and the countries will not benefit from specialisation and trade.

Solution 24.8 Answer: B

A production possibility curve shows the potential

output of two commodities a country can produce with its resources. Country Y has absolute advantage in producing both tractors and wheat and comparative advantage in producing wheat. It can produce three times more tractors than country X but four times more wheat. So country Y will specialise in wheat and will export to country X in exchange for tractors. Country X will concentrate on producing tractors and will export these to country Y. As there are differences in the relative efficiencies with which the countries can produce the goods, there is a potential for them to benefit from specialisation and trade.

Solution 24.9 Answer: **D**

A reduction in the level of protection faced by domestic producers means that home producers will face more competition from foreign producers.

At first glance the answer may appear to be option C, but a reduction in import quota levels would mean that fewer imported goods would be allowed into the country, and hence protection for home producers would be increased.

The introduction of exchange control would enable a government to control the value of imports and VAT is charged on both foreign and home-produced goods in the domestic market.

In contrast the acceptance of reciprocal tariff concessions proposed by WTO will mean a reduction in taxes on imports, which will make foreign goods more competitive than home products.

Solution 24.10 Answer: **B**

The pre-trade domestic production of the good is 0E. With free trade the quantity bought is 0G, where the domestic demand (DD) cuts the world supply (WS). Of this quantity, 0C is supplied by domestic producers and CG by foreign producers. When the tariff is imposed and price rises to P_Z, the new quantity bought is 0F (where DD cuts what is, in effect, a new supply curve running parallel with P_Z). Of this 0D is supplied by domestic producers and DF by foreign producers. So domestic producers increase their output by CD.

Solution 24.11 Answer: **C**

Both customs unions and free-trade areas remove tariff barriers between member countries. However, whereas customs unions also require member countries to impose a common external tariff, free-

trade areas allow member countries to decide their own external tariff policies.

Solution 24.12 Answer: **B**

Sunset industries are declining industries. If these are given protection, which is gradually removed, they can be allowed to go out of business gradually and employment can be reduced by means of 'natural wastage'.

A $\Rightarrow$ is an argument for protecting sunrise industries.

C $\Rightarrow$ Dumping may affect any industry and not just sunset industries.

D $\Rightarrow$ is an argument for protecting strategic industries

24.6 Essays

Example 24.13

Discuss the arguments for and against the use of import controls. **(25 marks)**

- Distinguish between arguments for selective and general import controls.
- Concentrate on the arguments rather than detailed descriptions of the different types of import control.

Solution 24.13

Protection limits the entry of goods into a country. It is usually imposed to protect domestic industries. The main argument against protection is that it prevents full advantage being taken of the principle of comparative advantage, which states that world output will be higher when countries specialise and engage in free trade. Moreover protection may reduce choice, reduce competition, create shortages, increase inefficiency and provoke retaliation.

However some economists argue that selective import controls should be placed on particular countries. These calls for selective controls are backed by a number of arguments. One reason given is that protection is necessary to enable infant industries to grow and take advantage of economies of scale.

At the other end of the industry age span, protection may be used to help industries decline gradually. The idea is that this will permit natural wastage to occur and avoid a sudden increase in unemployment.

Selective import controls may also be used to

prevent dumping, where foreign companies sell products at or below cost price. Predatory pricing benefits domestic customers in the short term. In the longer term, artificially low prices may eliminate domestic firms. Foreign producers can then use their monopoly position to raise prices.

General import controls may improve the terms of trade so that each export can be exchanged for more imports. This will occur if the imposition of tariffs or other forms of import control forces foreign producers to reduce their prices in order to remain competitive.

Import restrictions may also enable a country to diversify and avoid overspecialisation. If a country is highly specialised there is a danger that it will suffer if there is a fall in world demand or if there are supply problems, Protection of strategic industries guarantees a domestic supply of essential goods, for example weapons and food.

In some developing countries import controls are used to raise revenue, and both developing and developed countries may use import controls to gain a strong bargaining position or to retaliate against other countries' trade restrictions. However the danger is that a trade war may develop.

Countries may also use import controls to correct or prevent a balance of payments deficit. However import controls are usually only used as a last resort, and are likely to be combined with other measures to reduce the underlying tendency to purchase a high level of imports.

Some economists, including the Cambridge Economic Policy Group, urge the adoption of a system of general import controls in order to restructure the UK economy. They do not wish to reduce imports, merely to control their growth and to prevent an injection of government spending – designed to stimulate the UK economy – being largely spent on imports. Their main ideas is that a protective wall will enable UK industry to regain its efficiency and growth, creating a situation of full employment.

Example 24.14

(a) Explain the theory of comparative advantage.

(10 marks)

(b) To what extent is it a satisfactory explanation of the basis of international trade? **(15 marks)**

• Distinguish between absolute and comparative advantage.

• Explain comparative advantage and then consider the assumptions underlying the theory.

• Keep the numerical example simple. It should be designed to illustrate economic theory and not to prove elaborate mathematical skill.

Solution 24.14

(a) The theory of comparative advantage states that, provided that their opportunity cost ratios differ, even a more efficient country and a less efficient country will benefit from specialisation and trade with each other. However the simplicity and unreality of some of the assumptions upon which the theory is based have led to reservations about its applicability to the real world.

It is relatively straightforward to ascertain that countries with absolute advantages in different products will benefit from specialisation and trade.

However David Ricardo, in developing the theory of comparative advantage, went further. He stated that both countries will benefit from specialisation and trade, even if one country is more efficient at making both products concerned, provided that it is even better at making one of the two. It is relative and not absolute efficiency that is crucial.

	UK	USA
Units of output per factor: cars	10	50
Units of output per factor: wheat	20	200

In the example given above, the USA has absolute advantage in producing both cars and wheat since it can produce more of both. However it has comparative advantage in producing wheat since it is even better at growing this product, being able to produce ten times more wheat but only five times more cars than the UK. In contrast the UK has comparative advantage or lesser disadvantage in making cars since it is not so bad at making this product, producing one fifth of the quantity of cars but only one tenth of the quantity of wheat produced in the USA.

Another way of determining which product a country has a comparative advantage in is to examine the internal opportunity cost ratios. A country has comparative advantage in a product when producing it involves a lower opportunity cost than in another country.

Output will be increased by specialisation, and both

countries should be able to enjoy more goods than previously if the exchange rate lies between the internal opportunity cost ratios – in this case, 1 car: 2–4 wheat.

(b) However the applicability of the theory to international trade has been questioned on a number of grounds. It is often stated in terms of a few countries and a few products, whereas the real world is more complex. It also ignores transport costs. These will reduce the advantages of specialisation and trade – particularly in the case of low-price bulky goods.

The theory assumes constant opportunity costs as resources are moved from one industry to another, whereas in practice economies or diseconomies of scale may arise. The shifting of resources from one use to another also presumes perfect factor mobility, whereas some factors – particularly labour – may be immobile.

Indeed the theory presumes that perfect competition exists in the international and domestic markets. In practice completely free trade does not exist, and the presence of import restrictions reduces

specialisation. Also, there is not perfect knowledge, so it may be difficult to calculate comparative advantage. There may also be imperfect competition in the domestic markets. This is likely to mean that at least some prices do not accurately reflect domestic opportunity cost ratios. Countries also have different degrees of economic power, and in practice exchange rates are more likely to favour developed than developing nations.

The theory concentrates on the supply side. A country may specialise in making a product and yet still import it if home demand exceeds its output potential.

A country may also experience significant unemployment, and it maybe considered better to employ factors relatively inefficiently rather than not to employ them at all.

The theory of comparative advantage indicates that output will be increased by specialisation and trade, but the simplicity and unreality of some of the assumptions means that it does not fully explain the actual pattern of world trade.

Balance of Payments

25.1 Fact sheet

(a) Definition of the terms of trade

The *terms of trade* (ToT) is the ratio comparing export and import prices:

$$\text{ToT} = \frac{\text{index of export prices}}{\text{Index of import prices}} \times 100$$

A *favourable movement* means that the ToT get larger. Favourable movements are caused by:

(1) a rise in export prices;
(2) a fall in import prices;
(3) a rise in export prices and a fall in import prices;
(4) export prices rising faster than import prices;
(5) import prices falling faster than export prices.

(b) Causes of changes in the terms of trade

The ToT change in response to:

changes in demand – e.g. increased demand for raw materials during a boom;
(2) changes in supply – e.g. a crop failure;
(3) changes in value of the currency – e.g. a depreciation results in a fall in export prices and a rise in import prices:
(4) changes in the inflation rate – e.g. an acceleration in the inflation rate will result in higher export prices.

(c) Results of a favourable movement

(1) In the short term, higher export prices and lower import prices are likely to improve the current account balance before demand has had time to adjust.
(2) In the longer term:
  (a) if demand for exports is elastic, export revenue will fall;
  (b) if demand for imports is elastic, expenditure on imports will rise;
  (c) if demand for imports is inelastic, foreigners may experience a fall in income and reduce demand for UK exports;
  (d) UK subsidiaries abroad may suffer a decline in revenue.

(d) Composition of the balance of payments

The *balance of payments* (BoP) is a record of all economic transactions between residents in the UK and residents in the rest of the world, over a period of a year. The BoP has three components:

(1) the current account;
(2) UK external assets and liabilities;
(3) the balancing item.

(e) The current account

Particular attention is paid to the *current account*, which is made up of:

(1) The *visible balance* (also called the *balance of trade*), which shows exports and imports of tangible goods – e.g. cars, radios. A trade gap occurs when the value of visible imports exceeds the value of visible exports.

(2) The *invisible balance*, which shows the net total of:
  (a) *services*, including sea transport, civil aviation, travel, banking and insurance, expenditure on embassies abroad and staff stationed abroad;
  (b) *interest, profits and dividends* (investment income is included, whether it is remitted or retained for investment);
  (c) *transfers*, including government grants overseas, subscriptions to international organisations (including the EU) and private transfers in the form of payments to overseas dependents and charitable donations.

Visible balance + invisible balance = current account balance

(f) UK external assets and liabilities

This covers short-term and long-term capital movements and flows to and from reserves. It is made up of two sections:

(1) *Transactions in external assets*, comprising:
  (a) UK direct and portfolio investment overseas;
  (b) lending to overseas residents;
  (c) drawing on (+) and additions to (-) the reserves;
  (d) intergovernmental loans made by the UK and subscriptions to international lending bodies.

(2) *Transactions in external liabilities*, comprising:
  (a) overseas direct and portfolio investment in the UK;
  (b) borrowing from overseas residents by UK residents and banks;
  (c) intergovernmental loans to the UK, foreign currency borrowing from banks overseas and transactions with the IMF.

Transactions in external assets + transactions in external liabilities = net transactions

(g) The balancing item

The *balancing item* represents the net total of errors and omissions in the other items. The BoP always

balances, in the sense that the current account balance plus net transactions in external assets and liabilities plus the balancing item must equal zero.

Table 25.1 The 1993 UK balance of payments

	£ millions
Current account	
Visibles	−13 209
Invisibles	2 029
	−11 180
UK external assets and liabilities	
transactions in assets	−156 303
transactions in liabilities	164 724
Net transactions	8 421
Balancing item	2 759

Source: *Monthly Digest of Statistics*, February 1995 (CSO).

(h) Current account surplus

(i) Consequences

A current account surplus may be taken to be a sign of economic strength, but a large surplus may be considered to be disadvantageous because:

(1) it involves an opportunity cost in terms of forgone higher living standards;
(2) it results in an injection of demand into the economy, possibly contributing to demand-pull inflation;
(3) it is likely to increase the money supply, which may contribute to inflationary pressures;
(4) it may make the country unpopular with countries in deficit.

(ii) Measures to eliminate a current account surplus

(1) *Revalue the currency*: this will increase export prices and lower import prices.
(2) *Introduce a reflationary fiscal and/or monetary policy*, which will increase demand for imports.
(3) Reduce or abolish import controls.

(i) Current account deficit

(i) Consequences

(1) A *current account deficit* causes a *welfare gain*, since the country, consumes more than it produces.

(2) A country will eventually be unable to cover a current account deficit by drawing on reserves.
(3) A leakage in domestic demand.
(4) A decrease in the money supply.

(ii) Measures to correct a current account deficit

(1) Impose or increase import controls (protectionism) to switch expenditure from imports to home-produced goods.
2   Introduce a *deflationary fiscal and/or monetary policy* to reduce demand for imports and stimulate exports by lowering domestic demand.
(3) Encourage exports by, say, zero rating VAT on exports.
(4) *Devalue the currency*: this will decrease export prices and raise import prices.

(j)   The Marshall-Lerner condition

A devaluation of the pound sterling results in the following:

(1) An immediate deterioration in the BoP because of:
   (a) an immediate rise in the price of imports but a constant quantity of imports bought;
   (b) a fall in the price of exports but a constant quantity of exports bought.
(2) A longer-term improvement in the BoP as:
   (a) UK consumers buy fewer imports;
   (b) foreign consumers buy more exports.

The overall long-run effect of a devaluation of sterling depends on the *Marshall–Lerner condition*, which states that a devaluation improves the current account balance if the combined price elasticities of demand for exports and imports are greater than 1. The J effect in Figure 25.1 shows that a devaluation initially causes a deterioration in the current account balance (A to B) before demand and supply adjust to the new prices of exports and imports (B to C)

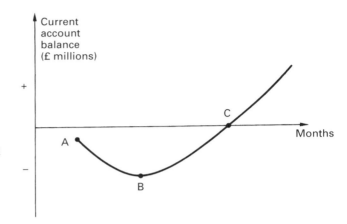

Figure 25.1 The J effect

25.2 Investigative study

Example 25.1

A study of the export performance of local businesses, including an analysis of changes in their performance.

25.3 Data response

Example 25.2

	Balance of payments figures in £ millions					GDP at constant factor cost index (1990 = 100)
Year	Exports	Imports	Services	Investment ncome	Transfers	
1988	80 346	101 826	3 957	4 424	23 518	97.3
1989	92 154	116 837	3 361	3 388	24 578	99.4
1990	101 718	120 527	3 689	981	24 896	100.0
1991	103 413	113 697	3 708	2271	21 383	97.9
1992	107 343	120 447	4 089	4 293	25 109	97.4
1993	121 414	134 623	4 942	3 062	25 106	99.4

Sources: *Economic Trends*, Annual Supplement, 1995, CSO; *The Pink Book 1994*; *Monthly Digest of Statistics*, February 1995

(a) In the context of the balance of payments, what is meant by investment income? **(3 marks)**

(b) Calculate:
  (1) the visible balance;
  (2) the invisible balance;
  (3) the current account balance. **(6 marks)**

(c) What do the data show about the relationship between changes in economic activity, as indicated by changes in GDP at constant cost, and the current account balance? **(6 marks)**

(d) Are your findings in (c) in accord with what the relationship economic theory would lead you to expect? **(6 marks)**

(e) What effect would a rise in economic activity abroad be likely to have on the current account position of the UK balance of payments?
(4 marks)

Solution 25.2

(a) Investment income refers to profits, interest and dividends. It is the amount UK citizens earn on their overseas financial and physical assets minus the amount overseas citizens earn on UK assets. Included in this category are, for example, dividends earned by a UK citizen on shares in a French company, interest paid on a loan made by a UK bank to a Canadian company and profits earned by a UK company based in Spain.

(b)

| | | (£ millions) | |
Year	Visible balance	Invisible balance	Current account balance
1988	−21 480	4 863	−16 617
1989	−24 683	2 171	−22 512
1990	−18 809	−226	−19 035
1991	−10 284	2 108	−8 176
1992	−13 104	3 273	−9 831
1993	−13 209	2 898	−10 311

(c)

Year	GDP at constant factor cost index (1990 = 100)	Direction of change	Current account balance (£ million)	Direction of change
1988	97.3		−16 617	
1989	99.4	↑	−22 512	↓
1990	100.0	↑	−19 035	↑
1991	97.9	↓	−8 176	↑
1992	97.4	↓	−9 831	↓
1993	99.4	↑	−10 311	↓

Note: Direction of change on current account: ↓ = deficit getting larger: ↑ = deficit getting smaller.

The table does not show a consistent pattern. In three years GDP and the current account position move in opposite directions and in two years they move in the same direction.

(d) Economic theory would suggest that GDP and the current account balance are likely to move in opposite directions, so that a rise in GDP would be accompanied by a deterioration in the current account of the balance of payments. This is because an increase in economic activity, unless generated by an increase in exports (export-led growth), is likely to suck in imports and divert goods from the export to the home market. However a fall in economic activity would tend to reduce the demand for imports and divert goods from the home to the overseas market.

The data is not entirely consistent with this view. Although the deficit did decline markedly at the start of the recession it is surprising that relatively large deficits were experienced in both years of the recession. Part of the answer for the not entirely consistent pattern may be found by examining the rate of change in GDP. In 1990 GDP rose and the current account position improved. However what was occurring in 1990 was a slowdown in economic growth from 2.2% in 1989 to 0.6%. In 1992 GDP fell and the current account position deteriorated. However the fall in GDP declined from 2.1% in 1991 to 0.5% in 1992.

(e) A rise in economic activity abroad, unless export led, is likely to improve the UK balance of payments. With higher incomes overseas consumers are likely to purchase more UK goods and services. In addition, with buoyant home markets, overseas producers may compete less rigorously abroad. This may enable UK producers to sell more in the UK and overseas.

25.4 Objective questions

Example 25.3

A favourable movement in the terms of trade occurs when:

A the price of exports rises relative to the price of imports

B the ratio of export to import earnings increases

C the volume of exports rises relative to the volume of imports

D the current account of the balance of payments moves into surplus

Example 25.4

The following figures show the UK's terms of trade:

1988:	98.6	1991:	100.2
1989:	98.8	1992:	101.4
1990:	100.0	1993:	103.9

Source: *Monthly Digest of Statistics*, December 1994.

Which of the following could account for the movement in the terms of trade shown in the table:
A Export prices fell faster than import prices
B Export prices rose faster than import prices
C Import prices rose while export prices remained constant
D Export prices fell while import prices remained constant

Example 25.5

Which of the following items would appear as a credit item in the invisible balance of the UK balance of payments?
A The spending of UK tourists in France
B The hiring of a UK ship by a Dutch oil company
C The purchase of UK government bonds by French residents
D The purchase by a German company of a china factory in Worcester

Example 25.6

	Exports		Imports	
	Price per unit (£000s)	Number of units (000s)	Price per unit (£000s)	Number of units (000s)
Year 1	20	20	25	8
Year 2	40	12	40	6

What changes took place in the terms of trade and the balance of trade between years 1 and 2?

	Terms of trade	Balance of trade:
A	improved	improved
B	improved	worsened
C	worsened	improved
D	worsened	worsened

Example 25.7

	£ million
Visible exports	2560
Visible imports	2620
Transfers	50
Interest, profits and dividends	70
Services	90
Net transactions	−20

What is the current account balance?
A −£60m   B £50m   C £150m   D £210m
In which of the following circumstance is a devaluation most likely to improve the visible balance?

Example 25.8

In which of the following circumstances is a devaluation most likely to improve the visible balance?

	Demand for imports:	Demand for exports:
A	price elastic	price elastic
B	price inelastic	price elastic
C	price inelastic	price inelastic
D	price elastic	price inelastic

Example 25.9

The following table shows a country's national income and domestic expenditure for three years:

	Year 1	Year 2	Year 3
National income	600	660	720
Consumer spending	360	360	390
Government spending	180	180	180
Investment	120	120	120

In which year(s) will a balance of trade deficit be experienced?
A 1 and 3   B 2 and 3
C 1 only   D 2 only

Example 25.10

Measures designed to improve a country's current account balance may be either expenditure-reducing or expenditure-switching. Which of the following is an example of an expenditure-reducing policy?
A Devaluation

B   A credit squeeze
C   The granting of export subsidies
D   The imposition of import controls

Example 25.11

Which of the following will appear in the external assets and liabilities section of the UK balance of payments?
A   Support costs of UK embassies abroad
B   Lending to Nigerian companies by British banks
C   Interest earned on UK funds held in American banks
D   Profits earned by British subsidiaries in Argentina

Example 25.12

The income elasticities of demand for imports and exports in four countries are given below. Which country's balance of payments position will benefit most from a world recession?

Country	Income elasticity of demand for imports	Income elasticity of demand for exports
A	1.8	0.8
B	1.2	1.2
C	1.0	1.6
D	0.8	2.0

25.5 Solutions to objective questions

Solution 25.3 Answer: A

A favourable movement in the terms of trade occurs when the index rises. This situation occurs when the price of exports rises in relation to the price of imports. This may result from, for example, a rise in the price of exports and/or a fall in the price of imports or even export prices falling by a lesser extent than import prices.

Solution 25.4 Answer: B

The figures in the table show a favourable movement in the terms of trade, i.e. the number has become higher. A favourable movement occurs when the price of exports rises in relation to the price of imports.

A, C and D ⇒ In each case there would be an unfavourable movement in the terms of trade.

Solution 25.5 Answer: B

The invisible balance includes services, interest, profits and dividends and transfers. A credit item on the invisible balance is one that represents money being paid to a UK resident or a firm in the UK, whereas a debit item represents a payment to a foreign resident by a UK resident. If a Dutch oil company hires a UK ship, money will be paid from the Netherlands to the UK.

A ⇒ represents a debit item in the UK invisible balance as it involves money going out of the UK to France.

C and D ⇒ are credit items in the net transactions section.

Solution 25.6 Answer: A

The terms of trade in year 1 were:

$$\frac{\text{index of export prices}}{\text{Index of import prices}} \times 100,$$

i.e. $\frac{20\ 000}{25\ 000} \times 100 = 80$

and in year 2:

$\frac{40\ 000}{40\ 000} \times 100 = 100$

Thus there has been an improvement in the terms of trade in the period shown.

The balance of trade in year 1 was value of exports (price × value) − value of imports (price × volume) in £000s:

$$400(20 \times 20) - 200(25 \times 8) = 200$$

and in year 2:

$$480(40 \times 12) - 240(40 \times 6) = 240$$

The balance of trade has improved with an increase in the surplus of £40 000.

Solution 25.7 Answer: C

The current account balance is the visible balance plus the invisible balance, i.e. −£60m (visible exports minus visible imports) plus £210m (net transfers + net interest, profits and dividends + net services) = £150m.

Solution 25.8 Answer: A

A devaluation is most likely to improve the balance of trade position when demand for both exports and imports is price elastic – the Marshall–Lerner condition.

Solution 25.9 Answer: **C**

The country will have a deficit on the balance of trade when its total demand (consumer spending + government spending + investment) exceeds its output (NY).

- In year 1 output is 600 but demand is 660, so there will be a deficit of 60.
- In year 2 output is 660 and so is demand. Therefore there will be equilibrium.
- In year 3 output is 720 and demand is 690, so there will be a surplus of 30.

Solution 25.10 Answer: **B**

Expenditure-reducing measures seek to improve a country's current account position by reducing the demand for all goods and services, both domestic and foreign. The fall in demand for imports will reduce import expenditure and the fall in demand for home-produced goods may encourage forms to switch production from the home to the foreign market.

In contrast expenditure-switching measures aim to improve the current account balance by switching from foreign to the home country's goods and services, i.e. from imports to domestic goods and from another country's exports to the home country's exports.

A credit squeeze is a measure designed to reduce the demand for all goods bought by the home country's residents.

A ⇒ is an expenditure-switching measure encouraging residents of the country to switch from buying imports to buying domestically produced goods and foreigners to switch from buying their own products or other countries' products to buying the devaluing country's products.

Solution 25.11 Answer: **B**

The external assets and liabilities section of the balance of payments includes investment into and out of the UK, lending to and borrowing abroad, intergovernmental lending and borrowing, drawing on and additions to the reserves. Lending to Nigerian companies by British banks would appear as a transaction in external assets.

A, C and D ⇒ would all appear in the invisible balance section of the balance of payments.

Solution 25.12 Answer: **A**

In a world recession, incomes are likely to fall. To gain the most benefit from a world recession, the demand for a country's exports should be income inelastic. Thus a fall in income results in a smaller percentage fall in the demand for its exports. In contrast its imports should be income elastic, so that a fall in domestic income results in a greater percentage fall in the demand for imports. If income elasticity of demand for imports is 1.8 – i.e. elastic – and income elasticity of demand for exports in 0.8 – i.e. inelastic – a fall in income will result in a greater reduction in import expenditure than in export earnings. Thus a current account deficit would be reduced or a surplus increased.

25.6 Essays

Example 25.13

Assess the measures a government may use to correct a deficit on the current account of the balance of payments. (**25 marks**)

- Briefly explain what is meant by a deficit on the current account of the balance of payments.
- Concentrate on three main measures of improving the current account balance.
- Examine both the internal and external effects of the measures.

Solution 25.13

The current account section of the balance of payments covers visible and invisible exports and imports. A deficit on the current account balance means that the country's population is spending more on goods and services from abroad than it is earning from the sale of goods and services abroad.

The measures a government will adopt to correct a deficit will be aimed at increasing income earned and/or reducing expenditure abroad. In considering which policies to adopt, a government will consider the cause of the deficit and the advantages and disadvantages of the measures.

One possible measure, provided the government is not committed to keeping the currency within set margins, is devaluation. This will mean lowering the price of exports in terms of foreign currencies and raising the price of imports in terms of the home currency. It is essentially an expenditure-switching measure, changing relative prices.

However, whether the policy will be successful in terms of improving the current account position will depend on whether there is elastic demand for imports, elastic demand for exports, elastic supply of exports, lack of import restrictions abroad and a low domestic marginal propensity to import, among other factors.

Lowering the value of the currency will affect not only a country's external trade position, but also its internal position. If exports rise and imports decline there will be a net injection into the circular flow of income, and national income should rise by a multiple amount. This should stimulate output and employment. However there may be inflationary effects arising from the increase in import prices and the net injection. While devaluation is associated with an increase in domestic economic activity, deflation is associated, in the short term at least, with a reduction in economic activity. Deflation involves reducing demand by restrictive fiscal and/or monetary policy. For instance a government may increase taxation in the expectation that, if people's disposable income declines, they will buy fewer imports. The higher the income elasticity of demand for imports the greater the effect will be. It will also be expected that demand for the home country's products will decline, so home producers will be forced to try to export more of their output. The interest rate may also be pushed up to deflate the economy. If deflation also reduces inflation the current account position will be further improved by the increase in price competitiveness. However deflation may, even if only in the short term, have an adverse effect on employment and growth.

An alternative to deflation is the imposition of import controls, either a general system or on selected industries. Import controls may prevent dumping, assist infant (sunrise) industries, allow sunset industries to decline gradually, improve the terms of trade and, of course, correct a current account deficit.

However import controls may prove to be inflationary. This is because imports are included in the retail price index, costs of production will rise if imported raw materials continue to be used and if unions press for wage rises to compensate for higher prices. UK firms may also be able to raise prices and remain competitive with more expensive imports.

Import controls may provoke retaliation from other countries and their use may be restricted by membership of trade blocs, e.g. the European Union and international organisations such as the World Trade Organisation.

Among other measures a country may employ are encouraging exports by, for instance, giving favourable loans to exporters and encouraging other countries to remove some of their import restrictions.

Example 25.14

(a) Explain what is meant by a surplus on the current account of the balance of payments and briefly discuss how it might arise.   **(7 marks)**

(b) Why may a government seek to eliminate such a surplus?   **(6 marks)**

(c) What measures could a government implement to achieve such an objective?   **(12 marks)**

- Define a surplus on current account.
- Discuss the main motives for eliminating a surplus.
- Discuss revaluation, reflation and other measures to eliminate a surplus.

Solution 25.14

(a) A surplus on its current account means that a country is earning more abroad than it is spending. This could arise as a result of a surplus on its visible balance and invisible balance, a visible balance surplus exceeding an invisible deficit or an invisible surplus exceeding a visible deficit.

A country may be earning more from the sale of its visible and invisible exports than it is spending on visible and invisible imports, for a number of reasons. The country's goods and services may be price competitive. They may be marketed very effectively, be of a high quality and provide, for example, good after sales service. Incomes abroad may be rising, which will increase demand. Incomes at home may be relatively low, which would keep down the demand for imports whilst forcing domestic producers to sell more abroad. The removal of import restrictions abroad would also enable the country to sell more exports.

(b) A country may wish to eliminate a surplus in order to improve the standard of living of its inhabitants. If a country has been experiencing a large current account surplus over a number of years, then the opportunity cost involved is the goods and services it could have bought with the currency it has been earning.

If a country has been experiencing large current account surpluses there may be pressure on it from other countries to reduce or eliminate the surplus. Measures a government may take to achieve this may not only restore its current account equilibrium, but also help deficit countries achieve current account equilibrium. A country trying to reduce a surplus is likely to buy more abroad and sell less. Considerable pressure has, in the past, been put on Germany and Japan to reduce their surpluses.

A country may also eliminate a surplus to reduce inflationary pressures. A surplus can result in an injection of demand into the domestic economy and an increase in the money supply.

(c) One possible measure to eliminate a surplus may be implemented with the prime objective of reducing inflationary pressures. A revaluation of the currency upwards will mean that more foreign currency will be obtained for the same value of the home currency. The home country's exports will be more expensive in terms of foreign currency, while its imports will be cheaper in terms of the domestic currency. The revaluation is likely to result in an increase in import expenditure and a fall in export revenue, assuming elastic demand for exports and elastic demand for imports.

An increase in the value of the currency means that imports are cheaper and these count in the retail price index. There may also be a reduction in the costs of production for home producers, as imported raw materials and components will be cheaper. The rise in the price of exports may force domestic exporters to cut their costs in order to remain competitive. Domestic producers selling in the home market will also have to keep their prices low in order to compete with cheaper imports. However there is the possibility that foreigners may raise the price of their goods in the knowledge that they may still be competitive.

Reflationary fiscal and/or monetary measures will increase the demand for all products. For instance an increase in government spending will result in a multiple rise in national income and, hence, demand. More imports will be purchased and the increase in domestic demand for home-produced goods may divert goods from the export to the home market.

A country may also seek to increase expenditure on imports by removing or reducing import restrictions. For instance lowering tariffs will reduce the price of imports on the home market and will result in an increase in expenditure on imports. Subsidies on domestic products could also be removed.

In addition, encouragement for exporters could be reduced or removed. For instance banks may no longer be directed to give preference to exporters when lending, and indirect taxation may be imposed or increased on exports.

Exchange Rates

26.1 Fact sheet

(a) The foreign exchange rate

The *exchange rate* is the price of one currency in terms of another currency. An exchange rate can be bilateral (£/$) or multilateral (a basket of currencies such as the *trade weighted sterling index*.

* A *devaluation* of sterling occurs when the UK government lowers the value of the pound from one fixed rate to another. *Depreciation* means that the value has fallen because of market forces. In both cases £1 would buy fewer units of another currency.

* A *revaluation* of sterling occurs when the UK government raises the value of the pound from one fixed rate to another. *Appreciation* means that the value has risen because of market forces. In both cases £1 would buy more units of another currency.

Table 26.1 The demand for and supply of the pound sterling

£s are demanded by	£s are supplied by
Foreign residents wishing to buy UK exports and pay for UK services	UK residents wishing to buy imports and pay for foreign services
People wishing to invest in the UK	UK residents wishing to invest abroad
Those wishing to take advantage of a future rise in the value of the pound	Those wishing to take advantage of a future rise in the value of another currency
Governments wishing to add sterling to their reserves	Governments wishing to replace the sterling in their reserves with other assets
A UK government wishing to raise the value of the pound	A UK government wishing to lower the value of the pound
Foreign governments wishing to lower the value of their currencies	Foreign governments wishing to raise the value of their currencies

- A *Eurocurrency* is any currency deposited in a financial institution outside its country of origin, e.g. French francs deposited in a bank in Singapore.
- The *London Foreign Exchange Market* consists of all those who deal in foreign exchange but have no formal meeting place.
- The *spot market* is that part of the foreign exchange market concerned with the buying and selling of currencies for immediate use.
- The *forward market* is concerned with agreeing the price of a currency now to buy or sell in the future.
- *Arbitrage* is movements of funds to take advantage of differences in exchange or interest rates, and this quickly eliminates any such differences.
- The *purchasing power parity theory* suggests that the prices of goods in countries will tend to equate under floating exchange rates so that people will be able to purchase the same quantity of goods in any country for a given sum of money.

(b)   Exchange rate systems

(1)   A *fixed exchange rate* is one that is maintained at a certain level (parity or par) by the government buying and selling currencies when necessary.

(2)   *Adjustable peg* is when the exchange rate is maintained within agreed margins around a central parity but with the possibility that the central parity may be changed.

(3)   *Crawling peg* is a form of adjustable peg where the central parity can be changed regularly on the basis of the previous trend in the exchange rate.

(4)   *Managed floating* is when the government occasionally intervenes in the exchange market to stabilise the exchange rate or move it in a desired direction.

(5)   *Free floating* occurs when the exchange rate is determined by demand and supply, without government intervention.

(c)   The exchange rate mechanism (ERM)

The *ERM* is an adjustable peg system that involves EU countries maintaining the value of their currencies within limited margins but being allowed to float their currencies against non-member currencies. If a currency within the ERM begins to move outside its margins, its government is expected to bring it back into line by:

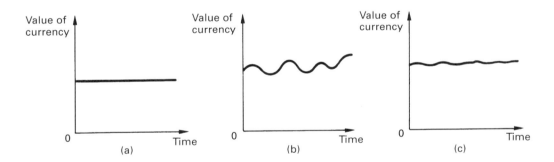

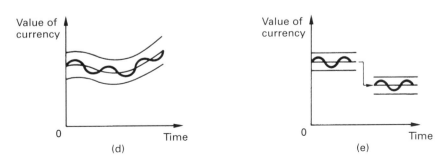

Figure 26.1 Exchange rate systems: (a) fixed; (b) floating; (c) managed floating; (d) crawling peg; (e) adjustable peg

(1) buying or selling its currency;
(2) changing its interest rate;
(3) seeking to realign its central parity with the agreement of the other members.

(d)   Advantages of the ERM

Membership of the ERM can confer a number of advantages on a country. It:

(1) provides greater discipline to reduce inflation as a fall in the exchange rate cannot be used to restore international competitiveness;
(2) gives the country a greater say in EU matters;
(3) helps to provide greater predictability of exchange rates within the EU, which in turn should promote trade in the EU;
(4) makes monetary union easier to achieve;
(5) discourages destabilising speculation;
(6) increases the chance of inflation rates converging.

(e)   Disadvantages of the ERM

The disadvantages of membership include:

(1) less opportunity to use the exchange rate as a policy tool, e.g. it cannot be reduced to increase employment;
(2) reduced independence of monetary policy, e.g. a government may have to raise its interest rate to prevent the value of its currency falling below the lower margin, even if this conflicts with domestic objectives;
(3) some currencies are more volatile than others and therefore are subject to more and wider fluctuations in demand and supply – this makes them harder to maintain within the agreed margins.

(f)   UK membership of the ERM

The UK joined the ERM in October 1990 at a central parity of 2.95 Deutschmarks. It left on 16 September 1992 'Black Wednesday' because:

(1) the value of the pound had been set too high and hence was difficult to maintain;
(2) the government wanted to be free to lower the interest rate to reflate the domestic economy;
(3) the value of the pound had come under downward pressure due to:
  (a) a rise in German interest rates;

(b) the Bundesbank president stating that the value of the pound was too high;
(c) concern over whether France would sign the Maastricht Treaty;
(d) speculation.

The UK government has stated it will only rejoin the ERM if there is:

(1) greater convergence of monetary policy in the EU;
(2) a stronger mechanism for helping currencies that come under pressure;
(3) a healthy UK economy.

(g)   International liquidity

International liquidity is an asset that is acceptable in settling international debts. Internationally acceptable assets are kept in countries' reserves. Forms of international liquidity are:

(1) Gold.
(2) Foreign currencies
(3) Reserve positions at the IMF, i.e. the ability to borrow from the IMF.
(4) *Special drawing rights* (SDRs), which are issued by the IMF and have been specifically created to act as international liquid assets. They are allocated to member countries on the basis of their quotas, and their value is expressed in terms of a weighted basket of five leading currencies.

(h)   Problems of international liquidity

The two current major problems are:

(1) Shortage of international liquidity.
(2) Which form international liquidity should take. Some economists have suggested the following:
  (a) Increased use of gold. This view overlooks the opportunity cost of using gold, and its inelastic supply. Some economists suggest the *demonetarisation* of gold, i.e. ceasing to use gold as a form of government money.
  (b) Increased reliance on foreign currencies. However this would mean that the growth of world reserves would depend on national policies. There may be a risk of destabilisation via movements from weakening to strengthening currencies.
  (c) Adoption of completely freely floating

exchange rates. This would eliminate the need for reserves.

(d) Increased government cooperation between central banks in order to make more effective use of existing reserves through coordinated intervention.

(e) Increased use of SDRs.

(i) International organisations

(1) The *International Monetary Fund* (IMF) was set up in 1944. Its main aims include:

(a) facilitating the expansion and balanced growth of world trade;

(b) promoting assistance to member countries with balance of payments difficulties;

(c) promoting exchange rate stability.

Member countries pay a quota based on their national income and share of world trade. The purpose of quotas is to make available a pool of foreign currency that can be borrowed by member countries in tranches, i.e. percentages of their quotas. The right to the first 25%, or gold tranche, is automatic but the right to subsequent tranches is subject to increasing conditionality.

(2) *The International Bank for Reconstruction and Development*, which is more commonly known as the World Bank. It was established in 1945 to help member countries recover from the Second World War. It now gives long-term loans to member countries for high priority infrastructure, agricultural, industrial and educational projects.

(3) The International Finance Corporation (a member of the World Bank group) was set up in 1956 to encourage private sector development by providing share and loan capital for companies, encouraging local capital markets and promoting the international flow of private capital.

(4) The *International Development Association* lends at low, subsidised interest rates to less developed countries. It too is a member of the World Bank group.

(5) The *World Trade Organisation* (WTO) replaced GATT (the General Agreement on Tariffs and Trade) in January 1955. It polices and administers the rules that govern world trade.

26.2 Investigative study

Example 26.1

An assessment of the impact of exchange rate changes on local businesses.

26.3 Data response

Example 26.2

Yen's Unstoppable Rise Threatens to End in Disaster

OFFICIALS in Tokyo have all but abandoned their efforts to hold down the value of the yen after it soared spectacularly to 88.7 to the dollar last week.

Foreign analysts now believe the yen will remain at historically high levels for at least another 12 months. Despite the serious drag that this rate of exchange is putting on Japan's recovery, the Bank of Japan appears to have no plans to cut the official discount rate (currently at a historic low of 1.75%) or continue its unilateral effort to prop up the dollar. In the past eight months the Bank of Japan has bought more than $14 billion in a futile effort to support the ever-weakening dollar and slow the yen's rise. As the Bank's dollar holdings have ballooned to $125 billion, the value of the dollar has slumped more than 10%.

Authorities in Tokyo last week were blaming hedge-fund speculators such as George Soros for the strengthening of the yen, but more fundamental economic factors were also at work. A Japanese current-account surplus of $129 billion last year, continuing restrictions on a wide range of imports and a tight monetary policy all contributed to make the yen one of the world's strongest currencies.

But the bubble is bound to burst because of the imminent collapse of the current-account surplus. Import volumes are growing 10% more rapidly than export volumes and will grow even faster when Japan's recovery picks up.

The underlying strength of the Japanese economy is powerfully revealed in several recent studies which show that Japanese companies will still be able to make useful profits, albeit reduced ones, if the exchange rate strengthens by another 5%.

"Even with the yen–dollar rate at 85, we believe economic recovery will continue," says Dick Beason, economist with James Capel Pacific in Tokyo. JP Morgan estimates that between 3% and 5% of expected profits will be wiped off the 1994 corporate results as a result of the yen falling from 98 to 90 to the dollar. Toyota, the largest Japanese carmaker and exporter, has announced it is losing Y1 billion (£6.6m) in annual sales for every one-yen drop in the dollar exchange rate.

"It remains highly unlikely that the Bank of Japan will cut the ODR (official discount rate) or that America's Federal Reserve will take the Fed Funds rate higher in response," says Beason.

Source: Garth Alexander, *The Sunday Times*, 12 March 1995.

(a) Why would a rise in the value of the yen put a 'drag' on Japan's recovery? **(5 marks)**

(b) Draw a diagram to show the effect of the Bank of Japan buying dollars and explain what it is showing. **(4 marks)**

(c) Explain what has caused the value of the yen to rise. **(5 marks)**

(d) What is meant by a current account surplus? **(2 marks)**

(e) What may cause a country to import more
goods? **(4 marks)**

(f) What may enable companies to make
'useful' profits despite a rise in the exchange
rate? **(5 marks)**

Solution 26.2

(a) A rise in the value of the Japanese yen will
increase the price of Japanese exports in terms of
foreign currency, and reduce the price of Japanese
imports in terms of yen. This is likely to reduce the
sales of Japanese goods both at home and abroad,
which in turn is likely to reduce output and
employment. So a rise in the value of a currency can
reduce the level of economic activity in a country.

(b) To purchase dollars the Bank of Japan will sell
yen. This will increase the supply of yen, lower its
price and increase the quantity trade on foreign
exchange markets.

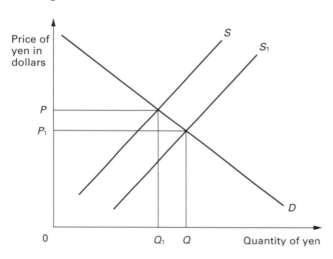

(c) The value of the yen rose because of the high and
increasing demand and decreasing supply. Speculators
had been purchasing yen in the expectation that it
would rise in the future. The country had a large
current account surplus so demand by foreigners to
purchase yen to buy exports exceeded the sale of yen
by the Japanese to buy imports. Supply of the yen was
also reduced by restrictions on imports and tight
monetary policy – both of which would have caused
the Japanese to buy fewer imports and hence sell
fewer yen.

(d) The current account of the balance of payments is
the visible balance plus the invisible balance. A
current account surplus means that more is earned

from the sale of visible and invisible exports than is
spent on visible and invisible imports. Export revenue
exceeds import expenditure.

(e) There are a number of factors that could cause a
country to import more goods. Domestic output may
be increasing so more raw materials may be
purchased from abroad. Higher incomes are likely to
result in increased demand for overseas finished
manufactured goods and services. The price
competitiveness of overseas products may rise, their
quality improve or they may be marketed more
effectively.

More imports may be purchased if import
restrictions are reduced or removed. A rise in the
value of the currency is also likely to result in more
imports being purchased.

(f) A rise in the exchange rate will reduce the price
competitiveness of domestic goods at home and
abroad. However a domestic company may still
continue to make normal or even supernormal profits
in a number of circumstances. It may be able to cut its
costs and hence lower its prices to keep its market
share and maintain profit levels. It may also be able to
improve its marketing or the quality of its products, so
they will still be demanded even at a higher relative
price. In overseas and home markets the company
may not experience a significant change in its profit
margin if the demand for its products is inelastic.

26.4 Objective questions

Example 26.3

On the foreign exchange market the value of the
pound depreciates from £1 = $1.5 to £1 = $1. If a UK
export firm allows the price of its goods to reflect this
depreciation, by what percentage will the price in the
USA of a £20 000 good change?

A +50%   **B** +10%   **C** −20%   **D** −33⅓%

Example 26.4

The following diagram shows the market for sterling.

If the government wishes to maintain the exchange
rate at 0P it should:

A buy XY sterling
B buy XZ sterling
C sell XY sterling
D sell XZ sterling

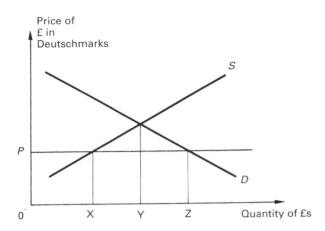

Example 26.5

Under a freely floating exchange rate system, which of the following will cause an appreciation of the pound sterling?

A   A rise in French interest rates
B   An increase in Japanese tourist expenditure in London
C   An increase in speculative sales of sterling
D   The purchase by a British company of a controlling interest in a company in Germany

Example 26.6

A British shirt manufacturer sells 60 shirts per week in the USA when the price is £10 per shirt and the exchange rate is £1 = $1.5. The US market has a unit elasticity of demand for these shirts. If the sterling price is unchanged, what is the maximum number of shirts the manufacturer can sell in the USA if the exchange rate changes to £1 = $2?

A   40   B   45   C   60   D   80

Example 26.7

Which of the following will impose downward pressure on the pound sterling?

A   A fall in US interest rates
B   A reduction in German import duties
C   A reduction in UK investment abroad
D   A reduction in foreign tourists coming into the UK

Example 26.8

Which of the following would be likely to cause a decrease in the UK's reserves under a fixed exchange rate?

A   The issue of SDRs by the IMF

B   A decrease in overseas investment by UK residents
C   A surplus on the current account of the balance of payments
D   Support of the pound sterling by the Exchange Equalisation Account

Example 26.9

Which of the following is a possible disadvantage of a fixed exchange rate?

A   Reserves will have to be held
B   There will be frequent changes in the value of the currency
C   Trade may be diminished because of exchange rate uncertainty
D   There will be an absence of external pressure to control inflationary pressures

Example 26.10

The exchange rate between country X and country Y is £1 = £2.0. To be as well off in country Y, a citizen of country X earning £24 000 per annum would need to earn £72 000. What is the purchasing power parity between the $ and £?

A   5:1   B   4:1   C   3:1   D   2:1

Example 26.11

The diagram below shows the market for the pound sterling.

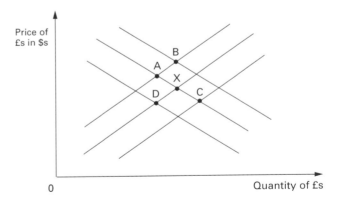

The initial equilibrium position is X. If there is an increase in overseas investment by British companies, will the new equilibrium position be **A, B, C** or **D**?

Example 26.12

If a UK company keeps the German price of its exports unchanged after a fall in the value of the pound the result will be:

A a decrease in the value of German sales valued in sterling

B an increase in the value of German sales valued in sterling

C a decrease in the demand for its products in Germany

D an increase in the demand for its products in Germany

26.5 Solutions to objective questions

Solution 26.3 Answer: **D**

Originally the £20 000 good would have sold in the USA for £20 000 × $1.5 = $30 000. After the depreciation it will sell for £20 000 × $1 = $20 000. This is a reduction of ($10 000/$30 000) × 100 = $33\frac{1}{3}$%.

Solution 26.4 Answer: **D**

At the exchange rate 0P, demand for the currency exceeds supply by amount XZ. To prevent the exchange rate rising the government would have to sell amount XZ to ensure that supply matches demand at this artificially low price.

Solution 26.5 Answer: **B**

An appreciation of the currency will occur if there is an increase in demand for the currency and/or a decrease in supply of the currency. A rise in Japanese tourist expenditure in London would mean an increase in Japanese demand for sterling.

A ⇒ A rise in French interest rates may result in a shift in investment finance from the UK to France. UK residents wishing to invest in France will change pounds into francs, thereby increasing the supply of sterling. Fewer foreigners will wish to invest in the UK and so the demand for sterling will fall.

C ⇒ Selling sterling increases supply and hence causes a fall in the price of the pound.

D ⇒ If UK residents buy more imports, more sterling will be sold to gain foreign currency, so again the supply of sterling will increase.

Solution 26.6 Answer: **B**

The initial price of a $10 shirt in the USA is £10 × $1.5 = $15. Sixty are sold, so the total revenue

is 60 × $15 = $900. The change in the exchange rate will cause the US price to rise to $20. As elasticity of demand for the shirt is unity, a rise in price will cause an equal percentage change in demand and total revenue will remain constant. Thus, as total revenue is $900 and each shirt sells for $20, the number of shirts sold is $900/$20 = 45.

Solution 26.7 Answer: **D**

Downward pressure on the pound sterling can arise as a result of an increase in the supply of sterling and/or a decrease in the demand for sterling. Fewer tourists coming into the UK would reduce demand for sterling.

A ⇒ A fall in US interest rates is likely to cause a rise in the value of the pound, as fewer UK citizens will invest in the USA and more foreigners will invest in the UK, as opposed to the USA.

B ⇒ If Germany reduces the taxes it places on imports the UK should be able to export more to Germany, and hence the demand for sterling will increase.

C ⇒ A reduction in UK investment abroad would reduce the supply of sterling on the world markets and hence increase its price.

Solution 26.8 Answer: **D**

If the EEA is supporting the pound it will buy up sterling. Most probably it will use foreign currencies in its reserves to do this.

A ⇒ The issue of SDRs by the IMF will increase the reserves of member countries, including the UK.

B ⇒ A decrease in overseas investment by UK residents may, in the short term, reduce the amount of money going abroad, and hence may enable less money to be drawn from the reserves or more money added to the reserves.

C ⇒ A current account surplus will mean more money being earned abroad than is spent abroad and some of this may be added to the reserves.

Solution 26.9 Answer: **A**

To maintain a fixed exchange rate, the authorities may have to buy the currency and to do this it will be necessary to hold reserves. Keeping reserves involves an opportunity cost.

B, C and **D** ⇒ Discouragement of trade, absence of external pressure to control inflationary pressures and frequent changes in the exchange rate are claimed by some economists to be disadvantages of a floating exchange rate.

Solution 26.10   Answer: **C**

The purchasing power parity theory states that the exchange rate between currencies will be such that the purchasing power of the money will be the same in both countries, i.e. the amount that can be purchased with the money concerned. If, in order to be as well off in country Y, a citizen earning £24 000 needs to earn £72 000, the value of the currencies is $3 to £1 in terms of what the currencies will buy. Thus the official exchange rate is not reflecting the purchasing power of the respective currencies.

Solution 26.11   Answer: **C**

An increase in overseas investment by UK companies will mean that more sterling will be exchanged into foreign currencies to invest abroad. The supply of sterling will increase, causing price to fall and demand to expand. The supply curve shifts to the right, intersecting the original demand curve at C.

Solution 26.12   Answer: **B**

A company can take advantage of a fall in the value of the currency either by allowing the foreign price of its product to fall, thereby raising demand for it, or by leaving the foreign price constant. The latter option will result in an increase in its revenue measured in its own currency. For example, if initially £1 = 10 marks, then a £6 good would sell in Germany for 60 marks. If, when the exchange rate falls to £1 = 5 marks, the company keeps the price in Germany at 60 marks, it will receive £12 per good when it changes its earnings from marks into pounds.

26.6 Essays

Example 26.13

Discuss the effects on the UK economy of a depreciation in the sterling exchange rate. (**25 marks**)

- Explain the meaning of depreciation.
- Examine the internal and external effects of a depreciation.

- Make use of the concept of price elasticity of demand.

Solution 26.13

Depreciation means a fall in the value of a currency in terms of another currency or currencies under a floating exchange rate system. It is caused by an increase in the supply of the currency and/or a fall in demand for the currency.

A depreciation will mean that exports, in terms of foreign currency, will be cheaper, while imports, in terms of pounds, will be more expensive. A depreciation not only makes exports more price-competitive, but also increases the competitiveness of those UK products sold on the home market that compete against imports.

In the short term the demand for both imports and exports will be inelastic, as there will not be time for the pattern of demand to change. However if the demand for exports is elastic, then total revenue earned from exports should rise, as the fall in price will cause a greater percentage rise in demand. Also, expenditure on imports should decrease, since a rise in their price will cause a greater percentage fall in demand. The Marshall Lerner condition states that if depreciation of a currency is to improve the balance of payments position, the elasticity for exports and imports must be greater than one.

Exporters may take advantage of the fall in the currency either by allowing the price of their goods to fall in foreign markets or by keeping their prices constant, raising their sterling profit margins.

If the depreciation results in a rise in export revenue and a fall in expenditure on imports, there will be a net injection in the circular flow of income. This will cause national income to rise by a multiple amount.

If more exports are sold, fewer imports are purchased and NY is rising, then employment is also likely to rise. This will occur unless there is already full employment or underemployment or unless a rise in output results entirely from increased capital or changes in technology.

While it is believed that the demand for UK exports is elastic, it is more doubtful whether some of the other conditions required for a depreciation to improve the balance of payments position will be met. If the demand for exports and imports is inelastic, then a fall in the value of the pound will result in more being spent on imports and less being earned from exports. This will cause a deterioration in the balance of payments position and will result in a leakage from the circular flow.

Even if the demand for exports is elastic, the country may not benefit if the supply of exports is inelastic. For instance, if there is full employment it may be difficult to meet any extra demand. The beneficial effects of a depreciation may also be affected by other countries devaluing their currencies.

A depreciation can accelerate inflation both directly and indirectly. Imports are counted in the retail price index, and a rise in their price will, *ceteris paribus*, raise the RPI. Also, home producers may raise their price because of increases in the cost of imported raw materials and components and/or because they can do so while still remaining competitive against more expensive imports. Trade unions may be stimulated to press for wage rises, since higher import prices will probably increase the cost of living.

Investment in the UK may be discouraged, especially if it is thought that there will be a future fall in the value of the pound. Some countries that have kept sterling in their reserves may decide to change to other currencies, and this will put increased pressure on the pound.

The effects of a depreciation are uncertain and may be beneficial or adverse, depending on a number of factors, including the elasticity of demand for exports and imports.

Example 26.14

(a) Explain how the ERM works. **(10 marks)**
(b) Discuss why the UK entered and left the ERM.
(15 marks)

- Include a diagram.
- Explain measures that can be used to keep currencies within the bands.
- Consider both immediate and fundamental reasons for the UK's departure.

Solution 26.14

(a) The exchange rate mechanism (ERM) is part of the European Monetary System, which was established in 1979 with the aim of increasing exchange rate stability between the member countries of the EU and thereby encouraging trade between the members.

The ERM is an adjustable peg system. Each currency in the ERM has a central rate (called parity)

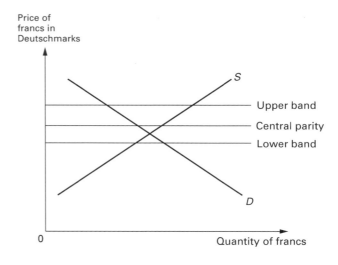

against the ECU and other member countries' currencies. It is permitted to fluctuate by a given percentage either side of the central parity. Initially this was 2.25%, although some countries were allowed a wider margin of 6%. In August 1993 the bands were widened to 15%. Figure 1 shows the central parity, the upper and lower bands, and the price of the French franc being within the bands.

If a currency moves too far away from its central parity, its government is expected to intervene by buying its currency if it is moving towards the lower band, and selling its currency if it is moving towards the upper band. If this does not work the government would be expected to raise its interest rate to raise the value of its currency or lower its interest rate to reduce the value of its currency.

If both these measures are unsuccessful and the central parity appears to be out of line with market forces, agreement of the other member countries would be sought to realign the currency.

(b) The UK entered the ERM in October 1990. In part this move was a step, albeit a hesitant one, towards greater economic and monetary union, but the main motive behind UK membership was the desire to gain the advantages of a more fixed exchange rate system. With less opportunity for the exchange rate to fluctuate, greater certainty is created and exporters and importers find it easier to plan for the future. There is also greater pressure on the government and firms to control inflation, and this was perhaps the main benefit the government was seeking. In a floating exchange rate system, if domestic inflation occurs the exchange rate will float down, which will restore firms' competitiveness in overseas markets. This is not possible to the same extent in an adjustable peg system, and if firms wish to stay competitive in export markets they will have to keep price rises down.

Membership of the ERM became a central part of the government's anti-inflation policy. However this may itself have contributed to the UK's departure from the ERM. A number of economists argued that the UK entered the ERM with an overvalued pound. The advantage of a high pound value is that it puts downward pressure on inflation. However an artificially high pound value is difficult to sustain and this is what the UK found in 1992.

The UK left the ERM on 'Black Wednesday', 16 September 1992. The immediate reason for the departure was the significant increase in the sale of sterling on foreign exchange markets throughout the world caused by the relatively high German interest rate, fears that France would not sign the Maastricht Treaty, and a growing belief that the pound was overvalued. The Bank of England tried to prevent the downward fall in the value of the pound by large-scale purchases of sterling and raising the interest rate by 5 percentage points in two days. As speculation built up

the government was unable to hold the value of the pound and the UK left the ERM.

More fundamental reasons for the UK's departure were the government's desire to gain more control over its monetary policy and concerns over the operation of the ERM. The government had wanted to cut the rate of interest to stimulate economic activity and reduce unemployment. However its ability to do this was constrained by its membership of the ERM. A cut in UK interest rates would have tended to cause an outflow of money from UK financial institutions to financial institutions in, for example, Germany. This would have caused the supply of sterling to increase, thereby putting downward pressure on the pound.

There was also increasing awareness of the fact that, if the ERM was to work, the economies of the member countries would have to converge. This was not occurring in the early 1990s, when some member governments were seeking to reduce inflation and others were seeking to promote output and employment.

Development Economics

27.1 Fact sheet

(a) Indicators of development

Possible indicators include:

(1) Real GDP capital.
(2) MEW.
(3) HDI.
(4) Average life span.
(5) Consumer durables per head.
(6) Access to health services.
(7) Proportion of labour force employed in different sectors.
(8) Infant mortality.

(b) Characteristics of development

Developing countries usually share most of the following characteristics:

(1) Low real income per capita.
(2) Low capital to labour ratio.
(3) Low level of literacy.
(4) High birth rate.
(5) High infant mortality.
(6) Low productivity.
(7) Poor industrial and social infrastructure.
(8) High proportion of the population employed in agriculture.

(c) Constrains of development

A developing country may experience problems increasing its output and productivity because of the following:

(1) Low level of investment.
(2) Low level of saving.
(3) Narrow tax base
(4) Dependency on a narrow export base.
(5) Unfavourable terms of trade.
(6) International debt, some arising on past loans.
(7) High dependency ratio.
(8) Low level of education.

(d) Development strategies

A developing country can seek to increase its output by using one or a combination of strategies. These include:

(1) Promoting export-led growth.
(2) Developing infant manufacturing industries.
(3) Improving productivity in the primary sector.
(4) Using overseas aid to improve infrastructure, education and health systems.

(e) Overseas aid

- *Bilateral aid* is assistance from one government to another.
- *Multilateral aid* is channelled through international organisations and charities to a number of countries.
- *Tied aid* is given on condition that the funds are used to purchase goods made in the donor country.

Countries give aid for the following reasons:

(1) Commercial: tied aid increases the exports of the donor country. As the assisted country becomes more prosperous it will tend to buy more goods from 'friendly' countries.
(2) Political: aid is given to win the support and cooperation of strategically important countries.
(3) Altruism: charitable concerns such as Oxfam are motivated by a concern for others.

(f) Problems of overseas aid

Less developed countries argue for trade on more favourable terms than aid, because:

(1) Aid may involve political interference.
(2) Aid may be inappropriate if, say, it promotes capital-intensive projects when labour-intensive activities are better suited to the economy.
(3) Loans impose future interest and repayment burdens, particularly if debts must be repaid in foreign currency.
(4) Tied aid involves a loss of freedom of choice.
(5) Aid in the form of products depresses the price of those goods in aided countries. Producers are then unable to sell their own output at a profit.

27.2 Intensive study

Example 27.1

An investigation into the causes of the rapid growth of China and the impact this is having on the Chinese economy.

27.3 Data response

Example 27.2

INCOME PER HEAD

Developing countries' populations are growing more quickly than those of industrial countries. Unless their output also grows faster, their relative real GDP per head will fall. In 1985–94, those in Asia, the Middle East and Europe raised output fast enough to avoid this. But while GDP per head soared in Asia by an average of 6.3% a year, in the Middle East and Europe it edged up by only 0.3% a year. Income per head fell in both Africa (down by 0.7% a year) and Eastern Europe (5.1%).

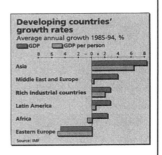

RICH AND POOR

Of the 24 emerging economies tracked by *The Economist*, Hong Kong has the highest income per head, $21,670 in 1993 (at purchasing-power parity). India's, $1,250, was the lowest.

Source: *The Economist*, 11 March 1995, p. 162.

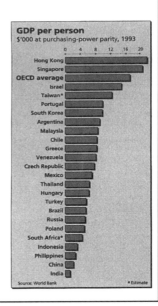

(a) Which part of the developing world experienced the most rapid growth between 1985 and 1994? **(2 marks)**
(b) Give two reasons for the high birth rate in many developing countries. **(2 marks)**
(c) Explain how the income per head figures in the second chart were compared. **(3 marks)**
(d) Which members of the EU had a GDP per capita below the OECD average? **(2 marks)**
(e) What economic characteristics are shared by the countries in second highest and second lowest ranking of GDP per person? **(7 marks)**
(f) Give three ways by which a developing country could increase its GDP per capita. **(6 marks)**

(g) Which areas of the world do you think are included in 'rich industrial areas'? **(3 marks)**

Solution 27.2

(a) Asia experienced the most rapid growth between 1985 and 1994. A number of Asian countries witnessed rapid growth in this period, including China, India, Korea and Singapore.

(b) The birth rate in a number of developing countries is high because of high infant mortality rates (which lead people to expect that only a proportion of their children will survive), lack of knowledge about and means by which to practice birth control, the proportion of the population who are of childbearing age and the perceived need to have children so as to be looked after when old.

(c) The GDP per capita figures were compared by using purchasing power parity. This involves calculating the price of a given basket of goods in different countries and then using this as a basis upon which to convert currencies. For example if the same basket of goods cost £90 in the UK and $108 in the US, GDP figures would be converted at the rate of £1 = $1.2.

(d) Both Portugal and Greece had GDP per capita figures below the OECD average.

(e) Singapore and China share a number of economic characteristics. They both have relatively high population densities but they also have high annual growth rates. They both draw on ideas from outside and are experiencing inward investment from overseas. In addition both have relatively high expenditure on secondary education and both are making advances in high-tech industries, albeit with China a later comer onto the scene, but a later comer with tremendous potential.

(f) There are a number of ways in which a developing country could develop, but none of these are easy to achieve. The country could devote more of its resources to education and training in an attempt to improve long-term growth. It could encourage inward investment from overseas to raise domestic employment and to learn new methods and ideas. It could also seek overseas assistance and possibly impose import restrictions. All these methods have their advantages and their costs.

(g) Currently 'rich industrial countries' include the Western European countries, the United States, Japan and the countries of Australasia, but this could change in the future.

27.4 Objective questions

Example 27.3

Multilateral aid is aid:
A from one country to another
B from one country directly to a number of other countries
C from one country to a number of other countries via an international agency
D from a group of countries to one country with conditions attached

Example 27.4

Which of the following is not usually a characteristic of a developing country?
A High infant mortality
B A high level of obesity
C A low level of literacy
D A low level of real GDP per capita

Example 27.5

In the poorest countries of the world most of the population is employed in:
A the primary sector
B the secondary sector
C the tertiary sector
D the quaternary sector

Example 27.6

Exports from developing countries traditionally have:
A price elasticity of demand greater than one
B price elasticity of supply greater than one
C income elasticity of demand less than one
D cross-elasticity of demand of zero

Example 27.7

Middle-income economies that are developing rapidly and gaining an increasing share of export markets are known as:
A lesser developed countries
B newly industrialised countries
C Third World countries

D Fourth World countries

Examples 27.8 and 27.9 refer to the following diagrams, which show the age distribution of the populations of four countries.

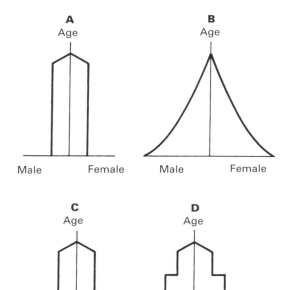

Example 27.8

Which diagram (**A**, **B**, **C** or **D**) most accurately depicts developing economy?

Example 27.9

Which diagram (**A**, **B**, **C** or **D**) most accurately depicts developed economy with a constant birth rate?

Example 27.10

What is likely to be the main motive for a country giving tied aid to another country?
A To increase the exports of the donor country
B To increase the international competitiveness of the recipient country
C To increase the choice of the recipient country in terms of the products it can buy
D To increase the birth rate of the recipient country, thereby reducing the average age of the population

Example 27.11

One possible development strategy is import substitution. What is meant by import substitution?

A Encouraging domestic firms to use the best raw materials irrespective of the country they come from
B Replacing imports from high-cost countries with imports from low-cost countries
C Using exports to buy manufactured imports rather than agricultural products
D Using tariffs and other forms of trade restriction to replace imports with domestic goods

Example 27.12

Which international organisation makes loans to poor countries at concessionary rates?
A IDA   **B** IFC   **C** IMF   **D** WTO

27.5 Solutions to objective questions

Solution 27.3 Answer: **C**

Multilateral aid comes mainly from international organisations such as the International Development Association.

Solution 27.4 Answer: **B**

Options **A**, **C** and **D** are all common features of a developing country. Due to the low levels of food consumption in development countries, obesity is unlikely to be a problem – it is, however, becoming an increasing problem in developed countries.

Solution 27.5 Answer: **A**

In the poorest countries most of the population are employed in agriculture. As economic development proceeds more of the population will move into the secondary sector and then into the tertiary and quaternary sectors.

Solution 27.6 Answer: **C**

Developing countries often export agricultural products. These usually have income inelastic demand since as income rises, the demand for foodstuffs rises by only a small amount. Food also usually has inelastic demand and inelastic supply (price) – options **A** and **B**. As one country's food and other products will compete with other countries' exports, cross-elasticity of demand will not be zero.

Solution 27.7 Answer: **B**

Newly industrialised countries, e.g. South Korea, are experiencing significant rises in GDP and are becoming major competitors in the export markets for manufactured products.

A, **C** and **D** ⇒ Lesser developed countries and Third World countries are poor countries with low per capita incomes, lack of human capital and a number of other common features. Fourth World countries are the world's poorest countries, e.g. Bangladesh.

Solution 27.8 Answer: **B**

Developing countries tend to have a high birth rate and a high death rate. As a result the base of the population pyramid is broad and the top narrow.

Solution 27.9 Answer: **A**

Developed countries tend to have both a low birth rate and a low death rate. Consequently the upper regions of the population pyramid are almost as broad as the base. The vertical slope of the pyramid indicates a constant birth rate.

C and **D** ⇒ also show developed countries, but the V-shaped base of the pyramid suggest that the birth rate is falling.

Solution 27.10 Answer: **A**

Tied aid is often given with the intention of increasing demand for the donor's goods. Indeed the aid may be given on condition that the recipient buys a certain quantity or value of the donor country's goods.

B and **D** ⇒ are very unlikely motives.

C ⇒ By its very nature, tied aid limits the recipient country's choice of which goods to buy and where to buy them from.

Solution 27.11 Answer: **D**

To switch from producing mainly primary products to mainly manufactured goods, i.e. to industrialise, some developing countries believe that manufacturing industries will need to be developed behind tariff walls. This is so that they can be protected until they can take full advantage of economies of scale – the

infant industry argument. The intention is to replace imported manufactured goods with home-produced manufactured goods.

Solution 27.12 Answer: **A**

The International Development Agency provides low-interest loans to development countries that often find it difficult to obtain loans from other sources. These loans are usually for government projects or for private sector projects supported by the government.

B ⇒ The International Finance Corporation seeks to promote private sector development by building up countries' capital markets and providing share and loan capital.

C ⇒ The International Monetary Fund seeks to promote world trade, to help countries in balance-of-trade difficulties and to encourage exchange rate stability.

D ⇒ The World Trade Organisation seeks to reduce trade restrictions and to promote world trade.

27.6 Essays

Example 27.13

(a) Why do the prices of primary products tend to be unstable? **(10 marks)**
(b) Is specialisation in the production of primary products a good method of encouraging economic development? **(15 marks)**

- Consider elasticities of demand and supply.
- Include a cobweb diagram.
- Consider price fluctuations, income elasticity of demand, and competition,

Solution 27.13

(a) The price of primary products tends to fluctuate by a significant amount because both demand and supply are inelastic, because supply can change by large and unexpected amounts and because it takes time to adjust output in line with price changes.

Primary products, including commodities and agricultural products, tend to have inelastic demand. For example many items of food may be regarded as necessities and some primary products are perceived as having few close substitutes, e.g. gold.

The supply of primary products is inelastic as they can take time to grow or extract and process. With

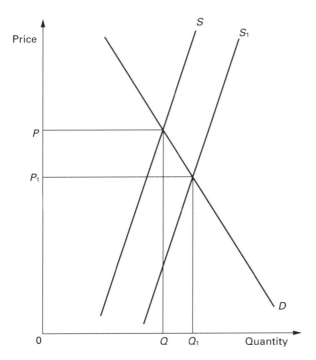

(b) It is widely considered that reliance on the production of primary products is not a good way of encouraging economic development. As has been shown above, the prices of primary products tend to be volatile. This creates uncertainty about income for producers and often leads to damaging changes in income. For example an increase in supply will tend to lead to a significant fall in price and a reduction in revenue. Similarly, whilst a decrease in supply, which raises price, will benefit some producers it will not help, for example, those farmers whose crop has failed. This last point is connected with another problem encountered in many primary product markets – the difficulty of controlling supply. For example favourable weather conditions could lead to a bumper supply of apples, which will lower their price.

Developing countries also have to compete in agricultural markets with developed countries, many of which give significant protection to their agricultural industries.

Over time world incomes usually rise and demand for agricultural products, in contrast with manufactured products, is income inelastic so producers of manufactured products gain at the expense of primary products. Non-oil primary products have seen a relative decline in their prices over time.

Fluctuations in income and hence economic activity can have a significant impact on the price of commodities. For instance a recession in developed countries will reduce the demand for petroleum.

Petroleum has the advantage over some primary products in that it can be stored, However, as with other primary products, problems can be encountered in operating producer cartels. There is a tendency for some members to break agreements in an attempt to gain a competitive advantage.

Primary producers also have the problem of trying to increase their market power because of the difficulty of product differentiation in primary markets.

In recent years the Third World countries that have seen the most rapid growth, e.g. China and South Korea, have been building up their manufacturing industries.

both inelastic demand and supply any change in the conditions of demand and/or supply will have a significant impact on price. Figure 1 shows an increase in supply causing price to fall.

The influence of weather conditions and diseases on agricultural products and new discoveries and speculation in commodity markets means that supply can change by significant amounts.

As it takes time to put primary products on to the market, demand and price conditions may have changed. Producers may base their output decisions on the prices prevailing in the previous season and this may lead to a shortage or a surplus. This tendency for prices to move around the equilibrium can be illustrated by a cobweb diagram. Figure 2 shows a convergent cobweb with price and output moving towards the long-run equilibrium.

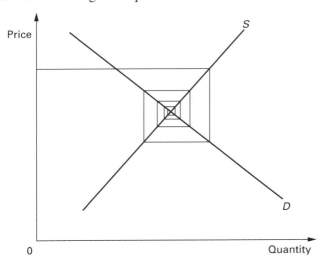

Example 27.14

(a) Explain what is meant by net emigration.

(3 marks)

(b) Why do most developing countries experience net emigration? **(7 marks)**

(c) What are the effects of net emigration on developing countries? **(15 marks)**

- Keep the definition brief.
- Consider both the advantages and disadvantages of net emigration.

Solution 27.14

(a) Net emigration means that more people are leaving a country than entering it. It arises when emigration exceeds immigration and results in a net loss of people from the country.

(b) Most developing countries experience net emigration because of their relatively low income levels, low job opportunities and low educational prospects. Some emigrants will initially go abroad to attend educational courses and then stay on. Others, unable to find jobs at home or dissatisfied with the wages on offer, will leave the country to gain employment abroad. For example a number of people from India and Pakistan are working in Gulf State countries. Related to higher incomes abroad, obviously, are higher living standards and, in some cases, better welfare provisions. Some emigrants will leave in search of asylum from political or religious persecution.

The number of people who emigrate will be influenced not only by their willingness to leave but also by the willingness of other countries to grant them entry.

(c) There are a number of possible economic effects of net emigration, although of course they will depend on the size of the net emigration. The country may move nearer to its optimum population size. However the size of the labour force is likely to be reduced as most of the emigrants will tend to be of working age. This may place a greater burden of dependency on remaining workers. Those who leave may be the more able and enterprising workers, which would reduce the overall quality of the remaining workforce. Also, a shortage of particular skills, e.g. medicine, may be created if it is mainly workers from particular categories who emigrate.

The sex distribution of the population is likely to be affected as it is usually men who emigrate. Those who emigrate often send money home to relatives and, in the case of a number of developing countries, transfers of money from people who have emigrated abroad form a significant credit item in their balance of payments.

John Kenneth Galbraith has suggested that emigration from developing countries can be a significant force in economic development. He argues that in addition to sending back money to relatives, emigrants send back ideas about the methods of production used abroad and the quality of life enjoyed there. People in the developing countries can copy these methods and can start to demand the goods, education, health provisions etc. enjoyed by those in developed countries. Dissatisfaction with the quality of their living standards may induce people to place greater pressure on their governments to adopt appropriate development strategies. Galbraith believes that emigration will break the acceptance of poverty in developing countries and relieve the pressure of overpopulation.

Managing the Economy

28.1 Fact sheet

(a) Government policy

There are three stages of government policy:

(1) *Objectives*: The aims of government policies.
(2) *Targets*: variables through which the government attempts to achieve its objectives.
(3) *Instruments*: policy tools over which the government has control and are implemented to influence target variables.

(b) Economic objectives

Governments have four main macroeconomic aims:

(1) High employment.
(2) Price stability.
(3) Balance of payments equilibrium.
(4) Economic growth.

• Governments may have a number of other macro objectives, such as a more equitable distribution of income. This requires state intervention through progressive taxation, income-related benefits etc.
• Governments may also have a number of micro objectives, such as protection of the environment or efficiency in the allocation of resources.

(c) Macroeconomic policies

A central issue in macroeconomics is whether or not markets automatically bring about equilibrium. If the free operation of market forces automatically results in a full employment level of national income with stable prices and economic growth, there is no need for government intervention to achieve equilibrium. However, if the economy is unstable or slow to reach satisfactory equilibrium, government economic policies will be required. These include:

(1) *Monetary policy*: the two main instruments are

Table 28.1 Examples of government policies

Policy	Instrument	Target	Objective
Monetary	Interest rate	Bank lending	Price stability
Fiscal	Government spending	Aggregate demand	Employment
Regional	Selective grants	Location of firms	Growth
Exchange rate	Exchange rate	Price of exports and imports	Balance of payments
Supply side	Supply side	Labour mobility	Growth

changes in the money supply and interest rates.

(2) *Fiscal policy*: the two main instruments are changes in government spending and taxation.

(3) *Prices and incomes policy* usually involves a limit on price rises and rises in incomes, particularly wages.

(4) *Regional policy*, where government measures help influence the location of industry and people.

(5) *Exchange rate policy*, which involves the government managing the exchange rate to achieve its aims – it may also be regarded as a form of monetary policy.

(6) *Import controls*, where, for example, tariffs are used to reduce or stabilise imports.

(d)   Fiscal policy

Fiscal policy covers any measure that changes the timing, amount or composition of government expenditure and/or taxation.

- *Direct taxes* are taxes on income and wealth.
- *Indirect taxes* are taxes on expenditure.
- As income rises a *progressive tax* takes a higher percentage of it in tax, a *proportional tax* takes the same percentage and a *regressive tax* takes a smaller percentage.
- *Government spending* covers spending on government investment projects, running government services and transfer payments.
- a *budget deficit* arises when government expenditure exceeds government revenue.
- A *cyclical deficit* is caused by a downturn in economic activity.
- A *structural deficit* is caused by a planned change in government spending and/or taxation.

(e)   Policy approaches

(1) Keynes argued that aggregate demand is the chief determinant of output and employment. Therefore demand management through macroeconomic policies is the best method of achieving policy objectives.

- *Reflationary policies* increase AD.
- *Deflationary policies* decrease AD.

(2) New classical economists generally argue that supply is the chief determinant of output and employment. Therefore microeconomic policies that increase supply are the best method of

achieving objectives. New classical economists favour measures such as reductions in tax rates or policies that reduce market distortions. These include:

(a) increasing the gap between earnings from employment and the job seekers' allowance to reduce voluntary and search unemployment;

(b) increasing, through training, the quality and flexibility of the labour force;

(c) privatising nationalised industries to make them subject to market forces;

(d) removing government restrictions to increase the efficiency of markets (*deregulation*);

(e) reducing the monopsony power of unions.

(f)   Government failure

Government failure occurs when government intervention does not improve the allocation of resources. All governments experience problems in managing the economy because:

(1) There may be a conflict between policy objectives. For instance, increased government spending may increase employment and growth but result in rising prices and a deficit in the current account of the balance of payments. *Tinbergen's rule* states that a government needs to have at least one instrument to achieve each objective. Fiscal policy can be directed at unemployment, exchange rate policy can be directed at the current account of the balance of payments, etc.

(2) Governments are faced with political constraints. For instance restrictive monetary policy may cause such high interest rates that mortgage payers refuse to vote for the government.

(3) Resistance from trade unions and professional bodies may act as a constraint.

(4) Policy instruments are interdependent. For example increased government spending may result in a rise in the PSBR and interest rates.

(5) Policy instruments can also become objectives, thereby reducing their flexibility. For example exchange rates and the money supply.

(6) There may be *time lags* between recognising a problem, deciding on the policy and then implementing that policy. In the meantime economic relationships may change. For example, if a government tackles unemployment by

reducing taxation, only to find that demand is rising anyway, this policy reinforces the cycle rather than acting *countercyclically*.

(7) The economy may not respond in the way anticipated. For example entrepreneurs may react to rises in demand by increasing prices rather than output.

(8) Some target variables are difficult to define. For example it is difficult to know which assets to include in a measure of the money supply.

(9) External shocks, e.g. a world recession, may undermine government policies.

28.2 Investigative study

Example 28.1

An investigation into alternatives to state pensions as a way of providing for the elderly.

28.3 Data response

Example 28.2

(a) What is the main source of government tax revenue **(2 marks)**

(b) Identify three direct taxes. **(3 marks)**

(c) What could cause, overtime, VAT revenue to increase? **(4 marks)**

(d) Identify one form of government expenditure that could be classified as 'regrettable'. **(2 marks)**

(e) Which forms of government expenditure are likely to fall with an increase in economic activity? **(10 marks)**

(f) From which sources can the government borrow? **(4 marks)**

Solution 28.2

(a) The main form of government tax revenue is income tax, which in 1993–94 accounted for 21% of total revenue.

(b) Direct taxes are taxes on the income of individuals and firms. Income tax, national insurance contributions and corporation tax are all examples of direct taxes.

(c) VAT revenue could increase if the rate of VAT increased, the number of goods subject to VAT was widened or if consumer expenditure rose.

(d) Expenditure on law, order, protective services and defence are forms of 'regrettable' expenditure. They do not cause living standards to rise. Increased expenditure on these items is usually undertaken to keep up with rising crime and perceived increases in threats to national security.

(e) Social security expenditure is likely to fall with increased economic activity. With higher output unemployment is likely to fall and this would reduce government expenditure on the job seekers' allowance, income support and housing benefit. This may have a significant impact on the level of government expenditure as total social security expenditure accounts for nearly a third of all government spending.

Increased economic activity is likely not only to reduce government spending on, for example, social

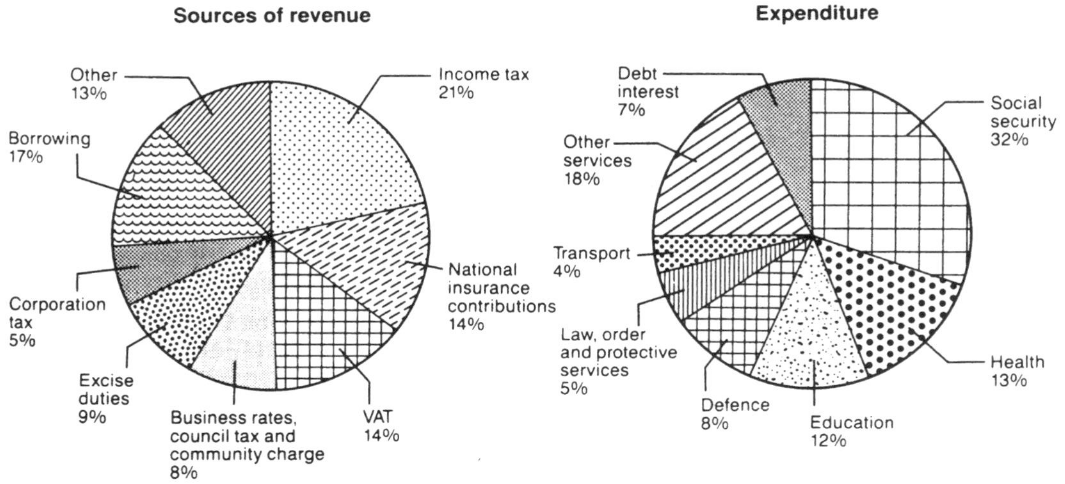

Figure 28.1 Government receipts and expenditure 1993–94
Note: As a result of rounding and omission of minor items, percentages do not add up to 100.
Source: HM Treasury.

security but also to raise tax revenue as more people will be in work and incomes will rise. This is likely to reduce any PSBR the government is running, and may even turn it into a PSDR. Hence debt interest payments may fall.

It is also possible that increased economic activity will reduce crime levels, thereby enabling expenditure on law, order and protective services to decline.

(f) The government can borrow from the Bank of England. This is often referred to as resorting to the printing press. It can also borrow from the retail banking sector. In both cases the borrowing will lead to an increase in the money supply. It can borrow from overseas, either in sterling or in a foreign currency. However most government borrowing is from the non-bank private sector.

28.4 Objective questions

Example 28.3

Which of the following policies would a government adopt to reduce both a surplus in the current account of the balance of payments and inflation?
A Revalue the currency
B Increase income tax
C Raise interest rates
D Impose import controls

Example 28.4

Which combination of events might cause a government to lower interest rates and reduce direct taxation?
A A deficit in the current account of the balance of payments and inflation
B A surplus in the current account of the balance of payments and inflation
C A surplus in the current account of the balance of payments and unemployment
D A deficit in the current account of the balance of payments and unemployment

Example 28.5

According to a supporter of supply-side economics, which of the following measures is most likely to reduce unemployment?
A Increasing the money supply
B Increasing public sector investment
C Increasing labour retraining schemes
D Increasing government payments to the unemployed

Example 28.6

Which of the following is an example of an automatic stabiliser?
A Child benefit
B Defence expenditure
C Education expenditure
D The job seekers' allowance

Example 28.7

A government is faced with both demand-pull inflation and a deficit in the current account of the balance of payments. Which of the following policy measures might simultaneously reduce both problems?
A Devaluation   B Revaluation   C Reflation
D Deflation

Example 28.8

An example of a restrictionist monetary instrument is:
A an increase in direct taxation
B a tight prices and incomes policy
C the conversion of long-term government debt into short-term government debt
D a switch of government borrowing from the banking sector to the non-bank private sector

Examples 28.9 and 28.10 are based on the following information. A country has a progressive income tax system. The first £6000 earned is tax-free. Thereafter the next £18 000 of earned income is taxed at 25% and all taxable income above that is taxed at 50%.

Example 28.9

A person earns £20 000. What proportion of this income is paid in tax?
A 50%   B 25%   C 17.5%   D 15.5%

Example 28.10

What is the marginal rate of tax paid when a person's income rises from £24 000 to £24 001?
A 0.8   B 0.5   C 0.3   D 0.1

Example 28.11

Which of the following is an example of fiscal policy?

A   Changes in interest rates
B   Changes in employees' National Insurance contributions
C   A change from expansionary to restrictionist open-market operations
D   A change from a floating to a managed exchange rate

Example 28.12

The diagram below shows government spending to be autonomous at a level of G. The initial tax structure is *T* and the initial level of National Income is 0*Y*. The full employment level of national income is 0*Y*$_{Fe}$. A new tax structure of T_1 is introduced.

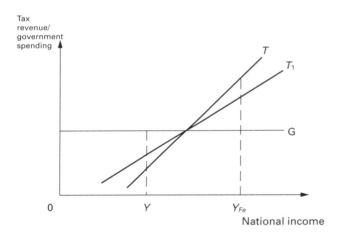

The change in taxes shows:

A   deflationary fiscal policy at 0*Y*
B   an expansionary fiscal policy at 0*Y*
C   an increase in the budget deficit at 0*Y*
D   an increase in the budget surplus at 0*Y*$_{Fe}$

28.5 Solutions to objective questions

Solution 28.3 Answer: **A**

Revaluing the currency is likely to result in expenditure on imports rising and export revenue falling. This will reduce a current account surplus. Inflationary pressure is likely to be reduced, since revaluation will reduce import prices, and imports count in the retail price index. Domestic producers are also likely to limit price rises in order to remain competitive at home and abroad.

Solution 28.4 Answer: **C**

Lowering interest rates and reducing direct taxation will increase demand in the home economy. This is likely to stimulate domestic output and employment. The increase in demand is also likely to increase imports and possibly reduce exports (as home producers switch from foreign markets to the home market). This will reduce a current account surplus and enable the home country to enjoy more goods and services.

Solution 28.5 Answer: **C**

Supporters of supply-side economics urge the use of microeconomic incentives to raise output and employment. They believe that, if the quantity and quality of factors of production are improved and markets operate more efficiently, growth and increases in employment will follow. Retraining schemes should increase the productivity of labour.

A ⇒ Supply-side economists believe that increases in the money supply, if greater than the increase in output, lead to higher prices but not to higher employment in the long term.

B ⇒ Increasing public sector investment will increase demand. Supply-side economists argue that governments should concentrate on increasing aggregate supply.

D ⇒ Increasing government payments to the unemployed would narrow the gap between unemployment income and income from employment. Supply-side economists favour the opposite course of action – ensuring that workers are better off in work. They believe that this will make people seek employment more quickly and settle for lower wages.

Solution 28.6 Answer: **D**

Automatic stabilisers offset changes in NY, without any direct change in government policy. If NY is falling, total expenditure on the job seekers' allowance will rise. This increase will reduce the fall in demand, and hence will act countercyclically.

A, B and **C** ⇒ will not adjust automatically with changes in NY. They are adjusted as a result of government decision and action.

Solution 28.7 Answer: **D**

Deflation involves reducing demand, usually by means of fiscal and/or monetary policy. This should reduce demand-pull inflation. It should also reduce a current account deficit by reducing expenditure on imports and possibly stimulating exports as a result of the fall in domestic demand.

A ⇒ Devaluation should assist the current account position, but may increase inflationary pressures as a result of the rise in export earnings and a rise in import prices.

B ⇒ Revaluation should reduce inflation by lowering import prices, but it is likely to have an adverse effect on the current account balance as a result of the fall in import prices and the rise in export prices.

C ⇒ Reflation means increasing demand, and this is likely to have an adverse effect on both the current account position and inflation.

Solution 28.8 Answer: **D**

When the government borrows from the retail banks, e.g. by selling treasury bills, it increases their liquid assets and hence their ability to lend. In contrast, when the government borrows from members of the non-bank private sector it merely makes use of existing money. Switching borrowing from the banking to the non-bank private sector will tend to reduce bank lending and hence reduce monetary expansion.

A ⇒ An increase in direct taxation is a deflationary fiscal policy.

B ⇒ A prices and incomes policy is a direct government policy influencing incomes.

C ⇒ Issuing more short-term government debt is an expansionary policy, since this will increase the supply of liquid assets

Solution 28.9 Answer: **C**

A person who earns £20 000 will have £6000 tax-free income and a taxable income of £14 000. The tax paid on this will be 25%, i.e. £3500. So the proportion income paid in tax is:

$$\frac{£3500}{£20\,000} \times 100 = 17.5\%$$

Solution 28.10   Answer: **B**

A person earning £24 000 will have £18 000 taxable income and hence will be in the 25% tax bracket. If the person's income rises by £1, this extra £1 will be

taxed at 50%, i.e. £0.5 will be taken in tax. So the marginal rate of tax is 0.5.

Solution 28.11   Answer: **B**

Fiscal policy involves changes in the amount, timing and/or composition of government spending and taxation. National Insurance contributions are a form of direct taxation.

A and **C** ⇒ are examples of monetary policy.

D ⇒ is an example of exchange rate policy, which can also be regarded as a form of monetary policy.

Solution 28.12   Answer: **A**

The new tax structure will result in a smaller budget deficit at $0Y$ than tax structure T. This will reduce demand.

B ⇒ An expansionary fiscal policy at $0Y$ would have been shown by a rise in the gap between government expenditure and taxation.

C ⇒ The budget deficit has fallen rather than risen at $0Y$.

D ⇒ At $0Y_{Fe}$ the budget surplus is smaller than with taxation structure T. There has been a decrease in the budget surplus.

28.6 Essays

Example 28.13

Should there be a shift from direct towards indirect taxation?   **(25 marks)**

• Define direct and indirect taxes.
• Consider the advantages and disadvantages of both indirect and direct taxation.

Solution 28.13

Direct taxes, e.g. income tax and corporation tax, are levied directly on a person's or firm's income or wealth. On the other hand indirect taxes, e.g. VAT and excise duty, are taxes on goods and services and are paid to the government through a third party. They are sometimes referred to as expenditure or outlay taxes.

The argument for moving the tax base towards greater reliance on indirect taxes and less reliance on direct taxation is based on the disadvantages of direct taxes and the advantages of indirect taxes.

It is claimed by some economists that direct taxation, particularly at a high level, acts as a disincentive to effort. However studies have shown that few people (less than 10%) change the hours they work when income tax rates are altered and that as many work fewer hours as work more hours.

A high level of corporation tax may discourage risk taking and may discourage investment, since most investment is financed by retained profits. Direct taxation may also reduce the savings of individuals, since the rich save more than the poor and savings may effectively be taxed twice: once when the income is earned and then when interest is received on the part of income that is saved.

In addition to reducing the disadvantages arising from direct taxation, a country would gain more of the advantages of indirect taxation by shifting the tax base. Indirect taxes are relatively cheap to administer and collect. For instance manufacturers and traders do most of the administrative work involved in VAT.

Indirect taxes can also be adjusted more quickly than direct taxes. While direct taxes can be changed at budget time and may involve complex revision of, for example, PAYE codings, indirect taxes can be changed relatively quickly.

Indirect taxes are difficult to evade as they are included in the price of the good. They may provide more freedom of choice in terms of payment, although if a wide range of goods are taxed, this may not be a significant advantage. Nevertheless it is thought that many people are unaware of the amount of tax they are paying when they buy goods, and this may reduce the resentment they feel about paying taxes.

Some economists argue that indirect taxes do not discourage effort, since the taxes are linked to spending rather than earning. However if certain goods, e.g. cars and colour TVs, are highly taxed, this may place them out of the reach of people who would have been prepared to work longer hours to buy them.

Indirect taxation can help to regulate the economy. At times of high demand, spending on goods will go up, which will cause the revenue from indirect taxation to go up, which in turn will reduce demand, although in real terms the burden of specific taxes will fall with inflation.

Indirect taxes can also be used for specific aims. Particular goods may be taxed in order to discourage the consumption of those goods, to protect domestic industries and even to encourage the production of certain goods by reducing the amount of tax levied on them. When indirect taxes are placed on goods for which the private costs of production are below the social costs, resources may be reallocated in a way that increases total economic welfare.

However increasing the percentage of tax revenue accounted for by indirect taxation may give rise to a number of disadvantages. Indirect taxes are regressive, since they take a higher percentage of the income of the poor than of the rich. This is thought to be one of the main disadvantages of indirect taxation, and although certain categories of goods may be zero-rated, the poor are less well protected than under direct taxation.

Indirect taxes may be inflationary as a rise in indirect taxes will cause a rise in prices. They may also distort consumers' patterns of expenditure and the allocation of resources. If, prior to the imposition of an indirect tax consumers were maximising their total utility, then the tax would reduce consumer satisfaction.

Some economists would also argue against shifting the tax base, on the grounds that the advantages of direct taxes are greater than those of indirect taxes. Direct taxes provide a high yield, and they are certain and convenient since most are deducted at source. They also have a stabilising effect, since during times of recession tax revenue will fall, while during periods of rising incomes tax revenue will rise. Direct taxes also have the advantage of equity as most are progressive, so those who are most able to pay bear the greater burden.

The main arguments advanced for moving towards a greater reliance on indirect taxation are a reduction in the disincentive effect and economy of collection. However, because of the relative merits and demerits of each, the government will continue to rely on both forms of taxation.

Example 28.14

(a) Explain what is meant by discretionary fiscal policy. **(4 marks)**

(b) How may discretionary fiscal policy influence aggregate demand? **(5 marks)**

(c) What problems may be experienced in the conduct of fiscal policy? **(16 marks)**

- Define discretionary fiscal policy and distinguish between it and automatic stabilisers.
- Consider the effect of expansionary and contractionary fiscal policy.

- Cover major areas of government failure, e.g. time lags, and relate them to fiscal policy.

Solution 28.14

(a) Discretionary or active fiscal policy is when the government takes a positive decision to alter government spending or taxation to alter demand. This contrasts with automatic stabilisers, which come into effect when tax revenue and government spending change independently of any deliberate government action.

(b) The level of aggregate demand could be raised by an expansionary policy. This could involve an increase in government spending and/or a reduction in taxation. An expansionary or reflationary fiscal policy would represent a net injection into the circular flow and would cause NY to rise by a multiple amount. It may be used to reduce a deflationary gap.

A deflationary or contractionary fiscal policy will result in a multiple fall in NY and will involve a fall in government expenditure and/or a rise in taxation. This may be introduced in order to reduce or eliminate an inflationary gap.

(c) There are a number of problems that may be encountered with fiscal policy. Some forms of government spending may not be easy to change. For instance a government committed to improving educational standards may find it difficult to reduce spending on education. Also, it will be difficult to reduce spending on a long-term investment project once it is underway.

Tax revenues may be difficult to predict. When the government alters indirect taxation it has to estimate the price elasticity of demand. An even more difficult calculation may prove to be the multiplier. If the government gets this wrong, it may inject too much or too little spending into the economy.

There is also likely to be a time lag involved with fiscal policy, which means that the government has to be able to forecast accurately future changes in economic variables. For instance a government may announce in a November budget a reduction in the standard rate of income tax, designed to raise spending. This may take two to three months to come into or take effect, by which time gross pay and demand may be rising anyway. So the policy will be contributing to the cycle rather than acting countercyclically.

The use of fiscal policy may have different effects on different government objectives. A contractionary fiscal policy may reduce inflation and a deficit in the current account of the balance of payments, but may have an adverse effect on employment and grants.

There is the possibility that the economy may not respond as anticipated to discretionary fiscal policy. For instance a government may raise income tax in order to reduce spending. However spending may not fall, or may not fall significantly if, for example, people choose and are able to work overtime to maintain their current spending patterns and/or if people choose to reduce saving rather than spending.

A fiscal policy measure may also have undesirable effects on other policy instruments and variables, or may itself be constrained by these. A rise in government spending, that is not financed by taxation may increase the money supply and/or raise interest rates. The latter may reduce private sector investment, which may, at least in part, offset the expansionary effect of the increase in government spending. The former may contribute, according to monetarist analysis, to inflation.

When past governments increased government spending to increase demand they encountered difficulties with the current account position of the balance of payments. This resulted in 'stop–go' cycles – i.e. governments adopted expansionary policies, whereupon NY and expenditure on imports rose, so deflationary fiscal policies were adopted to restore current account equilibrium.

Monetarists claim that an expansionary fiscal policy aimed at increasing employment and growth will have an impact on prices rather than output if it is based on increasing aggregate demand. They also consider that fiscal policy may have very uncertain effects, as it is difficult to predict future changes in economic variables. They believe that monetary policy is more important and effective.

Index

acmillan Work Out Series

For GCSE examinations
Accounting
Biology
Business Studies
Chemistry
Computer Studies
English Key Stage 4
French (cassette and pack available)
Geography
German (cassette and pack available)
Modern World History
Human Biology
Core Maths Key Stage 4
Revise Mathematics to further level
Physics
Religious Studies
Science
Social and Economic History
Spanish (cassette and pack available)
Statistics

For A Level examinations
Accounting
Biology
Business Studies
Chemistry
Economics
English
French (cassette and pack available)
Mathematics
Physics
Psychology
Sociology
Statistics